D0777183

COMPILER DESIGN AND CONSTRUCTION

COMPILER DESIGN AND CONSTRUCTION

Arthur B. Pyster, Ph.D.

University of California
Santa Barbara, California

Van Nostrand Reinhold
Electrical/Computer Science and Engineering Series

VAN NOSTRAND REINHOLD COMPANY
NEW YORK   CINCINNATI   ATLANTA   DALLAS   SAN FRANCISCO
LONDON   TORONTO   MELBOURNE

Van Nostrand Reinhold Company Regional Offices:
New York   Cincinnati   Atlanta   Dallas   San Francisco

Van Nostrand Reinhold Company International Offices:
London   Toronto   Melbourne

Library of Congress Catalog Card Number: 79-11216
ISBN: 0-442-24394-4

Manufactured in the United States of America

Published by Van Nostrand Reinhold Company
135 West 50th Street, New York, N.Y. 10020

Published simultaneously in Canada by Van Nostrand Reinhold Ltd.

15 14 13 12 11 10 9 8 7 6 5 4 3 2

Library of Congress Cataloging in Publication Data

Pyster, Arthur.
    Compiler design and construction.

    (Electrical /computer science and engineering
series)
    Includes index.
    1. Compiling (Electronic computers)   I. Title.
II. Series.
QA76.6.P9   001.6'425   79-11216
ISBN 0-442-24394-4

To Teena, Marli, and
Baggins

Van Nostrand Reinhold
Electrical/Computer Science and Engineering Series

SANJIT K. MITRA, SERIES EDITOR

HANDBOOK OF ELECTRONIC DESIGN AND ANALYSIS PROCE-
DURES USING PROGRAMMABLE CALCULATORS, by Bruce K.
Murdock

COMPILER DESIGN AND CONSTRUCTION, by Arthur Pyster

SINUSOIDAL ANALYSIS AND MODELING OF WEAKLY NON-
LINEAR CIRCUITS, by Donald D. Weiner and John F. Spina

Preface

This is an introductory text on compiler writing suitable for Juniors and Seniors in a Computer Science program which attempts to follow the guidelines set by both the ACM and the IEEE Computer Society for such a course. In addition, the computer professional who is seeking an applied approach to compiler writing should find this text a suitable introduction to the field.

I presume that the reader has taken a data structures course such as (CS-7 of the ACM recommendations or SE-2 and SE-3 of the IEEE recommendations), a "principles of programming languages" course (CS-8, CS-15 or SE-5) and a computer architecture course (CS-6, CS-9 or CO-3), although the student could "get by" without either the languages or architecture course.

In order to write a compiler, a student must know both the source and the target languages of interest quite well, especially the former. This text is structured around the presentation of a PASCAL compiler which generates IBM 360/370 assembly language. The features of PASCAL are explained as they are presented, but I really do presume some exposure to PASCAL elsewhere. Similarly, the target language, IBM 360/370 assembly language is overviewed in Appendix B, but the student will need a more complete reference manual. This machine was chosen because of its general popularity and its relatively versatile (though dated) architecture and instruction set.

I believe that no compiler course is complete without a major project in which each student writes a working compiler. This text presents the design and specification of CANTOR, a compiler which translates RASCAL (rudimentary PASCAL) into IBM 360/370 assembly language. RASCAL is a variant of PASCAL, mostly drawing features from the original PASCAL defined by Niklaus Wirth. However, RASCAL deviates from the standard in a few places, either to simplify the compilation problem or to study a feature not specifically found in standard PASCAL, such as a variable length string data-type.

The compiler itself is implemented using step-wise refinement; consequently, the actual implementation language is not nearly so important as it might otherwise be. For concreteness, the pseudo-code is structured around the PASCAL language, deviating from it for convenience in several places, so that the compiler is written in a language which is quite similar to the language it compiles. With the implementation language so closely related to the compiled language, the student is able to concentrate on just two languages throughout the book, RASCAL and IBM 360/370 assembly language.

In most cases, compiler modules are refined only to some intermediate step short of executable code. The intermediate coding language is a mixture of PASCAL and English, leaving the student with the task to complete the refinement process, thereby creating a working compiler.

HOW TO USE THIS TEXT

The text itself is broken into three major parts: The first part overviews general compiling principles and develops the concepts and notations needed for specifying CANTOR, the compiler which is studied in the second and third parts of this book. Beginning in Chapter 4, Part 2 lays out the specifications for a challenging subset of RASCAL including such features as unformatted input/output and **while** loops. I strongly urge the reader to work through this material in the order in which it is presented: Part 2 should take about one quarter to complete. The third part, Chapters 8 through 11, specify the remainder of the compiler in which such interesting features as arrays and block structure are developed. Part 3 should also take one quarter to complete and is intended for a follow-up course on compiling methods. The language and compiler features presented in the third part have been described independently so that the instructor may select from among them without loss of clarity and cohesion. However, the reader should complete the implementation of all RASCAL features in Part 2 before beginning the implementation of any advanced features.

EXERCISES

At various points in the development of CANTOR and RASCAL, design decisions are made which may seem somewhat arbitrary. Sometimes the road taken is motivated by a drive for simplicity in order to keep the project manageable. At other times the choice is admittedly an expression of my own prejudices. At a number of these forks, I suggest alternative designs as exercises. Pursuing these alternatives will make it possible for the reader to carefully examine the consequences of various design decisions. Other exercises given at the end of each chapter vary from suggestions on how to test CANTOR, to problems designed to test the reader's understanding of the material presented in that chapter. The reader is strongly urged to work at least some of the latter type of exercises. It goes almost without saying that it is critical for each compiler writer to thoroughly test his product within the time constraints that the university calendar permits. Therefore, the reader should either try the testing procedures recommended here or should work up his own with equal rigor and attention to boundary conditions and other special cases where programs which otherwise seem correct often fail.

DOCUMENTATION

Any piece of software is useless unless prospective users understand what it does, what data it expects and what output it generates. The people who document programs are the unsung heroes of the software business. Many a program has sat idly on a shelf simply because its documentation was so poor that no one could understand how to properly use it; a compiler being no exception to this rule. Documentation takes two forms, *internal* and *external:* Internal documentation is created in the form of comments embedded in the source compiler code. External documentation for this project will be in the form of a *user's manual* which will explain such important matters as how to invoke the compiler, what language statements it can process, what error processing capabilities it has, and so forth. The table of contents of the manual and some suggestions on writing are given in Appendix A. The reader should not slight the importance of the user's manual. Learning to write clear effective documentation is an important lesson which is useful in many areas beyond compiler writing.

PARSING METHODS

Because this text is really a case study, it concentrates on the development of LL(1) parsing, the method chosen for implementing CANTOR, the compiler of interest. However, to avoid slighting bottom-up parsing, Chapter 2 contains a discussion of LR parsing in general and SLR(1), in particular. This material is not needed in order to understand CANTOR and may be skipped if desired. In order to avoid inflating the text unduly, I have *not* explicitly shown how to incorporate the SLR(1) parsing algorithm into a syntax-directed translator, but the alert reader should be able to see the analogy between bottom-up and top-down syntax-directed translation well enough to rewrite CANTOR using a bottom-up method.

Acknowledgments

I am deeply grateful to the many people who encouraged me in this effort and whose assistance made this book possible. I am especially grateful to Paul Anderson, Al Carlson, Toni Guckert, Sandy Hartman, Steve Johnson, Ramachandran Krishnaswamy, Reg Meeson, Sanjit Mitra, Teddi Potter, John White, and the many others who reviewed this text and suggested countless improvements.

The algorithms developed in Figures 2-8, 2-30 and 2-31 originally appeared on pages 178-179, 207, and 208, respectively, in PRINCIPLES OF COMPILER DESIGN by Aho and Ullman, copyright © 1977 by Bell Laboratories and published by Addison Wesley Publishing Co., Reading, Massachusetts. The author and publisher are grateful to the authors, Addison Wesley, and Bell Laboratories for their courtesy in granting permission to use this material.

Contents

COMPILER DESIGN AND CONSTRUCTION

Part 1.
General Compiling Principles

Part 1 is an overview of the basic principles of compiler design and a discussion of the various components into which compilers are classically divided. In this section of the text many of the terms and notations which are needed in order to specify both CANTOR and RASCAL are defined and explained. A first glimpse at both language and its implementation are given in this part. RASCAL is more carefully defined in the second and ᵗᵈ parts of the text.

   Chapter 1 describes the basic components of a compiler and how they relate to one another. A micro-version of RASCAL is used as an example language throughout. In Chapter 2 the formalism for describing the syntax of programming languages is defined, the *context-free grammar. Parsing*, the generation of a grammatical description of a program is studied here, as well. The first part closes with a discussion of *translation grammars* in Chapter 3. These grammars are a modification of the context-free grammar which not only enable us to describe the syntax of the language which we wish to compile, but also let us specify how its translation is to be generated (hence its name). CANTOR is specified by a translation grammar.

1
Compiler Overview

1.1 INTRODUCTION

A *translator* is a program which takes text written in one language (the *source* language) and converts it into equivalent text in a second language (the *target* or *object* language). If the source is an *abstract* or *high-level* language, and the target is a *low-level assembly* or *machine* language, then the translator is a *compiler*.

Compilers are among the most valuable tools in any computer system. A typical machine language instruction set is very primitive, manipulating bits and bytes through a limited number of high-speed registers and slower, main memory storage. Programming in assembly or machine language requires an intimate knowledge of the computer architecture. Such low-level languages do not facilitate (and in fact greatly hinder) an abstract view of the problem which is being programmed. It is well known that the relative difficulty of most problems is to a large extent dependent upon the tools available with which to solve them. This is especially true in programming, where the tool of the programmer is the language in which he expresses the algorithm that solves his problem. High-level languages such as FORTRAN, PASCAL, SNOBOL, and PL/I give the programmer varying abilities to express his solution in a notation (language) far more suited to the problem space in which he is working than is typically possible via low-level languages. However, in order for a high-level language to be truly useful, its instructions must be made "intelligible" to the computer. One common way of doing this is to translate the instructions of the high-level language into the machine instructions which the computer can directly execute; a compiler does this translation (by definition). Figure 1-1 shows the steps typically taken to execute a high-level programming language.

High-level programming languages are "custom designed" to facilitate programming efforts in particular applications. For example, SNOBOL4 is suited to string processing, GPSS to discrete simulation, COBOL to business data processing and FORTRAN to numeric computation. The first commonly available programming language, FORTRAN, was designed about 25 years ago. In the past quarter century literally hundreds of

3

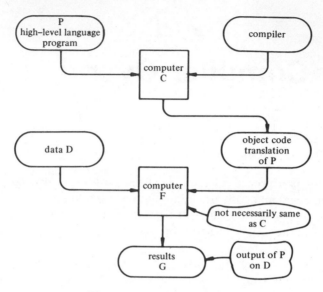

Fig. 1-1. Executing a Program.

different high-level languages have been developed and implemented. Today there are over 150 high-level languages in active use, although most of the activity centers around a mere handful of languages, especially COBOL, FORTRAN, PL/I and BASIC. The number of active languages has held fairly constant over the past five years, although the individual languages in the active roster have changed. The study of language implementation is an important part of any computer scientist's education.

1.2   A MICRO-LANGUAGE

The best way to begin a study of almost any complex subject is with an example in order to build the reader's intuitions about the area. We have chosen a handful of features from RASCAL for this purpose and show briefly how they are compiled. Since the tools for formally describing RASCAL will not be available until Chapter 2, we introduce these features informally here, using English and examples. Of course, the discussion of how RASCAL is compiled is quite superficial in this chapter but hopefully will give the reader some insight into how compiling is performed.

   LITTLE RASCAL, as our micro-language is called, has four statement types:

1. **program**
2. assignment
3. **begin-end**
4. declaration

Every LITTLE RASCAL program begins with a single **program** statement, which also gives the name of the program. This statement is followed by the declaration of all variables referenced in the program. LITTLE RASCAL has only one data-type, *integer,* so all variables are declared to hold *integer* values. The series of declarations are followed by a single **begin-end** statement, which has zero or more assignment statements nested inside it. Figure1-2 shows a sample LITTLE RASCAL program called, appropriately enough, *trivial.*

Note that in the last paragraph, the word "integer" is printed in italics and the terms "program" and "begin-end" are in bold face type. All data-types in this text appear in italics when discussed in prose. We do so to distinguish the language type *integer* from the numeric concept of integer. Similarly for "real," "char," "boolean," and so forth. For example, the *real* numbers of programming languages do not in general coincide with the real numbers of mathematics. This textual difference will remind us of that fact.

In virtually all programming languages, there are words which have a special meaning. These *keywords,* as they are called, are distinguished in this text from other words by writing them in bold face type; for example, the keywords of LITTLE RASCAL are:

div, var, begin, end, program, integer

Full RASCAL has many more keywords which will be introduced later in the text. In *trivial,* variables *x, y, and z* are not keywords. Many languages and language implementations forbid the use of keywords outside their

```
program   trivial;
             {this is a trivial program which illustrates the fea-
             tures of LITTLE RASCAL.}
      var   x,y,z: integer;
             a: integer;
      begin
             {this program has four assignment statements.}
             x := 23 + 5;
             z := x div −3;
             y := z + 18 * 3;
             a := x + (y−2) div 4;
      end.
```

Fig. 1-2. The Program *trivial.*

special context. In this case, the keyword is said to be *reserved*. In LIT-
TLE RASCAL, all keywords are reserved. Note that this is a property of
the language itself and not just the implementation, which we call
GEORG. Hence, the sample program shown in Fig. 1-3 is not legal because the reserved words **var** and **program** are declared as variables. By
reserving keywords, a language improves the readability of the code, and
an implementation simplifies the analysis of the program; later chapters
will amplify these facts.

The program name and all variables and keywords are collectively
known as *identifiers*. In LITTLE RASCAL, identifiers may be arbitrarily
long. An implementation such as GEORG could impose a restriction on
the permissible length of names for the sake of efficient compilation, but
this should be a characteristic of the *implementation*, not the language
definition. A clearer example of the distinction between implementation
and definition is in the specification of a valid range of *integer* values.
Clearly, the permissible range must be intimately bound to the word size
of the machine on which the language is implemented. For a language
definition to impose such a constraint would be impractical. Machines
with short word sizes (e.g., INTEL 8080, PDP-11) cannot reasonably
allow the same range of values as machines with long words (e.g., CDC
6600, IBM 360); of course, this results in a loss of program portability, the
price we must pay for the efficiency we need. As a general rule, restrictions which seem more a result of implementation concerns than language
issues should be left out of the language definition.

It is often necessary to specify a series of statements which are to be
treated as a group for some purpose. A heading and trailing marker must
delineate the endpoints of this group. For example, the keyword "**pro-**

```
program   incorrect;
            {this program illustrates the restriction in LITTLE RASCAL
            that keywords may not be used as variables.}
    var   x,a,var: integer;   {the declaration of var as a variable is illegal.}
        program: integer;   {we can't use program here either.}
    begin
        var := 1; x := 8;   program := var * x div 3;
        {note that several statements may appear on a single line.
        this is legal in LITTLE RASCAL and in full RASCAL as well.}
        program :=
            x;
        {a single statement may also be spread over any number of
        lines desired.}
    end.
```

Fig. 1-3. Illegally Used Reserved Words.

gram" marks the beginning of a program, and a period ends it; these are explicit end markers. Sometimes one of the markers may be implicit; e.g., the end of the variable declarations is indicated by the beginning of the next program section—the executable statements. RASCAL has one general set of group markers which appears in several contexts-**begin-end.** The statements to be grouped are sandwiched between a **begin** and an **end.** In LITTLE RASCAL these brackets are used only to group all executable commands together. The control structures of full RASCAL also require this bracketing to denote the scope of control.

Confusion in the treatment of **begin-end** often occurs because this bracket is also treated as a *statement.* This confusion largely results from the fact that the opening and closing brackets are identifiers, not special symbols (such as '{' and '}' found in the C programming language). They *look like* a statement. Thus, we talk about a *simple* statement, such as an assignment, which cannot be broken down further into constituent statements and about a *compound* statement, which is actually a series of statements (some of which may themselves be compound) bracketed by a **begin-end.** We expect that the reader has been exposed to this statement elsewhere and will not dwell on its problems further.

With one exception, every statement in LITTLE RASCAL ends in a semicolon. The final statement terminates with a period to indicate that the end of a program has been reached. It is quite common for languages to select one or more symbols to denote the end of statements. Both PL/I and ALGOL 60 use semicolons for this purpose; for COBOL it is the period.

In LITTLE RASCAL, every variable which occurs in an assignment statement must be declared. This restriction runs counter to the philosophy of many established languages. FORTRAN, for example, does not require the programmer to explicitly declare the type of a variable. If there is no declaration, then a *default* data-type is assigned to the variable. In FORTRAN the rule for assigning defaults is quite simple. If the variable name begins with any of the letters A–H or O–Z, then the variable is *real;* otherwise, it is *integer.* PL/I also assigns default attributes to undeclared variables. However, its default structure is considerably more complex, since in PL/I many attributes other than simply *type* can be specified, including precision and number base of numeric variables. There is evidence that programs which do not explicitly declare their variables are harder to debug and more error prone than those which do. By disallowing programs which do not declare variables, LITTLE RASCAL enforces the good programming habit of declaring all variables.

Figure 1-4 depicts a clear indication of how relying on default attributes can lead a programmer into trouble. Variable name *nexttoken* has been

```
program  default;
         {this program illustrates how misspelling identifier
          names is caught in a language
          which requires each name
          to be declared prior to referencing it.}
var      nexttoken: integer;
             . . .
begin

             . . .
         nexttoken := 0;  {misspelt variable name!}
             . . .
end.
```

Fig. 1-4. Misspelling A Variable.

misspelled by the programmer in statement n as *nextoken*. In a reasonably large program, as we shall imagine *default* to be, such a typographical error could easily go unnoticed by the programmer. A FORTRAN compiler would not detect such an error, since *nextoken* is perfectly legal in this context. It has the default type *integer;* it is just the *wrong* statement with respect to the intentions of the programmer. Note, however, that any reasonable implementation of LITTLE RASCAL would flag statement *n* at compile time as having an undeclared variable.

Another interesting feature of LITTLE RASCAL is the symbol for the assignment operation; namely,

$$:= $$

Most available languages denote assignment by the simpler token

$$ = $$

Unfortunately, the equal sign has a common mathematical meaning quite different from that intended by assignment. In fact, many of these same languages use the equal sign for the test of equality between two operands. The meaning of '=' varies with the context in which it is used. This is a well-known point of confusion for the beginning programmer, especially when he encounters such seemingly absurd statements as the assignment

$$ x = x + 1 $$

in FORTRAN. Just as restricting the appearance of keywords to their special context simplifies compilation and improves program readability, so does distinguishing more clearly between assignment and equality. When a single token may be given different meanings in different contexts, it is a source of confusion. The equal sign and the left and right parentheses are all examples of commonly *overworked* tokens. The practical reason for this phenomenon is an inadequate number of symbols available on keypunches, terminals, lineprinters, and other input/output devices. The situation is improving, but it will be some time before a language designer can safely assume that even the full ASCII character set (for example) is almost universally available. Some languages, such as APL, indicate assignment with a left pointing arrow '←'. Such a unique symbol is clearly preferable to the ad hoc solution of concatenating a colon and an equals sign. However, few input/output devices have '←' at this time, so we must settle for ':=' instead.

The assignment statements of LITTLE RASCAL follow the pattern common to most languages. The four arithmetic operators are '+', '−', '*', and **'div'**; only the latter is peculiar, in that normally '/' is used to denote division. In RASCAL there are two division operators: one for *real* division, denoted by '/'; the other for *integer* division, denoted by **'div'**. One of the most common errors made in arithmetic computation involving *integer* and *real* quantities is the unexpected truncation of the quotient resulting from the division of one *integer* by another *integer*. It is often quite subtle, introducing difficult and nasty bugs into programs. RASCAL tries to minimize this problem by forcing the programmer to use different symbols when requesting *integer* and *real* division. The **'div'** operation is only defined on *integer* operands and always truncates the fraction, yielding an *integer* result. The precise definition of truncation when the signs of the divisor and dividend differ is a source of constant controversy. See exercise 1-7 for more on **"div"**. The '/' operator is defined on either *integer* or *real* operands but never truncates, always yielding a *real* result. Perhaps a symbol such as '÷' would be better than the more artificial **'div'**, but since most input/output devices do not have this character available, **'div'** is a reasonable compromise.

Arithmetic expressions are evaluated from left to right, with '*' and **'div'** having higher precedence than '+' and '−'. There is no exponentiation operator in LITTLE RASCAL (or even in full RASCAL, for that matter). Parentheses can be applied in the normal manner to override the implicit precedence relationships between operators. Figure 1-5 presents several examples of arithmetic expressions and their evaluation.

This completes the informal introduction to LITTLE RASCAL. If this language is anything, it is skimpy. LITTLE RASCAL has no input/output facilities, no control structures and no data-type other than *integer*. The description here has been intentionally vague but hopefully gives the reader insight into many of the design considerations of LITTLE RAS-

$$3 + 7 * 2 \textbf{ div } 3$$
$$= \quad 3 + 14 \textbf{ div } 3$$
$$= \quad 3 + 4$$
$$= \quad 7$$

$$12 - (4 \textbf{ div } 3 + 6 - (18 * 3))$$
$$= \quad 12 - (1 + 6 - (18 * 3))$$
$$= \quad 12 - (7 - (18 * 3))$$
$$= \quad 12 - (7 - 54)$$
$$= \quad 12 - -47$$
$$= \quad 59$$

$$(32 - 6) \textbf{ div } (6 - 32)$$
$$= \quad 26 \textbf{ div } (6 - 32)$$
$$= \quad 26 \textbf{ div } -26$$
$$= \quad -1$$

Fig. 1-5. Evaluating Arithmetic Expressions.

CAL as drawn from PASCAL. A more complete and rigorous definition of LITTLE RASCAL and the other features of RASCAL follow in Parts 2 and 3 of this text.

We have devoted a large part of this section to *why* the language features have their particular characteristics. When the remainder of RASCAL is revealed, we shall continue the practice of motivating features as they are introduced. We shall be especially interested in those features of RASCAL which facilitate easy or more efficient compilation.

1.3 INSIDE THE BLACK BOX

With the introduction to LITTLE RASCAL complete, we turn to the structure of a compiler for it. The first step in decomposing a compiler is to overview the seven major components common to most existing compilers and to examine their interconnections. These seven components are the:

1. scanner
2. parser
3. intermediate code generator
4. semantic processor
5. optimizer
6. code generator
7. tables

A block diagram of these components showing roughly the flow of control and information between them is given in Fig. 1-6. Not all compilers have

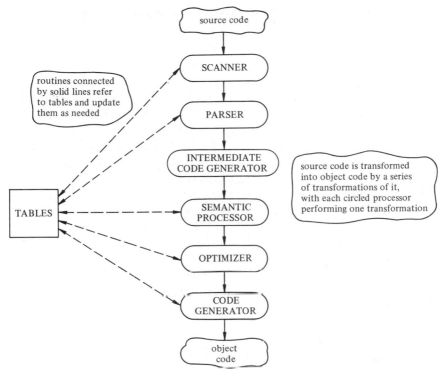

Fig. 1-6. A Block Diagram of A Compiler.

each of these modules as physically independent entities. Some functions of the scanner, for example, may be integrated into the parser; conceptually, however, it is easier to decompose any compiler into these seven components.

1.3.1 Scanner

When a program is first input into a compiler, it is just one long stream of characters, perhaps broken into lines or records reflecting the input medium. The scanner converts this external view of the source program into an internal format more suited for further manipulation by the remainder of the compiler.

The scanner has several roles:

1. identify the basic lexical units of the program, which are called *tokens;*

2. remove extraneous blanks, carriage returns and other characteristics of the input medium;
3. remove comments;
4. report errors which it discovers.

Consider the program *trivial* defined earlier. Figure 1-7 shows this same program but written as card images reflecting the input medium. Statements appear within columns 1 through 72 reflecting the IBM norm. Typically, a scanner will make one pass over the text in its original form, carrying out its four tasks as this pass proceeds and output the program in some internal format, a token at a time, to the parser upon request or as one large file of tokens. The exact manner of operation of the scanner depends on how the compiler is organized. This is further discussed in section 1.5 on *multi-pass* compilers. Usually, the scanner examines the text character by character. Based upon the symbol it is currently examining, plus its knowledge of the text it has previously seen, the scanner determines whether the symbol it is currently processing is part of a comment, an extraneous blank, the beginning of a new token, the continuation of an old token or some illegally placed symbol. The scanner then takes the appropriate action with respect to the output it must generate.

Figure 1-8 shows one possible output of the scanner for *trivial*. In this case, the scanner identifies each token or lexical unit of the program, separating consecutive tokens by a ' #', which we presume cannot otherwise occur in the string. Markers of the external organization of the program text, such as line feeds and carriage returns, have been removed; no

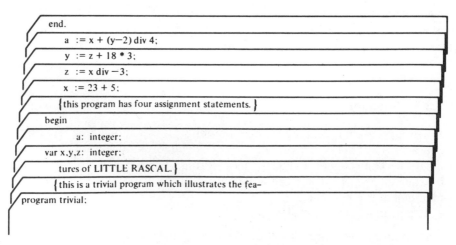

Fig. 1-7. *Trivial* as seen by the Scanner.

#program#trivial#;#var#x#,#y#,#z#:#integer#;#a#:#integer#;#
begin#x#:=#23#+#5#;#z#:=#x#div#−#3#;#y#:=#z#+#18#∗#
3#;#a#:=#x#+#(#y#−#2#)#div#4#;#end#.#

Fig. 1.8. Output of A "String-Oriented" Scanner on *trivial*.

comments or extraneous blanks appear in the program text in its revised form. Since this is a valid LITTLE RASCAL program, the scanner does not generate any error messages for it. If we assume that GEORG imposes a limit on the permissible length of identifiers, then a violation of that limit might be detected here by the scanner.

This scanner does not convert tokens into some internal format; it has, in some sense, merely *normalized* the program's representation in order to simplify the work of the parser which receives the output of the scanner. The parser must be able to process tokens in this form. Depending on the tools available for implementing the parser, this may be a reasonable burden to place upon it; if not, then a more suitable format must be devised. If the parser is implemented in a string-processing language, such as SNOBOL4, then the parser can reasonably assume the responsibility of handling tokens in this format. If the parser is implemented in a language such as PASCAL, which has relatively poor string manipulation features, then it is probably better to have the scanner replace the character oriented tokens with a numeric form, in order to reduce the complexity of the parser; hence, the scanner just presented is one which a SNOBOL4 implementation of LITTLE RASCAL might reasonably have.

For languages in which string manipulation is more awkward, such as PASCAL, we consider a second type of scanner. The output of this scanner on *trivial* is shown in Fig. 1-9. This scanner emits tokens in the form of ordered pairs of (PASCAL-like) enumerated constants, *(tag,class)*, where *tag* identifies which particular source symbol is being represented and *class* indicates which type of symbol was encountered. (Enumerated constants or just enums are used to avoid an arbitrary numbering. In Chapter 9 we shall see that the implementation of such constants is quite easy and efficient.) There are four classes: special symbol, keyword, non-keyword identifier and *integer;* they are shown in Fig. 1-10. For all symbols except *integers* and non-keyword identifiers, we predefine the tag assigned to them; this correspondence is also shown in Fig. 1-10. For *integers* and non-keyword identifiers (which in this language are just variables and the program name) we assign consecutive integers as tags beginning with one. The tags are assigned in the order in which the symbols are encountered in the program scan. Each tag greater than one is also found in the *symbol table* which holds information about each *integer* and non-keyword identifier. Figure 1-11 shows the table with entries for the scan of *trivial*. This

(program, keyword)
(var, keyword)
('y', non_key_id)
(colon, spec_sym)
('a', non_key_id)
(semicolon, spec_sym)
(assign, spec_sym)
('5', integer)
(assign, spec_sym)
(minus, spec_sym)
('y', non_key_id)
(plus, spec_sym)
('3', integer)
(assign, spec_sym)
(left-paren, spec_sym)
('2', integer)
('4', integer)
(period, spec_sym)

('trivial', non_key_id)
('x', non_key_id)
(comma, spec_sym)
(integer, keyword)
(colon, spec_sym)
(begin, keyword)
('23', integer)
(semicolon, spec_sym)
('x', non_key_id)
('3', integer)
(assign, spec_sym)
('18', integer)
(semicolon, spec_sym)
('x', non_key_id)
('y', non_key_id)
(right_paren, spec_sym)
(semicolon, spec_sym)

(semicolon, spec_sym)
(comma, spec_sym)
('z', non_key_id)
(semicolon, spec_sym)
(integer, keyword)
('x', non_key_id)
(plus, spec_sym)
('z', non_key_id)
(div, keyword)
(semicolon, spec_sym)
('z', non_key_id)
(asterisk, spec_sym)
('a', non_key_id)
(plus, spec_sym)
(minus, spec_sym)
(div, keyword)
(end, keyword)

(a) Symbolic Form

Fig. 1-9. Output of "Enum-Oriented" Scanner on *trivial*.

Keyword substitution

program	'program'
var	'var'
integer	'integer'
end	'end'
begin	'begin'
div	'div'

Special symbol substitution

semicolon	';'
comma	','
colon	':'
assign	':='
plus	'+'
minus	'−'
asterisk	'*'
period	'.'
left_paren	'('
right_paren	')'

token classes

keyword
spec_sym
non_key_id
integer

Fig. 1-10. Substituting Enums for Tokens.

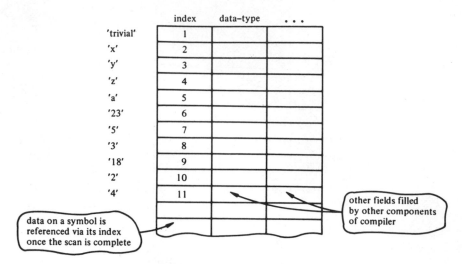

Fig. 1-11. Symbol Table for *trivial*.

table is referenced frequently by the compiler as it fills in more information about each item as the compilation proceeds.

1.3.2 Parser

Each programming language has its own set of grammar rules characteriz-
ing the correct form of programs in that language. The *parser* or *syntactic
analyzer* accepts the output of the scanner; i.e., tokens, and verifies that
the source program satisfies the grammatical rules of the language being
compiled. In English, the grammar rules are normally not stated with
great precision. Each person's view of what constitutes correct English
seems highly dependent on the quirks of his high school English teachers.
However, the syntax of each programming language is simple enough so
that it can be written in a precise mathematical notation called a *context-
free grammar*. Using such a schema, it is possible to mechanically classify
programs into those which do and do not belong to the language under
consideration. (Actually, things are not quite that simple: A number of
programs which should not belong to the language on *semantic* grounds
will be admitted on syntactic ones. The grammar of a real programming
language typically describes a *superset* of the intended language; this is
discussed in more detail in Chapter 2.) The parser does this mechanical
classification; furthermore, the parser can construct a complete syntactic
description of the program much as sentences are diagrammed in English.
The description takes the form of a labelled, ordered tree. Figure 1-12

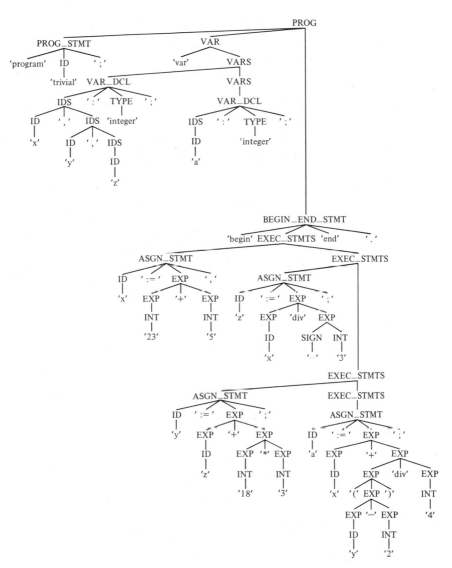

Fig. 1-12. Possible Parse of *trivial*.

shows one such tree for *trivial*. The tokens of *trivial* are the frontier of the tree. The internal nodes represent grammatical categories in much the same way that 'noun phrase' represents a collection of related sentence fragments in English. The generation of grammatical descriptions, such as those of Fig. 1-12 is relatively complex, consuming most of Chapter 2; however, it is, along with scanning, the best understood part of the compilation process.

The parser may not generate a tree for the entire program; it might, for example, parse the program statement by statement, discarding the parse of the last statement when it begins its work on the next. Information, located in earlier statements, which is required to emit code for the current statement, is saved in various structures, such as stacks and tables, eliminating the need to keep the parse of those earlier statements around indefinitely; this can enormously reduce the storage requirements needed by the compiler.

1.3.3 Intermediate Code Generator

The tree output by the parser is transformed into a "program" of sorts written in an *intermediate code,* which is closer in form to assembly language than the source text and yet is in a form which makes further manipulation easier than if actual assembly (or machine) code were emitted. Since the intermediate level code is machine-like in character, but not in form, it will normally vary with the machine for which the object code is being generated. For example, the intermediate code generated by a compiler for a computer with a stack architecture such as the B5500 will probably differ from that for a computer which has a more conventional Von Neumann structure; Fig. 1-13 shows possible intermediate code which will eventually be transformed into IBM 360/370 assembly language (hereafter referred to simply as *360AL*). Note that no registers are mentioned in the code. Register assignment is delayed until object code generation, which is discussed in section 1.3.6. UC San Diego has released an extremely successful version of Pascal in which the compiler translates Pascal source into an intermediate language, P-code. P-code is the language for a virtual P-machine (where P stands for Pascal). The UC San Diego system, available on a variety of computers including the TEL 8080, Z80, and PDP-11, includes a software interpreter which directly executes P-code. In this case, the intermediate code is the object code as well.

Intermediate Code	*Purpose*
(prologue,'trivial')	initialize program called *trivial;* establish base registers and so forth
(add,'23','5','@T')	add 23 to 5 and store the result in @*T,* a compiler-generated location used to hold intermediate results
(store,'@T','x')	store value of @*T* into *x*
(div,'x','−3','@T')	divide *x* by −3 and store the result in @*T*
(store,'@T','z')	store value of @*T* into *z*
(mult,'18','3','@T')	multiply 18 by 3 and store the result in @*T*
(add,'z','@T','@T')	add *z* to @*T* and store the result in @*T*
(store,'@T','y')	store value of @*T* into *y*
(sub,'y','2','@T')	subtract 2 from *y* and store the result in @*T*
(div,'@T','4','@T')	divide @*T* by 4 and store the result in @*T*
(add,'x','@T','@T')	add *x* to @*T* storing result in @*T*
(store,'@T','a')	store value of @*T* into *a*
(epilogue)	terminate program execution and emit storage for variables, literals, compiler generated constants, and so forth

> symbolic names have been used in the intermediate code rather than indices to the symbol table for clarity in the presentation, but a commercial compiler would probably not use these symbolic names

Fig. 1-13. Intermediate Code for *trivial.*

1.3.4   Semantic Processor

Virtually all active programming languages have features which cannot be captured by any context-free grammar. This grammar model has its formal limitations which we shall briefly examine in Chapter 2. Other features may be formally expressed within a context-free grammar but only at the expense of clarity and brevity in the grammar specification. To address those language features which, for one reason or another, are not captured by the grammar, we define a special component—the *semantic processor.* Those language aspects specified in the grammar are said to be *syntactic;* all other aspects are by definition *context-sensitive* or *semantic.* LITTLE RASCAL is so simple that GEORG has little need for a semantic processor; however, even LITTLE RASCAL has one feature which cannot be checked by a context-free grammar, no matter how awkward we are willing to make that grammar. No context-free grammar can capture the fact that a variable must be declared *exactly once* if referenced in an assignment statement. The semantic processor of GEORG would check for violations of this rule.

In full RASCAL the semantic processor is more useful. Each operator expects operands from a specific set of data-types. The semantic processor will check the symbol table where the type information about each operand is kept, in order to verify that the operands are of the expected types; if not, it can report the error.

The semantic processor for the most part just checks the validity of code; as such it will not change that code unless it discovers an error. In that case, the processor may attempt to *repair* the error in some way by changing the code so that it becomes valid. The semantic processor makes an "intelligent" guess at what the programmer intended. Alternatively, the semantic processor might simply note that an error had been uncovered and not attempt to repair it. Chapter 8 addresses *error processing* in which we shall study this problem in some detail.

1.3.5   Optimizer

Intermediate code can be converted directly into the object language by the code generator. However, it is not uncommon to insert another component between the semantic processor and the code generator; namely, the *optimizer*. If the code generator transforms intermediate level text into assembly language in a straightforward manner, the generated object code is probably not as efficient with respect to execution time and storage space as it might be. If a compiler is more than superficially concerned with producing efficient code, as most commercial compilers must be, it will include a module specifically designed to improve some combination of time and space characteristics of the code. The optimizer modifies the code which it is given into a more efficient version. Sophisticated compilers, such as the *PL/I F* and *PL/I optimizing* compilers have so many different optimizing strategies, some of which conflict with one another (time versus space), that they give the user the opportunity to specify whether he prefers space or time optimization or a mixture of both.

Some optimization strategies depend on the particular target language; e.g., *register allocation* can be improved to reduce the number of loads and stores from main memory. The particulars of this strategy depend on the register structure of the target machine. For a stack machine such as the PDP-11 which has few registers, these strategies are less important. Other optimization strategies are relatively independent of the target machine; e.g., moving a computation which is invariant with respect to a program loop outside the scope of the loop, so that it is executed only once. For LITTLE RASCAL, with its very simple sequential flow of control, the only significant optimizations we mention here are efficient register allocation and performing *compile-time arithmetic;* there are others, of course. The code generator will actually perform register allocation, so this particular optimization cannot be performed yet. Note that the intermediate code does *not* refer to specific registers.

If the values of all operands of an operation are known at compile-time, and these values cannot change at execution-time, then the *compiler* itself can *execute* the operation and substitute the computed result for the original expression; for example, in the LITTLE RASCAL assignment statement:

$$x := y + 3 * 6 - z;$$

the subexpression:

$$3 * 6$$

can be replaced by:

$$18$$

without changing the value assigned to x:

$$x := y + 18 - z;$$

A more subtle and more interesting situation arises when the compiler applies the *commutative law of addition* (for example):

$$x := 3 + y - z + 8;$$

is equivalent to:

$$x := 3 + 8 + y - z;$$

which is equivalent to:

$$x := 11 + y - z;$$

Figure 1-14 shows the output of the optimizer on the intermediate code generated for *trivial;* note that the code for the first and third assignment statements has been altered to reflect the compile-time arithmetic performed by the optimizer.

1.3.6 Code Generator

The code generator takes the intermediate code it receives from the optimizer and produces assembly or machine language code (the object program); obviously, code generation is highly *machine-dependent*. Hence, whenever the object machine is altered, the code generator must be extensively revised. On the other hand, the other components are somewhat more insensitive to the machine for which code is being gener-

Intermediate Code	*Purpose*
(prologue,'trivial')	initialize program called *trivial;* establish base registers and so forth
(store,'28','x')	store 28 into x
(div,'x','−3','@T')	divide x by -3 and store the result in $@T$
(store,'@T','z')	store value of $@T$ into z
(add,'z','54','@T')	add z to 54 and store the result in $@T$
(store,'@T','y')	store value of $@T$ into y
(sub,'y','2','@T')	subtract 2 from y and store the result in $@T$
(div,'@T','4','@T')	divide $@T$ by 4 and store the result in $@T$
(add,'x','@T','@T')	add x to $@T$ storing result in $@T$
(store,'@T','a')	store value of $@T$ into a
(epilogue)	terminate program execution and emit storage for variables, literals, compiler generated constants, and so forth

optimized

Fig. 1-14. Optimized Intermediate Code for *trivial*.

ated; however, none of the compiler modules is, in general, totally immune to a change in the target machine. Figure 1-15 shows the assembly language code output by the code generator for the input displayed in Fig. 1-14 from the optimizer.

1.3.7 Tables

The algorithms which make up most compilers are largely driven by tables which summarize information about the program being compiled and about the source and target languages in general. For example, the scanner may build a symbol table of identifier names. The parser and semantic processor may add additional information (called *attributes*) about each identifier in the table. The parser often has the context-free grammar definition of the language converted into a table for more convenient processing. The error messages associated with each detected error may all be stored in one large table. As we shall see in Parts 2 and 3, CANTOR has a number of tables, which, along with the *stack,* are the primary data structures manipulated by the compiler.

1.4 DIAGNOSTIC TOOLS

A topic often overlooked in compiling textbooks is that of *diagnostic tools.* No commercial compiler is marketable unless it generates informative commentary about each program that it processes. A compiler which generates correct object code but does nothing more is unusable and unsellable; at a bare minimum, any compiler must give some indication

TRIVIAL	CSECT		
	STM	14,12,12(13)	save registers
	BALR	12,0	set up base register
	USING	*,12	
	ST	13,@SAV+4	save loc old save area
	LA	13,@SAV	load addr new save area
	MVC	@I0(4),=F'28'	x := 28
	L	2,@I0	x div −3
	SRDA	2,32	
	D	2,=F'−3'	
	ST	3,@I2	z := @T
	A	3,=F'54'	z + 54
	ST	3,@I1	y := @T
	S	3,=F'2'	y − 2
	SLDA	2,32	@T div 4
	SRDA	2,32	
	D	2,=F'4'	
	A	3,@I0	x + @T
	ST	3,@I3	a := @T
	L	13,@SAV+4	restore loc old save area
	LM	14,12,12(13)	restore old registers
	BR	14	return
@SAV	DS	18F	@SAV
@I0	DS	F	x
@I1	DS	F	y
@I2	DS	F	z
@I3	DS	F	a
	END		

Fig. 1-15. Assembly Language Code for *trivial*.

when it encounters an error in a program. Any reasonable compiler also makes extensive checks for errors (so it has something to report), as well. If the error occurs at execution-time, then perhaps the operating system may report the error, although in Chapter 8 we shall analyze the wisdom of such a practice, but all errors detected during compilation should be reported by the compiler itself; hopefully, the compiler identifies the nature and location of the error in some detail.

Besides reporting errors, a compiler may also generate other informative commentary which aids a programmer in documenting and debugging his program; for example, two common aids are the cross-reference map and a dump of the values of variables upon request. Figure 1-16 shows one format for a cross-reference map of *trivial*. More and more implementations are offering a *profile* option which permits a programmer to see at a glance how many times each statement of his program was executed on a particular run. The profile option permits the programmer to quickly identify possible bottlenecks in his program, as well as detect code which is

CROSS-REFERENCE MAP

NAME	TYPE	REFERENCED IN LINE NUMBER
trivial	entry	1
x	integer	4,8,9,11
y	integer	4,10,11
z	integer	4,9,10
a	integer	5,11

Fig. 1-16. Cross Reference Map for *trivial*.

not executed at all, possibly indicating a logical error. Dozens of other tools are found in the literally thousands of language implementations available today; they range from the relatively trivial indication of how much time the compiler took to compile a program, to an elaborate analysis of the flow of control of a particular program run.

Language definitions typically do not mandate the presence of any tools in an implementation; diagnostic tools are, however, required in any common sense implementation which is to be usable. The advanced CANTOR compiler includes error detection and reporting capabilities, a cross-reference map, and a facility for dynamically dumping the value of program variables, among other diagnostic tools.

1.5 MULTI-PASS COMPILERS

A compiler can be organized so that all transformations which convert the source text into the object code are performed in a single pass over the original source code; such compilers are called *single-pass compilers*. CANTOR is a single-pass compiler. It is quite easy to imagine a different strategy in which the compiler is broken into several modules, each of which makes a complete pass over some form of the program being compiled before the next module is given control; such compilers are called *multi-pass compilers* to reflect the way in which they process the source program. Normally the module which performs a given pass reads its input from secondary storage where the previous pass has left it, performs whatever transformations on that input it is supposed to make, and outputs the resulting code back onto secondary storage. The first pass of a five-pass compiler might scan the program, the second parse the output of the scanner, and so forth, until the fifth phase generated object code which it might place on secondary storage for further processing.

Conceptually, it is easier to understand compilation when it is broken into passes as just described; besides conceptual clarity, its chief advantages are:

1. increased modularity achieved by the division of the compiler into passes;
2. an improved ability to perform global analysis of the program (especially important in optimization), since the i-th pass has the complete output of the (i-1)st pass available to it;
3. decreased space requirements, since the code for each pass need only be present during the execution of that pass and may be overlayed by new code for the next pass when no longer needed.

The third reason is especially important in computers with small memories such as today's typical microcomputer. The chief disadvantage (and a very important one) is that if secondary storage is used to store the output of each pass (not required by the definition of multi-pass compilers, but often the only feasible approach), a considerable amount of time may be spent on the overhead of reading and writing operations.

EXERCISES

1-1. Take a compiler which is available in your installation and determine whether it is a single-pass or a multi-pass compiler. If it has more than one pass, determine the function of each in the overall compilation process. If possible, dump the output of each pass so you can examine it.

1-2. If you have two implementations of the ''same'' language for which a standard exists, such as FORTRAN or ALGOL 60, then compare the two implementations for conformance to that standard. Find features of each implementation which are extensions of the standard. Find other features mentioned in the standard which are not part of the implemented constructs. Does the available documentation for these implementations point out the discrepancies with the standard in a clear and understandable manner?

1-3. Obtain a copy of the definition of ALGOL 60 and FORTRAN IV (see bibliography). Read each of the documents for clarity and completeness. How easy a task do you think it would be to implement either of these languages given only these documents as guidelines for the features included? Write out a list of places in the document where you feel the specification is either unclear or ambiguous.

1-4. Investigate the overhead in your computer installation for having a multi-pass compiler which requires extensive references to secondary store versus one which could keep all intermediate phases in core. Do so by writing a small program which fills up a large amount of core memory with data, then performs four trivial modifications to the data, one at a time. Determine how much total time and space were required for this program. Now repeat this process, except modify the program to read and write this data on secondary memory instead of in core.

1-5. Select a programming language which you know reasonably well, and list all of the keywords in it. Are these words reserved within the language? By the implementation which you have used?

1-6. Take any language which you know well and analyze it to determine in how many different ways parentheses are used; the keyword 'END' is used; the comma is used.

1-7. Integer division is more complex than it might at first seem. Does the remainder have the same sign as the quotient? For example, is $3/(-2)$ equal to -1 (remainder $-\frac{1}{2}$) or -2 (remainder $\frac{1}{2}$)? Most languages specify the former, and are said to truncate *towards zero*. RASCAL will follow this policy. Devise a more rigorous definition of **integer** division which (a) truncates towards zero; (b) truncates away from zero.

BIBLIOGRAPHY

The early history of programming languages and their compilers is somewhat difficult to decipher. There were several predecessors to FORTRAN, the first widely available high-level programming language, which was developed at IBM [Backus, et al 57]. [Sammet 68, 72] and [Knuth and Pardo 76] are excellent sources for the history and folklore of early programming language efforts. The early work of Konrad Zuse reported in [Knuth and Pardo 76] is especially fascinating because of speculation on what the current state of languages might be if his work had surfaced soon after World War II. Zuse developed a language, Plankalküls, in 1945 which was not equaled until ALGOL 60 appeared years later. There are several texts on the market dealing with the general compiling topic, including [Gries 71], [Cocke and Schwartz 70], [Lewis, Rosenkrantz, and Stearns 76], [Aho and Ullman 77], and [Lee 74].

In order to appreciate the difficulty of writing a compiler which is consistent with a language definition, the reader should examine some sample language definition documents. [ANSI 66], [ANSI 76] define FORTRAN, [ANSI 76] defines PL/I, and [Naur 63] presents the official ALGOL 60 definition. PASCAL was promulgated in [Wirth 71]. [Hoare and Wirth 71] axiomatized its semantics in what has proven to be a fundamental paper on language semantics. [Jensen and Wirth 75] is the standard reference manual on the language, although more recently, texts such as [Conway, et al 77] offer a more lucid explanation of many facets of PASCAL. At the time this volume is going to press, ANSI and the IEEE are jointly working toward a standard for Pascal as part of an international standardization effort ([ANSI 79]).

2
Context-Free Languages

2.1 INTRODUCTION

In order to write a compiler, an implementor must have a clear unambiguous definition of the language to be implemented. Some aspects of language definition have yielded to analysis quite handily, most notably those aspects dealing with the *form* or *syntax* of programs. Other aspects, concerned with the behavior of programs, or their *semantics,* have been far more stubborn in yielding to formalization. We will use one formal tool for describing programming language syntax, the *context-free grammar.* To specify language semantics, we will rely upon English and examples, which despite their inadequacies and imprecisions, is a satisfactory method for our purposes here.

The context-free grammar, originally motivated by studies of natural languages, is the primary tool by which language designers specify the form of programs in a language. Using a context-free grammar, it is possible to specify a computationally tractable and quite intuitive syntactic description of each program in a language. The descriptions are well-behaved, easy to understand, relatively concise and completely rigorous. In the next section we will examine a grammar for LITTLE RASCAL expressions and point out how the syntactic structures which describe programs enhance our understanding of the language being defined.

Unfortunately, the context-free grammar has its limitations. There are certain features common to almost all programming languages which cannot be modelled using the context-free grammar; for example, there is no context-free grammar for LITTLE RASCAL which will generate all and only programs which do not have multiply declared identifiers. It is not a question of cleverness on the part of the grammar designer; rather, it is a provable inadequacy of the context-free model for language. However, in virtually every language actually used, there is a context-free grammar which very closely approximates the desired language. By using ad hoc means (the semantic processor) to further restrict the approximation language, it can be made to coincide with the desired language. More often than not, the ad hoc method is English when specifying the language. These English restrictions on programs typically become routines in the semantic processor.

Sometimes a feature which can, in fact, be captured by a context-free grammar should not be, because it would be awkward to do so; blanks are particularly notorious in this respect. In some languages blanks are required only where ambiguity might result if they were omitted, such as in:

$$\text{beginx:} = \text{yend};$$

rather than:

$$\text{begin} \quad \text{x:} = \text{y} \quad \text{end};$$

Semantically, it makes no difference how many blanks (more than one) are actually inserted in such a case. We can write a grammar which incorporates these facts, but it would appear cluttered. Since one of the motivations for a formal grammar is clarity, we typically push the handling of blanks (and other ugly forms such as comments and quoted strings) onto the scanner. Since the scanner's job is relatively simple compared to that of the parser, it seems better to increase scanner complexity and simplify the parser's load (see exercises 2-24 and 2-25).

Recognizing the inadequacies of English for precisely stating restrictions on the form of programs, various groups have proposed rigorous augmentations of the context-free grammar. One of the most important, the *Van Wijngaarden grammar,* is a modification of the context-free grammar which gives it the power to formally and rigorously specify the context-sensitive constraints on languages which the context-free grammar cannot do; for example, a language which has many context-dependent constraints that cannot be expressed by any context-free grammar, ALGOL68, has been completely defined by a Van Wijngaarden grammar without reliance on any English or other supplements. However, for our purposes, the added precision which such systems offer is more than offset by the increased complexity of their description. For such a simple language as RASCAL, such powerful tools are not warranted; we shall rely upon a context-free grammar, English, and examples to define RASCAL's features. The interested reader is referred to the references in the bibliography for further information on grammar models more powerful than the context-free grammar.

2.2 INFIX ARITHMETIC EXPRESSIONS

The language chosen to illustrate the context-free grammar is familiar to all programmers: *parenthesized arithmetic expressions,* drawn from LITTLE RASCAL. To simplify the presentation, we break the grammar into two components: The first defines the operands of expressions; namely, variables and *integer* literals; the second grammar applies these operands in arithmetic expressions.

The first language can be described in English by:

"Each sentence of the language is either an *integer* or an identifier. An *integer* is a string of one or more digits optionally preceded by '+' or '−'. An identifier is an English letter followed by zero or more English letters or digits."

This English description is somewhat awkward and is incomplete, in that it assumes the reader knows which characters constitute the English alphabet and the digits. The formal specification of a context-free grammar for this same language will leave nothing to chance, since it explicitly indicates the alphabet over which the sentences of the language are defined. More important, however, the context-free grammar not only provides a means of determining which strings are in the language under consideration, it also details an underlying syntactic structure which is lacking in the English version.

Several sample sentences from OPERANDS, the name of the first language, are:

pascal,   nexttoken,   3,   w3,   help,   −274

The following strings are *not* in OPERANDS:

1a,   ++2,   2.,   ss*,   2+3,   x0:

Note that the set of operands falls quite naturally into two classes, *integers* and identifiers; the English description even makes that distinction. This can be written as:

1. OPERAND → ID │INTEGER

or as:

1'. OPERAND → ID
    OPERAND → INTEGER

or as:

1″. OPERAND → ID
    → INTEGER

where " │" means "or." Here we are stating that an operand can be viewed either as an ID (identifier) or as an INTEGER (*integer*). We can continue this process, breaking up an ID or an INTEGER into its possible subcomponents. An ID can be a single letter followed by a list of zero or more letters and digits:

2. ID → LETTER   LIST

A letter is one of the 26 characters of the English alphabet.

3. LETTER → 'a' |'b' |'c' |'d' |'e' |'f' |'g' |
            'h' |'i' |'j' |'k' |'l' |'m' |'n' |
            'o' |'p' |'q' |'r' |'s' |'t' |'u' |
            'v' |'w' |'x' |'y' |'z'

A list is iteself just a letter or a digit followed by another list, or it is just the string of length zero, which we denote by the Greek letter *lambda*, λ:

4. LIST → LETTER LIST |
          DIGIT LIST |
          λ

A digit is any numeral from zero to nine:

5. DIGIT → '0' |'1' |'2' |'3' |'4' |'5' |'6' |'7' |'8' |'9'

An *integer* is a digit followed by a possibly empty list of digits optionally preceded by a sign:

6. INTEGER → SIGN DIGIT DIGITS |
             DIGIT DIGITS

A sign is either '+' or '−':

7. SIGN → '+' |'−'

A list of digits is itself a digit followed by a list of digits or is just lambda:

8. DIGITS → DIGIT DIGITS |
            λ

These 8 "major" rules, 48 rules in all, in some sense completely capture the form of correctly written operands; in fact, these rules are called *productions* of a context-free grammar, because they indicate how to produce a sentence of the language. Each of the symbols in quotation marks can be part of a language sentence; such symbols are called *terminals* or *tokens*. The upper case words correspond to grammatical categories in English such as "noun phrase" or "preposition;" they are called *nonterminals*. Since the strings are operands, we distinguish the nonterminal OPERAND from the others and call it the *axiom*. The set of strings composed just of terminals which can be derived from the axiom are the *sentences* of the language.

Figure 2-1 shows a pictorial representation of the analysis of 'az3' using the grammar just presented; it is in the form of a *labelled ordered tree*. The *root* of the tree is the axiom OPERAND; the *frontier* is the string 'az3'. The structure of the tree between the root and the frontier gives a grammatical analysis of 'az3' in terms of this particular grammar. Figure 2-2 shows the *parse tree*, as such trees are called, for the operand '+450'.

Before we can formally define a context-free grammar, we must intro-

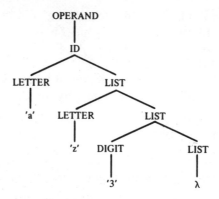

Fig. 2-1. Parse Tree of 'az3'.

duce one supportive concept about strings. Suppose S is a set of strings. The *concatenation closure*, S*, of S is defined recursively by:

1. $\lambda \epsilon S^*$;
2. if $\alpha \epsilon S$, then $\alpha \epsilon S^*$;
3. if $\alpha \epsilon S$ and $\beta \epsilon S^*$, then $\alpha \beta \epsilon S^*$ and $\beta \alpha \epsilon S^*$.

S* is the concatenation of an arbitrary number of members of S in any order. If S is not empty, then S* always has an infinite number of distinct elements in it. We also define the *λ-free concatenation closure*, S⁺, which is $S^* - \{\lambda\}$.

A *context-free grammar* is a 4-tuple (N, Σ, A,P), where (i) N is a finite set of *nonterminals*; (ii) Σ is a finite set of *terminals* or *tokens*; (iii) A ∈ N is the grammar *axiom;* and (iv) P is a finite set of *productions* of the form (B, α), where B ∈ N and α ∈ (N∪Σ)*. We often write (B, α) ∈ P as "B → α". N∪Σ is sometimes called the *vocabulary,* V.

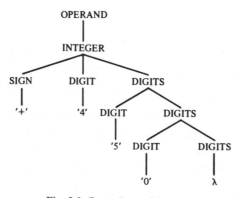

Fig. 2-2. Parse Tree of '+450'.

To aid the reader in distinguishing between the several types of symbols we shall encounter, we adopt the following scheme: (i) upper case Roman letters are nonterminals; (ii) lower case Roman letters a–k are members of Σ; (iii) lower case Roman letters l–z are members of Σ^*; and (iv) lower case Greek letters are members of V or V^*. So, for example, in the definition of context-free grammar, the fact that a production is shown in the form "$B \rightarrow \alpha$" indicates that the left-hand side is a nonterminal, while the right-hand side is a member of $V.^*$

Technically, the productions of our example grammar do not satisfy the definition of "production" just given; rather, they are given in a convenient alternate format. If each production in a set of productions has the same left-hand side:

$$B \rightarrow \alpha_1$$
$$B \rightarrow \alpha_2$$
$$. . .$$
$$B \rightarrow \alpha_n$$

then alternatively we can write them either as:

$$B \rightarrow \alpha_1 \ | \alpha_2 \ | . . . \ | \alpha_n$$

or as:

$$B \rightarrow \alpha_1$$
$$\rightarrow \alpha_2$$
$$. . .$$
$$\rightarrow \alpha_n$$

Productions with the same left-hand side are said to be *alternative* productions.

Formally then, OPERANDS is the language of context-free grammar $G_1 = (N, \Sigma, OPERAND, P)$ where:

1. N = {OPERAND, ID, INTEGER, LETTER, LIST, DIGIT, DIGITS, SIGN}
2. Σ = {'a', . . . , 'z', '0', . . . , '9', '+', '−'}
3. P is the set of 48 productions given previously.

We can now describe the second grammar. In this grammar we will assume that OPERAND is a terminal symbol in that we shall not bother to detail again how operands are analyzed. In fact, a complete grammar of arithmetic expressions, would repeat the details of grammar G_1 just defined; i.e., it would classify OPERAND as a nonterminal and include all of the nonterminals, terminals, and productions of G_1. We are treating OPERAND as a token class, which appears as a terminal in the grammar.

A scanner would take the actual characters which compose the operand and classify them jointly as an OPERAND. This strategy simplifies our second grammar enormously.

The language EXPRESSIONS is the language of grammar $G_2 = (N_2, \Sigma_2, \text{EXPRESS}, P_2)$ where:

1. N_2 = {EXPRESS, OP}
2. Σ_2 = {'(', ')', '+', '*', '−', 'div', OPERAND}

P_2 has the productions:

1. EXPRESS → EXPRESS   OP   EXPRESS |
            '('   EXPRESS   ')' |
            OPERAND
2. OP   → '+' |'−' |'*' |'div'

A parse tree for the string 'a+bc*2' is shown in Fig. 2-3; a second parse tree for the same string is shown in Fig. 2-4; hence, it is not always true that a string has a unique parse tree. If *every* string generated by a grammar has exactly one parse tree, then that grammar is said to be *unambiguous*. The grammar, G_1, given earlier is unambiguous. If *one or more* strings in the language of a grammar has two parse trees, then that grammar is said to be *ambiguous*. This second grammar is ambiguous since the sentence 'a+bc*2' has the two distinct parse trees shown in Figs. 2-3 and 2-4.

The string 'a+bc*2' can reasonably be evaluated in either of two ways; the addition can precede the multiplication, or conversely, the multiplication can precede the addition. The answer computed will vary, depending on the order in which these two operations are performed. If 'a+bc*2' were rewritten as a fully parenthesized expression, then the choice in ordering operations would disappear. Expressions 2.1 and 2.2 have just one interpretation, since the parentheses force an ordering on the evaluation of the operations.

$$((a+bc)*2) \qquad\qquad (2.1)$$
$$(a+(bc*2)) \qquad\qquad (2.2)$$

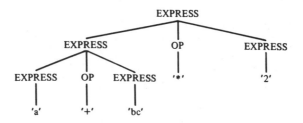

Fig. 2-3. First Parse Tree of 'a+bc*2'.

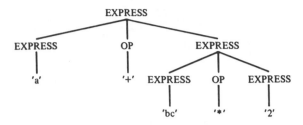

Fig. 2-4. Second Parse Tree of 'a+bc*2'.

In Fig. 2-3 operands 'a' and 'bc' are grouped together under the addition operator, while in Fig. 2-4, both 'bc' and '2' are grouped together under the multiplication sign. Viewing these groupings within a parse tree as being equivalent to parenthesizing the string, the tree Fig. 2-3 corresponds to evaluation 2.1, and Fig. 2-4 corresponds to evaluation 2.2. Expressions which have multiple interpretations are normally shunned in programming languages. It would be rather disconcerting if a program gave different results on the same data because an expression was interpreted one way for one run of the program and another way for a second run.

There are an infinite number of distinct grammars for the same language; some may be ambiguous, others may not. If the grammar is to drive the parser of a compiler, then an unambiguous grammar is usually selected by the compiler writer. In this way, each string has a unique, grammatical description. Alternatively, the compiler writer might use a grammar which is ambiguous but apply some extra-grammatical means to *disambiguate* it; i.e., remove the ambiguity. We shall see an example of disambiguation when control structures are studied in Chapter 6.

The next grammar is an unambiguous grammar for EXPRESSIONS. (Recall that G_2 is ambiguous.) In addition, the derivation trees of this new grammar G_3 express all of the implicit *precedence* common to most programming languages (including RASCAL) so that multiplication and division are performed before addition and subtraction, scanning left to right across an expression:

Grammar $G_3 = (N_3, \Sigma_3, \text{EXPRESS}, P_3)$ where:

1. N_3 = {EXPRESS, MDOP, ASOP, FACTOR, TERM}
2. $\Sigma_3 = \Sigma_2$

The productions of P_3 are:

1. EXPRESS → TERM
   → EXPRESS ASOP TERM
2. TERM → FACTOR
   → TERM MDOP FACTOR

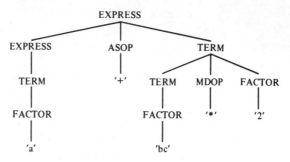

Fig. 2-5. Unique Parse Tree of 'a+bc∗2'.

3. FACTOR   → '(' EXPRESS ')'
          → OPERAND
4. ASOP   → '+' |'−'
5. MDOP   → '∗' |'div'

The unique parse tree of string 'a+bc∗2' is pictured in Fig. 2-5. The reader should verify that no tree which indicates addition should be performed before multiplication can be constructed for the string 'a+bc∗2' using grammar G_3 (see exercise 2-16).

Even though G_3 is unambiguous, it still has certain negative properties which will be studied in the next section. CANTOR actually employs a somewhat different grammar in its syntactic analysis of expressions, one which does not have these negative properties.

2.3 TOP-DOWN PARSING

In the previous discussion, we ignored how a parse tree is constructed when we were given just the grammar and the string to be analyzed. The generation of the parse tree for a string is said to be *parsing,* and the program which performs this task is said to be a *parser.* In the next two sections we shall analyze one particular class of parsers called *top-down.* They are so called because they construct the parse tree from the root to the frontier, and, by custom, the root of a tree is its 'top'. In sections 2.5 and 2.6 we shall explore the other common parsing orientation called *bottom-up.*

We shall illustrate some of the problems which arise in parsing by showing how to parse 'a+bc∗2', using grammar G_3 from section 2.2; however, before doing so, we first introduce the concepts of a *derivation* and that of a *sentential form.* If $\alpha B \beta \epsilon V^+$, where $\alpha, \beta \epsilon V^*$, and $B \epsilon N$, and there is a production $B \rightarrow \gamma$ in P, then $\alpha \gamma \beta$ is said to be *directly derivable* from $\alpha B \beta$. We show this by:

$$\alpha B \beta \Rightarrow \alpha \gamma \beta$$

A string δ is said to be *derivable* from $\alpha B \beta$ if either (i) $\delta = \alpha B \beta$; or (ii) there is a set of strings $\delta_1, \ldots \delta_r$ for some $r \geq 0$ such that:

$$\alpha B \beta \Rightarrow \delta_1 \Rightarrow \ldots \Rightarrow \delta_r \Rightarrow \delta$$

If δ is derivable from $\alpha B \beta$, we write this as:

$$\alpha B \beta \overset{*}{\Rightarrow} \delta$$

The set of strings in V^* derivable from the axiom A is called the set of *sentential forms*. The *sentences* of a language are just the sentential forms in Σ^*.

It is sometimes useful to indicate which production was applied in deriving one string from another, and, at which point of the string being modified, the production was applied. If we number the productions, then we write:

$$\alpha B \beta \overset{m}{\underset{n}{\Rightarrow}} \alpha \gamma \beta$$

to indicate that the m-th production was applied at the n-th character from the left of $\alpha B \beta$. (Note that there may be several occurrences of B in $\alpha B \beta$ since α and β are arbitrary members of V^*, so the number n is not superfluous in general.) A sequence:

$$\alpha B \beta \overset{m_0}{\underset{n_0}{\Rightarrow}} \delta_1 \overset{m_1}{\underset{n_1}{\Rightarrow}} \ldots \overset{m_{r-1}}{\underset{n_{r-1}}{\Rightarrow}} \delta_r \overset{m_r}{\underset{n_r}{\Rightarrow}} \delta$$

is said to be a *derivation* of δ from $\alpha B \beta$. If, in addition, $n_i \leq n_j$ for $0 \leq i \leq j \leq r$, then the derivation is said to be *leftmost*. For leftmost derivations, we usually omit the integers below the arrows since in that case they are superfluous.

A derivation is a *history* of how a particular string is derived from the axiom. A derivation is leftmost if the *leftmost* nonterminal is always expanded by the application of a production at each derivation step. There is a parse tree associated with each derivation. The derivation gives the order in which the subtrees of unit height are composed into the parse tree when it is constructed. Typically, there are many derivations associated with a single tree. Figure 2-6 presents two derivations of 'a+bc*2' for the tree given in Fig. 2-5; the second derivation is leftmost. Each derivation tree has a unique leftmost derivation associated with it; thus, leftmost derivations are a *normal form* for general derivations. Many parsing algorithms generate a leftmost derivation of a sentence; in

$$\text{EXPRESS} \overset{1.2}{\underset{1}{\Rightarrow}} \text{EXPRESS ASOP TERM} \overset{4.1}{\underset{2}{\Rightarrow}} \text{EXPRESS '+' TERM} \overset{1.1}{\underset{1}{\Rightarrow}}$$

$$\text{TERM '+' TERM} \overset{2.2}{\underset{3}{\Rightarrow}} \text{TERM '+' TERM MDOP FACTOR} \overset{2.1}{\underset{1}{\Rightarrow}}$$

$$\text{FACTOR '+' TERM MDOP FACTOR} \overset{3.2}{\underset{1}{\Rightarrow}} \text{'a' '+' TERM MDOP FACTOR} \overset{5.1}{\underset{4}{\Rightarrow}}$$

$$\text{'a' '+' TERM '*' FACTOR} \overset{2.1}{\underset{3}{\Rightarrow}} \text{'a' '+' FACTOR '*' FACTOR} \overset{3.2}{\underset{3}{\Rightarrow}}$$

$$\text{'a' '+' 'bc' '*' FACTOR} \overset{3.2}{\underset{5}{\Rightarrow}} \text{'a' '+' 'bc' '*' '2'}$$

$$\text{EXPRESS} \overset{1.2}{\underset{1}{\Rightarrow}} \text{EXPRESS ASOP TERM} \overset{1.1}{\underset{1}{\Rightarrow}} \text{TERM ASOP TERM} \overset{2.1}{\underset{1}{\Rightarrow}}$$

$$\text{FACTOR ASOP TERM} \overset{3.2}{\underset{1}{\Rightarrow}} \text{'a' ASOP TERM} \overset{4.1}{\underset{2}{\Rightarrow}} \text{'a' '+' TERM} \overset{2.2}{\underset{3}{\Rightarrow}}$$

$$\text{'a' '+' TERM MDOP FACTOR} \overset{2.1}{\underset{3}{\Rightarrow}} \text{'a' '+' FACTOR MDOP FACTOR} \overset{3.2}{\underset{3}{\Rightarrow}}$$

$$\text{'a' '+' 'bc' MDOP FACTOR} \overset{5.1}{\underset{4}{\Rightarrow}} \text{'a' '+' 'bc' '*' FACTOR} \overset{3.2}{\underset{5}{\Rightarrow}}$$

$$\text{'a' '+' 'bc' '*' '2'}$$

Fig. 2-6. Two Derivations of 'a+bc*2'.

particular, the top-down parsing algorithm which we shall describe here will do so.

The parsing method which we shall study is called *recursive descent;* it is so called because it is implemented by a set of recursive procedures, one to correspond to each nonterminal of the grammar. The parser descends the tree, actually constructing the tree during the descent. In general, the recursive descent parser is too inefficient for practical use; however, under special conditions which we shall study, it becomes quite efficient.

Consider the problem of generating the leftmost derivation of 'a+bc*2' with respect to grammar G_3 of the last section. We rewrite the productions of G_3 for convenient reference exactly as they appeared earlier:

1. EXPRESS → TERM
   → EXPRESS ASOP TERM
2. TERM → FACTOR
   → TERM MDOP FACTOR
3. FACTOR → '(' EXPRESS ')'
   → OPERAND

4. ASOP $\rightarrow$ '+'
           $\rightarrow$ '$-$'
5. MDOP $\rightarrow$ '*'
           $\rightarrow$ 'div'

The operating principle of brute force recursive descent parsing is to "guess" at which production should be applied next in constructing the leftmost derivation, try it, and then back out of the consequences of that choice, if it proves to be incorrect, trying another "guess" in its place.

All leftmost derivations begin with the axiom, EXPRESS, so, initially, the leftmost derivation of 'a+bc*2' must be just the single token:

EXPRESS   (2.3)

At this point, there are two *alternative* productions which can be applied, productions 1.1 and 1.2. Having no other basis upon which to decide at this time, we opt for trying the first alternative; if that fails to lead to the desired derivation, *and we can recognize that fact,* then we will return to the state of derivation 2.3 and try production 1.2., instead.

EXPRESS $\Rightarrow$ TERM   (2.4)

The first alternative of production 2 replaces TERM by FACTOR.

EXPRESS $\Rightarrow$ TERM $\Rightarrow$ FACTOR   (2.5)

This, in turn, leads to:

EXPRESS $\Rightarrow$ TERM $\Rightarrow$ FACTOR $\Rightarrow$ '(' EXPRESS ')'   (2.6)

At this point, the sentential form '(' EXPRESS ')' has been derived from the axiom.

A *prefix* of any string $w_1 \ldots w_n$ of vocabulary symbols is $w_1 \ldots w_i$ for some $0 \leqslant i \leqslant n$. If $i = 0$, then the prefix is λ. The longest prefix of '(' EXPRESS ')' consisting solely of terminals is '('. This prefix can be matched against the first token of 'a+bc*2', the string being parsed. If the longest prefix of terminal symbols of the latest sentential form derived is not also a prefix of the string being parsed, then the latest sentential form cannot derive the string being parsed; hence, the leftmost derivation being constructed is incorrect.

At this point, the parser must back out of its guess that production 3.1 was correct and try production 3.2, instead.

EXPRESS $\Rightarrow$ TERM $\Rightarrow$ FACTOR $\Rightarrow$ OPERAND   (2.7)

For purposes of this example, we are ignoring how OPERAND is further analyzed, so we rewrite derivation 2.7 as:

$$\text{EXPRESS} \Rightarrow \text{TERM} \Rightarrow \text{FACTOR} \Rightarrow \text{'a'} \qquad (2.8)$$

Derivation 2.8 matches the first character of 'a+bc∗2' correctly; unfortunately, there are no nonterminals in sentential form 'a', but there are other tokens in 'a+bc∗2'. Therefore, we must again back out of derivation 2.8. Since there are no more alternatives to production 3, the "erroneous guess" must have come earlier than derivation 2.5. Returning to derivation 2.4 and trying production 2.2 instead we have:

$$\text{EXPRESS} \Rightarrow \text{TERM} \Rightarrow \text{TERM} \quad \text{MDOP} \quad \text{FACTOR} \qquad (2.9)$$

This choice too is wrong, because the original choice in step 2.4 was wrong; however, the parser as described using the two rejection strategies:

1. reject a derivation if the longest terminal prefix of the last step is not a prefix of the string being parsed;
2. reject a derivation if the derivation terminates and the last step is not equal to the string being parsed;

will never discover this error! It will continue searching unsuccessfully for a leftmost derivation indefinitely; a partial history of this unsuccessful search is shown in Fig. 2-7.

Grammar G_3 is said to be *left recursive*. It is the left recursion which causes the difficulties pointed out in parsing 'a+bc∗2'. A production of a

EXPRESS

EXPRESS $\Rightarrow$ TERM

EXPRESS $\Rightarrow$ TERM $\Rightarrow$ FACTOR

EXPRESS $\Rightarrow$ TERM $\Rightarrow$ FACTOR $\Rightarrow$ '(' EXPRESS ')'

EXPRESS $\Rightarrow$ TERM $\Rightarrow$ FACTOR $\Rightarrow$ 'a'

EXPRESS $\Rightarrow$ TERM $\Rightarrow$ TERM MDOP FACTOR

EXPRESS $\Rightarrow$ TERM $\Rightarrow$ FACTOR MDOP FACTOR

EXPRESS $\Rightarrow$ TERM $\Rightarrow$ '(' EXPRESS ')' MDOP FACTOR

EXPRESS $\Rightarrow$ TERM $\Rightarrow$ 'a' MDOP FACTOR

EXPRESS $\Rightarrow$ TERM $\Rightarrow$ 'a' '∗' FACTOR

EXPRESS $\Rightarrow$ TERM $\Rightarrow$ 'a' 'div' FACTOR

EXPRESS $\Rightarrow$ TERM $\Rightarrow$ TERM MDOP FACTOR MDOP FACTOR

. . .

Fig. 2-7. Attempted Construction of Leftmost Derivation of 'a+bc∗2'.

context-free grammar:

$$B \to \gamma \tag{2.10}$$

is said to be *directly left recursive* if γ has the form $B\rho$ where $\rho \neq \lambda$. Such a production leads to derivations of the form:

$$B \Rightarrow B\rho \Rightarrow B\rho\rho \Rightarrow B\rho\rho\rho \ldots$$

If there is a derivation:

$$B \Rightarrow \gamma \overset{*}{\Rightarrow} B\rho$$

where $\rho \epsilon V^+$, then production 2.10 is said to be *indirectly left recursive*. A production which is directly or indirectly left recursive is said to be left recursive. The left-hand side of a left recursive production is a *left recursive nonterminal*. A grammar which has one or more left recursive nonterminals is itself a *left recursive grammar*.

The solution to the problem of left recursion is to modify the left recursive grammar into one which is *equivalent;* i.e., one which generates the same language, and yet is not left recursive. An algorithm to eliminate direct left recursion is in Fig. 2-8a. One to eliminate general left recursion appears in Fig. 2-8b. The algorithm assumes that the grammar has no *cyclic nonterminals;* i.e., no nonterminals which derive themselves in one or more steps as in derivation 2.11:

$$B \Rightarrow \gamma \overset{*}{\Rightarrow} B \tag{2.11}$$

where $\gamma \epsilon V^+$, and it also assumes that there are no productions of the form:

$$B \to \lambda$$

called *lambda productions.*

There are algorithms eliminating both lambda productions and cyclic nonterminals from arbitrary context-free grammars which can be applied to a grammar before trying to eliminate left-recursion; however, we leave the specification of those algorithms as exercises for the reader.

Grammar G_3 can be given to the direct left-recursion elimination algorithm as is, yielding a new grammar, G_4, which has no left-recursion.

```
1. EXPRESS    → TERM  EXPRESSES
2. EXPRESSES  → ASOP  TERM  EXPRESSES
              → λ
3. TERM       → FACTOR  TERMS
4. TERMS      → MDOP  FACTOR  TERMS
              → λ
5. FACTOR     → '('  EXPRESS  ')'
              → OPERAND
```

6. ASOP $\qquad$ → '+'

$\qquad\qquad\qquad$ → '−'

7. MDOP $\qquad$ → '*'

$\qquad\qquad\qquad$ → 'div'

Two new nonterminals were added to our grammar, EXPRESSES and TERMS, formed by pluralizing EXPRESS and TERM. EXPRESSES generates the "second half" of an EXPRESS followed by any number of EXPRESSES (zero or more); similarly for TERMS. A parse of 'a+bc*2' with respect to this new grammar is given in Fig. 2-9.

Our example grammar does not require the full power of the algorithm in Fig. 2-8b; in fact, if we order the nonterminals:

1. EXPRESS
2. TERM
3. FACTOR
4. ASOP
5. MDOP

To eliminate direct left recursion among productions whose left-hand side is B, group these productions as:

$$B \rightarrow B\alpha_1 \mid B\alpha_2 \mid \ldots \mid B\alpha_m \mid \beta_1 \mid \beta_2 \mid \ldots \mid \beta_n$$

where no β_i begins with a B. Replace these n+m productions by:

$$B \rightarrow \beta_1 B' \mid \beta_2 B' \mid \ldots \mid \beta_n B'$$
$$B' \rightarrow \alpha_1 B' \mid \alpha_2 B' \mid \ldots \mid \alpha_m B' \mid \lambda$$

(a) Direct Left Recursion

To eliminate left recursion from a grammar with no cyclic nonterminals and no lambda productions, execute:

function   eliminate(G: context-free grammar) : context-free grammar;
$\quad$ **var**   i,j: **integer;**
$\quad$ **begin**
$\qquad$ *arrange the nonterminals, $B_1, \ldots , B_n$, in any order;*
$\qquad$ **for** i := 1 **to** n **do**
$\qquad\quad$ **begin**
$\qquad\qquad$ **for** j := 1 **to** i−1 **do**
$\qquad\qquad\quad$ *replace each production $B_i \rightarrow B_j\delta$ by productions $B_i \rightarrow \rho_1\delta \mid \ldots \mid \rho_k\delta$, for*
$\qquad\qquad\quad$ *$\delta\epsilon V^*$, where $B_j \rightarrow \rho_1 \mid \ldots \mid \rho_k$ are the current productions with left-hand side*
$\qquad\qquad\quad$ *B_j;*
$\qquad\qquad$ *eliminate direct left-recursion among the B_i productions;*
$\qquad\quad$ **end;**
$\qquad$ *return the revised grammar;*
$\quad$ **end;**

(b) General Left Recursion

Fig. 2-8. Algorithm to Remove Left Recursion from A Context-Free Grammar.

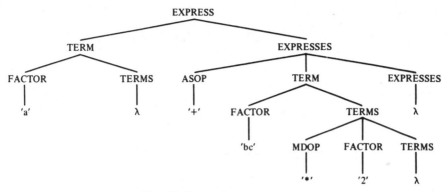

Fig. 2-9. Parse of 'a+bc∗2' by G_4.

then there are no productions of the form: $B_i \rightarrow B_j \, \delta$ and this algorithm yields grammar G_4. To illustrate the generality of Fig. 2-8b, we must reorder the nonterminals, interchanging TERM and EXPRESS:

1. TERM
2. EXPRESS
3. FACTOR
4. ASOP
5. MDOP

Here n is 5. Initializing i to 1, the inner loop is skipped. Eliminating direct left recursion among the TERM productions yields:

$$\text{TERM} \rightarrow \text{FACTOR} \quad \text{TERMS}$$
$$\text{TERMS} \rightarrow \text{MDOP} \quad \text{FACTOR} \quad \text{TERMS}$$
$$\rightarrow \lambda$$

Variable i is incremented to 2, j is set to 1 and the inner loop is executed once. One production:

$$\text{EXPRESS} \rightarrow \text{TERM}$$

satisfies the form specified in the inner loop:

$$B_2 \rightarrow B_1 \, \delta$$

where $B_2 = \text{EXPRESS}$, $B_1 = \text{TERM}$, and $\delta = \lambda$. This production is replaced by

$$\text{EXPRESS} \rightarrow \text{FACTOR} \quad \text{TERMS}$$

We next eliminate direct left-recursion from the EXPRESS productions replacing:

$$\text{EXPRESS} \quad \rightarrow \text{EXPRESS} \quad \text{ASOP} \quad \text{TERM}$$

by:

$$\begin{aligned}
\text{EXPRESS} &\rightarrow \text{FACTOR TERMS EXPRESSES} \\
\text{EXPRESSES} &\rightarrow \text{ASOP TERM EXPRESSES} \\
&\rightarrow \lambda
\end{aligned}$$

At this point we have grammar G_5:

$$\begin{aligned}
\text{EXPRESS} &\rightarrow \text{FACTOR TERMS EXPRESSES} \\
&\rightarrow \text{FACTOR TERMS} \\
\text{EXPRESSES} &\rightarrow \text{ASOP TERM EXPRESSES} \\
&\rightarrow \lambda \\
\text{TERM} &\rightarrow \text{FACTOR TERMS} \\
\text{TERMS} &\rightarrow \text{MDOP FACTOR TERMS} \\
&\rightarrow \lambda \\
\text{FACTOR} &\rightarrow \text{'(' EXPRESS ')'} \\
&\rightarrow \text{OPERAND} \\
\text{ASOP} &\rightarrow \text{'+'} \\
&\rightarrow \text{'}-\text{'} \\
\text{MDOP} &\rightarrow \text{'*'} \\
&\rightarrow \text{'div'}
\end{aligned}$$

Further steps of the algorithm will not yield any new changes; note that G_5 differs from G_4 only in the EXPRESS productions.

The inner loop, which is the most complex step, removes one level of intermediacy between nonterminals B_i and B_j, so that $B_i \rightarrow B_j \delta$ and $B_j \rightarrow B_1 \rho$ are replaced by $B_i \rightarrow B_1 \rho \delta$ in the modified grammar. The indirect left-recursion thereby becomes direct left-recursion which can then be removed; in general, any level of indirection in the left-recursion can be removed by repeated application of this step. Exercise 2-20 addresses this issue further.

With the elimination of left recursion, the brute force recursive descent parser will always find a leftmost derivation of a candidate sentence if one exists and will halt and reject that string if no such derivation exists. Figures 2-10 to 2-16 are a program which returns the *boolean* value, *true*, if a string is a sentence, and *false* if it is not. It does not actually emit the leftmost derivation, it merely recognizes whether a string is a sentence. However, it makes that determination by stepping through the leftmost derivation. It is a rather easy modification to have the program also emit the leftmost derivation as it constructs it. This task is left as an exercise for the reader (see exercise 2-18).

The program given in Figs. 2-10 through 2-16 must "back out" of a bad choice; i.e., when a predicate of an **if** statement is false. To do so it must "erase" all effects on the data structures manipulated by that program

{Token pointer initially points to first token. Pointer is advanced after matching current token with terminal symbol of a production.}

```
function   express: boolean;
                {look for an EXPRESS}
        begin
          save token pointer value;
          express := true;
          if term then   {production 1}
            if expresses then return;
          restore token pointer value;
          express := false;
        end;
```

Fig. 2-10. *Express.*

which the incorrectly called routines have had. In this case, the effect in question is the advancement of the "token pointer" which moves across the candidate sentence as the parsing proceeds. When a request for the "next token" is made, this pointer is advanced to the next token in the string. Bad choices could advance the pointer further to the right. To recover to an earlier point in the derivation, we must not only unwind from the recursive routine calls, but restore the token pointer as well to that point in the string where it was prior to the incorrect calls. The pseudo-code instructions in Figs. 2-10 through 2-16 which "restore" the token pointer which it earlier "saved" have this effect. Note that the pointer is only restored when the called routine returns "false," indicating that it was incorrectly called.

Despite the fact that left recursion can be eliminated by the method just discussed, two other problems remain. The first and most serious is the abysmal time which this parser can in general take to complete its work, $O(k^n)$, for some integer constant $k,$ where n is the length of the input string being parsed. This is caused by the need to constantly recover from

```
function   expresses : boolean;
                {look for an EXPRESSES}
        begin
          save token pointer value;
          expresses := true;
          if asop then   {production 2.1}
            if term then
              if expresses then return;
          restore token pointer value;   {production 2.2}
        end;
```

Fig. 2-11. *Expresses.*

```
function  term: boolean
          {look for a TERM}
     begin
       save token pointer value;
       term := true;
       if factor then    {production 3}
          if terms then return;
       restore token pointer value;
       term := false;
     end;
```

Fig. 2-12. *Term.*

```
function:  terms: boolean;
          {look for a TERMS}
   begin
     save token pointer value;
     terms := true;
     if mdop then   {production 4.1}
        if factor then
           if terms then return;
     restore token pointer value;   {production 4.2}
   end;
```

Fig. 2-13. *Terms.*

```
function  factor: boolean;
          {look for a FACTOR}
   begin
     save token pointer value;
     factor := true;
     if next token = '(' then   {production 5.1}
        if express then
           if next token = ')' then return;
     restore token pointer value;   {production 5.2}
     if next token is an operand then return;
     restore token pointer value;
     factor := false;
   end;
```

Fig. 2-14. *Factor.*

```
function   asop: boolean;
           {look for an ASOP}
    begin
      save token pointer value;
      asop := true;
      if next token = '+' then return;    {production 6.1}
      restore token pointer value;
      if next token = '−' then return;    {production 6.2}
      restore token pointer value;
      asop := false;
    end;
```

Fig. 2-15. *Asop.*

erroneous "guesses" as to which is the correct production to apply given a set of alternatives. The second problem is that the new grammar obtained by applying the algorithm which eliminates left recursion "mars" the appearance of the original grammar. Grammar, G_4, with its revised productions, does not look as "natural" as does G_3, even though they are equivalent.

There is no clean solution to the second problem without a resulting loss of efficiency in the parser. The method described in the next section reduces parsing time to $O(n)$ for a certain class of languages which seem to encompass all programming languages of interest, but only parses grammars of a special form; e.g., they may not be left recursive. The new method adopted here requires a more obscure grammar but is more efficient; also, it is not necessary to have just one version of a grammar available. A clearer more natural version can be made available for documentation. A second more obscure version can be given to the parser. However, once the reader becomes accustomed to the form which these restricted grammars take, they will become almost as natural to him as more general context-free grammars.

```
function   mdop: boolean;
           {look for an MDOP}
    begin
      save token pointer value;
      mdop := true;
      if next token = '*' then return;    {production 7.1}
      restore token pointer value;
      if next token = 'div' then return;    {production 7.2}
      restore token pointer value;
      mdop := false;
    end;
```

Fig. 2-16. *Mdop.*

2.4 TOP-DOWN PARSING WITHOUT BACKTRACKING

Let us return to grammar G_4. There is a technique by which we can choose between alternative productions in G_4 and be certain that we shall never choose incorrectly; however, in order to apply this technique, we must analyze the grammar itself more carefully. By first performing a fixed amount of work *before* trying to parse any sentences with G_4, it will be possible to avoid the overhead incurred by backtracking when we actually begin to parse. It is most important to recognize that the analysis of the grammar must be done only *once*. The same information derived from that analysis may be applied when parsing *any* string.

Consider a partial leftmost derivation as shown in 2.12. The sentential form $wB\beta$ has been derived so far. The

$$A \overset{*}{\Rightarrow} wB\beta \overset{*}{\Rightarrow} wbr\epsilon\Sigma^+ \tag{2.12}$$

nonterminal B must be expanded next. Suppose there are two alternative productions which can be applied in this situation

$$B \rightarrow \alpha \tag{2.13}$$
$$B \rightarrow \gamma \tag{2.14}$$

and the string we are parsing is wbr, where $b\epsilon\Sigma$, and $r\epsilon\Sigma^*$. If we knew that none of the terminal strings derivable from $\alpha\beta$ began with 'b', while at least one terminal string derivable from $\gamma\beta$ did begin with 'b', then we could unhesitatingly choose production 2.14 to apply. Production 2.13 could not possibly be correct. If wbr is a sentence, then production 2.14 must be correct. If wbr is not a sentence, then the reason for it failing to be a sentence has not yet surfaced in the leftmost derivation.

We continue by formalizing the ideas just presented. For $\alpha\epsilon V^+$, define $GEN(\alpha)$ to be

$$\{w\epsilon\Sigma^* \mid \alpha \overset{*}{\Rightarrow} w\}$$

$GEN(\alpha)$ is just the set of terminal strings derivable from α. Furthermore, define $FIRST(\alpha)$ to be the set of the first characters of the members of $GEN(\alpha)$; i.e., $FIRST(\alpha) =$

$$\{d\epsilon\Sigma \mid dz\epsilon GEN(\alpha) \quad \text{for} \quad z\epsilon\Sigma^*\}$$

For a grammar G, if it is always true that whenever there are two leftmost derivations:

$$A \overset{*}{\Rightarrow} wB\beta \overset{*}{\Rightarrow} w\gamma\beta \overset{*}{\Rightarrow} wz\epsilon\Sigma^+$$
$$A \overset{*}{\Rightarrow} wB\beta \overset{*}{\Rightarrow} w\rho\beta \overset{*}{\Rightarrow} wv\epsilon\Sigma^+$$

$\rho \neq \gamma$ implies FIRST(z) $\neq$ FIRST(v), then that grammar is said to be *LL(1)*. An LL(1) grammar can always be parsed top-down without backtracking. Given two alternative productions, we can tell by examining the next token which must be derived which production to apply.

The term LL(1) comes from the fact that the string being parsed is scanned from *L*eft to right, that the decision of which production to apply is made by examining the *L*eftmost tokens that production will derive, and that we look at the *first* token which must be derived next in making that choice. In our example shown in derivation 2.12, this symbol is 'b', which is also called the *lookahead* symbol. The lookahead string can be expanded to any length k, and need not be a single symbol. This gives rise to the definition of *LL(k)* grammars. For our purposes, it is enough to consider such grammars when $k=1$. The bibliography points to the literature on general LL(k) grammars for the interested reader.

We have not yet shown how we can easily conclude that a grammar satisfies the LL(1) condition, nor have we shown how to select a production from alternatives in a particular grammar and a particular situation. For LL(1) grammars we construct a *selection set* for each production. This set permits us to select the correct production in any situation (hence the name).

The selection set of production "B $\rightarrow$ α" is defined as

$$\text{SELECT}(B \rightarrow \alpha) =$$

$$\{d \epsilon \text{FIRST}(\alpha\beta) \mid \text{there is a derivation from axiom A}$$

$$A \overset{*}{\Rightarrow} wB\beta \Rightarrow w\alpha\beta \quad \text{for} \quad w \epsilon \Sigma^*, \ \beta \epsilon V^+\}$$

The algorithm for computing the selection set of each production is not that complex, but it is tedious; it is included in Appendix C. For simple grammars, the selection set can often be computed by hand by inspection of the grammar; in general, however, it is necessary to reply upon more formal means.

If the selection sets of alternative productions (i.e., productions with the same left-hand side) are mutually disjoint, then whenever a nonterminal B must be expanded, there will be at most one production whose selection set includes the next token in the string being parsed. In our example, this token is 'b'. Choose that unique production, if it exists. If there is no production, then the string being parsed is not a sentence.

There is just one problem with the LL(1) parsing algorithm as just presented: There is no lookahead symbol for the last token of a string being parsed. Hence, the parsing algorithm will not work correctly unless we can modify either it or the language being parsed to overcome this problem. The solution is to simply concatenate an *endmarker* to the right of every string being parsed. This endmarker, which we shall denote by

'¢', is not otherwise in the terminal or nonterminal alphabets of the grammar. The selection sets are computed on the premise that all sentences of the language end with '¢'. In that way, '¢' becomes part of the selection sets of certain productions but *not* a symbol in any of the productions of the grammar. With this modification, the lookahead symbol is always defined and the parsing algorithm will function correctly. The algorithm in Appendix C, which computes selection sets, presumes than an endmarker is concatenated to the right end of each string being parsed. Figure 2-17 shows a general grammar-driven LL(1) parsing algorithm. It presumes that the selection set of each production has already been computed. The driver works for any LL(1) grammar and requires no stacks or other auxiliary data structures beyond the grammar productions themselves.

We now rewrite the productions of G_4 with the selection set of each production to its right:

1. EXPRESS   → TERM   EXPRESSES   {OPERAND, '('}
2. EXPRESSES → ASOP   TERM   EXPRESSES   {'−', '+'}
                        → λ   {')', '¢'}
3. TERM   → FACTOR   TERMS   {OPERAND, '('}
4. TERMS   → MDOP   FACTOR   TERMS   {'div', '*'}
                        → λ   {'¢', '−', ')', '+'}
5. FACTOR   → '(' EXPRESS ')'   {'('}
                        → OPERAND   {OPERAND}
6. ASOP   → '+'   {'+'}
                        → '−'   {'−'}
7. MDOP   → '*'   {'*'}
                        → 'div'   {'div'}

The selection set of each production was computed using the algorithm described in Appendix C. The selection sets of alternative productions are mutually disjoint; therefore, this grammar is LL(1). Figure 2-18 shows the parsing action of the parser given in Fig. 2-17 for "a+bc*2." Figures 2-19 through 2-25 give an alternative formulation of the parser in which the grammar rules are "embedded" into the code itself.

Simply because a grammar is not left recursive does not guarantee that it is LL(1); however, no left recursive grammar is ever LL(1). Here we are assuming that there are no "useless" productions, in that for each production there is at least one sentence whose leftmost derivation includes an application of that production; the proof of this fact is left as an exercise. There is a standard set of transformations which are applied to convert non-LL(1) grammars into LL(1) grammars. The algorithm given in Fig. 2-8 which eliminates left recursion is one such grammar transformation. For most programming languages these transformation rules

```
function  LL_parser(candidate: string): boolean;
          {grammar – driven LL(1) parser.}
          {algorithm presumes grammar used to drive parser is LL(1).}
var       sent_form: string;   sent_form_ptr: ↑string;
          token_ptr: ↑string;
begin
          LL_parser := true;   {presume candidate is a sentence.}
          sent_form := grammar axiom;
          candidate := candidate ||'¢';   {add endmarker}
          sent_form_ptr := address of sent_form;
          token_ptr := address of candidate;
          while sent_form_ptr↑ is defined do
            if sent_form_ptr↑ is a terminal then
              if token_ptr↑ = sent_form_ptr↑ then begin
                advance token_ptr;   advance sent_form_ptr;   end;
              else begin
                  LL_parser := false;   {candidate is not a sentence}
                  return ; end ;
            else if there is a production whose left-hand side is sent_form_ptr↑, and whose
                    selection set includes token_ptr↑ then
                      replace sent_form_ptr↑ by the right-hand side of that production in
                      sent_form;
              else begin
                  LL_parser :– false;   {candidate is not a sentence}
                  return ; end ;
end;
```

Fig. 2-17. LL(1) Parsing Algorithm.

EXPRESS	begin with the axiom
TERM EXPRESSES	next symbol is 'a'
FACTOR TERMS EXPRESSES	next symbol is still 'a'
'a' TERMS EXPRESSES	next symbol is still 'a'
'a' EXPRESSES	next symbol is '+'
'a' ASOP TERM EXPRESSES	next symbol is still '+'
'a' '+' TERM EXPRESSES	next symbol is still '+'
'a' '+' FACTOR TERMS EXPRESSES	next symbol is 'bc'
'a' '+' 'bc' TERMS EXPRESSES	next symbol is still 'bc'
'a' '+' 'bc' MDOP FACTOR TERMS EXPRESSES	next symbol is '*'
'a' '+' 'bc' '*' FACTOR TERMS EXPRESSES	next symbol is still '*'
'a' '+' 'bc' '*' '2' TERMS EXPRESSES	next symbol is '2'
'a' '+' 'bc' '*' '2' EXPRESSES	next symbol is '¢'
'a' '+' 'bc' '*' '2'	next symbol is still '¢'

Fig. 2-18. LL(1) Parsing of 'a+bc*2'.

```
function  express: boolean;
          {look for EXPRESS—current token should be one of:
                              operand   '('                    }
     begin
       if current token in [operand,'('] then
         if term then
           if expresses then express := true;
           else express := false;
         else express := false;
       else express := false;
     end;
```

Fig. 2-19. *Express* for LL(1) Parser.

```
function  expresses: boolean;
          {look for an EXPRESSES}
     begin
       if current token in ['−','+'] then
         if asop then
           if term then
             if expresses then expresses := true;
             else expresses := false;
           else expresses := false;
         else expresses := false;
       else if current token in ['¢', ')'] then expresses := true;
         else expresses := false;
     end;
```

Fig. 2-20. *Expresses* for LL(1) Parser.

```
function  term: boolean;
          {look for a TERM}
     begin
       if current token in [operand,'('] then
         if factor then
           if terms then term := true;
           else term := false;
         else term := false;
       else term := false;
     end;
```

Fig. 2-21. *Term* for LL(1) Parser.

```
function   terms: boolean;
           {look for a TERMS}
   begin
     if current token in ['div','*'] then
        if mdop then
          if factor then
             if terms then terms := true;
             else terms := false;
          else terms := false;
        else terms := false;
     else if current token in ['¢','−',')','+'] then terms := true;
          else terms := false;
   end;
```

Fig. 2-22. *Terms* for LL(1) Parser.

work; however, they are heuristic in that they are not guaranteed to always convert a non-LL(1) grammar into an equivalent LL(1) grammar. Some of these transformations are given in Appendix C.

LL(1) grammars and languages have interesting properties; we state several of them without proof here. The interested reader is referred to the literature cited in the bibliography for details on why these results are true.

```
function   factor: boolean;
           {look for a FACTOR}
   begin
     if current token in ['('] then
        begin
          advance token pointer;
          if express then
             begin
               if current token in [')'] then
                  begin advance token pointer; factor := true;   end;
               else factor := false;
             end;
          else factor := false;
        end;
     else if current token in [operand] then
        begin
          advance token pointer;
          factor := true;
        end;
     else factor := false;
   end;
```

Fig. 2-23. *Factor* for LL(1) Parser.

```
function   asop: boolean;
              {look for an ASOP}
    begin
      if current token in ['+'] then
        begin
          advance token pointer;
          asop := true;
        end;
      else if current token in ['-'] then
          begin
            advance token pointer;
            asop := true;
          end;
        else asop := false;
    end;
```

Fig. 2-24. *Asop* for LL(1) Parser.

Theorem. There are context-free languages which have no LL(1) grammar.

Theorem. There is an algorithm which can determine whether an arbitrary context-free grammar is an LL(1) grammar.

Theorem. There is no algorithm which can determine whether an arbitrary context-free language has an LL(1) grammar which defines it.

Theorem. There is an algorithm which can determine whether two arbitrary LL(1) grammars generate the same language.

```
function   mdop: boolean;
              {look for an MDOP}
    begin
      if current token in ['*'] then
        begin
          advance token pointer;
          mdop := true;
        end;
      else if current token in ['div'] then
            begin
              advance token pointer;
              mdop: = true;
            end;
          else mdop := false;
    end;
```

Fig. 2-25. *Mdop* for LL(1) Parser.

The first and third results are quite negative. There are languages which have no LL(1) grammar, and it is not in general possible to examine arbitrary languages and well if they have an LL(1) grammar. Despite these facts, it is true that nearly all *actual* programming languages of interest do have LL(1) grammars which approximate them. The languages which present problems are not generally of interest to us in language design. The exercises at the end of this chapter address non-LL(1) grammars and languages more carefully.

LL(1) parsing is one method to eliminate backtracking. The overhead of computing the selection set of each production and then matching the next token in the string being parsed to the selection sets of alternative productions reduces the parsing time to a *linear* function of the length of the input. Note that the computational overhead in selecting a production is quite small. The selection set of each alternative production must be examined. For any practical grammar, there will typically be a handful of alternative productions; by organizing the selection sets in some collating sequence, the search through each set can be performed in $\log_2 m$ time, where m is the size of the selection set. An even more efficient scheme is possible if a *parsing action* table is set up which summarizes the information contained in the grammar and its selection sets. The rows of the table may be labelled by the nonterminals of the grammar while the columns are labelled by the possible lookahead symbols. Legal combinations of nonterminals and lookahead symbols can have an entry which is the number of the production to apply in that situation. Entries for illegal combinations can be calls to various error routines. Figure 2-26 shows such a table for G_4 which can drive the parser in Fig. 2-17.

	OPERAND	'('	')'	'+'	'−'	'*'	'div'	'¢'
EXPRESS	1	1						
EXPRESSES			2.2	2.1	2.1			2.2
TERM	3	3				4.1	4.1	
TERMS			4.2	4.2	4.2			4.2
FACTOR	5.2	5.1						
ASOP				6.1	6.2			
MDOP						7.1	7.2	

Fig. 2-26. Parsing Action Table for G_4.

One final comment on LL(1) parsing concerns the ability of such parsers to detect errors at the earliest possible moment in a left to right scan of the source string. A string, δ, is said to be a *viable prefix* if there is some sentential form $\delta\alpha$. An LL(1) parser rejects a string as soon as it discovers a terminal prefix of that string which is not viable. Hence, no effort is wasted parsing a string which cannot be a sentence simply because the parser cannot detect that fact from the characters of the string it has seen. As we will see in Chapter 8, this also improves the error processing capabilities of a compiler with an LL(1) parser driving it.

2.5 LR PARSING

The last section showed how to efficiently construct a parse tree from the root down. LL parsing, the method described, is a *top-down* parsing method. Another strategy is to build the tree up from the frontier elements to the root. Parsers which behave in this way are, appropriately enough, called *bottom-up*. A number of different bottom-up parsing algorithms have been used throughout the past fifteen years including simple, operator and mixed precedence parsers, bounded context parsers, and LR parsers. The bibliography contains references to each of these methods. This section concentrates only on the LR method, which has largely replaced other bottom-up techniques in recent years.

In many respects, LR parsing is the most general bottom-up parsing method. It subsumes all other common parsing methods in power. Originally due to Knuth, LR parsing is more complex than LL parsing and is much less intuitive in its operation; however, it has one major advantage over LR parsers which has made it widely adopted. Although LR parsers also require grammars to be in a special form, many more "common" grammars fit this form than fit the form required for LL parsers. For example, grammar G_3, with only a trivial modification, is an LR grammar, even though it is not LL. Left recursion causes no problem for LR parsers.

Like LL parsers, LR parsers have the *viable prefix* property. They scan the candidate string from left to right. An LR parser will never scan further into a string than its longest viable prefix. This facilitates error processing because the parser will not "waste time" scanning past the point where the error occurs. The significance of the viable prefix property will be better appreciated after Chapter 8, where error processing is examined.

Recall that LL parsers are classified by the length of the lookahead strings found in their selection sets. Thus, we have LL(1), LL(2), . . . , LL(k) parsers, although section 2.4 only examined LL(1) parsers. LR parsers also use a lookahead string. Depending on the length of that string, we have LR(1), LR(2), . . . , LR(k) parsers. Here we will deal only with LR(1) parsers.

The letters 'LR' are an acronym for how the parser operates; i.e., scanning the input *l*eft to right, generating an inverse *r*ightmost derivation. A leftmost derivation is one in which the leftmost nonterminal is expanded at each step; similarly, a rightmost derivation is one in which the rightmost nonterminal is expanded. Figure 2-27 gives the rightmost derivation of 'a+bc*2' with respect to G_3, and the inverse of that derivation. Figure 2-28 shows the step-wise construction of the tree corresponding to the inverse derivation of Fig. 2-27. An LR(1) parser for G_3 would perform this step-wise construction.

```
EXPRESS ⇒
TERM EXPRESSES ⇒
TERM ASOP TERM EXPRESSES ⇒
TERM ASOP TERM ⇒
TERM ASOP FACTOR TERMS ⇒
TERM ASOP FACTOR MDOP FACTOR TERMS ⇒
TERM ASOP FACTOR MDOP FACTOR ⇒
TERM ASOP FACTOR MDOP '2' ⇒
TERM ASOP FACTOR '*' '2' ⇒
TERM ASOP 'bc' '*' '2' ⇒
TERM '+' 'bc' '*' '2' ⇒
FACTOR TERMS '+' 'bc' '*' '2' ⇒
FACTOR '+' 'bc' '*' '2' ⇒
'a' '+' 'bc' '*' '2'
```

(a) Rightmost Derivation of 'a+bc*2'

```
'a' '+' 'bc' '*' '2' ⇒
FACTOR '+' 'bc' '*' '2' ⇒
FACTOR TERMS '+' 'bc' '*' '2' ⇒
TERM '+' 'bc' '*' '2' ⇒
TERM ASOP 'bc' '*' '2' ⇒
TERM ASOP FACTOR '*' '2' ⇒
TERM ASOP FACTOR MDOP '2' ⇒
TERM ASOP FACTOR MDOP FACTOR ⇒
TERM ASOP FACTOR MDOP FACTOR TERMS ⇒
TERM ASOP FACTOR TERMS ⇒
TERM ASOP TERM ⇒
TERM ASOP TERM EXPRESSES ⇒
TERM EXPRESSES ⇒
EXPRESS
```

(b) Inverse Rightmost Derivation of 'a+bc*2'

Figure 2-27. Derivations of 'a+bc*2'

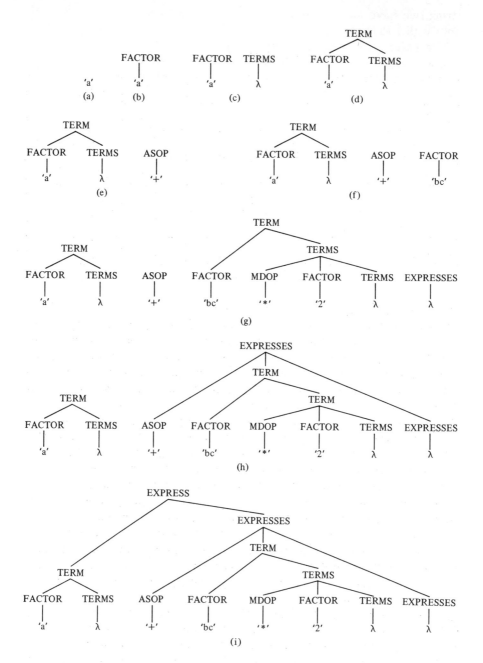

Fig. 2-28.

When parsing top-down, we *expand* a nonterminal. A nonterminal is replaced in the derivation by the right-hand side of one of its alternatives. When parsing bottom-up, we replace the right-hand side of a production by its left-hand side. Such a replacement is called a *reduction*.

When parsing top-down, there is never any doubt which nonterminal to expand next. When parsing bottom-up, it is not clear where in the derivation to reduce; for example, in the inverse rightmost derivation of 'a+bc*2', the first few steps are:

$$
\begin{array}{ll}
a + bc * 2 & \Rightarrow \\
\text{FACTOR} + bc * 2 & \Rightarrow \\
\text{TERM} + bc * 2 & \Rightarrow \\
\text{EXPRESS} + bc * 2 & \Rightarrow \\
\text{EXPRESS} + \text{FACTOR} * 2 & \Rightarrow \\
\text{EXPRESS} + \text{TERM} * 2 & \Rightarrow \\
\text{EXPRESS} + \text{TERM} * \text{FACTOR}
\end{array}
$$

Notice that if we had performed the leftmost possible reduction in the last step we would have had instead:

$$\text{EXPRESS} * 2$$

Of course, this reduction would have been incorrect. How does the parser know which substring of the current sentential form to reduce? The correct substring is the *handle*. In every bottom-up parser without back-up, previous analysis of the grammar allows correct determination of the handle. The primary difference between the various bottom-up methods lies in their abilities to locate the handle and, in cases where there are two productions:

$$
\begin{array}{l}
A \rightarrow \beta \\
B \rightarrow \beta
\end{array}
$$

in their abilities to choose between them when the handle is β. For an LR parser, this analysis is summarized in two tables.

An LR(1) parser requires that two *tables* be constructed from the grammar in question. These tables, the *parsing action* and *goto* tables, "drive" the parser. It is important to isolate the table construction from parsing. By examining the grammar, the parsing action and goto tables are built. Once these tables which are peculiar to the grammar have been constructed, a parsing algorithm references the tables to parse a string. This algorithm does not change with the grammar—just the tables change.

As originally conceived by Knuth in 1965, these tables proved to be impractically large for grammars defining actual programming languages. It was not until 1969 that F.L. DeRemer and A.J. Korenjak discovered that in many cases the tables could be "compacted" by merging some of the rows, while still maintaining the correctness of the parser. The reductions in table size were substantial enough that LR became practical. The parsing method is the same in all cases; i.e., the tables in all cases have the same format and are used in the same way; it is only the *table construction algorithms* which differ. DeRemer described what are called *simple LR grammars* (SLR), while Korenjak defined the *look-ahead* LR grammars (LALR). A language which has an LR(k), SLR(k) or LALR(k) *grammar* is said to be an LR(k), SLR(k) or LALR(k) *language,* respectively.

Not every LR(k) grammar is LALR(k), and not every LALR(k) grammar is SLR(k); however, this difference does *not* extend to languages. For any k, the set of LR(k), SLR(k) and LALR(k) languages are all equal; furthermore, these languages do not form a true hierarchy. For any k, j, the LR(k) languages are the same as the LR(j) languages; similarly so for SLR and LALR languages. Contrast this with the LL languages for which the LL(k) languages are a proper subset of the LL(k+1) languages for any k $\geq$ 1. In practice, the only grammars used are SLR(1) and LALR(1), because the tables are too large for k $>$ 1. Now that the general character of LR parsing has been described, we shall present the parsing algorithm and the SLR(1) table construction algorithm. Our running example of arithmetic expressions will be parsed by an SLR(1) parser.

Figure 2-29 depicts an LR parser. It has an input string with endmarker ¢ attached, a push-down stack, and two parsing tables. The input is read from left to right, one symbol at a time. The endmarker serves the same purpose in LR parsing as it did in LL parsing. The stack is a string of the form:

$$s_0 \ X_1 \ s_1 \ X_2 \ . \ . \ . \ s_{m-1} \ X_m \ s_m$$

where s_m is on top. Each X_i is a vocabulary symbol, while each s_i is a *state* symbol. Each state symbol captures the information contained in the stack below it and serves to direct parser action. Actually the grammar symbols are superfluous and are included only to aid in the explanation of the parser; in a real implementation, they could be omitted.

Each step of the parser begins by examining the next input symbol a_i and the state s_m currently on top of the stack. It then consults ACTION $[s_m, a_i]$, the parsing action table. Each table entry can have one of four values:

    1. shift   s

2. reduce B → β
3. accept
4. error

The last two actions are the easiest to explain. If ACTION $[s_m, a_i]$ = accept, the parser halts and accepts the string; it is a sentence of the grammar's language. Alternatively, if ACTION $[s_m, a_i]$ = error, the parser rejects the candidate string; it is not a sentence. The first two are only slightly more complex. If ACTION $[s_m, a_i]$ = shift s, then the input pointer of the parser shifts one character (token) to the right and pushes a_1 and state s onto the stack. Finally, if ACTION $[s_m, a_i]$ = reduce B → β, then several actions occur: First, the top 2r symbols are popped off the stack, where r is the length of β; this leaves:

$$s_0 \ X_1 \ s_1 \ X_2 \ . \ . \ . \ s_{m-r-1} \ X_{m-r} s_{m-r}$$

on the stack. Second, it looks up s = GOTO $[s_{m-r}, B]$ in the goto table. Third, it pushes B and s onto the stack, giving:

$$s_0 \ X_1 \ s_1 \ X_2 \ . \ . \ . \ s_{m-r-1} \ X_{m-r} s_{m-r} \ B \ s$$

The current input symbol remains unchanged.

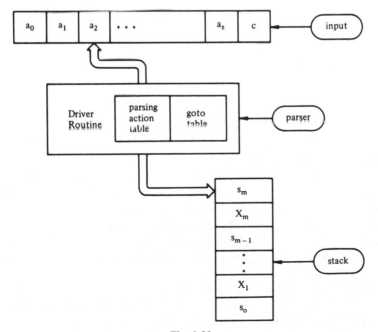

Fig. 2-29.

That is the entire LR parsing algorithm. Initially, the parser begins with a designated start state on the stack and the input pointer at the far left end of the candidate string. The LR, SLR, and LALR parsers all use this algorithm; only the table constructors differ.

We would like to guarantee that when the handle reduces to the grammar axiom, we can immediately accept the string. Ordinarily this will not be possible; for example, axiom EXPRESS of G_3 can occur at places other than the root of the parse tree. To circumvent this situation, we ordinarily *augment* any grammar with a new axiom and a rule:

$$A' \to A$$

where A is the old axiom. We augment grammar G_3 with axiom E' and the rule:

$$0. \ E' \to E$$

yielding G'_3.

The first step in generating the tables is to augment the grammar. After this, we must construct what is called the collection of *LR(0) items*. Intuitively, these are the states of a finite-state automaton which accepts the viable prefixes of sentential forms of the grammar. Note that this is *not* the same as accepting the *sentences* of the grammar. From this collection we will be able to construct the tables directly.

An item is a production of the grammar with a dot at some position of the right-hand side; for example, the following are all items using production 1.2 of G_3:

$$\text{EXPRESS} \to .\text{EXPRESS ASOP TERM}$$
$$\text{EXPRESS} \to \text{EXPRESS .ASOP TERM}$$
$$\text{EXPRESS} \to \text{EXPRESS ASOP .TERM}$$
$$\text{EXPRESS} \to \text{EXPRESS ASOP TERM.}$$

The production $B \to \lambda$ generates only one item; i.e., $B \to . \ .$

Intuitively, an item represents how much of a production's right side has been seen in the current sentential form. For example, the first item above shows that none of the production has yet been seen, while the last one indicates that all three right side components have been found. Informally, a *completed* item, one in which the dot is at the far right, "signals" the parser that this right side is the handle, and a reduction using this production is in order.

Items are grouped into sets; each set is a state of the automaton which accepts viable prefixes. To construct the collection of sets we need, we must define two functions, *CLOSURE* and *GOTO*. CLOSURE is shown in Fig. 2-30. Given set of items $\{[E' \to .\text{EXPRESS}]\}$, its closure, CL, is:

$$E' \rightarrow .\text{EXPRESS}$$
$$\text{EXPRESS} \rightarrow .\text{TERM}$$
$$\text{EXPRESS} \rightarrow .\text{EXPRESS ASOP TERM}$$
$$\text{TERM} \rightarrow .\text{FACTOR}$$
$$\text{TERM} \rightarrow .\text{TERM MDOP FACTOR}$$
$$\text{FACTOR} \rightarrow .\text{'(EXPRESS)'}$$
$$\text{FACTOR} \rightarrow .\text{OPERAND}$$

Intuitively, the closure operation indicates that since we are "looking for" E' by looking for an EXPRESS, we should also be looking for those strings which are derived from EXPRESS; in this case, there are two such forms, TERM and EXPRESS ASOP TERM. Extending this reasoning, we conclude that in seeking TERM we should look for FACTOR and TERM MDOP FACTOR. This finally leads us to add '(EXPRESS)' and OPERAND to the list of substrings to be sought, as shown in the closure of { [E' → .EXPRESS] }.

If I is a set of items and X is a vocabulary symbol, then $GOTO(I,X)$ is simply the closure of the set of all items $[B \rightarrow \alpha X. \beta]$ such that $[B \rightarrow \alpha. X \beta]$ is in I. Intuitively, if I is the set of items that are *valid* for viable prefix γ, then $GOTO(I,X)$ is the set of items valid for γX. Item $B \rightarrow \beta_1 . \beta_2$ is said to be *valid* for viable prefix $\alpha\beta$, if there is a *rightmost* derivation $A' \Rightarrow \alpha\beta\omega \Rightarrow \alpha\beta_1\beta_2\omega$. $GOTO$ (CL, EXPRESS) is:

$$E' \rightarrow \text{EXPRESS}.$$
$$\text{EXPRESS} \rightarrow \text{EXPRESS .ASOP TERM}$$
$$\text{ASOP} \rightarrow .\text{'+'}$$
$$\text{ASOP} \rightarrow . \text{'−'}$$

Now that we have the two basic functions needed, we can construct the collection of the set of items. The algorithm is given in Fig. 2-31. Its input is augmented grammar G'; its output is the collection of sets of items. Figure 2-32 shows the collection of sets of items for augmented grammar G_3. Each set of items has been consecutively numbered from zero. To the

```
function closure (I : set of items) : set of items;
   begin
      repeat
         for   each item B → α C β in I and each production C → γ in G such that C →. γ is
               not in I  do
               add C →. γ to I;
         until no more items can be added to I;
      closure : = I ;
   end;
```

Fig. 2-30. *Closure.*

function collection (G' : grammar) : collection of sets of items;
  begin
    collection : = {closure ({A' → .A})};
      repeat
        for   *each set of items I in collection and each vocabulary symbol X such that*
              GOTO (I, X) ≠ Φ and is not in collection **do**
              add GOTO(I, X) to collection;
      until *no more sets of items can be added to collection;*
  end;

Fig. 2-31. *Collection.*

right of each set is the viable prefix which that set represents. Sets I_{13}, I_{15}–I_{16}, I_{18}–I_{20}, I_{22}, I_{23}, and I_{25}–I_{30} all duplicate existing sets.

I_0 : E'   → .EXPRESS   {λ}
       EXPRESS → .TERM
       EXPRESS → .EXPRESS ASOP TERM
       TERM   → .FACTOR
       TERM   → .TERM MDOP FACTOR
       FACTOR → .'(' EXPRESS ')'
       FACTOR → .OPERAND

I_1 : E'   → EXPRESS   {EXPRESS}
       EXPRESS → EXPRESS .ASOP TERM
       ASOP   → .'+'
       ASOP   → .'−'

I_2 : EXPRESS → TERM.   {TERM}
       TERM   → TERM .MDOP FACTOR
       MDOP   → .'*'
       MDOP   → .'div'

I_3 : TERM   → FACTOR.   {FACTOR}

I_4 : FACTOR → '(.EXPRESS ')'   {'('}
       EXPRESS → .TERM
       EXPRESS → .EXPRESS ASOP TERM
       TERM   → .FACTOR
       TERM   → .TERM MDOP FACTOR
       FACTOR → .'(' EXPRESS ')'
       FACTOR → .OPERAND

I_5 : FACTOR → OPERAND.   {OPERAND}

Fig. 2-32. Collection of Sets of Items.

I_6 : EXPRESS → EXPRESS ASOP .TERM   {EXPRESS

      TERM → .FACTOR   ASOP }

      TERM → .TERM MDOP FACTOR

      FACTOR → .'(' EXPRESS ')'

      FACTOR → .OPERAND

I_7 : ASOP → '+'.   {EXPRESS

                                           '+' }

I_8 : ASOP → '−'.   {EXPRESS

                                           '−' }

I_9 : TERM → TERM MDOP .FACTOR   {TERM

      FACTOR → .'(' EXPRESS ')'   MDOP}

      FACTOR → .OPERAND

I_{10} : MDOP → '*'.   {TERM}

I_{11} : MDOP → 'div'.   {TERM

                                          'div' }

I_{12} : FACTOR → '(' EXPRESS .')'   {'(

      EXPRESS → EXPRESS .ASOP TERM   EXPRESS}

      ASOP → .' +'

      ASOP → .'−'

I_{13} : EXPRESS → TERM.   {'(

same TERM → TERM .MDOP FACTOR   TERM}

 as   MDOP → .'*'

I_2 : MDOP → .'div'

I_{14} : TERM → FACTOR.   {'(

                                        FACTOR}

I_{15} : FACTOR → '(' .EXPRESS ')'   {'('

same EXPRESS → .TERM   '('}

 as   EXPRESS → .EXPRESS ASOP TERM

I_4 : TERM → .FACTOR

      TERM → .TERM MDOP FACTOR

      FACTOR → .'(' EXPRESS ')'

      FACTOR → .OPERAND

Fig. 2-32 (continued).

I_{16} : FACTOR $\rightarrow$ OPERAND. $\left\{\begin{array}{l}\text{'('}\\ \text{OPERAND}\end{array}\right\}$
same
  as
I_5

I_{17} : EXPRESS $\rightarrow$ EXPRESS ASOP TERM. $\left\{\begin{array}{l}\text{EXPRESS}\\ \text{ASOP}\\ \text{TERM}\end{array}\right\}$
      TERM $\rightarrow$ TERM .MDOP FACTOR
      MDOP $\rightarrow$.'*'
      MDOP $\rightarrow$.'div'

I_{18} : TERM $\rightarrow$ FACTOR. $\left\{\begin{array}{l}\text{EXPRESS}\\ \text{ASOP}\\ \text{FACTOR}\end{array}\right\}$
same
  as
I_3

I_{19} : FACTOR $\rightarrow$ '(' .EXPRESS ')' $\left\{\begin{array}{l}\text{EXPRESS}\\ \text{ASOP}\\ \text{'('}\end{array}\right\}$
same EXPRESS $\rightarrow$ .TERM
  as   EXPRESS $\rightarrow$ .EXPRESS ASOP TERM
I_4 TERM $\rightarrow$ .FACTOR
       TERM $\rightarrow$ .TERM MDOP FACTOR
       FACTOR $\rightarrow$.'(' EXPRESS ')'
       FACTOR $\rightarrow$ .OPERAND

I_{20} : FACTOR $\rightarrow$ OPERAND. $\left\{\begin{array}{l}\text{EXPRESS}\\ \text{ASOP}\\ \text{OPERAND}\end{array}\right\}$
same
  as
I_5

I_{21} : TERM $\rightarrow$ TERM MDOP FACTOR. $\left\{\begin{array}{l}\text{TERM}\\ \text{MDOP}\\ \text{FACTOR}\end{array}\right\}$

I_{22} : FACTOR $\rightarrow$ '(' .EXPRESS ')' $\left\{\begin{array}{l}\text{TERM}\\ \text{MDOP}\\ \text{'('}\end{array}\right\}$
same EXPRESS $\rightarrow$ .TERM
  as   EXPRESS $\rightarrow$ .EXPRESS ASOP TERM
I_4 TERM $\rightarrow$ .FACTOR
       TERM $\rightarrow$ .TERM MDOP FACTOR
       FACTOR $\rightarrow$.'(' EXPRESS ')'
       FACTOR $\rightarrow$ .OPERAND

Fig. 2-32 (continued).

I_{23} : FACTOR → OPERAND.
same
 as
I_5

$\left\{\begin{array}{l}\text{TERM}\\\text{MDOP}\\\text{OPERAND}\end{array}\right\}$

I_{24} : FACTOR → '(' EXPRESS ')'.

$\left\{\begin{array}{l}\text{'('}\\\text{EXPRESS}\\\text{')'}\end{array}\right\}$

I_{25} : EXPRESS → EXPRESS ASOP .TERM
same TERM → .FACTOR
 as   TERM → .TERM MDOP FACTOR
I_6 FACTOR → .'(' EXPRESS ')'
    FACTOR → .OPERAND

$\left\{\begin{array}{l}\text{'('}\\\text{EXPRESS}\\\text{ASOP}\end{array}\right\}$

I_{26} : ASOP   → '+'.
same
 as
I_7

$\left\{\begin{array}{l}\text{'('}\\\text{EXPRESS}\\\text{'+'}\end{array}\right\}$

I_{27} : ASOP   → '−'.
same
 as
I_8

$\left\{\begin{array}{l}\text{'('}\\\text{EXPRESS}\\\text{'−'}\end{array}\right\}$

I_{28} : TERM   → TERM MDOP .FACTOR
same FACTOR → .'(' EXPRESS ')'
 as   FACTOR → .OPERAND
I_9

$\left\{\begin{array}{l}\text{EXPRESS}\\\text{ASOP}\\\text{TERM}\\\text{MDOP}\end{array}\right\}$

I_{29} : MDOP   → '*'.
same
 as
I_{10}

$\left\{\begin{array}{l}\text{EXPRESS}\\\text{ASOP}\\\text{TERM}\\\text{'*'}\end{array}\right\}$

I_{30} : MDOP   → 'div'
same
 as
I_{11}

$\left\{\begin{array}{l}\text{EXPRESS}\\\text{ASOP}\\\text{TERM}\\\text{'div'}\end{array}\right\}$

Fig. 2-32 (continued).

From the collection of sets of items and the *GOTO* function, we can construct a deterministic finite state automaton which accepts all viable prefixes of the sentential forms generated by a grammar. Each set of items is a state, and *GOTO* is the transition function. Figure 2-33 shows the state transition diagram of this automaton for G_3'. Each state shown is a final state. There is one "reject" state not shown. If we included all transitions in the diagram, those not shown in Fig. 2-33 would lead to the reject state.

Recall that an item $B \to \beta_1 . \beta_2$ is *valid* for viable prefix $\alpha\beta_1$ if there is a rightmost derivation $A' \overset{*}{\Rightarrow} \alpha B w \Rightarrow \alpha\beta_1\beta_2 w$. An item is typically valid for many viable prefixes. From the fact that $B \to \beta_1 . \beta_2$ is valid for $\alpha\beta_1$, we can decide whether to shift or reduce when we encounter $\alpha\beta_1$ on the stack. If $\beta_2 = \lambda$, the end of the handle would appear to have been reached, and a reduction via $B \to \beta_1\beta_2$ would seem in order; otherwise, we have not yet seen the entire handle and a shift seems correct. Of course a single state may have several items which can indicate conflicting actions for the same viable prefix. By looking at the next symbol, we can resolve some of the conflicts—but not necessarily all. The various LR techniques use different methods for resolving such conflicts.

The SLR (1) parsing action table for G_3' is shown in Fig. 2-34; states label the rows, terminals label the columns. There are three types of entries indicating to shift, reduce or accept. A blank entry indicates error.

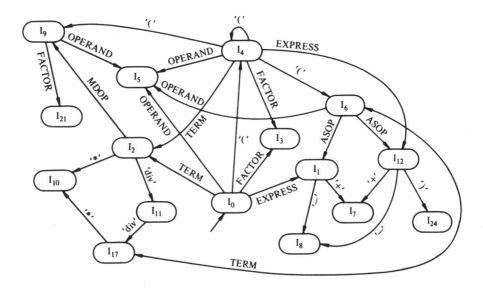

Fig. 2-33.

State	Operand	(	+	−	*	div	)	¢
0	S5	S4						
1			S7	S8				Accept
2			R1.1	R1.1	S10	S11	R1.1	R1.1
3			R2.1	R2.1	R2.1	R2.1	R2.1	R2.1
4	S5	S4						
5			R3.2	R3.2	R3.2	R3.2	R3.2	R3.2
6	S5	S4						
7	R4.1	R4.1						
8	R4.2	R4.2						
9	S5	S4						
10	R5.1	R5.1						
11	R5.2	R5.2						
12			S7	S8				
17			R1.2	R1.2	S10	S11	R1.2	R1.2
21			R2.2	R2.2	R2.2	R2.2	R2.2	R2.2
24			R3.1	R3.1	R3.1	R3.1	R3.1	R3.1

Fig. 2-34. Parsing Action Table for SLR(1) Parser for Augmented G_3'.

An "*sj*" entry means shift and enter state *j*. Entry "*rj*" means reduce using production *j*. The algorithm for constructing the table references the *GOTO* function and the FOLLOW set of each nonterminal. The latter is shown in Fig. 2-35. The algorithm is straightforward. Suppose COLL = $\{I_0, I_1, \ldots, I_n\}$ is the collection of sets of items.

1. If $[B \rightarrow \alpha.b\beta] \in I_1$ and GOTO $(I_1,b) = I_j$, then ACTION $[i,b]$ = "sj."
2. If $[B \rightarrow \alpha.] \in I_1$, then ACTION $[i,b]$ = "rn" for all b $\in$ FOLLOW (B). Here, n is the number of production $B \rightarrow \alpha$.
3. If $[A' \rightarrow A.] \in I_1$, then ACTION $[i, ¢]$ = "accept."

	Operand	(	+	−	*	div	)	¢
EXPRESS			✓	✓			✓	✓
TERM			✓	✓	✓	✓	✓	✓
FACTOR			✓	✓	✓	✓	✓	✓
MDOP	✓	✓						
ASOP	✓	✓						
E'								✓

Fig. 2-35. FOLLOW (B) for Each Nonterminal of Augmented G_3.

If any conflicts arise, the grammar is not SLR (1), and a more powerful LR method or perhaps a non-LR method must be used; alternatively, the grammar can be modified to eliminate the conflict.

The *GOTO* table, shown in Fig. 2-36, only has state transitions for nonterminals. Transitions for terminals are embedded in the parsing action table in the shift entries; again, all blanks are really "error." The initial state of the parser is the closure of $\{[A' \rightarrow .A]\}$.

Figure 2-37 shows the sequence of transitions taken by this parser on 'a+bc*2'. Figure 2-38 shows the transitions on the nonsentence 'a+*bc'; note that the parser rejects the string before scanning past the erroneously placed '*'.

Two types of conflicts occur:

shift/reduce
reduce/reduce

Shift/reduce conflicts occur when a state has two items:

$$B \rightarrow \alpha.b\gamma$$
$$C \rightarrow \beta.$$

where b is in FOLLOW(C). The first item forces a shift when b is seen, while the second forces a reduction using $C \rightarrow \beta$. Reduce/reduce conflicts occur when a state has two items:

$$B \rightarrow \alpha.$$
$$C \rightarrow \beta.$$

Both completed items indicate a reduction is necessary, but via two distinct productions.

State	EXPRESS	TERM	FACTOR	MDOP	ASOP
0	1	2	3		
1					6
2				9	
3					
4	12	2	3		
5					
6		17	3		
7					
8					
9			21		
10					
11					
12					6
17				9	
21					
24					

Fig. 2-36. Goto Table for SLR(1) Parser for Augmented G_3'.

There are three ways to resolve the conflict:

1. use a more powerful LR method,
2. force a choice,
3. modify the grammar.

The first option would probably mean choosing either the LALR(1) or LR(1) table construction methods. These methods, by doing more thorough analyses of the grammar, cut down on the number of entries in the parsing action table. In some cases, this may eliminate an entry which is the source of a conflict. These more sophisticated methods increase the number of states, refining the division of viable prefixes.

Stack	*Input*
s_0	a + bc * 2 ¢
s_0 a s_5	+ bc * 2 ¢
s_0 FACTOR s_3	+ bc * 2 ¢
s_0 TERM s_2	+ bc * 2 ¢
s_0 EXPRESS s_1	+ bc * 2 ¢
s_0 EXPRESS s_1 + s_7	bc * 2 ¢
s_0 EXPRESS s_1 ASOP s_6	bc * 2 ¢
s_0 EXPRESS s_1 ASOP s_6 bc s_5	* 2 ¢
s_0 EXPRESS s_1 ASOP s_6 FACTOR s_3	* 2 ¢
s_0 EXPRESS s_1 ASOP s_6 TERM s_{17}	* 2 ¢
s_0 EXPRESS s_1 ASOP s_6 TERM s_{17} * s_{10}	2 ¢
s_0 EXPRESS s_1 ASOP s_6 TERM s_{17} MDOP s_9	2 ¢
s_0 EXPRESS s_1 ASOP s_6 TERM s_{17} MDOP s_9 2 s_5	¢
s_0 EXPRESS s_1 ASOP s_6 TERM s_{17} MDOP s_9 FACTOR s_{21}	¢
s_0 EXPRESS s_1 ASOP s_6 TERM s_{17}	¢
s_0 EXPRESS s_1 accept	¢

Fig. 2-37. Parsing of 'a+bc*2'.

The second option quite often is satisfactory. We simply force the parser to choose one way or the other by erasing a conflicting entry in the parsing action table. YACC, an LALR(1) parser generator, which is part of the Unix operating system software, has a default "tie-breaking" strategy which guarantees that for *any* context-free grammar, YACC will produce a table. Of course, the conflicts must be settled in a satisfactory way if the parser is to be useful. Having the ability to break ties quite

Stack	*Input*
s_0	a + * bc ¢
s_0 a s_5	+ * bc ¢
s_0 FACTOR s_3	+ * bc ¢
s_0 TERM s_2	+ * bc ¢
s_0 EXPRESS s_1	+ * bc ¢
s_0 EXPRESS s_1 + s_7	* bc ¢

error—no entry in parsing action table in row number 7, column *.

Fig. 2-38. Parsing of 'a+*bc'.

often enables the compiler writer to simplify his grammar. Ambiguous grammar G_2 will lead to the parsing action table shown in Fig. 2-39. Note the conflicts in state 11, which represents viable prefix 'EOE'. It is precisely at this point the ambiguity arises. Should we reduce, causing left to right evaluation of the expression, or shift, causing right to left evaluation. If we prefer left to right, then striking out the 'S6' entries in Fig. 2-39 will achieve this.

The third option to resolve conflicts is not necessary nearly as often as for LL(1) grammars. There is not the same standard set of obvious transformations to perform as we have for LL(1) grammar. We will not discuss this option further.

2.6 SUMMARY

Programming languages are often defined using a formalism called the *context-free grammar*. The language of a context-free grammar, a *context-free language,* is the set of strings derivable from it. Using this formalism, we can define languages such as that of infix arithmetic ex-

	(	+	−	*	div	)	OPERAND	¢
1	S3						S4	ACCEPT
2		S6	S7	S8	S9	R0		
3	S3						S4	
4		R1.3	R1.3	R1.3	R1.3	R1.3		R1.3
5	S3						S4	
6	R2.1						R2.1	
7	R2.2						R2.2	
8	R2.3						R2.3	
9	R2.4						R2.4	
10		S6	S7	S8	S9	S12		
11		R1.1 S6	R1.1 S6	R1.1 S6	R1.1 S6	R1.1		R1.1
12		R1.2	R1.2	R1.2	R1.2	R1.2		R1.2

Fig. 2-39. SLR(1) Parsing Action Table for G_2.

pressions over the *integers* and variables and the operations of '+', '−', '*', and **'div'**. Some grammars for this and other languages are *ambiguous* in that a single sentence may have more than one *parse tree* for it. Ambiguity is usually shunned where possible. The generation of a *derivation* of a string is called *parsing*. In order for *top-down parsers* to be practical, they must operate without significant *backtracking;* otherwise, their execution time is unacceptably long. One top-down scheme for parsing without backtracking uses what are called *LL(1) grammars,* a special type of context-free grammar. Such parsers have very fast execution times, $O(n)$, where n is the length of the string being parsed; however, LL(1) grammars are often not as "natural" as we would like. The price paid in this case for parsing speed is clarity in the grammar rules.

A second class of parsers works *bottom-up*. The most popular of these is the family of *LR parsers* which also have $O(n)$ execution times. The *simple LR(1) parsing* algorithm can parse many common grammars with only trivial modification-including grammar G_3. Left recursion causes LR parsers no problems. Both LR and LL parsers display the viable prefix property, which improves parsing speed and facilitates error processing.

EXERCISES

2-1. Construct the parse tree(s) for the following sentences of grammar G_1 defined in the chapter:

    a. 'a0bc'
    b. '305'
    c. '7'

2-2. For each parse tree you constructed in 2-1, write the corresponding leftmost derivation.

2-3. A derivation is *rightmost* if the rightmost nonterminal is expanded in each step. Formalize this notion in the same manner as we did for leftmost derivations.

2-4. Write the rightmost derivation of '(a+bc)*2' with respect to grammars G_2, G_3, and G_4.

2-5. Devise an algorithm which eliminates "useless" productions from an arbitrary context-free grammar. A production is "useless" if it does not appear in a derivation of any sentence of the grammar.

2-6. Devise an algorithm which eliminates all "cyclic" productions from a context-free grammar. A production B → w is cyclic if $w \overset{*}{\Rightarrow} B$.

2-7. Devise an algorithm which eliminates all productions of the form "B → λ" from a context-free grammar.

2-8. Implement the LL(1) parser defined in the text for G_4 in your favorite programming language and test it on a number of candidate sentences.

2-9. Implement the pseudo-code program which eliminates left recursion from a context-free grammar.

2-10. Show the history of the LL(1) parser for G_4 on 'bc+(a*b **div** c) * (30 + x)'.

2-11. Prove that no LL(1) grammar is left recursive.

2-12. Prove that an LL(1) parser rejects a candidate string as soon as the prefix of the string being parsed is no longer viable.

2-13. Prove that an LL(1) parser works in $O(n)$ time, where n is the length of the string being parsed.

2-14. For each of the following languages, find an LL(1) grammar which generates it:

    a. $\{0^n1^n \mid n > 0\}$
    b. $\{b^nc^{2n} \mid n > 0\}$
    c. $\{wcw^{reverse} \mid w \in \{d,e\}^*\}$
    d. $\{b^nc^n \mid n > 0\} \cup \{c^nb^m \mid 0 > n > m\}$

2-15. Write an LL(1) grammar for the FORTRAN **if** statement; for the ALGOL 60 **if-then-else** statement.

2-16. Show that there is no parse for string 'a+bc*2' with respect to G_3 which indicates addition should be performed before multiplication.

2-17. Implement the parser for grammar G_4 of the chapter text in your favorite programming language.

2-18. Modify the parser for G_4 to emit the leftmost derivation of a candidate sentence if there is one and to emit the longest partial leftmost derivation if the candidate string is not a sentence.

2-19. Step through the construction of the selection set of each production of grammar G_4 from the chapter using the algorithm in Appendix C.

2-20. Eliminate the left recursion in the following context-free grammar:

$$N = \{E,P,T\}$$
$$\Sigma = \{`[`, `]`, `(`, `)`\}$$
$$\text{Axiom} = E$$
$$P = \{E \rightarrow E\ P$$
$$P \rightarrow E\ T$$
$$P \rightarrow T$$
$$T \rightarrow `[`\ E\ `]`$$
$$P \rightarrow `(`\ E\ `)`$$
$$E \rightarrow P$$
$$T \rightarrow `[`\ `]`$$
$$P \rightarrow `(`\ `)`\}$$

2-21. Construct the selection set of each production in the grammar you constructed in problem 2-20. Is the grammar LL(1)? If not, where is the selection set conflict?

2-22. Prove that no LL(1) grammar is ambiguous.

2-23. Convert the following non-LL(1) grammar into an LL(1) grammar and give the selection set of each production:

$$G = (\{S,T,U\}, \{c,x,y\}, S, P) \text{ where P is}$$

$$S \rightarrow S \text{ x } U$$
$$S \rightarrow X \text{ U}$$
$$T \rightarrow S$$
$$T \rightarrow c$$
$$U \rightarrow T \text{ y}$$

2-24. Define a grammar for LITTLE RASCAL. Blanks, comments, and line boundaries are *not* to be included in the grammar. For example, the grammar rule for the **program** statement might be:

$$\text{PROG\_STMT} \rightarrow \text{'program' NAME ';'}$$

2-25. Rewrite the grammar of exercise 2-24 so that blanks, comments, and line boundaries *are* accounted for in the grammar. (Note the difference in grammar size and complexity.)

2-26. Given the following grammar:

```
BEXP   → 'not'  BEXP
       → REXP
REXP   → AEXP  ROP  AEXP
       → AEXP
ROP    → '='
       → '<'
AEXP   → AEXP  AOP  ATERM
       → ATERM
AOP    → '+'
       → 'or'
ATERM → ATERM  MOP  AFACT
       → AFACT
MOP    → 'and'
       → 'div'
       → '*'
AFACT → '('  BEXP  ')'
       →      OPERAND
```

where BEXP is the axiom, and OPERAND is a terminal:

a. List all operators in *decreasing* order of precedence.
b. Rewrite the grammar so that the operators have the following precedence:

```
(     )      |
div   *
+
=     <         decreasing
not   ↓         precedence
and
or
```

2-27. Prove than an SLR(1) parser operates in O(n) time, where n is the length of the input string.

2-28. Determine if each LL(1) grammar you constructed in solving exercise 2-14 is also SLR(1).

2-29. Prove that if a grammar is ambiguous, its SLR(1) parsing action table will have at least one conflict.

2-30. Prove that the error (blank) entries of the *GOTO* table are superfluous; i.e., that the parser can never reference GOTO (j,B) if GOTO (j,B) = error.

2-31. Prove that the automaton shown in Fig. 2-33 recognizes all of the viable prefixes of G_3'.

2-32. Prove that for augmented grammar G', the automaton constructed by the algorithm given in section 2.5 will recognize all of its viable prefixes.

2-33. Is the grammar:

$$S \rightarrow AS \mid b$$
$$A \rightarrow SA \mid a$$

SLR(1)? Construct the parsing action table. If there is a conflict, indicate where.

2-34. Develop a general strategy to construct a grammar for binary expressions over operators $op_1, \ldots, op_n$ for some $n \geq 1$, where the expressions are to be evaluated from left to right within precedence. The operators are partitioned in $k \geq 1$ groups of arbitrary size where two operators are in the same group if they have the same precedence.

2-35. Can removing shift/reduce conflicting entries in SLR(1) parsing action tables affect the *language* which the parser accepts? (Hint: consider what happens in Fig. 2-39 if we remove R1.1 instead of S6 in state 11.)

2-36. Can removing reduce/reduce conflicting entries in SLR(1) parsing action tables affect the *language* which the parser accepts?

2-37. Modify the proper entries in Fig. 2-39 to make the parser evaluate expressions right to left.

2-38. Can you force multiplication and division to be performed before addition and subtraction by modifying the entries in Fig. 2-39?

BIBLIOGRAPHY

The notion of a *context-free grammar* arises from the study of natural languages. [Chomsky 56, 59] published the fundamental work in this area, and is considered to be the "father of formal language theory." John Backus, who also headed the FORTRAN project for IBM, independently invented a notation equivalent to the context-free grammar; this notation, Backus-Naur Form, today bears his name. Its first widespread appearance was in [Backus 59] and later in [Naur 63]. Since then, context-free grammar theory has received intense interest to the point that it is one of the most analyzed and well-understood areas of computer science. [Ginsburg 66] is a thorough study of the properties of context-free languages known up to that point. [Hopcroft and Ullman 69] is the classic text on formal language theory and their processing automata. [Salomaa

73] is a more recent study of formal languages, including many results obtained since [Hopcroft and Ullman 69] was published.

Numerous parsing techniques have been developed over the years. Some of the earliest were the *precedence parsers* ([Floyd 63], [Wirth and Weber 66], [McKeeman 66], [Ichbiah and Morse 70]). These techniques were heavily employed in compilers constructed in the Sixties and early Seventies; since then, however, these methods have been largely replaced by the more powerful LL and LR techniques.

LL grammars and parsers are developed in [Lewis and Stearns 68]. The general theory of LL(1) grammars is presented in [Rosenkrantz and Stearns 70]. [Lewis, Rosenkrantz, and Stearns 76] is a theoretical compiler text employing LL parsing as a base. [Bauer and Eickel 74] discusses the relative tradeoffs between LL and LR parsing. The left-recursion elimination algorithm is taken from [Aho and Ullman 77], the selection set computation algorithm from [Lewis, Rosenkrantz, and Stearns 76].

LR parsers are developed in [Knuth 65]. Initially, they were deemed impractical because the parser requires large tables which are unmanageable, despite the fact that in power, the LR technique subsumes all other common parsers. [Korenjak 69] and [DeRemer 69, 71] later described simplifications to the original method, which made LR parsing practical. They showed that, in many cases, the size of the tables could be reduced significantly without a corresponding loss in parsing power. LR parsing is now widespread because so many common grammars can be parsed by this technique.

Programming language syntax was originally described chiefly in English for lack of a better notation. ALGOL 60 was the first language defined by a context-free grammar ([Naur 63]). Backus-Naur Form, the style of context-free grammar presented in the ALGOL 60 report, has become, in one of its many variants, the standard for syntax specification. PASCAL is presented in an interesting variation in [Jensen and Wirth 75], replacing the linear productions with two dimensional *bead* diagrams. Chapters 4 through 7 include definitions of RASCAL subsets using the bead notation.

The *Van Wijngaarden grammar* is an extension of the context-free grammar which permits the language specifier to capture formally the context-sensitive constraints on the language. ALGOL 68 was officially reported via a Van Wijngaarden grammar ([Van Wijngaarden, et al 74]). The system's complexity has impeded its widespread acceptance. Part of the difficulty in acceptance may also stem from the most widely referenced document containing a major example of the grammar form, the ALGOL 68 report. This report is "recursively unreadable" and has been widely criticized; [Cleaveland and Uzgalis 77] is a lucid explanation of the Van Wijngaarden grammar.

3
Translation Grammars

3.1 INTRODUCTION

Although a context-free grammar specifies a language, our goal is not to recognize strings of a language but to *translate* a source language program into equivalent text in the target language. In this chapter, we show how to transform a context-free grammar into a more powerful system called the *translation grammar* which does precisely that. The translation grammar contains information needed to parse the source program *and* to generate object code from it. As a leftmost derivation of the input string is constructed, a series of *actions* are executed as directed by calls to various *action routines* which are defined as part of the translation grammar. If these routines arc properly specified, their action can be to emit intermediate, assembly, or machine language codc which is equivalent to the input string. Thus, a translation grammar can specify a translation from the source language to some target language. CANTOR, as described in later chapters, is essentially a translation grammar in which the input to the compiler or translation grammar processor is RASCAL code and the output is the equivalent 360AL code. This chapter introduces the translation grammar by an example given in section 3.2. We remain informal throughout, since the notation required to formalize such grammars is more imposing than we wish to consider.

3.2 PROCESSING LITTLE RASCAL DECLARATIONS

LITTLE RASCAL declarations are easily compiled by a translation grammar. We illustrate this by defining a translation grammar which creates correct symbol table entries for LITTLE RASCAL variable declarations and emits correct 360AL instructions to reserve the necessary storage. Variables in LITTLE RASCAL, you will recall, are declared in statements of the form:

$$\text{id}_1, \ldots, \text{id}_n : \text{integer};$$
$$\cdots$$
$$\text{id}_m, \ldots, \text{id}_r : \text{integer};$$

where the *id*'s become variable names by the action of these declarations. In full RASCAL, the data-type of such variables could be any of numerous types, including *real, boolean,* and *set,* but in LITTLE RASCAL only the *integer* data-type is allowed. To process a declaration we must:

1. create an entry in the symbol table for each variable declared;
2. determine if any variable is multiply declared (an illegal act which is checked semantically, not syntactically);
3. allocate storage for each variable declared.

To simplify the example, we shall assume that the only possible error is for a variable to be declared more than once. Other errors, such as illegal variable names, or an illegal data-type, will be ignored.

The symbol table which we shall construct holds information about each declared variable. In addition, it must also have an entry for a number of other symbol types, two of which are the program name as specified in the program statement and all literals which appear in assignment statements such as

$$+3 \qquad 56 \qquad -310 \qquad 27$$

As we shall see in Part 2, there are other quantities which require symbol table entries, but these need not concern us here.

The format of a suitable symbol table, shown in Fig. 3-1, has three columns labelled: *internal name, type,* and *mode.* The *external name* of a symbol, the name appearing on the source LITTLE RASCAL statement, is the index or key into the symbol table. In general, there are many external names which are not legal 360AL symbolic names; e.g., LITTLE RASCAL variable names may be arbitrarily long, but the assembler restricts symbolic names to eight or fewer characters. Literals such as '+3' cannot be used as symbolic labels for "Define Constant" statements. Therefore, we shall uniformly substitute compiler generated names for LITTLE RASCAL external names which have the form '@n' where n is a non-negative integer. Initially, n is given the value zero, and as each new symbol is entered into the table, the value of n is incremented by one.

There are only two data-types of interest at this point: *integer* and *prog_name* (program name). The *mode* of a name refers to the permanence of the value assigned to it. The value of a variable may change repeatedly during execution, depending on the series of assignments executed. Literals, on the other hand, such as '4', cannot change value during execution, their values being fixed by the language definition. Symbols may have one of two modes, *mutable* or *immutable,* depending on whether or not their values can change during execution.

Having explained the format of the symbol table and the significance of

external name

keys into
table

internal name   type   mode

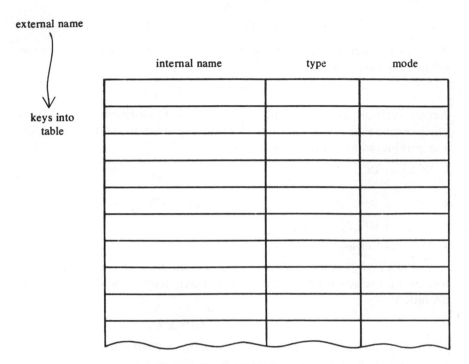

Fig. 3-1. Symbol Table Format.

the entries in it, we next consider how this table will actually be filled. A translation grammar is a context-free grammar in which the terminal symbols are partitioned into two categories: *source* and *action* symbols. The source symbols are tokens of the source language which occur in the program text being translated. Action symbols, on the other hand, do not appear in the source program. Their appearance in the source program would be an error. Action symbols are calls to functions which actually perform the translation.

We continue with the description of a translation grammar which translates LITTLE RASCAL declarations into "Define Storage" pseudo-instructions and symbol-table entries. In this example, we shall assume that a scanner (or something equivalent) passes tokens to the translation grammar processor so that we need not consider how individual characters are combined to form identifier names, and so forth. The translation grammar, TRANSDCL, has four nonterminals:

DCLS, DCL, IDS, TYPE

There are five source symbols:

$$\text{`:', `;', `,', `integer', ID}$$

Here ID is a special token *class* which stands for any identifier. There are also two action symbols:

$$insert(x,y,\text{`mutable'}),\quad alloc(x)$$

Action symbols are written in italics to visually distinguish them from other terminal symbols rather than enclosing them in quotation marks. The productions of this grammar are:

1. DCLS → DCL   DCLS
        → λ

2. DCL   → IDS$_x$ `:'   TYPE$_y$   `;' *insert(x,y,'mutable')*   *alloc(x)*

3. IDS   → ID   (`,'   IDS | λ)

4. TYPE → `integer'

A new abbreviation has been introduced in production 3 whose purpose will become clear later in this section when parsing is discussed. By definition,

$$\text{w (x | y) z = w x z | w y z} \tag{3.1}$$

where x, y, and z are *string patterns*. A string pattern is either i) a string; ii) the concatenation of string patterns; iii) the alternation of string patterns; iv) the parenthesization of a string pattern. Equation 3.1 is also called the *distributive law of strings over alternation and concatenation*. Note that the parentheses in Eq. 3.1 are not tokens, but part of the metalanguage in which productions are expressed, just as → is. If a parenthesis is to be used as a token, it must be surrounded by quotation marks, as `(' or `)'. In our original notation, either with or without alternation, production 3 could be rewritten as:

$$\text{IDS → ID `,'   IDS | ID}$$

or as:

$$\text{IDS → ID `,'   IDS}$$
$$\text{→ ID}$$

In production 2, nonterminals IDS and TYPE have been subscripted by an x and a y, respectively. These variables, which are assigned character strings as values, will be the arguments of the action routines *insert* and *alloc*.

When a leftmost derivation involving production 2 is constructed, nonterminals IDS and TYPE eventually derive a list of identifiers and a datatype, respectively; for example, in parsing the string:

pascal,power:**integer**;

the following leftmost derivation is generated (ignoring action symbols momentarily):

$$DCLS \Rightarrow DCL \quad DCLS$$
$$\Rightarrow IDS \quad \text{':'} \quad TYPE \quad \text{';'} \quad DCLS$$
$$\stackrel{*}{\Rightarrow} \text{'pascal,power'} \quad \text{':'} \quad \text{'integer'} \quad \text{';'}$$

where IDS derives 'pascal,power' and TYPE generates 'integer. The grouping of tokens in the last sentential form of the derivation is intended to facilitate understanding the example and is not inherent in the problem. These terminal strings generated by IDS and TYPE can be viewed as their *value* for this particular derivation. All nonterminals can have values assigned to them in this manner; for example, the entire statement being parsed can be viewed as the value of the DCLS which roots the parse tree. The value of a nonterminal becomes defined as soon as the terminal string which it generates is produced in the derivation, after which it can be referenced. To facilitate referencing the value of a nonterminal, we assign that value to a variable (in this case x and y) which is positioned in the lower right hand corner of the nonterminal.

Both *insert* and *alloc* are functions, specified in the definition of TRANSDCL, which use x and y as arguments for their calls. *Insert* has three arguments: The first is a list of external names; the second and third are the *type* and the *mode* of the names in the list of external names. Note that all such names have the same *type* and *mode*. A call to *insert* creates an entry in the symbol table for each member of the list of external names. In production 2, the first two arguments of the call to *insert* are variables x and y.

Alloc, as the reader has probably guessed, is a function with one argument which emits storage when called, the list of external names for which it is to allocate storage. *Alloc*(x) will look up the attributes of each element of the list in x in the symbol table and emit the proper "Define Storage" pseudo-instructions. In CANTOR, this function will be generalized to emit "Define Constant" pseudo-instructions as well for names such as *integer* literals. Implementations of *insert* and *alloc* are shown in Figs. 3-2 and 3-3.

The components of TRANSDCL have now been presented. We next explain how a translation grammar processor would process the string:

pascal,power:**integer**;
fortran,fool:**integer**;

Before we begin parsing, we wish to ensure that the parsing can proceed

procedure   insert(external_names : **string**; in_type: [prog_name,integer]; in_mode: [muta-
          ble,immutable]);
              {create an entry in the symbol table for each identifier in the list of external
              names given as the first argument. It is an error to attempt to create an entry
              under an external name for which an entry already exists.}
    var   name: **string**;
    begin
        break next name from list of external_names;
          {name will be lambda when no names are left in the list.}
        while   name <> lambda **do**
          begin
            if   *symbol_table[name] is defined* **then**
                process error—multiple name definition;
            else   {create a symbol table entry}
                symbol_table[name] := (gen_internal_name, in_type, in_mode);
              break next name from the list of external names;
          end;
    end;

Fig. 3-2. Implementation of *Insert.*

without back up, so we rewrite the first production of TRANSDCL with
selection sets so that the LL(1) parsing strategy is applicable. Endmarker
' ¢' is added to the end of each string being parsed so that the lookahead
symbol is always defined. Only the first production has alternatives, so we
list a selection set only for each alternative of the first production.

    1. DCLS → DCL   DCLS   {ID}
            → λ   {'¢'}

procedure   alloc(external_names: **string**);
          {allocate storage for entries in external_names.}
    var   name: **string**;
    begin
        break next name from the list of external names;
        while   name <> lambda **do**
          begin
            *emit a "DS" pseudo-instruction with label field = internal_name[name], operand
            field = 'F', and comment field = name;*
            break next name from the list of external names;
          end;
    end;

Formally, *emit* has four arguments: label, opcode, operand, and
comment. We do not bother to detail it further here.

Fig. 3-3. Implementation of *Alloc.*

In addition, we must specify how to choose between the alternatives given in production 3.

3. IDS → ID (‘,’ IDS |λ)

Two strategies are obvious: The first assigns selection sets to the alternatives within the single production:

3'. IDS → ID (‘,’   IDS {‘,’} |λ {‘:’})   {ID}

Since the selection sets are disjoint, this maintains the LL character of the grammar. The second strategy permits back up at this point to try alternatives one at a time in the order in which they appear (for lack of a better ordering scheme). We opt for the first strategy, totally eliminating the need for backtracking.

The importance of this new notation becomes clearer when we rewrite production 3 with selection sets using the original alternation format:

3″. IDS → ID ‘,’ IDS   {ID}
    → ID   {ID}

Both alternatives have the same selection set. When written in unparenthesized form, the production has a selection set conflict, and the LL(1) parsing strategy does not apply. When written in the new parenthesized notation, this conflict is eliminated by the *factoring* of a substring common to the right-hand sides of both alternatives, a technique discussed further in Appendix C. An alternative approach which would achieve the same result, but is somewhat more awkward, introduces a new nonterminal specifically for the purpose of eliminating the selection set conflict.

IDS → ID NEW
NEW → ‘,’ IDS   {‘,’}
    → λ   {‘:’}

We opt for the more elegant solution which embeds selection sets instead of introducing extraneous nonterminals.

The leftmost derivation must begin with the axiom:

DCLS

Since the first token of the source text is ‘pascal’, production 1.1 is selected:

DCLS ⇒ DCL   DCLS

There is no choice in the next step of the derivation:

$$\text{DCLS} \Rightarrow \text{DCL}\quad \text{DCLS}$$
$$\Rightarrow \text{IDS}_x\quad \text{':'}\quad \text{TYPE}_y\quad \text{';'}$$
$$insert(x,y,\text{'mutable'})\quad alloc(x)\quad \text{DCLS}$$

This is the first point where action symbols are introduced into a sentential form of the derivation. The calls to the action routines are not made at this time. The calls will not be made until the parser has successfully matched all of the symbols to the left of the action symbols with the source text. Furthermore, in a string of contiguous action symbols, the calls to action routines are made in the order in which the symbols appear from left to right, so that *insert* will be called before *alloc* in this case. Since *alloc* references information in the symbol table which is entered by *insert,* the relative order of execution of these action routines is important. Note that at this point in the derivation neither x nor y has been assigned a value.

Skipping to the point in the derivation where IDS and TYPE have derived terminal strings:

$$\text{DCLS} \Rightarrow \text{DCL}\quad \text{DCLS}$$
$$\overset{*}{\Rightarrow} \text{'pascal,power'}\quad \text{':'}\quad \text{'integer'}\quad \text{';'}$$
$$insert(x,y,\text{'mutable'})\quad alloc(x)\quad \text{DCLS}$$

x has the value 'pascal,power' and y has the value 'integer'. The text 'pascal,power:integer;' is a terminal prefix of the string being parsed, so at this time, the translation grammar processor calls *insert* with the indicated arguments, creating a table entry for each variable in the list of external names; i.e., each identifier in x. *Insert* also checks for duplicate names and reports any errors it uncovers. After *insert* has returned, the processor examines the next symbol to the right of the call to *insert*. (Note that the processor does not try to match the action symbols to the source text.) This symbol, a call to *alloc*, initiates the execution of *alloc* with argument x, leading to the storage emission shown in Fig. 3-5. *Alloc* then returns, and the processor continues its work. The processor will eventually generate a leftmost derivation of the source string and in doing so will make two more calls to action routines, one call each to *insert* and *alloc* for the second declaration, 'fortran,fool:integer'. Figures 3-6 and 3-7 show the symbol table and total storage emitted after the second calls to *insert* and *alloc* have taken place.

3.3   FORMALISMS

The last section having introduced the translation grammar in a very informal manner, we continue by defining the translation grammar and its

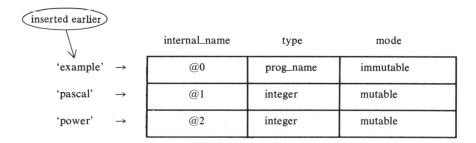

Fig. 3-4. Symbol Table after First Call to *Insert*.

supporting concepts somewhat more rigorously. A *translation grammar* has eight components. The first component is SU, a set of *subscripts*. N is a finite set of *nonterminals,* some of which may be subscripted by a member of SU. AR is a finite set of function definitions also called *action routines*. In this text, the function definitions are written in pseudo-PASCAL. AS is a finite set of *action symbols*. Each action symbol has the form "$f(a_1, . . . ,a_n)$," where $f:D_1 \times . . . \times D_n \to R$ is a function defined in AR. For $1 \le i \le n$, either $a_i \in D_i$ or a_i is a subscript from SU, and D_i is a set of strings. SS is a finite set of *source symbols;* together, SS and AS form the set of *terminal symbols*. The terminals and nonterminals together form the *vocabulary*, V. A$\in$N is the *axiom*. P is a set of *productions* of the form "B $\to$ α," where B$\in$N and $\alpha\in$V*. Finally, the eighth component is a set of *data structures,* DS, which may be manipulated by the functions defined in AR.

All of the components should be familiar to the reader after working through the example of the last section. Data structures such as the symbol table from the earlier example are included in the definition of the translation grammar because the translation of a source sentence depends on the history of changes to those structures during the generation of the leftmost derivation of a sentence.

The translation grammar as defined is still not restrictive enough to guarantee well-defined translations. We must place the following two additional constraints on a translation grammar:

1. The same subscript may not appear more than once in a single production.

| @1 | DS | F | pascal |
| @2 | DS | F | power |

Fig. 3-5. Storage Emitted by First Call to *Alloc*.

	internal_name	type	mode
'example' $\rightarrow$	@0	prog_name	immutable
'pascal' $\rightarrow$	@1	integer	mutable
'power' $\rightarrow$	@2	integer	mutable
'fortran' $\rightarrow$	@3	integer	mutable
'fool' $\rightarrow$	@4	integer	mutable

Fig. 3-6. Symbol Table after Second Call to *Insert*.

2. If a production has the form

$$B \rightarrow \alpha \quad f(a_1, \ldots, a_n) \quad \beta$$

where $f(a_1, \ldots, a_n)$ is an action symbol, $\alpha \epsilon V^+$, and $\beta \epsilon V^*$, then if a_1 is a subscript, it is the subscript of a nonterminal in α.

We shall assume in what follows that all translation grammars under discussion obey these two additional constraints, guaranteeing that the action calls are well-defined; for example, the production:

$$B \rightarrow C_x \quad D_x \quad f(x)$$

violates the first restriction. It is not clear which value of x should be the argument of f when that function is called. Of course, we could arbitrarily rule that the rightmost occurrence of x (for example) has the "current" value when f is called; however, this leaves one wondering why C was subscripted to begin with.

Production:

$$B \rightarrow C_x \quad D_y \quad f(z) \quad E_z$$

violates the second restriction. When f is called, z will not have a value, and the result of the call will be undefined.

Before we consider precisely how translations are generated by these grammars, it is necessary to introduce a special function, *emit*. *Emit* may

@1	DS	F	pascal
@2	DS	F	power
@3	DS	F	fortran
@4	DS	F	fool

Fig. 3-7. Storage Emitted after Second Call to *Alloc*.

be called either directly from a production as an action symbol or from within the definition of some member of AR in order to emit target code; for example, *alloc* of the last section called *emit* (see Fig. 3-3) in order to output "Define Storage" pseudo-instructions. The particular arguments of *emit* and the form of the output generated will vary from grammar to grammar, depending on the nature of the object code being produced. For example, *emit* as defined in section 3.2 has four arguments and outputs text in 80 character records, the four arguments corresponding to the four fields of 360AL instructions. Different target languages could require different formatting details; however, we reserve the unique name *emit* to refer to that function which actually outputs the target code. The other action routines and functions called within activations of these routines all merely support, in some sense, the all important calls to *emit*.

The action routines are called during the derivation of the source text from the axiom. Suppose TG is a translation grammar as defined earlier. Let LD be a leftmost derivation of sentential form:

$$\delta = \alpha \ \ f(a_1, \ . \ . \ . \ ,a_n) \ \beta$$

LD is:

$$A \Rightarrow \delta_1 \Rightarrow \delta_2 \Rightarrow \ . \ . \ . \Rightarrow \delta_r = \delta$$

where $\alpha\epsilon\Sigma^*$, $\beta\epsilon V^*$, and $f(a_1, \ . \ . \ . \ ,a_n)$ is the leftmost action symbol in δ which has not yet been *activated*. (Initially, no action symbols are activated.) There is some step in LD:

$$\delta_i \Rightarrow \delta_{i+1}$$

in which $f(a_1, \ . \ . \ . \ ,a_n)$ was first introduced into a sentential form by the application of some production p =

$$B \rightarrow \gamma \ \ f(a_1, \ . \ . \ . \ ,a_n) \ \phi$$

where γ , $\phi\epsilon V^*$. Then $f(a_1, \ . \ . \ . \ ,a_n)$ is *activated* by calling f with arguments $\bar{a}_1, \ . \ . \ . \ ,\bar{a}_n$ where $\bar{a}_i = a_i$ if $a_i \epsilon D_i$ and $\bar{a}_i$ is the value of the corresponding nonterminal in p if a_i is a subscript. The *activity sequence* of a derivation is the sequence of function calls made by activating action symbols. This sequence may manipulate any or all of the members of DS, changing them as needed. The *enlarged language*, EL(TG), of translation grammar, TG, is the set of terminal strings derivable from the grammar axiom. Recall, however, that our goal is not to translate strings from Σ^* but from SS*. Consequently, we also define the *language*, L(TG), of translation grammar, TG, to be the set obtained by deleting action symbols from the members of EL(TG). The members of L(TG) are the valid inputs to a translator which is driven by TG.

Let LD be a leftmost derivation of w ϵ V*. Suppose y is the string obtained by deleting all action symbols from w and that the activity sequence of LD is:

$$\phi = \phi_1, \; \phi_2, \; \phi_3, \; . \; . \; . \; , \; \phi_n$$

If:

$$\sigma = \sigma_1 \quad \sigma_2 \quad \sigma_3 \quad . \; . \; . \quad \sigma_n$$

is the output of *emit* for sequence ϕ, then σ is the *translation* of y with respect to LD. If there is more than one leftmost derivation of w, or there is more than one w which becomes y when action symbols are removed, there may be several translations of y. The translation of y with respect to LD is denoted TRANS(y,LD). The entire set of translations of y induced by TG is denoted TRANS(y); in general, TRANS(y) may be infinite. (See the exercises at the end of this chapter.) However, for a compiler we normally wish TRANS(y) to contain just a single member. Note that the translation of a string is defined in terms of a complete leftmost derivation. Because the translation is not dependent upon the parsing method used to generate that leftmost derivation, a parsing method which employs backtracking must guarantee that the translation eventually output by the translator is not affected by erroneous selections of alternative productions.

3.4   IMPLEMENTING A TRANSLATION GRAMMAR PROCESSOR

Presuming the translation grammar is LL(1), so that it may be parsed without backtracking, the translation grammar processor may be implemented quite simply. Figures 3-8 through 3-11 are an implementation of a translator driven by TRANSDCL. The major differences between a straight LL(1) parser and a translation grammar processor are the inclusion of the action calls as needed and the code necessary to assign values to the subscripts of the nonterminals in TRANSDCL. Because these

```
function   dcls: string;
              {look for DCLS and emit its translation.}
       begin
          if current token not in [id,'¢'] then process error;
          if current token in [id] then
              dcls := dcl || dcls; {concatenate dcl and dcls}
          else
              dcls := λ;
       end;
```

Fig. 3-8. *Dcls* in Translation Grammar.

```
function   dcl: string;
           {look for DCL and emit its translation.}
  var x,y: string;
  begin
    if current token not in [id] then process error;
    x := ids;
    if current token not in [':'] then process error;
    advance token pointer;
    y := type;
    if current token not in [';'] then process error;
    advance token pointer;
    dcl := x || ':' || y || ';' ;
    insert(x,y,'mutable');
    alloc(x);
  end;
```

Fig. 3-9. *Dcl* in Translation Grammar.

```
function   ids: string;
           {look for IDS and emit its translation.}
  var temp: string;
  begin
    if current token not in [id] then process error;
    temp := current token;
    advance token pointer;
    if current token not in [',', ':'] then process error;
    if current token in [','] then
       begin
         temp := temp || ',' ;
         advance token pointer;
         ids := temp || ids;
       end;
    else
       ids := temp;
  end;
```

Fig. 3-10. *Ids* in Translation Grammar.

```
function   type: string;
           {look for a TYPE and emit its translation}
  begin
    if current token not in {'integer'} then process error;
    type := current token;
    advance token pointer;
  end;
```

Fig. 3-11. *Type* in Translation Grammar.

routines now return *strings* rather than a *boolean* value, the logic of error processing must change somewhat. When an error occurs (because a string is not a sentence), an error processing routine will be called instead of merely setting a variable to the *boolean* value, *false*. Since at this point we are not overly concerned with error processing, we will not dwell on how these routines work until Chapter 8.

In Chapter 2 we introduced a grammar-driven LL(1) parser which obviates the need for coding each set of alternative productions into a function, a concept which generalizes to translation grammars as well. A grammar-driven translation grammar processor (GDTGP) which has been implemented at the University of California at Santa Barbara is shown in Figs. 3-12 and 3-13. A GDTGP actually has two components: a translation grammar analyzer (TGA) and a skeletal translator (ST). The TGA accepts as input a translation grammar such as the one shown in Fig. 3-14, and produces two files: an internal format for the grammar, which must be read in by the compiler, and a procedure called *takeact* which structures the calls to action routines. The latter file is in PASCAL, and is embedded into ST at the indicated points along with the action routine definitions. Once ST has been "fleshed out" in this manner, it is a complete compiler (CC) presumably written in PASCAL. After compiling CC, we have a compiler for the original translation grammar. Hence, the basic steps to produce an executable version of CC are:

1) execute TGA on translation grammar;
2) embed generated files into ST;
3) embed action routines into ST producing CC;
4) compile CC.

The translation grammar is input to TGP in two stages: First, the vocabulary is specified. Each line begins with '%a' (for axiom), '%n' for nonterminal, '%l' for literal, or '%g' for group. Exactly one axiom must be specified. If a vocabulary symbol is used in a production, then it must be declared in this part of the grammar input. Terminals are divided into two categories: literal and group. A literal stands for itself in a production, such as '=' or ';' in Fig. 3-14, while a group stands for a set of actual tokens such as ID which represents the whole set of identifiers in productions. A scanner, *nexttoken,* which must be one of the action routines, will, during the actual processing of a candidate sentence, determine whether a token is a *literal* or a *group.* If it is a literal, that token's *class* is set to λ; otherwise, the *class* is set to the group name, such as ID. In either case, the actual characters which make up the token in the candidate are assigned to the token's *value*.

Productions follow '%%' and are written at most one to a line, but any

```
program   translation_grammar_analyzer(keepfile, input, output, actfile, ingram):
        {generate the parser from an LL(1) grammar}
    type
      style = (literal,nonterminal,group,action);
      right = record   {element of rhs of a production}
                    value:  string;
                      {name of vocabulary symbol or string it generates}
                    casesel:  0. .maxint;
                      {action routine is assigned a case number}
                    kind:  style;
                  end;
      production = record
                      lhs:  string;
                      rhs:  list of right;
                      select:  list of right;
                    end;
      grammar = record
                      axion:  string;
                      nonterm:  list of strings;
                      lit:  list of strings;
                      groups:  list of strings;
                      prods:  list of productions;
                    end;
    var
      keepfile:  file of char;   {where grammar for skeletal compiler is stored}
      ingram:  file of char;   {where grammar written by user is stored}
      actfile:  file of char;   {where action code is stored in a big case statement for inclu-
                                sion in parser}
      nextact:  integer;   {case number of next action routine}
      gram:  grammar;   {the grammar to be stored in keepfile}
    procedure process_action_routine;   {process an action routine.}
      begin
        nextact := nextact + 1;   {another action is being processed}
        with the current rhs element of the current production do begin
          value := '';          {action routines have no value}
          casesel := nextact;   {for the case stmt in takeact}
          writeln(actfile,'      ',casesel, ': begin');
          kind := action;
          get the next character;
          while the current character <> '}' do begin
                {process the action routine}
            if eoln(ingram) then writeln(actfile);
            if current character = '$' then begin
                {is char following $ a digit?}
              get the next character;
              if the current character is a digit then begin
                    {replace string in action rotuine}
                  write(actfile, 'sentform[sentptr−');
```

Fig. 3-12. *Translation_grammar_processor.*

```
                write(actfile, difference between the position of the action routine in the rhs
                        and the position of the symbol being referenced);
                write(actfile, '].value')
                end;
              else
                write(actfile,dollar);
              end;
            else
              write(actfile,current character);
              get the next character;
          end;
        get the next character;   {skip past brace}
        writeln(actfile);
        writeln(actfile,'              end; {', nextact, '}');
        end;   {with}
      end;   {process action routine}

begin
    {set up the header for the case statement in which all action routines are called.}
    rewrite(actfile);
    writeln(actfile, 'procedure takeact(sentptr: integer; ', 'actionnum: integer); ');
    writeln(actfile,' begin');
    writeln(actfile,' case actionnum of');
    writeln(actfile,'         0: ;');
    reset(ingram);
        {get everything before the productions}
    add the end of string marker to the set of literals;
repeat
    readln(ingram, line);
    if (first character = '%') and (second character <> '%') then using second character to
        determine which type of information is on this line, add a new literal, group to the list of
        vocabulary symbols;
until   (first two characters are both '%');
                {get the productions}
nextact := 0;   {initially there are no action routines}
get the first line;
while current character <> '%' do begin
            {get the lhs of the current production}
    with the current production do begin
        skip past all initial blanks;
        lhs := all characters up to next blank of '=';
        skip past all blanks and '=';
        end;   {with}
            {get the rhs of the current production}
    with the current production do
        while curchar <> '[' do begin
            if curchar = '{' then process_action_routine;
            else
```

Fig. 3-12 (continued).

```
  with current rhs element do begin
      value   :=  all characters up to blank or '[';
      casesel   :=  0;
      kind   :=  whatever vocabulary type current symbol is;
      end;
  skip past all blanks between this rhs element and the next rhs element;
  end;
  {get the selection set of the current production}
with current production do begin
  skip past the open brace;
  skip any blanks;
  while current character <> ']' do
     {search for next selection set member}
     with current rhs element do begin
      value   :=  all characters up to next blank or ']';
      casesel   :=  0;
      kind   :=  literal or group depending on its vocabulary type;
      skip all blanks up to next member of ']';
      end;   {with}
  end;   {with}
  skip past the rest of the line of input from ingram;
  end;   {while}
  {terminate the case statement in which all action calls are located}
writeln;
writeln(actfile, ' end;  {case}');
writeln(actfile, code to mark the action routine just executed to show that it has);
writeln(actfile, ' end;  {takeact}');
                   {save the grammar on disk.}
rewrite(keepfile);
keepfile↑:=  gram;
put(keepfile);
end.
```

Fig. 3-12 (continued).

production can extend over multiple lines if necessary. Each production
has the form:

$$lhs = rhs\ sel$$

where *lhs* is the left-hand side nonterminal, '=' is equivalent to '→', *rhs* is
the right-hand side, and *sel* is the selection set. *Rhs* and *sel* elements are
separated by one or more blanks. The selection set is enclosed by square
brackets, action code by curly brackets. The *lhs* can be omitted for alternative productions after the first. Action code is a sequence of PASCAL
statements. The definition of any routines, variables, constants, etc.
mentioned in action code must be placed into ST when fleshing it out. In
this example that would include *insert, alloc,* and the symbol table. In
place of subscripts on symbols, the action routines use '$n' where *n* is the

```
program   skeletal_compiler(input, output, listing, object, keepfile, candfile);
                                    {translate a candidate string}
   type
      style = (literal, nonterminal, group, action);
      right = record
                  value: string;
                     {name of vocabulary symbol or string it generates}
                  casesel:  0. . maxint;
                     {action routine is assigned a case number}
                  kind:   style;
               end;
      production = record
                     lhs:   string;
                     rhs:   list of right;
                     select:   list of right;
                  end;
      grammar = record   {other components are not needed}
                  axiom:   string;
                  prods:   list of productions;
               end;
      tok = record
               value:   string;
                  {the literal token}
            class:   string;
            end;
      sentential = record
                     value:   string;
                     casesel:   0. . maxint;
                     kind:   style;
                  end;
   var
      candfile: file of char;   {where candidate program is stored}
      listing: file of char;   {where listing is printed}
      object: file of char;   {where object code is stored}
      keepfile: file of char;   {where grammar is stored}
      sentform: array[1. . 100] of sentential;
         {the stack of vocabulary symbols constituting the sentential form}
      sentptr: 0.  100;
         {the pointer to the vocabulary symbol currently being examined}
      tos: 0. . 100;
         {the top of the sentential form stack}
      gram: grammar; {the grammar on which the parsing is based}

procedure parse;   {parse the candidate}
   var
         change: boolean;   {did a compress change sentptr?}
         error: boolean;      {was the next token in the selection set of the alternatives of the
                              next element of the sentential form}
         derefsen: sentential;   {sentential form pointed to by sentptr}
```

Fig. 3-13. *Skeletal_compiler.*

sentptr: 1. . **maxint;**   {pinpoint current symbol in sentential form}
{include the supporting declarations needed for action routines}
{include the supporting routines such as nexttoken and all action routines}

procedure expand(derefsen: sentential; **var** error: **boolean**);
{expand the nonterminal in the sentential form}
   begin
     error := **false;**
        {presume there is no error − production will be found}
     determine whether there is a production whose lhs is sentvalue and whose selection set includes token. If so, then return the index to that production;
     if *search succeeds* **then**
        {a production has the token in its selection set.}
      with *production found* **do begin**
        insert the rhs on top of sentform so that the parent of each new rhs element points to the member of sentform which corresponds to lhs;
        sentptr := sentptr + 1;
          {have just finished with current sentence element}
        tos := tos + *the size of rhs;*
        if *production is a lambda production* **then**
         perform the reduction now by decreasing sentptr by 1, setting value to '',
         casesel to 0, and kind to literal;
        end;   {with}
     else
        {there is no alternative production with this token, this candidate is not a sentence.}
        error := **true;**
   end;   {expand}

procedure compress(**var** change: **boolean**);
{compress the stack of sentential forms}
  begin
    change := **false;**   {presume no change to the stack}
    while *all siblings of tos element are ready for reduction* **do begin**
      change := **true;**
      reset value of parent of tos element to be that of the string it generated, changing its kind to literal;
      tos := tos − *size of rhs of which tos element is a part;*
      sentptr := *parent of current tos element;*
      end;
  end;   {compress}

procedure abort;
{to recover from a syntactic error, terminate the compilation}
  begin
    writeln(*error message that syntactic error occurred, what token was encountered, what tokens would have been acceptable, and that compilation is being terminated*);
    exit from parse;
  end;

Fig. 3-13 (continued).

```
begin   {parse}
  initialize sentform to be the axiom;
  sentptr  :=   1;  {point to first token of sentform}
  while sentptr <= tos do begin
                            {derivation isn't finished}
    derefsen  :=   sentform[sentptr];
          {the component of the sentential form to be analyzed next.}
    if (current symbol is a literal and token matches) or
       (current symbol is group and the token class matches) then begin
      sentform[sentptr] value  :=   current token value;
            {replace the group name (if present) with the actual token value}
      mark sentform[sentptr] as having been processed;
      get the next token;
      compress(change);
      sentptr  :=   sentptr + 1;
      end;
    else
      case derefsen. kind of
        literal, group: abort;
        nonterminal: begin
          expand(derefsen, error);
          if error then abort;
          else if lambda production then begin
            compress(change);
            if change then
                {lambda production has been compressed}
              sentptr  :=   sentptr + 1;
            end;
          end;  {nonterminal}
        action: begin
            takeact(sentptr, derefsen. casesel);
            compress(change);
            sentptr  :=   sentptr + 1;
            end;  {action}
        patch: begin
          compress(change);
          sentptr  :=   sentptr + 1;
          end;  {patch}
      end;  {case}
    end;  {while}
  if current token value <> end of candidate then abort;
  {we have only matched against a part of the candidate. The candidate is not a sen-
                            tence.}
  end;  {parse}

begin   {main program}
    reset(keepfile);
    read the grammar in from keepfile;
    reset(candfile);
    parse;
end.
```

Fig. 3-13 (continued).

```
%a DCLS
%n DCL   IDS   TYPE
%n ID   NEW
%l :   ;   ,   integer
%g ID
%%
        DCLS = DCL   DCLS        [ID]
             =                   [@]
        DCL  = IDS   :   TYPE   ;
               {insert($1,$3,'mutable');
                 alloc($1)}      [ID]
        IDS  = ID   NEW          [ID]
        NEW  = ,   IDS           [,]
             =                   [:]
        TYPE = integer           [integer]
%%
```

Fig. 3-14. Translation Grammar for TRANSDCL.

relative position of the symbol on the right-hand side. If the action code is the k-th symbol in *rhs*, then $1 \le n < k$.

TGA maps the grammar into an internal form which can be included in ST to form CC. The action code is embedded into procedure *takeact*, which essentially consists of one **case** statement where each case is an action code sequence with the 'n' items replaced by the proper variables. TGA numbers each action code sequence from 1 as it encounters it. This number becomes the **case** label for the sequence in *takeact*. The internal grammar form used by CC contains an indicator to show that the original grammar had action code at that point which can be found at the specified case label in *takeact*.

CC manipulates an array of the current sentential form, each array element being a vocabulary symbol. Initially it is just the axiom. As tokens from the candidate string are examined, CC searches the internal grammar form for an alternative production whose selection set includes the current token, and expands the current nonterminal it is positioned at in the sentential form when it finds one. Literals and groups in the sentential form are matched directly against tokens in the candidate. Action code in *takeact* is executed when the corresponding element in the sentential form is processed. When nonterminal B has been completely expanded into α, the value of α is stored into B within the sentential form array and α is erased from that array. This way each nonterminal, literal, or group symbol is assigned a value which can be referenced by an action symbol, but once no action symbol can reference a value, that nonterminal, literal, or group symbol is erased from the sentential form.

At this stage the only error processing is to terminate translation if an error is found. Chapter 8 details more advanced error processing methods.

3.5 SUMMARY

The *translation grammar* is an extension of the context-free grammar which permits us to *translate* a string as well as recognize it. A *translation grammar processor* is easily implemented as an extension of the *top-down recursive descent parser,* provided that the parser does not back up. *Backtracking* with a translation grammar can be particularly expensive, in that arbitrarily complex data structures may be manipulated during the calls to *action routines*—the functions which actually perform the translation.

EXERCISES

3-1. Implement the translation grammar of the chapter example in your favorite programming language.

3-2. Modify grammar G_4 of Chapter 2 for infix arithmetic expressions so that it becomes a translation grammar. The target language is that of prefix arithmetic expressions. For example, if 'a+bc*2' is the source string being parsed, then '+a*bc 2' is the output.

3-3. Write a translation grammar whose source language is the Roman numerals, and whose target language is the arabic numerals. The output of the translator for input string x should be the arabic equivalent of x.

3-4. Rewrite the definition of a translation grammar for a scheme which generates the rightmost derivation of a string, rather than its leftmost derivation.

3-5. Write a translation grammar which accepts FORTRAN FORMAT statements as input and converts them into PL/I FORMAT statements.

3-6. Why do we include an entry in the symbol table for the mutability of a name's value? Cite a specific instance in LITTLE RASCAL where this information is needed after the entry is made.

3-7. The translation of a sentence can be an infinite set. Prove this is so by defining a translation grammar which has one such source sentence. (Hint: consider a grammar with a production which is cyclic.)

3-8. Construct a translation grammar based on the grammar G_2 of Chapter 2. The target language is that of postfix arithmetic expressions. Since the source grammar G_2 is ambiguous, sentences may have more than one translation. Show the steps of your translation grammar processor for sentences:

    a. a+bc*2
    b. (a+bf)*(c−q **div** 32)
    c. 3 **div** a − d

3-9. Construct a translation grammar which maps FORTRAN logical IF statements into ALGOL 60 logical IF statements.

3-10. Construct a translation grammar which maps ALGOL 60 IF-THEN-ELSE and IF-THEN statements into FORTRAN logical IF statements.

3-11. Construct a translation grammar which will map LISP conditional statements into PL/I IF statements.

3-12. Construct a translation grammar which outputs the reverse of the input string for input alphabet {b,c}.

3-13. Construct a translation grammar which maps postfix arithmetic expressions into infix expressions.

3-14. Construct a translation grammar which will map the **while** construct of PASCAL into the more primitive loop formed from an **if** statement and a **goto**. Show the action sequence of your translation grammar on

$$\textbf{while } x < 0 \textbf{ do } \textbf{ begin } x:=x+1; y:=y*x \textbf{ end}$$

3-15. Figures 3-12 and 3-13 show a pseudo-code grammar-driven LL(1) translation grammar processor. Complete the implementation.

3-16. You are given the following LL(1) grammar, G, with axiom DCL:

DCL → NON_KEY_ID ':' TYPE ';'	{NON_KEY_ID}
TYPE → 'INTEGER'	{'INTEGER'}
→ 'RECORD' ';' DCLS 'END'	{'RECORD'}
DCLS → DCL (DCLS {NON_KEY_ID} ׀λ {'END'})	{NON_KEY_ID}

NON_KEY_ID, which represents the set of non-keyword identifiers, is treated like a terminal here. Each sentence of the language generated by this grammar is a variable declaration. A variable may be declared to be an integer (a *simple* declaration):

    x: INTEGER;

or a record

    x: RECORD;
      y: INTEGER;
      z: RECORD;
        a: INTEGER;
        b: INTEGER;
        END;
      END;

Note that a record field may itself be a record. Convert G into a translation grammar which will:

1. emit a simple declaration unchanged and
2. translate a record declaration into a sequence of simple declarations for fully qualified variable names reflecting the structure of the record.

For example,

    x: INTEGER;

is passed unchanged but:

    x: RECORD;
      y: INTEGER;
      z: RECORD;
        a: INTEGER;
        b: INTEGER;
        END;
      END;

becomes:

    x.y: INTEGER;
    x.z.a: INTEGER;
    x.z.b: INTEGER;

3-17. The equivalent of a translation grammar for bottom-up methods can also be devised. In this case, however, all action symbols appear to the extreme right of the right-hand side of a production:

$$B \rightarrow \beta \ \ w_1 \ \ w_2 \ldots w_n$$

where $w_1, \ldots, w_n$ are action symbols, possibly referencing the value of a nonterminal in β. These routines are called *only* when a reduction $B \rightarrow \beta$ occurs.

Formalize the notion of a bottom-up translation grammar and demonstrate its viability by writing such a translation grammar to:

    a). translate infix arithmetic expressions to postfix;
    b). translate LITTLE RASCAL declarations as we did in the text body.

BIBLIOGRAPHY

The notion of a *syntax-directed translation,* in which a context-free grammar *drives* the translator, is attributed to [Irons 61, 63]. [Brooker, et al 63] describes a *compiler-compiler* or *translator-writing system,* which is a system to partially automate the generation of syntax-directed translators; numerous others have examined both the theory and practice of syntax-directed translation. The GDTGP described at the end of this chapter is one such translator-writing system. [Lewis and Stearns 68], [Aho and Ullman 69], and [Pyster and Buttelmann 78] study the formal properties of syntax-directed translation. [McKeeman, et al 70] is a detailed examination of XPL, a compiler-compiler which has been widely implemented. [Feldman and Gries 68] overview the art of translator-writing systems in the late Sixties.

Although we have not developed the equivalent of the translation grammar for bottom-up parsers in the main body of the chapter, the concept is easily transferred to such parsing techniques. One or more action routines can be called each time a reduction is performed whether the parser is precedence, LR, or some other model. [Gries 71] develops such a scheme with detailed examples of their application to numerous language constructs. [Aho and Ullman 77] is another excellent source for such material; exercise 3-17 addresses this further.

[Knuth 68, 71] superimposes a semantic model atop the context-free grammar, the *attributed grammar.* This scheme has been developed in [Pyster and Buttelmann 78] and in [Krishnaswamy and Pyster 77] into methodologies for formal translation of programming languages. [Lewis, Rosenkrantz, and Stearns 74, 76] developed attributed translators and translation grammars in large part based on the work of Knuth.

Part 2
A Simple Rascal
Compiler

Part 1 developed the basic concepts and notations necessary to specify both the RASCAL language and its compiler, CANTOR. Now that this background material has been presented, we continue with a four part specification of a major subset of RASCAL and a compiler for this language. Each chapter in this section will introduce new aspects of both the language and its compiler. By the completion of Chapter 7, which ends Part 2, the reader will have explored the implementation of the following RASCAL features:

1. *integer* and *boolean* data-types
2. *integer* and *boolean* variables
3. *integer* and *boolean* constants
4. *integer* and *boolean* literals
5. arithmetic, *boolean* and relational expressions
6. declarations
7. assignment statements
8. **if-then** statements
9. **if-then-else** statements
10. **while** statements
11. **repeat** statements
12. **program** statements
13. **begin-end** statements
14. null statements
15. **read** and **readln** procedures
16. **write** and **writeln** procedures

The specifications of CANTOR are complete enough so that the reader should be able to implement a working version of a compiler for programs which incorporate these 16 features. As a major concession to simplicity, error processing is not handled in this part of the text. We shall assume that only valid programs will be input to CANTOR throughout Part 2, delaying error processing techniques until Part 3 because at this point the reader has quite enough to master without being concerned about error processing. However, in the refinements presented, we shall often anticipate the introduction of error processing capability by including references to error processing routines. These routines will not be expounded upon in Part 2, merely mentioned here so that when errors are finally handled in Part 3, very little of the compiler will need to be reorganized to correctly process them.

The 16 language features of RASCAL presented in Part 2 enable us to write some fairly complex programs in a reasonable manner. RASCAL and its parent language, PASCAL, encourage good programming practices by the inclusion of certain "structured programming" constructs. As these features are introduced, their importance in good programming may be briefly discussed. Note that RASCAL as defined in Part 2 (and also Part 3) excludes both labels and **goto** statements. This exclusion facilitates optimization of the object code generated by CANTOR and also reflects the tendency of recent language designers to discourage the use of the **goto** statement. Actually, if RASCAL were to be proposed as a commercial language, then either the **goto** statement or some additional supplements to the control structures defined in RASCAL would have to be offered; however, since RASCAL is defined only for pedagogical purposes, the elimination of labels and **goto** statements is not a problem.

4
Stage 0: Skeleton

4.1 INTRODUCTION

The compiler developed in this chapter is called *skeleton* because the features of RASCAL presented here are so skimpy that RASCAL is a "bare bones" language. The only features of RASCAL here are the **program** statement, the declaration of *integer* and *boolean* variables and constants, and a lone **begin-end** statement which is the main body of the program. There are no *executable statements* in stage 0 RASCAL. Despite the paucity of features in stage 0 RASCAL, its compilation is no small task, which is precisely why such a small subset of RASCAL was selected for initial study. For example, a scanner, parser, semantic processor and code generator must be constructed in order for CANTOR to be able to compile even such limited RASCAL programs (hereafter referred to simply as *RASCAL/0* for convenience). As new and more powerful features augment RASCAL in later chapters, these components will become increasingly sophisticated as greater demands are placed upon them; however, the overall structure of the compiler established in this chapter will be retained throughout the text.

In this and succeeding chapters, we shall first present the new features of RASCAL which are being implemented in that chapter. The syntactic features will be introduced formally through an LL(1) grammar, while all context-sensitive constraints such as not declaring the same identifier twice will be discussed in English and illustrated by example where appropriate. At those points where RASCAL departs significantly from PASCAL, we shall explicitly indicate how it differs, and why we have made the change. After RASCAL/i features (generalizing on the notation RASCAL/0 to indicate the stage of the language) have been presented, we shall continue with the problem of compiling programs which exercise those features.

4.2 RASCAL/0 LANGUAGE FEATURES

It is critical that we isolate those aspects of RASCAL dictated by the *implementation* from those features central to the *language definition* itself. For example, the definition of RASCAL/0 in this section does not detail in which columns of a line statements may appear, but the next section on implementation features will. The position of statements on a line (for example) should probably not be important to the language designer. Some languages such as FORTRAN violate this rule, imposing the constraint *within the language definition* that statement labels be located in columns 1–5 of a line. This imposes unnecessary constraints on the language users. Sometimes the implementation constraints on the location of a statement on a line are highly dependent on the environment in which the program is being compiled; for example, PL/I comments begin with the token '/*'. This same token, when written in columns one and two of a line, has a special meaning to OS/360 (end of file marker). Consequently, the IBM 360 implementations of PL/I do not permit statements to begin in column one to avoid the potential problem of someone accidently terminating his program when he thought he was beginning a comment. For other environments and other languages, this restriction would be absurd.

We begin the presentation of RASCAL/0 with some general comments on the form of programs. All keywords of the language are reserved, of which there are nine in stage 0:

**program, const, var, integer, boolean,
begin, end, true, false**

Any use of these words outside their special context is illegal. PASCAL does not reserve **integer, boolean, true,** and **false.** Rather it establishes them as *pre-defined constants;* i.e., identifiers which have a constant value assigned to them at program entry. PASCAL allows a programmer to redefine the value of these four identifiers through declarations. Such a redefinition of such fundamental identifiers can only be tremendously confusing to anyone trying to read such code and is a very poor programming practice. RASCAL simply disallows their redefinition entirely.

All RASCAL statements but one *terminate* with a semicolon, a policy at variance with PASCAL in which the semicolon is inserted *between* statements. We follow the PL/I convention because experience has shown that the PASCAL policy is more error-prone and is also more difficult to compile. The RASCAL policy will, in general, mean that more semicolons will appear in programs than would be found in their PASCAL counterparts. By increasing the "noise" level within the program by requiring additional semicolons, it becomes easier to recover from errors encountered in the program. The lone exception to the semicolon rule is the **begin-end** statement which brackets the executable code of all RASCAL programs. It ends with a period (following the PASCAL standard) in order to indicate the end of a *program,* as opposed to the end of a *statement*.

Some languages, such as FORTRAN, are essentially insensitive to the insertion of blanks in code (except within *character* literals); for example, the two FORTRAN statements:

$$A = B\ C \qquad D + 5 * \qquad * T$$
$$A = BCD + 5 * *T$$

have exactly the same meaning, but in RASCAL this is not true. Blanks are token *delimiters;* i.e., no token (excluding *character* literals which are not of interest in Part 2) can have embedded blanks. Hence, two identifiers can never be adjacent, having to be separated by at least one blank or another delimiter. The general rule is that if two tokens are adjacent, then one of them must be composed solely of special characters. In RASCAL/0 the special characters are:

$$':' \quad ',' \quad ';' \quad '=' \quad '+' \quad '-' \quad '.'$$

Comments are begun by '{' and terminated by '}'. They may appear anywhere a blank is allowed without changing the meaning of the program. A comment may be any text not containing an embedded '}'. We continue with a description of the tokens of RASCAL/0 defined by a context-free grammar. At this point, we are not indicating how these tokens are assembled into legal RASCAL/0 statements:

1. KEYWORD   → 'program' | 'begin' | 'end' | 'var' | 'const' | 'integer' | 'boolean' 'true' | 'false'

2. SPEC_SYM   → '=' | ':' | ',' | ';' | '.' | '+' | '-'

3. NON_KEY_ID → ALPHA   ALPHANUMS

4. ALPHA   → 'a' | 'b' | 'c' | 'd' | 'e' | 'f' | 'g' | 'h' | 'i' | 'j' | 'k' | 'l' | 'm' | 'n' | 'o' | 'p' 'q' | 'r' | 's' | 't' | 'u' | 'v' | 'w' | 'x' | 'y' | 'z'

5. NUM   → '0' | '1' | '2' | '3' | '4' | '5' | '6' | '7' | '8' | '9'

6. ALPHANUM → ALPHA | NUM

7. ALPHANUMS → ALPHANUM   ALPHANUMS

             → λ

8. INTEGER   → NUM   NUMS

9. NUMS   → NUM   NUMS

             → λ

10. TOKEN   → KEYWORD |NON_KEY_ID |SPEC_SYM |INTEGER

So a token in RASCAL/0 is either a keyword, a non-keyword identifier, a special symbol or an *integer,* which is always unsigned.

Now that the tokens have been identified, we continue with an LL(1) context-free grammar for RASCAL/0 in which the selection sets of alternative productions are given to the right of each alternative. This grammar breaks programs into *tokens,* not individual characters. As such, the lookahead strings may be several characters long but will be only one token long. Actually, we shall use either the *tag* or the *class* of a token in the grammar and its processor as needed. The token grammar given earlier defines the classes of interest:

1. PROG   → PROG_STMT CONSTS VARS BEGIN_END_STMT
                                              {'program'}

2. PROG_STMT   → 'program' NON_KEY_ID ';'   {'program'}

3. CONSTS   → 'const' CONST_STMTS   {'const'}

                        → λ   { 'var','begin'}

4. VARS   → 'var' VAR_STMTS   {'var'}

                        → λ   {'begin'}

5. BEGIN_END_STMT → 'begin' 'end' '.'   {'begin'}

6. CONST_STMTS   → NON_KEY_ID '=' (NON_KEY_ID {NON_KEY_ID}
                          | LIT   {'true','false',INTEGER,'+','−'})
                          ';' (CONST_STMTS {NON_KEY_ID} | λ {'var','begin'})
                                                {NON_KEY_ID}

7. VAR_STMTS   → IDS ':' TYPE ';' (VAR_STMTS {NON_KEY_ID} | λ
                        {'begin'})   {NON_KEY_ID}

8. IDS   → NON_KEY_ID (',' IDS {','} | λ {':'}) {NON_KEY_ID}

9. TYPE   → 'integer'   {'integer'}

                        → 'boolean'   {'boolean'}

10. LIT   → INTEGER   {INTEGER}

                        → BOOLEAN   {'false','true'}

                        → '+' INTEGER   {'+'}

                        → '−' INTEGER   {'−'}

11. BOOLEAN   → 'true'   {'true'}

                        → 'false'   {'false'}

There are several context-sensitive constraints not expressed by the grammar rules:

1. Each identifier may be declared at most once.
2. Keywords are reserved.
3. The program name is not declared.
4. An identifier which occurs to the right of '=' in a constant declaration must itself be a previously declared constant.

```
program   notmuchhere;
   const   yes = true; no = false;
           small = 0; smalleryet = −1;
           big = 1; biggeryet = 2;
   var     some, many : integer;
           right, wrong: boolean;
   begin
   end
```

Fig. 4-1. A Legal RASCAL/0 Program.

An example of a legal RASCAL/0 program is given in Fig. 4-1, while two illegal RASCAL/0 programs are shown in Fig. 4-2. The comments within the programs indicate why the latter two are illegal.

4.3 CANTOR/0 IMPLEMENTATION FEATURES

We impose several constraints on RASCAL/0 programs at this point. These constraints are motivated by implementation concerns. As such they do not properly belong to the language definition:

1. A statement may be located anywhere in columns 1–72 of a line. For an interactive environment such as the rule for PDP-11 shops, this constraint would probably be omitted; however, since we are assum-

```
program   badegg;
           {illustrate erroneous use of RASCAL/0 features.}
   var   x: integer;
         y,z+: boolean;       {z+ is an illegal name.}
         asis: integr;        {'integer' misspelt.}
   const   help = 32;         {const section must precede var section.}
         x = true;            {x may not be redefined.}
         s,t = 0;             {no lists of constants allowed.}
   begin   end;               {program ends with a period, not a semicolon.}

program   evenworse;
           {illustrates more erroneous uses of RASCAL/0 features.}
   const   var = 2;           {keyword misused.}
           silly: boolean;    {need a literal and '=' for a constant.}
   const   raid = −34;        {only one occurrence of 'const' allowed.}
           wrong = 3.5;       {no real numbers in RASCAL/0.}
           po or = 0;         {no embedded blanks in a token.}
           s = b;             {referencing an undefined constant}
           b = 36;
   begin   begin   end;   end.     {only one begin-end statement allowed.}
```

Fig. 4-2. Two Illegal RASCAL/0 Programs.

ing a typical IBM card-oriented environment, this constraint is reasonable.

2. A statement may freely extend over any number of lines without any special markers to denote the continuation. A *newline* is equivalent to a blank as a delimiter, so that no token may extend over more than one line.

3. There is a maximum and a minimum valued *integer*. For all versions of CANTOR they are 2^{31}-1 and -2^{31}, respectively. These values, motivated by the range of *integer* values easily manipulated on an IBM 360/370 computer would likely change for another target machine.

4. The symbol table will hold up to 256 entries. This number is arbitrary but is large enough to accommodate most "student" programs.

5. The generated code must all be addressable by one base register. For the short test programs which will be run through CANTOR, this constraint is no problem.

A language implementation must do far more than just generate correct object code. It must also return information to the user about each program it compiles. The format of the output of CANTOR/0 (the compiler for RASCAL/0) is shown in Fig. 4-3. Each listing begins with a banner message which is followed by a listing of the program, then a trailer message, and finally the object code generated by CANTOR/0 (not shown until Fig. 4-5). Normally, commercial compilers print the generated object code only on demand from the programmer. Here we will uniformly emit the object code, since the student will be studying this code both to better understand compilation and also to debug his compiler.

In Fig. 4-3 the lines are numbered consecutively to facilitate referencing specific lines of code. Also note that a vertical bar, '|', is printed before the first character of the source line image and after the 72nd column of the

```
       CANTOR COMPILER: STAGE 0     JUN 7, 1979     12:17
LINE NO.                    SOURCE STATEMENT
   1 |        program   notmuchhere;                              |
   2 |        const   yes = true; no = false;                     |
   3 |                small = 0; smalleryet = −1;                 |
   4 |                big = biggeryet = 2;                         |
   5 |        var     some, many : integer;                       |
   6 |                right, wrong: boolean;                       |
   7 |        begin                                               |
   8 |        end.                                                |
       COMPILATION TERMINATED        0 ERRORS ENCOUNTERED
```

Fig. 4-3. Output of CANTOR/0 on Program from Fig. 4-1.

source line image as a visual aid to help the programmer recognize in which columns his statements appear. The right boundary marker is especially important, because the compiler will ignore characters which appear beyond column 72 of a line. The vertical bar aids the programmer in detecting characters accidentally placed beyond column 72, an error which is quite subtle and difficult to detect without some such device.

4.4 OVERALL COMPILER STRUCTURE

In this section the overall framework of CANTOR/0 is designed, including the main routine and the interfaces between that routine and its major components. CANTOR/0 (and for that matter, all versions of CANTOR) is organized as a translation grammar processor. The translation grammar intended for this purpose is shown next. The grammar given in section 4.2 for RASCAL/0 is an LL(1) grammar so that the processor can generate a leftmost derivation of programs without backtracking. The grammar given next includes the action symbols needed to translate source code into 360AL, the selection sets having been omitted in order to avoid clutter:

1. PROG   → PROG_STMT CONSTS VARS
                                         BEGIN_END_STMT

2. PROG_STMT   → 'program' NON_KEY_ID$_x$ ';'
                                         code('program',x) insert(x,prog_name,immutable,x,no)

3. CONSTS   → 'const' CONST_STMTS

                          → λ

4. VARS   → 'var' VAR_STMTS

                          → λ

5. BEGIN_END_STMT   → 'begin' 'end' '.' *code('end','.')*

6. CONST_STMTS   → NON_KEY_ID$_x$ '=' (NON_KEY_ID$_y$ ⏐ LIT$_y$) ';'
                                         insert(x,which_type(y),immutable,which_value(y),yes,1)
                                         (CONST_STMTS ⏐ λ)

7. VAR_STMTS   → IDS$_x$ ':' TYPE$_y$ ';'
                                         insert(x,y,mutable,,yes,1)
                                         (VAR_STMTS ⏐λ)

8. IDS   → NON_KEY_ID (',' IDS ⏐λ)

9. TYPE   → 'integer' ⏐ 'boolean'

10. LIT   → INTEGER ⏐ BOOLEAN ⏐ '+'
                           INTEGER ⏐ '−' INTEGER

11. BOOLEAN   → 'true' ⏐ 'false'

Note that in production 6, subscript y is used twice. This does not contradict restriction 1 on the form of valid productions of a translation grammar, however, since y is subscripting alternatives. Production 6 is actually an abbreviation for *two* productions; hence, y can never be the value of both alternatives simultaneously and no conflict can arise.

There are just four action routines called in this simple translation grammar:

1. *insert (external_names, type, mode,value,allocate,units)*
2. *code(operator,operand1,operand2)*
3. *which_type(external_name)*
4. *which_value(external_name)*

These routines are explained further in the following sections of this chapter. Figure 4-4 shows a parse tree of the program in Fig. 4-1. When the processor has completed the generation of the leftmost derivation of this program, it will have emitted the object code shown in Fig. 4-5, and generated the activity sequence shown in Fig. 4-6.

We continue with the main program for CANTOR/0. It is extremely simple, reflecting the fact that most of the actual processing is performed by the parser. Figure 4-7 shows the pseudo-code for the main program, which is for the most part self-explanatory. There is one important deviation from standard PASCAL (and full RASCAL), both here and in later refinements; namely, we shall not declare internal procedures explicitly to avoid cluttering the pseudo-code. So, for example, there is no declaration of the procedures which create listing headers and trailers and the parser itself in Fig. 4-7. The data-type *string* found in this routine is not from standard PASCAL. A variable of type *string* may be assigned any string of length greater than or equal to zero (length zero strings are lambda). Standard PASCAL's poor string manipulation facilities would cause awkward coding, which would detract from the presentation, so we simply extend PASCAL as needed.

The symbol table has been defined in Fig. 4-7 because this data structure is so pervasively referenced throughout the compiler. We again extend PASCAL to include a *table* data-type which is referenced in this case by the external name of an entry. So, for example, to reference the entry in the table for the external name 'trivia', we simply write:

symbol_table['trivia']

If there is no entry under that index, then the value referenced is *undefined*. Our goal in this organization is to avoid having to detail how look-up of entries is actually performed. We presume the reader is familiar with *hashing* and other table searching techniques. The bibliography con-

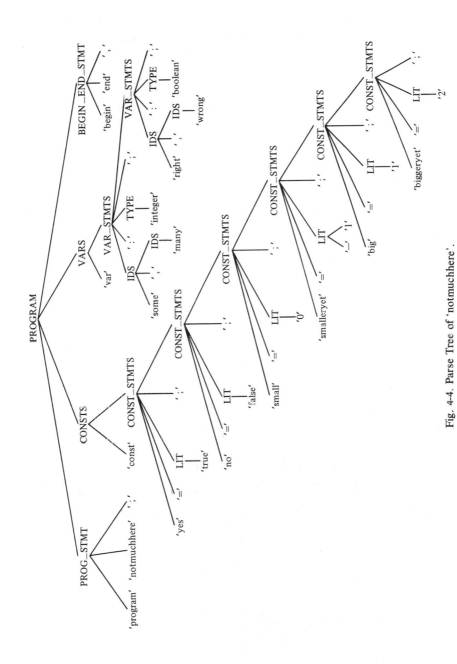

Fig. 4-4. Parse Tree of 'notmuchhere'.

111

```
NOTMUCHH    CSECT
            STM       14,12,12(13)      save registers
            BALR      12,0              set up base register
            USING     *,12
            ST        13,@SAV+4         save loc old save area
            LA        13,@SAV           load loc new save area
@END        L         13,@SAV+4         restore loc old save area
            LM        14,12,12(13)      restore old registers
            BR        14                return
@SAV        DS        18F               @SAV
@B0         DC        1F'−1'            yes
@B1         DC        1F'0'             no
@I0         DC        1F'0'             small
@I1         DC        1F'−1'            smalleryet
@I2         DC        1F'1'             big
@I3         DC        1F'2'             biggeryet
@I4         DS        1F                some
@I5         DS        1F                many
@B2         DS        1F                right
@B3         DS        1F                wrong
            END
```

Fig. 4-5. Object Code for Program in Fig. 4-1.

tains several references to material on table organization and searching for review. Note the use of symbolic constant, *table_size* in Fig. 4-7. By defining this symbolic constant and using it wherever the table size is needed, any decision to change its value will mean *only* a change in the constant declaration, independent of how many references to this value are made in the body of the compiler code.

4.5 CREATE LISTING HEADER AND TRAILER

The main procedure calls a routine which creates the banner message on the program listing generated by CANTOR/0. It is a simple routine shown

```
code('program','notmuchhere')
insert('notmuchhere','prog.name_immutable,'notmuchhere',no)
insert('yes',boolean,immutable,true,yes,1)
insert('no',boolean,immutable,false,yes,1)
insert('small',integer,immutable,0,yes,1)
insert('smalleryet',integer,immutable,1,yes,1)
insert('big',integer,immutable,1,yes,1)
insert('biggeryet',integer,immutable,2,yes,1)
insert('some,many',integer,mutable,,yes,1)
insert('right,wrong',boolean,mutable,,yes,1)
code('end','.')
```

Fig. 4-6. Activity Sequence for 'notmuchhere'.

```
program  cantor(source,listing,object);
         {This program is the CANTOR compiler. It will accept RASCAL input from the
         source file and output to the object file. Additionally, it will generate a listing of
         the program plus other information on the listing file.}
const    table_size = 256;   {size of symbol table}
type     store_types = (int_s, byte_s, double_s, char_s, bool_s, prog_name, ad-
         dress_s);
         allocation = (yes,no);
         modes = (mutable, immutable);
         entry = record   {define symbol table entry format}
                     internal_name: string;
                     data_type:   store_types;
                     mode:   modes;
                     value:   string;
                     alloc:   allocation;
                     units:   integer;
                 end;
var  symbol_table: table[table_size] of entry;
     source, listing, object: file of char;
begin
   create listing header;
   parse contents of source file and translate it, generating listing;
   create listing trailer;
end.
```

Fig. 4-7. Main Program of CANTOR.

on Fig. 4-8 which prints a line identifying the compiler and giving the date and time of day. *Create_listing_trailer,* which prints a message stating that the compilation has terminated, is given in Fig. 4-9.

4.6 PARSER

The third routine specified in the main program is the parser, whose refinements are shown in Figures 4-10 through 4-17. The action calls have been inserted into the productions. In the parser coding, we practice that art of "defensive" programming. In particular, each parser routine ex-

```
procedure  create_listing_header;
   begin
      skip to the top of the next page;
      print 'CANTOR COMPILER: STAGE 0', DATE, TIME OF DAY;
      skip two lines;
      print 'LINE NO.', 'SOURCE STATEMENT';
         {line numbers and source statements should be aligned under these headings.}
   end;
```

Fig. 4-8. *Create_listing_header.*

```
procedure  create_listing_trailer;
  begin
    skip two lines;
    print 'COMPILATION TERMINATED', '0 ERRORS ENCOUNTERED';
  end;
```

Fig. 4-9. *Create_listing_trailer.*

```
procedure  parser;
  var  token: string;
         {token is the next token.}
       charac: char;
         {charac is the next character of the source file.}
  begin
    next_char (char);
    {charac must be initialized so that it is the first character of the source file.}
    {a call to next_token has two effects: (1) the variable, token, is assigned the value of
    the next token; (2) the next token is read from the source file in order to make the
    assignment. The value returned by next_token is also the next token.}
    if next_token(token) not in ['program'] then
      process error—keyword 'program' expected;
    prog(token);
  end;
```

Fig. 4-10. *Parser.*

```
procedure  prog(var token: string);
             {process production 1}
             {token should be 'program'}
  begin
    if token not in ['program'] then
      process compiler error—keyword 'program' expected;
    prog_stmt(token);
    if token in ['const'] then consts(token);
    if token in ['var'] then vars(token);
    if token not in ['begin'] then
      process error—keyword 'begin' expected;
    begin_end_stmt(token);
    if token not in [end-of-file] then
      process error—no text may follow 'end';
  end;
```

Fig. 4-11. *Prog.*

```
procedure   prog_stmt(var token: string);
            {process production 2}
            {token should be 'program'}
   var   x: string;
   begin
     if token not in ['program'] then
       process compiler error—keyword 'program' expected;
     x := next_token(token);
     if token not in [NON_KEY_ID] then
       process error—program name expected;
     if next_token(token) not in [';'] then
       process error—semicolon expected;
     next_token(token);
     code('program', x);
     insert(x, prog_name, immutable, x, no, );
   end;
```

Fig. 4-12. *Prog_stmt.*

```
procedure   consts(var token: string);
            {process production 3}
            {token should be 'const'}
   begin
     if token not in ['const'] then
       process compiler error—keyword 'const' expected;
     if next_token(token) not in [NON_KEY_ID] then
       process error—non-keyword identifier must follow 'const';
     const_stmts (token);
   end;

procedure   vars(var   token: string);
            {process production 4}
            {token should be 'var'}
   begin
     if token not in ['var'] then
       process compiler error—keyword 'var' expected;
     if next_token(token) not in [NON_KEY_ID] then
       process error—non-keyword identifier must follow 'var';
     var_stmts(token);
   end;
```

Fig. 4-13. *Consts* and *Vars.*

```
procedure  begin_end_stmt(var token: string);
        {process production 5}
        {token should be 'begin'}
begin
   if token not in ['begin'] then
      process compiler error—keyword 'begin' expected;
   if next_token(token) not in ['end'] then
      process error—keyword 'end' expected;
   if next_token(token) not in ['.'] then
      process error—period expected;
   next_token(token);
   code('end','.');
end;
```

Fig. 4-14. *Begin_end_stmt.*

```
procedure  const_stmts(var  token: string);
        {process production 6}
        {token should be NON_KEY_ID}
var  x,y: string;
begin
   if token not in [NON_KEY_ID] then
     process compiler error—non-keyword identifier expected;
   x := token;
   if next_token(token) not in ['='] then
     process error— '=' expected;
   y := next_token(token);
   if y not in ['+', '−', NON_KEY_ID, 'true', 'false', INTEGER] then
     process error—token to right of '=' illegal;
   if y in ['+', '−'] then begin
     if next_token(token) not in [INTEGER] then
        process error—integer expected after sign;
     y := y || token; end;
   if next_token(token) not in [';'] then
     process error—semicolon expected;
   insert(x, which_type(y), immutable, which_value(y), yes, 1);
   if next_token(token) not in ['begin', 'var', NON_KEY_ID] then
     process error—non-keyword identifier, keyword 'begin' or keyword ''var' expected;
   if token in [NON_KEY_ID] then const_stmts(token);
end;
```

Fig. 4-15. *Const_stmts.*

```
procedure   var_stmts(var   token: string);
            {process production 7}
            {token should be NON_KEY_ID}
   var   x, y: string;
   begin
      if token not in [NON_KEY_ID] then
         process compiler error—non-keyword identifier expected;
      x := ids(token);
      if token not in [':'] then
         process error— ':' expected;
      if next_token(token) not in ['integer', 'boolean'] then
         process error—illegal type follows ':';
      y := token;
      if next_token(token) not in [';'] then
         process error—semicolon expected;
      insert(x, y, mutable, , yes, 1);
      if next_token(token) not in ['begin', NON_KEY_ID] then
         process error—non-keyword identifier or keyword 'begin' expected;
      if token in [NON_KEY_ID] then   var_stmts(token);
   end;
```

Fig. 4-16. *Var_stmts.*

```
function   ids(var   token: string) : string;
           {process production 8}
           {token should be NON_KEY_ID}
   var   temp: string;
   begin
      if token not in [NON_KEY_ID] then
         process compiler error—non-keyword identifier expected;
      ids := token;
      temp := token;
      if next_token(token) not in [',', ':'] then
         process error— ',' or ':' expected;
      if token in [','] then begin
         if next_token(token) not in [NON_KEY_ID] then
            process error—non-keyword identifier expected;
         ids := temp II ',' II ids(token);   end;
   end;
```

Fig. 4-17. *Ids.*

pects the current token to be among a certain set of values when that routine is called. If the parser is performing properly (i.e., has no bugs), then each routine's input *will* be what it should be. However, if there are any errors in the compiler, a routine could be called under improper conditions; e.g., *prog* could be called with the current token something other than '**program**'. Such an erroneous call could propagate errors indefinitely through any number of other routines until it were caught (if at all). Rather than assume the compiler is correct, we presume it might very well have bugs and test whether each parser routine is being called under the right circumstances. If not, an error processing routine is called to handle the problem, otherwise, compilation continues unabated. The price paid for this additional check is the added cost to test the value of the current token against the set of expected tokens, a small price to pay during development for the additional error detection capability. If CANTOR were installed as a working compiler, the compiler implementor could choose to remove these additional checks prior to installation if he felt CANTOR's performance would be unduly limited by their inclusion. In Figs. 4-15 and 4-17 we indicate concatenation of strings by '||', which we borrowed from PL/I, since PASCAL has no concatenation operator.

The parser refinements deviate from the translation grammar in a few places for the sake of efficiency; for example, in Fig. 4-15, the variable y is assigned to the next token, then it is determined whether y is a literal, a non-keyword identifier or an illegal token. This preassignment of y simplifies the code. Since the two nonterminals, TYPE and BOOLEAN, always have a single token for their value, the one token lookahead of the parser does the work of the call to the routine associated with each of these nonterminals, so, we have not bothered to create procedures to correspond to these two nonterminals. In general, this optimization strategy is applicable whenever the value of a nonterminal can be just a single token.

In chapter 3 we defined a grammar-driven translation grammar processor (GDTGP). This processor can be used here and throughout the construction of CANTOR to save an enormous amount of coding effort and to reduce the size of the compiler by a factor of several times with virtually no loss in the efficiency of the compilation process. If this method is chosen, then only slight modification to the translation grammar is needed. The first production must be changed to

> PROG → *create_listing_header*   PTOG_STMT   CONSTS
> VARS   BEGIN_END_STMT
> *create_listing_trailer*

because all actions must be embedded in the grammar. The declarations in the main routine become part of the *support declarations* which are embedded into the table-driven translator. With this change, all of the parsing procedures in Figs. 4-10 through 4-17 are eliminated.

There are no error processing facilities described for GDTGP as yet. These facilities are not discussed until chapter 8. The current reaction to a syntax error by GDTGP is to print a message that a fatal error has been encountered and to halt.

4.7 ACTION ROUTINES

4.7.1 Insert

Insert creates entries in the symbol table. It is an extension of the *insert* routine defined in section 3.2 and given in Fig. 3-2; however, since the activities of CANTOR/0 are far more complex than those of the declaration processor described in Chapter 3, *insert* has taken on more substance. It now has six arguments:

1. a *list* of external names
2. the *type* of the list members
3. the *mode* of the list members
4. the *value* of the list members
5. whether or not *storage* will be emitted
6. the number of storage *units* to be emitted (if any)

The symbol table has entries which have six fields as defined in Fig. 4-7: The first field is the internal name which corresponds to an external name; the second through sixth fields of the table entries correspond to the second through sixth arguments of *insert*. Figure 4-18 is the definition of *insert*.

Note that *insert* calls *gen_internal_name*, a function which has one argument, the *type* of the name being inserted. Recall that we shall convert names appearing in the source program (*external* names) into ones which we know are valid 360AL symbolic names. *Gen_internal_name* returns a unique internal name each time it is called. As a visual aid, we shall use different forms of internal names for each data-type of interest. The general form is:

$$@dn$$

where *d* denotes the data-type of the name ('I' for *integer*, 'B' for *boolean*) and *n* is a non-negative integer. Figure 4-5 clearly shows the effects of calling *gen_internal_name*. Four *boolean* and six *integer* internal names were generated for this program. CANTOR itself will also need to generate names to appear in the 360AL object code. Since CANTOR is

```
procedure  insert(external_name: string; in_type: store_types;
                  in_mode: modes; in_value: string;
                  in_alloc: alloc; in_units: integer);
              {create symbol table entry for each identifier in list of external names. Multiply
              inserted names are illegal.}
  var  name: string;
  begin
    break next name from list of external names;
      {name will be lambda when none are left in the list.}
    while name <> lambda do
      begin
        if symbol_table[name] is defined then
          process error—multiple name definition;
        else  if name is a keyword then
                process error—illegal use of keyword;
        else  {create table entry}
          if name begins with '@' then {it is compiler generated so internal and external
                                        names are the same}
            symbol_table[name] := (name, in_type, in_mode, in_value, in_alloc, in_units);
          else  symbol_table[name] := (gen_internal_name(in_type), in_type, in_mode,
                in_value, in_alloc, in_units);
        break next name from the list of external names;
      end;
  end;
```

Fig. 4-18. *Insert.*

defining these itself, there is no need to convert these names into any other form. The external and internal forms are the same, both beginning with '@'. The code for *insert* treats any external name beginning with '@' as one defined by CANTOR.

4.7.2 Code

Code, the code generator of CANTOR, is quite simple, having either one, two or three arguments, although in this stage, all calls have two arguments. The first argument is the operation being coded, while the second and third arguments are the operands of the first argument. All operations take zero, one or two arguments. In this stage, however, all operations take exactly one argument. The definition of *code* is in Fig. 4-19. The code for the operations 'program' and 'end' is given in Fig. 4-20. The program prologue and epilogue are standard in which we save all registers when beginning a program and restore them before termination. There is a lone base register, which in this case is register 12. Arithmetic and logical computations (which will not appear until stage 1) will be done in general registers 2 through 11.

procedure   code(operator, operand1, operand2: **string**);
{the code generator of CANTOR, which emits 360AL for the operator and operands which are its arguments.}
begin
   case   operator   **of**
  'program':   *emit prologue;*
  'end':   *emit epilogue;*
   end;
   otherwise   *process error—compiler error since code should not be called with illegal arguments;*
end;

Fig. 4-19. *Code.*

Figure 4-19 contains an interesting augmentation of PASCAL. The **case** statement is normally not defined if the value of the parameter is not the label of an alternative statement, which is of questionable wisdom, since errors in programs will often leave the value of a parameter to be other than expected. We have added an "error clause" to the **case** statement in the form of "**otherwise** statement," where the statement following **otherwise** may be any pseudo-PASCAL statement. If the value of the parameter is not one of the labels in the **case** statement, then the **otherwise** clause is executed.

procedure   emit_prologue(program_name: **string**);
     {emit the program prologue}
  begin
   emit up to first eight characters of program_name labelling 'CSECT';
   emit(,'STM','14,12,12(13)','save registers');
   emit(,'BALR','12,0','set up base register');
   emit(,'USING','*,12');
   emit(,'ST','13, @SAV+4','save loc old save area');
   emit(,'LA','13, @SAV','load loc new save area');
   insert('@SAV',integer,mutable,,yes,18);
  end;

procedure   emit_epilogue;
     {emit the program epilogue}
  begin
   emit('@END','L','13,@SAV+4','restore loc old save area');
   emit(,'LM','14,12,12(13)','restore old registers');
   emit(,'BR','14','return');
   emit_storage;   {generate all DS and DC instructions}
   emit(,'END');
  end;

Fig. 4-20. *Emit_prologue* and *Emit_Epilogue.*

The function *emit* is as defined in Fig. 3-3, having four arguments: The first is the *label* of the 360AL statement; the second is the *operator;* the third is the *operands;* and the fourth is a *comment. Emit* outputs code to the object file in 80 character records to correspond to the normal input expected by the 360AL assembler.

The next to the last function call in Fig. 4-20 is to *emit_storage.* Up to this point, no actual "Define Constant" or "Define Storage" pseudo-instructions have been emitted. Following common convention for assembly language programming, we shall always emit all data after all executable instructions. *Emit_storage* will examine the entries in the symbol table, and for each entry for which the *alloc* field is *yes, emit_storage* will output the appropriate pseudo-instruction. Finally, after emitting all storage, *emit_epilogue* outputs an "END" pseudo-instruction to terminate the object program. Figure 4-21 is the code defining *emit_storage.* Note that the *boolean* data-type uses a full-word to represent *true* and *false.* Actually, only one bit is needed; however, as we shall see later in stage 2, the use of full-words will ease some compilation problems related to *boolean* operations. In this case, we shall trade processing ease for the additional space it takes to store *boolean* values using the full-word scheme. Figure 4-22 shows *emit_boolean_storage.*

```
procedure  emit_storage
          {emit DS and DC pseudo-instructions.}
    var   row: entry;{of symbol table}
    begin
      row := first entry from symbol table;
      while row is defined do
        begin
          with row do
            if alloc = yes then
              case data_type of
                int_s: emit integer storage;
                byte_s: emit byte storage;
                double_s: emit double storage;
                char_s: emit character storage;
                bool_s: emit boolean storage;
                address_s: emit address storage;
              end;
              otherwise compiler error—illegal data type or data_type for which alloc should
                      be no;
          row := the next entry in symbol_table, if any;
        end;
    end;
```

Fig. 4-21. *Emit_storage.*

procedure emit_boolean_storage(row: entry, external_name: **string**);
  begin
    with row **do**
      case value **of**
        'true': emit(internal_name, 'DC', units || 'F''−1''', external_name);
        'false': emit(internal_name, 'DC', units || 'F''0''', external_name);
        lambda: emit(internal_name, 'DS', units || 'F', external_name);
      end;
      otherwise *compiler error − since no illegal value should ever be inserted into the*
          symbol table;
  end;

Fig. 4-22. *Emit_boolean_storage.*

4.7.3 *Which_*type and Which_value

These two simple functions just tell what is the *type* and *value* of their argument, respectively. Figure 4-23 is the definition of *which_type* and *which_value.*

4.8 SCANNER

The scanner of CANTOR, *next_token,* is referenced repeatedly in Figs. 4-10 through 4-17, which defined the parser. *Next_token* is a function which always returns the next token; in addition, it always assigns the value it returns to the variable *token,* so that the value is easily referenced after the call is completed (an extension to PASCAL). The scanner itself calls a routine which returns characters to it, called *next_char; next_char* also assigns the value it returns to a variable for each referencing, *charac.* *Next_char* in turn calls a routine, *get_line,* when it has passed all of the characters in the current line from the source file to *next_token.* We have taken great care to "hide" the actual details of the input medium's characteristics from the parser and the scanner so that they are relatively independent of changes in that medium and its characteristics. Furthermore, this independence simplifies their design and helps ensure greater reliability. Figure 4-24 shows the definition of *next_token* and Fig. 4-25 of *next_char.* We do not bother to detail *get_line.* Note how nicely the **case** statement can be used to organize the scanner. We have taken the liberty in Fig. 4-24 of listing the letters, digits and special symbols by their *token classes,* rather than list each element in order to simplify the scanner presentation.

    The scanner can also be organized as a finite state automaton, and often is. We have opted for a simpler presentation here. Aho and Ullman [77] offer an extensive discussion of scanners viewed as finite-state automata.

```
function  which_type(name: string) : store_types;
          {tells which data-type a name has}
   begin
    if name is a literal then
       if name is an integer literal then which_type := int_s;
       else which_type := bool_s;
    else  {name is an identifier and hopefully a constant}
       if symbol_table[name] is defined then
          which_type := types of symbol_table[name];
       else  process error—reference to undefined constant;
   end;

function  which_value(name : string) : string;
          {tells which value a name has}
   begin
    if name is a literal then
       which_value := name;
    else  {name is an identifier and hopefully a constant}
    if symbol_table[name] is defined and has a value then
       which_value := value of symbol_table[name];
       else  process error—reference to undefined constant;
   end;
```

Fig. 4-23. *Which_type* and *Which_value*.

INTRODUCTION TO SYNTAX CHARTS

At the close of each of Chapters 4 through 7, we present a pictorial view of the RASCAL version implemented in that chapter. These pictures, called *syntax charts* or *bead diagrams,* are included so that the reader can more easily grasp the entire language he is implementing. In the text body of Chapters 5, 6, and 7, we offer only a context-free grammar of the *changes* to the original grammar given in Chapter 4. By focusing on the changes alone, it is easy for the reader to lose sight of the language as a whole. The bead diagrams should compensate for this. Also, because they are pictorial, they are easier to read than a standard grammar.

The meaning of a diagram is quite straightforward. All alternative productions of a single nonterminal appear in one diagram. The name in the upper left-hand corner is equivalent to the left-hand side of a production. Rectangular boxes represent nonterminals, ovals represent tokens. An arrow from box x to box y indicates x is followed by y in a sentential form. Alternatives are represented by multi-way branching arrows. The reader is encouraged to match up the diagrams which follow with the grammar productions which appeared in section 4.2.

```
function   next_token(var   token : string) : string;
            {Returns the next token or end of file marker.}
      begin
        token := λ;
        while token = λ do
          case   charac of
            '{': begin   {process comment}
                  while next_char(charac) is not end of file or '}' do
                    next_char(charac);
                  if charac is end of file then
                    process error—end of file unexpectedly encountered;
                  else next_char(charac);
                  end;
            '}': process error—'}' cannot begin token;
            ' ': next_char(charac);   {skip spaces}
            special character:   begin token=charac; next_char(charac); end;
            letter:   begin token:= charac;
                while next_char(charac) is letter or digit do
                  token := token ‖ charac; end;
            digit: begin token := charac;
                while next_charac(charac) is digit do
                  token := token ‖ charac; end;
            end of file marker: token := charac;
          end;
          otherwise   process error—illegal symbol;
          next_token := token;
      end;
```

Fig. 4-24. Next_token.

```
function   next_char(var   charac : char) : char;
            {Returns the next character or end of file marker.}
    begin
      if end of line has been reached then
        get the next line;
      charac and next_char are assigned the next character in the line unless end of file in
      which case assign an end of file marker;
    end;
```

Fig. 4-25. Next_char.

4.9   SUMMARY

RASCAL/0 and CANTOR/0 have been presented. RASCAL/0 has the most rudimentary of features: *integer* and *boolean* literals, constants, and variables, the **program,** declaration and **begin-end** statement. Despite the paucity of features found in RASCAL/0, its compilation is nontrivial requiring essentially all major components of CANTOR in order to compile RASCAL/0, although they are not implemented in as complex a form here as they will later become.

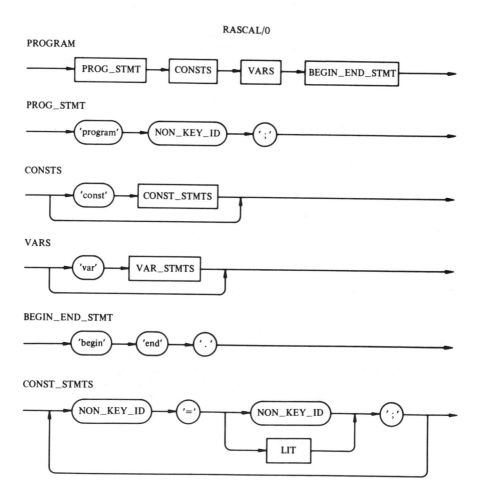

RASCAL/0

VAR_STMTS

IDS

TYPE

LIT

BOOLEAN

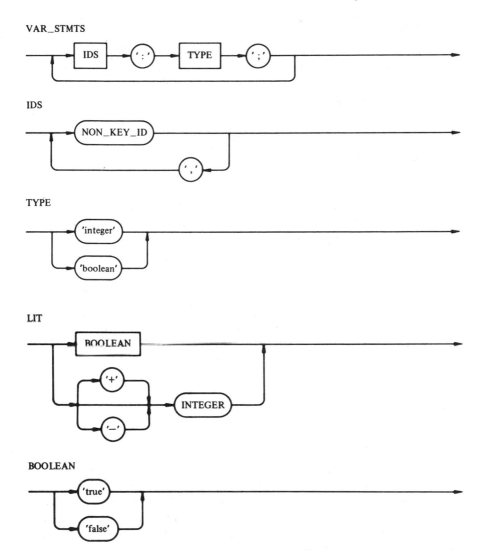

EXERCISES

4-1. The definition of the FORTRAN language states that no keywords are reserved. Check one or more implementations available to you to determine if your implementations impose the constraint that keywords are reserved.

4-2. RASCAL and its parent language PASCAL indicate the physical end of a program with a period. What end of program markers do:

ALGOL 60, FORTRAN, PL/I, SNOBOL

employ? Are these symbols allowed in other contexts?

4-3. Determine whether blanks are delimiters in each of the following languages:

ALGOL 60, FORTRAN, PL/I, SNOBOL

If a blank is not a delimiter, then what constraint does that impose on the language syntax?

4-4. Is the null program; i.e., the program consisting solely of the empty string, λ, a legal RASCAL/0 program?

4-5. What changes would we have to make to the LL(1) grammar which defines RASCAL/0, if the scanner passed characters rather than tokens? Try to determine how much more complex the grammar would become.

4-6. Is it legal to have a variable declaration section which has just 'var' in it; i.e., is the following tiny program legal in RASCAL/0:

```
program   emptyvar;
var   ;
begin
end.
```

4-7. Is it legal to have a constant declaration section which has just 'const' in it; i.e., is the following tiny program legal in RASCAL/0:

```
program   emptyconst;
const ;
begin
end.
```

4-8. Is the following RASCAL/0 program legal:

```
program   zglish;
const   x = 3;
        v = y;
        y = true;
var   x: integer;
begin
  begin   end;
end.
```

If not, then pinpoint each illegal aspect of the program.

4-9. Why do we not specify the maximum and minimum value of an *integer* within the definition of RASCAL/0? Do you know of any language definition which violates this policy?

4-10. The PASCAL language definition states that a correct implementation of PASCAL must allow variable names to be any length but need only recognize the first eight characters of the name. For example,

thisisaverylongname
thisisaveryverylongname

might not be considered distinct names by a PASCAL implementation, but the similar:

thisisaverylongname
thisisalongname

must be distinct names in any PASCAL implementation which obeys the standard. Why do you think this constraint was placed into PASCAL, and do you think it is a good idea? Does RASCAL/0 follow this pattern?

4-11. Suppose CANTOR/0 was modified to emit storage for constants, variables and compiler-generated quantities in-line rather than at the end of the object code through *emit_storage*. Show the output of CANTOR/0 on the program of Fig. 4-1 with this revised scheme. Compare the length of this code with that of Fig. 4-5. Is there any significant difference in this stage? Do you expect this to remain so in later stages? Why?

4-12. A scanner is often structured as a finite state transducer; i.e., a finite state automaton whose input is a stream of characters and whose output is a stream of tokens. Compare this organization with that of CANTOR's scanner. Show how you would map between these two organizations.

TESTING HINTS

Test CANTOR/0 on programs which have:
a. no **const** section and no **var** section;
b. no **const** section, but a **var** section;
c. no **var** section, but a **const** section;
d. a **const** and a **var** section;
e. constants of both *boolean* and *integer* types; this should include both *boolean* literals and also both signed and unsigned *integers;*
f. end-of-line interpreted as a blank on continued lines.
g. enough identifiers to fill the symbol table;
h. constants whose value is a previously defined constant;
i. continuation lines to ensure the scanner works;
j. comments at numerous places;
k. blank lines, including the first line;
l. *integers* with leading zeroes;
m. variable declarations which have a list of identifiers in a single statement;
n. variable declarations which have a lone identifier in a single statement;
o. multiple statements per line;

BIBLIOGRAPHY

[Bauer and Eickel 74] has an excellent discussion of "what the compiler should tell the user"; however, for the most part, this topic has been largely ignored in compiling textbooks.

5
Stage 1: Assignment

5.1 INTRODUCTION

Probably the most fundamental executable statement is the *assignment* (at least in most languages). We shall add the assignment statement to our skeletal language in this chapter, enabling us to write very simple but not totally trivial programs. Several new concepts will be introduced in this chapter. Because arithmetic operations require the use of registers on an IBM 360/370 computer, we shall be concerned with the assignment of registers to operands. Two *allocation and assignment* schemes will be presented. The first, although quite simple and transparent, is also quite inefficient with respect to the time and space of the executable code generated by CANTOR/1. The second register scheme makes more "intelligent" assignments of operands to registers but requires considerably more bookkeeping on the part of CANTOR/1. We recommend that the student study the first scheme so that he understands the basic considerations of allocation and assignment but that he implement the more complex scheme if possible.

Another new concept introduced here is that of *temporary variables,* which are generated by the compiler, not by explicit program direction. The target machine's architecture requires that complex arithmetic expressions be broken into simpler subexpressions, each of which is evaluated separately in turn. The result of one subexpression is an operand of another subexpression. Each result is given a name by the compiler for easy reference and is called a *temporary;* for example, the expression:

$$A := B + C * 2;$$

in RASCAL/1 would instead be compiled as if it were:

$$TEMP1 := C * 2;$$
$$TEMP1 := B + TEMP1;$$
$$A := TEMP1;$$

in which one statement is broken into three.

5.2   RASCAL/1 LANGUAGE FEATURES

Five new keywords are added to our language:

mod,   div,   not,   and,   or

The first two are *integer* arithmetic operators, while the last three are *boolean* operators.

Nine new tokens have been added to RASCAL:

':='   '*'   '<>'   '<='   '>='   '<'   '>'   ')'   '('

Four of them are two symbol tokens. These are the first such tokens which are not also numbers or identifiers. The scanner will have to be adjusted so that when it encounters ':' (for example), it checks whether the next character is '='. This token, of course, is the assignment operator. The second token indicates multiplication of *integer* operands. The next five are relational operators. The last two are parentheses for grouping expressions.

We continue as before, with a context-free grammar for RASCAL/1 features along with their selection sets, not bothering to repeat productions given in earlier chapters unless those productions have changed to accommodate new aspects of the language. In this case only production 5 has changed.

Revised Productions:

1. BEGIN_END_STMT → 'begin'   EXEC_STMTS   'end'   '.'   {'begin'}

New Productions:

2. EXEC_STMTS   → EXEC_STMT EXEC_STMTS   {NON_KEY_ID}
                   → λ   {'end'}

3. EXEC_STMT   → ASSIGN_STMT   {NON_KEY_ID}

4. ASSIGN_STMT   → NON_KEY_ID ':=' EXPRESS
                     ';'   {NON_KEY_ID}

5. EXPRESS   → TERM EXPRESSES   {'not','true','false',
                                 '(', '+','−',INTEGER,NON_KEY_ID}

6. EXPRESSES   → REL_OP TERM   {'<>','=', '<=','>=','<','>'}
                   → λ   {')',';'}

7. TERM   → FACTOR TERMS   {'not','true','false','(',
                                 '+','−',INTEGER,NON_KEY_ID}

8. TERMS   → ADD_LEV_OP FACTOR TERMS   {'−','+','or'}
                   → λ   {'<>','=','>=','<=','<','>',')',';'}

9. FACTOR   → PART FACTORS   {'not','true',
                                 'false','(' '+','−',INTEGER, NON_KEY_ID}

10. FACTORS   → MULT_LEV_OP   PART   FACTORS
                                                       {'*','div','mod','and'}
                         → λ   {'<>','=','>=','<=','<','>',')',';', '−','+','or'}

11. PART   → 'not' PART   {'not'}
                         → '(' EXPRESS ')'   {'('}
                         → '+' ('(' EXPRESS ')' {'('} |
                           INTEGER {INTEGER} |
                           NON_KEY_ID {NON_KEY_ID})   {'+'}

                         → '−' ('(' EXPRESS ')' {'('} |
                           INTEGER {INTEGER} |
                           NON_KEY_ID {NON_KEY_ID})   {'−'}
                         → INTEGER   {INTEGER}
                         → BOOLEAN   {'true','false'}
                         → NON_KEY_ID   {NON_KEY_ID}

12. REL_OP   → '='   {'='}
                         → '<>'   {'<>'}
                         → '<='   {'<='}
                         → '>='   {'>='}
                         → '<'   {'<']
                         → '>'   {'>'}

13. ADD_LEV_OP   → '+'   {'+'}
                         → '−'   {'−'}
                         → 'or'   {'or'}

14. MULT_LEV_OP   → '*'   {'*'}
                         → 'div'   {'div'}
                         → 'mod'   {'mod'}
                         → 'and'   {'and'}

The data-type of the result of an operation depends upon the operation itself. The result of an arithmetic operation is always *integer;* that of a *boolean* operation is *boolean;* and that of a relational operation is also *boolean*. In addition, there are several context-sensitive constraints on RASCAL/1 programs based on the data-types and attributes of operands:

1. Every identifier which is referenced in an assignment statement must have been previously declared as a variable or constant name.
2. The identifier to the left of the assignment operator, ':=', must be a variable name and declared to be the same type as the expression to the right of the ':=' operator.
3. The operands of the binary operators:

   '+' '−', **'div'** **'mod'** '*

   must be *integer* valued expressions.
4. The operands of the unary operators:

   '+' '−'

   must be *integer* valued expressions.

5. The operands of the logical operators:

'and' 'or' 'not'

must be *boolean* valued expressions.

6. The operands of the relational operators:

'<' '>' '<=' '>='

must be *integer* valued but for the two relational operators:

'=' '<>'

the operands may either both be *integer* valued or both be *boolean* valued (but not mixed).

An example of a legal RASCAL/1 program is given in Fig. 5-1 while two illegal RASCAL/1 programs are shown in Fig. 5-2. The comments within the programs indicate why the latter two are wrong.

One feature of RASCAL/1 is somewhat unusual—the precedence relationships between operators. For the most part, RASCAL/1 follows the precedence relationships common to most programming languages. These relationships, enforced in the grammar, are shown graphically in Figure 5-3. Note that 'and' has the same precedence as '*', 'div' and 'mod', and that 'or' has the same precedence as binary '+' and '−'. This is unusual and can lead to unexpected syntactic errors for a programmer not familiar with this fact. For example, statement 5.1 is illegal:

$$w := p < q \text{ and } r > s; \qquad (5.1)$$

where variables $p,q,r,$ and s are type *integer* and w is type *boolean* because it is equivalent to the parenthesized:

$$w := p < (q \text{ and } r) > s; \qquad (5.2)$$

```
program  hohum;
        {demonstrate correct usage of RASCAL/1 features.}
    const  zero = 0;  five = 5;
    var  a,b,c:  integer;  w,z:  integer;
         d:  boolean;
    begin
     a := five * (3 + 34);
     b := a +a ;
     z := b + −5 mod a;
     c := (b + z) * (a − b);
     w := a + b div c;
     b := w + −5 mod a ;
     d := z > zero;
    end  .
```

Fig. 5-1. A Valid RASCAL/1 Program.

```
program   yetanotherdud;
          {illustrate improper use of RASCAL/1 features.}
   const   x = 13;
           y = false;
   var   b,c: integer;
         d,e: boolean;
   begin
     f := 14;          {f has not been declared.}
     x := 3;           {constants may not be assigned values.}
     d := 1;           {boolean variable may not be assigned an integer value.}
     d := true or 3;   {'or' requires boolean operands.}
   end.


program   notanotherone;
          {illustrates more improper usage of RASCAL/1 features.}
   const   q = true;   r = false;
   var   b,c : integer;   d,e: boolean;
   begin
     b := 3 + −5 div 2 mod 6;   {this statement is ok.}
     c := b + q;                {addition requires integer operands.}
     d := c > b or d = e;       {'or' requires boolean operands.}
   end.
```

Fig. 5-2. Two Invalid RASCAL/1 Programs.

rather than the intended:

$$w := (p < q) \text{ and } (r > s);$$

Until a variable has been assigned a value, it is illegal to refer to its value, which is *undefined*. In Chapter 8, we shall examine methods for enforcing this restriction. As it stands, we shall presume that no RASCAL/1 program violates this constraint. Although good diagnostic compilers, such as WATFIV, a variant of FORTRAN, do detect this error, many commercial compilers do not. In such implementations, the value of a variable which is technically undefined is actually just whatever value is left in the storage from some previous usage of that memory location. Other implementations sometimes initialize variables to a special value at

```
'not'   '−' (unary)  '+' (unary)          ↓
'*'   'div'  'mod'  'and'              decreasing
'+' (binary)  '−' (binary)  'or'
'='   '<'  '>'  '<='  '>='  '<>'       precedence
':='                                       ↓
```

Fig. 5-3. Precedence Relations.

compile-time, in which case a variable is never undefined. The Stony-brook PASCAL compiler initializes *integer* variables to zero, even though the language definition does not specify such an initialization. In SNOBOL all variables are initially assigned the value of the null string as part of the *language definition*.

In RASCAL/1, the arithmetic and logical operators obey common mathematical laws:

1. The *integers* obey the commutative law over '+' and '*'.
2. The *integers* obey the associative law over '+' and '*'.
3. If i is an *integer* valued expression, then

$$i = -(-i) \qquad i = +i$$

4. The *booleans* obey the commutative law over '**and**' and '**or**'.
5. The *booleans* obey the associative law over '**and**' and '**or**'.
6. If b is a *boolean* valued expression, then

$$b = \textbf{not not } b$$

This list is obviously incomplete but serves to remind the reader of the flexibility possible in forming equivalent logical and arithmetic expressions. We shall take advantage of some of these properties to optimize object code produced by the implementation.

5.3 CANTOR/1 IMPLEMENTATION FEATURES

We must again impose several constraints on RASCAL/1 programs which are motivated by implementation concerns. Recall that there is a maximum valued *integer* and a minimum valued *integer* (with different magnitudes) in programs accepted by CANTOR. The evaluation of any expression which yields an *integer* valued result must yield one in this range; namely, -2^{31} up to $2^{31}-1$ inclusive. Specifically, if *op* is a binary operator, and *a* and *b* are *integer* valued expressions, then:

$$-2^{31} \leq a \leq 2^{31}-1$$
$$-2^{31} \leq b \leq 2^{31}-1$$
$$-2^{31} \leq a \text{ op } b \leq 2^{31}-1$$

If *op* is a unary operation, then:

$$-2^{31} \leq a \leq 2^{31}-1$$
$$-2^{31} \leq \text{op } a \leq 2^{31}-1$$

Otherwise, the operation is ill-defined. Again, we presume that all RASCAL/1 programs of interest obey this constraint.

5.4   CANTOR/1 TRANSLATION GRAMMAR

Fourteen new production groups and one revised production were introduced in section 5.2 to define the additions to RASCAL made in this chapter. Translation grammar productions must be specified for these rules.

Revised Productions:

1. BEGIN_END_STMT → 'begin' EXEC_STMTS 'end' '.'   *code* ('*end*', '.')

New Productions:

2. EXEC_STMTS   → EXEC_STMT EXEC_STMTS
                        → λ

3. EXEC_STMT   → ASSIGN_STMT

4. ASSIGN_STMT   → NON_KEY_ID$_x$ *push_operand*(x) ':='
                        push_operator(':=') EXPRESS ';'
                        code(*pop_operator, pop_operand, pop_operand*)

5. EXPRESS   → TERM EXPRESSES

6. EXPRESSES   → REL_OP$_x$ *push_operator*(x) TERM
                        code(*pop_operator,pop_operand,pop_operand*)
                        → λ

7. TERM   → FACTOR TERMS

8. TERMS   → ADD_LEV_OP$_x$ *push_operator*(x) FACTOR
                        code(*pop_operator,pop_operand,pop_operand*) TERMS
                        → λ

9. FACTOR   → PART FACTORS

10. FACTORS   → MULT_LEV_OP$_x$ *push_operator*(x) PART
                        code(*pop_operator,pop_operand,pop_operand*)   FAC-
                        TORS
                        → λ

11. PART   → 'not' *push_operator*('not') PART
                        code(*pop_operator,pop_operand*)
                        → (NON_KEY_ID$_x$ | INTEGER$_x$ | BOOLEAN$_x$)
                        push_operand(x)
                        → '(' EXPRESS ')'
                        → '+' ('(' EXPRESS ')' |
                        (INTEGER$_x$ |NON_KEY_ID$_x$) *push_operand*(x))
                        → '−' ('(' EXPRESS ')' *code*('neg',*pop_operand*) |
                        INTEGER$_x$ *push_operand*('−' || x) |
                        NON_KEY_ID$_x$ *code*('neg',x))

12. REL_OP   → '=' | '<>' | '<=' | '>=' | '<' | '>'

13. ADD_LEV OP   → '+' | '−' | 'or'

14. MULT_LEV_OP   → '*' | 'div' | 'mod' | 'and'

There are five action routines referenced in the translation grammar productions:

1. *code(operator,operand1,operand2)*
2. *push_operator(operator)*
3. *pop_operator*
4. *push_operand(operator)*
5. *pop_operand*

The first routine is the familiar code generator, although now *code* is called with new types of arguments for the more varied language constructs of RASCAL/1. The other four routines are all related to the manipulation of two auxiliary stacks which are needed to process RASCAL/1 source programs: *operator_stk* and *operand_stk*, holding, quite naturally, a list of operators and operands, respectively. The behavior of *code* on its new argument values, as well as refinements of the four utility routines for our two stacks are given next.

The last chapter detailed how the translation grammar would be converted into pseudo-code in Figs. 4-10 through 4-17. By this point, the pattern of conversion should be quite clear, so that from here on we shall give only the translation grammar productions and leave their relatively mechanical conversion to pseudo-code to the reader. If the reader is using the GDTGP, then the translation grammar can be input to it with only modest changes. We similarly leave the scanner modifications to the reader, as well, with the sole caveat that he must be cautious when encountering either ':', '<', or '>' as the first character of a token and check whether the next character in the input stream is a continuation of that same token.

5.5 OPERAND_STK AND OPERATOR_STK

As mentioned in section 5.1, complex expressions (whether logical, arithmetic, or relational) cannot be directly evaluated on the IBM 360/370 family of computers. Complex expressions must be broken into smaller subexpressions which can be directly evaluated. The proper combination of the results of evaluating these subexpressions yields the value of the original expression. The algorithm employed here by CANTOR for subexpression evaluation and analysis requires two auxiliary stacks, *operator_stk* and *operand_stk*. The first stack holds operators, the second holds the operands of these operators, or more correctly, it holds their names.

Before stepping through the algorithm for evaluating expressions, we must first clarify one point about the behavior of *code*. When *code* is called upon to emit target text which computes a "result" which must later be referenced (as is the case for unary and binary arithmetic, logical and relational operations), it gives a symbolic name to that result. This name is created internally by CANTOR and has no relationship to the names used for identifiers in RASCAL source code. Since the result of such a call is to be referenced later in code generation, *code* pushes the symbolic name of that result onto *operand_stk*. The names CANTOR uses for these results have a form similar to the internal names given to external identifiers; i.e., "@Tn," where n is a non-negative integer. With these facts about *code* in mind, we step through the code generation process for the single statement:

$$w := (a + b) * (2 \ \mathbf{div} \ c) \ ; \tag{5.4}$$

where all variables are *integer* valued.

Since we are interested in translating a single assignment statement, the derivation must begin with the nonterminal ASSIGN_STMT rather than PROG. Figure 5-4 shows the parse tree of statement 5.4, excluding action symbols. In place of token *classes* such as INTEGER or NON_KEY_ID, we have instead given the literal *tags* which appear in statement 5.4. The activity sequence for this derivation, with the actual values of the arguments of the action routines substituted for the variable names is:

$$push\_operand('w') \tag{5.5}$$
$$push\_operator(':=') \tag{5.6}$$
$$push\_operand('a') \tag{5.7}$$
$$push\_operator('+') \tag{5.8}$$
$$push\_operand('b') \tag{5.9}$$
$$code('+', 'b', 'a') \tag{5.10}$$
$$push\_operator('*') \tag{5.11}$$
$$push\_operand('2') \tag{5.12}$$
$$push\_operator('div') \tag{5.13}$$
$$push\_operand('c') \tag{5.14}$$
$$code('div', 'c', '2') \tag{5.15}$$
$$code('*', '@T1', '@T0') \tag{5.16}$$
$$code(':=', '@T0', 'w') \tag{5.17}$$

Figure 5-5 shows the changes to the two stacks, *operator_stk* and *operand_stk*, during the calls to these action routines. Initially, both stacks are empty. The first five action calls push three operands and two operators onto *operand_stk* and *operator_stk*, respectively, Figure 5-5a through 5-5f showing these successive changes. Call 5.10 adds *a* to *b*, pushing the result *@T0* onto *operand_stk*. When call 5.15 is made, code to divide 2 by *c* is emitted, and the result is given the name *@T1*, which is

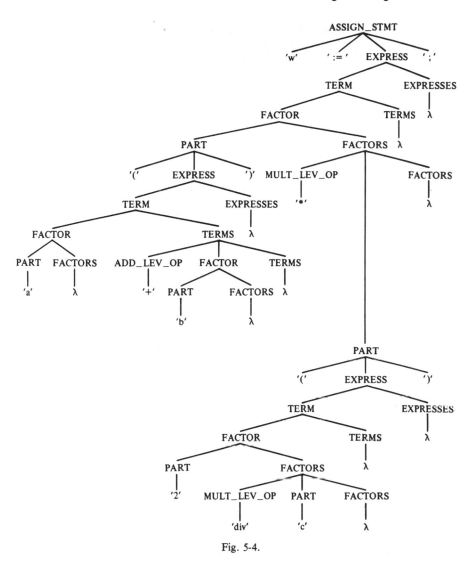

Fig. 5-4.

pushed onto *operand_stk* as shown in Fig. 5-5l. Because the second operand of a binary operation is on the top of *operand_stk, code (operator, operand1, operand2)* actually generates code to perform:

operand2   operator   operand1

Fig. 5-5n shows the result of executing call 5.16. " *@T0*" is reused to name the new result just computed; namely,

@T1 ∗ @T0

This is possible because the old value of @T0, $a + b$, cannot be referenced once it is multiplied by the value of variable b. After call 5.16 has
been completed, the code which computes the value of the expression on
the right hand side of ':=' will store its result in a location named *@T0*.
Call 5.17 emits code to store that value in variable w. Various exercises at
the end of this chapter address other features, such as logical and relational operations not covered in this example. The reader is strongly
urged to work at least some of them in order to completely familiarize
himself with the workings of this absolutely critical component of CAN-
TOR. As new features are added to RASCAL, these two push-down
stacks will be increasingly exercised. Their correct manipulation is essential to the proper execution of CANTOR.

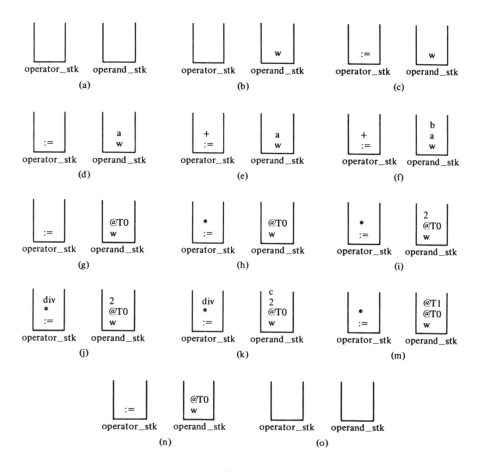

Fig. 5-5.

```
procedure   push_operator(name: string);
        {push name onto operator_stk.}
  begin
    if   operator_stk is not full then
        push name onto stack;
    else   process error—stack overflow;
  end;
```

```
procedure   push_operand(name: string);
        {push name onto operand_stk.   if name is a literal, also create a symbol table
        entry for it.}
  begin
    if   operand_stk is not full then
      begin
        if   name is a literal and has no symbol table entry then
            insert symbol table entry, calling which_type to determine the data type of the
            literal;
        push name onto operand_stk;
      end;
    else   process error—stack overflow;
  end;
```

Fig. 5-6. *Push_operator* and *Push_operand*.

Having completed an example which shows how *operand_stk* and *operator_stk* are manipulated by our action routines, we continue with a more rigorous development of those routines. First we discuss the utility routines for pushing and popping objects onto and from the two stacks. Figure 5-6 shows the refinements of *push_operator* and *push operand*. Figure 5-7 shows the refinements for the corresponding pop routines. The push routines include a check for stack overflow, the pop routines for

```
        function   pop_operator: string;
                {pop name from operator_stk}
          begin
            if   operator_stk is not empty then
                pop_operator := top element removed from stack;
            else
                process error—stack underflow;
          end;

        function   pop_operand: string;
                {pop name from operand_stk}
          begin
            if   operand_stk is not empty then
                pop_operand := top element removed from stack;
            else
                process error—stack underflow;
          end;
```

Fig. 5-7. *Pop_operator* and *Pop_operand*.

stack underflow. These checks for *compiler* errors, not errors in the RASCAL source code are simply more examples of defensive programming. How the stacks are themselves implemented is left open here. The *external,* not the internal, form of names is pushed onto the operand stack. Since external names can be arbitrarily long, it is unlikely that a commercial compiler would use external names here; rather, for the sake of time and space, the shorter internal names would instead be pushed onto the stack. However, CANTOR is a pedagogical tool, and it is critical that the student understand the internal behavior of his compiler when he is writing and debugging it. By pushing external names onto *operand_stk,* the student will find it much easier to understand the dynamic behavior of the compiler when he dumps the contents of the stacks during debugging. For our purposes, the added clarity of the compiler's operation far outweighs considerations of efficiency. The only place in CANTOR where the internal form of names will be needed is in the final generation of "Define Storage" and "Define Constant" pseudo-instructions during the execution of *emit_epilogue* and in references in the object code to that storage.

5.6 CODE

5.6.1 Introduction

In Chapter 4 *code* was relatively simple, but now, far greater demands are being placed upon it as many new features have been added to RASCAL. The structure of *code* remains unchanged, as we merely add new alternatives to the **case** statement in Fig. 4-19. These new alternatives are shown in Fig. 5-8.

WARNING.

Throughout we have been quite informal as to how pseudo-code is written. In one particular place this informality could be a source of confusion. Several translation grammar calls to *code* have the form:

code(*pop_operator, pop_operand, pop_operand*)

We have presumed a left to right evaluation of all argument lists. Since *pop_operand* alters *operand_stack,* this premise is important. It is somewhat unusual to insist on a left to right evaluation of arguments, but it does simplify the specification of calls to *code* enough to warrant this unusual feature.

END OF WARNING.

procedure   code(operator, operand1, operand2: **string**);
{the code generator of CANTOR, which emits 360AL for the operator and operands which are its arguments. May have side effect of pushing result of operation onto *operand_stk.*}
begin
  case operator **of**
'program':   *emit prologue;*
'end':   *emit epilogue;*
'+':   *emit addition code;*   {this must be binary '+'}
'−':   *emit subtraction code;*   {this must be binary '−'}
'neg':   *emit negation code;*   {this must be binary '−'}
'*':   *emit multiplication code;*
'div':   *emit division code;*
'mod':   *emit modulo code;*
'and':   *emit and code;*

    . . .

'=':   *emit equality code;*
':=':   *emit assignment code;*
  end;
  otherwise *process error—compiler error since code should not be called with illegal arguments:*
end;

Fig. 5-8. *Code.*

The refinements which generate 360AL code for the first two alternatives, **'program'** and **'end'** were given in Chapter 4. Here we offer refinements for five of the numerous operations added to RASCAL in stage 1:

'+'   **'div'**   **'and'**   '='   ':='

Each operation is from a different class or illustrates some new aspect of compilation not revealed in the others. We first offer a very simple allocation and assignment scheme, which is unfortunately also quite inefficient. After analyzing the weaknesses of this scheme, we will consider a more sophisticated method which requires more bookkeeping on the part of CANTOR, but which produces considerably tighter code.

5.6.2   Register Allocation and Assignment—Scheme One

In the first register allocation and assignment scheme, only a single pair of general purpose registers will be involved in any arithmetic, relational, or logical operations. For concreteness, we shall choose registers 2 and 3, but any pair from registers 2–11 (the others are reserved for other purposes) may be selected.

Whenever an operation is to be performed which requires that one of the operands be located in a register, that operand will be loaded into either register 2 or 3 from memory (the choice depends upon the operation). None of the operations found in RASCAL/1 require that both operands be simultaneously located in registers before the operation can be performed. After loading the operand, the operation will be performed. If the result of that operation is itself in a register, it is stored in a compiler-created *"temporary"* location for later reference. At that point, registers 2 and 3 are free to be reused to hold to next operand as required; so the basic execution sequence is:

1. load operand when needed into register 2 or 3
2. perform operation
3. store result, if any, in memory

In addition to emitting 360AL code to perform these actions, CANTOR must also push onto operand_stk the name of the location where it stored the result.

With this particular allocation scheme, there can be an arbitrary number of temporary locations required to hold intermediate results. To evaluate:

$$a_1 + a_2$$

requires one temporary location to hold the result of the addition (here a_i is a general quantity and not a RASCAL identifier). The evaluation of:

$$(a_1 + a_2) + (a_3 + a_4)$$

requires two temporary locations, one for each parenthesized subexpression. The evaluation of:

$$(a_1 + a_2) + (a_3 + a_4) + (a_5 + a_6))$$

requires three temporary locations. In general, the evaluation of:

$$(a_1 + a_2) + ((a_3 + a_4) + ((a_5 + a_6) + ((a_7 + a_8) + . . . + (a_{n-1} + a_n)) . . .)$$

$$(5.18)$$

requires $n/2$ temporaries to store all of the intermediate results. Figure 5-9 shows the assignment of temporaries to expression 5.18. Note that temporaries are reused wherever possible.

Since the number of temporary locations required depends upon the expressions being compiled, CANTOR/1 cannot allocate storage for these temporaries in advance with assurance of allocating enough; rather, it must allocate storage as needed, or allocate a fixed number and risk not

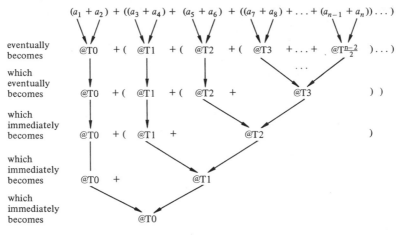

Fig. 5-9.

having enough. In practice, only a handful of temporaries would be used, so that it is fairly safe to allocate 10 temporaries. However, it is not much harder to handle the general case, so we will do so here.

Boolean and *integer* values both occupy one full-word, so temporary locations may freely be used to hold either value type. Hence, only one type of temporary storage will have to be allocated—full word temporaries. If we had stored *boolean* values in more compact storage, such as one byte or even one bit, then separate temporaries would have to be maintained for *integer* and *boolean* values, complicating the allocation and assignment scheme further. Since we shall be using one temporary location for both types of storage, we shall have to adjust the symbol table entry for the temp whenever the storage type changes. This is necessary in order to test whether the data-types of operands are correct for the operators they appear with.

5.6.3 Emitting Code

Figure 5-10 shows the refinement of the routine which emits 360AL code that performs addition. Note that for the IBM 360/370 architecture, the choice between loading the operand into register 2 or register 3 is arbitrary.

Division is slightly more complex because the IBM 360/370 architecture requires a double register in order to perform this operation, registers 2 and 3 forming that double register. *Operand2* is loaded into register 2 and shifted right into register 3, propagating the sign bit of *operand2* through-

procedure   emit_addition_code(operand1, operand2: **string**);
      {add *operand1* to *operand2*.}
  begin
    if   *type of either operand is not integer* **then**
      process error—illegal type;
    emit instruction to load operand2 into register 2;
    emit instruction to add operand1 to the contents of register 2;
    if   *operand1 or operand2 is a temporary* **then**
      adjust books to show these temporary names may be reused;
    adjust books to assign the next free temp to the sum located in register 2 and change
      type of temp in symbol table to integer;
    push name of result onto operand_stk;
    emit instruction to store the contents of register 2 into location of temporary;
  end;

Fig. 5-10. *Emit_addition_code.*

out register 2. The contents of this double register is then divided by *operand1,* leaving the quotient in register 3. (Note: the quirks of this division algorithm are peculiar to the IBM 360/370 architecture and vary considerably from machine to machine.) Figure 5-11 shows the refinement for division. We presume that no program ever attempts to divide by zero, which is, of course, illegal and is trapped by the hardware.

The logical operation **and** is performed between *boolean* operands. Recall from Chapter 4 that the internal representation of **false** is *integer* 0 (32 bits of zeroes) and that the internal representation of **true** is *integer* -1 (32 bits of ones). There is an instruction in the IBM 360/370 repertoire, N, which "ands" the operands bit-wise. Figure 5-12 shows the refinement of **and,** which is quite similar to the refinement for addition.

procedure   emit_division_code(operand1,operand2: **string**);
      {divide *operand2* by *operand1*.}
  begin
    if   *type of either operand is not integer* **then**
      process error—illegal type;
    emit instruction to load operand2 into register 2;
    emit instruction to shift contents of register 2 into register 3 propagating sign bit;
    emit instruction to divide contents of double register 2 and 3 by operand1;
    if   *operand1 or operand2 is a temporary* **then**
      adjust books to show that these temporary names may be reused;
    adjust books to assign the next free temp to the quotient located in register 3 and
      change type of temp in symbol table to integer;
    push name of result onto operand_stk;
    emit instruction to store the contents of register 3 into location of temporary;
  end;

Fig. 5-11. *Emit_division_code.*

procedure emit_and_code(operand1, operand2: **string**);
　　　　{"and" *operand1* to *operand2*.}
　begin
　　if *type of either operand is not boolean* **then**
　　　　process error—illegal type ;
　　emit instruction to load operand2 into register 2;
　　emit instruction to 'and' bit-wise operand1 and the contents of register 2;
　　if *operand1 or operand2 is a temporary* **then**
　　　　adjust books to show that these temporary names may be reused;
　　adjust books to assign the next free temp to the conjunct located in register 2 and change
　　　　type of temp in symbol table to boolean;
　　push name of result onto operand_stk;
　　emit instruction to store the contents of register 2 into location of temporary;
　end;

Fig. 5-12. *Emit_and_code.*

The relational operation '=' is performed between any two operands of the same type. There is an instruction which compares two quantities and sets the condition code depending on the result of that comparison which does not require a register. The value of the next temporary which will hold the result is set to **true** or **false,** depending on the outcome of that comparison. Figure 5 13 shows the refinement.

Finally, the assignment operation requires no registers at all. A "move character" instruction simply copies the value of the first operand into the location named by the second operand. Since assignment is legal only

procedure emit_equals_code(operand1,operand2: **string**);
　　　　{test whether *operand1* equals *operand2*.}
　　begin
　　　if *types of operands are not the same* **then**
　　　　　process error—incompatible types ;
　　　emit instruction to compare operand1 to operand2 in memory;
　　　if *operand1 or operand2 is a temporary* **then**
　　　　　adjust books to show that these temporary names may be reused;
　　　get the next available temporary name, call it "temp";
　　　change type of temp in symbol table to boolean:
　　　emit instruction to store logical 'false' (32 binary zeros into
　　　temp; {presume *operand1* ≠ *operand2*}
　　　emit instruction to branch around the next instruction if the
　　　　　condition code indicates operand1 ≠ operand2;
　　　emit instruction to store logical 'true' (32 binary ones)
　　　　　into temp; {change result if *operand1* = *operand2*}
　　　push temp onto operand_stk;
　　end;

Fig. 5-13. *Emit_equals_code.*

```
procedure   emit_assign_code(operand1,operand2: string);
              {assign the value of operand1 to operand2.}
   begin
     if types of operands are not the same then
       process error—incompatible types;
     emit code to move the value of operand1 into operand2;
       if operand1 is a temporary then
         adjust books to show that the temporary name may be reused;
       {operand2 can never be a temporary since it is to the left of ':=' in a RASCAL/1
         source statement}
   end;
```

Fig. 5-14. *Emit_assign_code.*

between operands of the same data-type, no conversion is necessary. Figure 5-14 shows the refinement for ':='.

All five code emitting procedures just given refer to "books" which must be "adjusted" to reflect changing uses of temporary locations. When a new temporary is needed, one must be created. When an old temporary is no longer needed, it must be discarded. There are two utility routines for this called *get_temp* and *free_temp,* respectively. *Get_temp* returns the name of the next temporary, and if necessary, will force allocation of a full-word to correspond to that name. *Free_temp* releases the name of the last temporary created by a call to *get_temp*; however, the storage (if any) allocated by the earlier call to *get_temp* remains allocated after the call to *free_temp*. Once storage for a temporary has been allocated, it may not be deallocated. The definitions of *free_temp* and *get_temp* are given in Figs. 5-15 and 5-16, respectively. Note that both refer to global quantities, *current_temp_no* and *max_temp_no,* which should be declared in the definition of the parser routine, and initialized to -1 to reflect the fact that initially no temporaries are allocated (*@T0* will be the first temporary name used).

We have completed the explanation of how code is generated under the first allocation scheme. Figure 5-17 shows the code which will be generated using this scheme for the program depicted in Fig. 5-1. This code,

```
procedure   free_temp;
   begin
     current_temp_no. := current_temp_no − 1;
     if   current_temp_no <−1 then
       process error—compiler error, current_temp_no should be greater than or equal to
         −1;
   end;
```

Fig. 5-15. *Free_temp.*

```
function   get_temp: string;
   begin
      current_temp_no := current_temp_no + 1;
      get_temp := '@T' || current_temp_no;
      if   current_temp_no > max_temp_no then
         begin
            insert('@T' || current_temp_no, , mutable, , yes, 1);
            max_temp_no := max_temp_no + 1;
         end;
   end;
```

Fig. 5-16. *Get_temp.*

HOHUM	CSECT		
	STM	14,12,12(13)	save registers
	BALR	12,0	set up base register
	USING	*,12	
	ST	13,@SAV+4	save loc old save area
	LA	13,@SAV	load addr new save area
	L	2,@I7	3 + 4
	A	2,@I8	
	ST	2,@T0	
	L	3,@I1	five * @T0
	M	2,@T0	
	ST	3,@T0	
	MVC	@I2(4),@T0	a := @T0
	L	2,@I2	a + a
	A	2,@I2	
	ST	2,@T0	
	MVC	@I3(4),@T0	b := @T0
	L	2,@I9	−5 mod a
	SRDA	2,32	
	D	2,@I2	
	ST	2,@T0	
	L	2,@I3	b + @T0
	A	2,@T0	
	ST	2,@T0	
	MVC	@I6(4),@T0	z := @T0
	L	2,@I3	b + z
	A	2,@I6	
	ST	2,@T0	

Fig. 5-17. Object Code for Fig. 5-1.

```
            L       2,@I2             a − b
            S       2,@I3
            ST      2,@T1
            L       3,@T0             @T0 * @T1
            M       2,@T1
            ST      3,@T0
            MVC     @I4(4),@T0        c := @T0
            L       2,@I3             b div c
            SRDA    2,32
            D       2,@I4
            ST      3,@T0
            L       2,@I2             a + @T0
            A       2,@T0
            ST      2,@T0
            MVC     @I5(4), @T0       w := @T0
            L       2,@I9             −a mod a
            SRDA    2,32
            D       2,@I2
            ST      2,@T0
            L       2,@I5             w + @T0
            A       2,@T0
            ST      2,@T0
            MVC     @I3(4), @T0       b := @T0
            L       2,@I6             z > zero
            C       2,@I0
            MVC     @T0(4), =F'0'     @T0 := false
            BNH     *+10
            MVC     @T0(4), =F'1'     @T0 := true
            MVC     @B0(4),@T0        d := @T0
@END        L       13,@SAV+4         restore loc old save area
            LM      14,12,12(13)      restore old registers
            BR      14                return
@SAV        DS      18F               @SAV
@I0         DC      1F'0'             zero
@I1         DC      1F'5'             five
@I2         DS      1F                a
@I3         DS      1F                b
@I4         DS      1F                c
@I5         DS      1F                w
@I6         DS      1F                z
@B0         DS      1F                d
@I7         DC      1F'3'             3
@I8         DC      1F'34'            34
@T0         DS      1F                @T0
@I9         DC      1F'−5'            −5
@T1         DS      1F                @T1
            END
```

Fig. 5-17. Object Code for Fig. 5-1 (continued).

while correct, is also quite verbose. Consider the translation of the assignment statement:

$$w := a + b \; \textbf{div} \; c; \qquad\qquad (5.19)$$

into:

```
      L    2,@I3        b div c              (5.20)
      SRDA 2,32
      D    2,@I4
      ST   3,@T0
      L    2,@I2        a + @T0
      A    2,@T0
      ST   2,@T0
      MVC  @I5(4),@T0   w := @T0
```

This code could easily be rewritten by hand into a more compact:

```
      L    2,@I3        b div c              (5.21)
      SRDA 2,32
      D    2,@I4
      A    3,@I2        @T0 + a
      ST   3,@I5        w := @T0
```

The eight instructions of 5.20 have been reduced to just five instructions in 5.21, a compaction possible because the allocation and assignment scheme described here does not take advantage of previously compiled subexpressions in order to eliminate redundant loads and stores. After an operation has been performed, the result of that operation may be sitting in a register and not need to be stored and then reloaded in order to be available as an operand. In this particular case, after b was divided by c, the quotient was located in register 3. Instead of storing that result into a main memory location, we could simply add the value of variable a to the contents of register 3 to obtain the value of:

$$a + b \; \textbf{div} \; c \qquad\qquad (5.22)$$

Note that we also took advantage of the commutativity of addition in this case, since we actually computed:

$$b \; \textbf{div} \; c + a$$

rather than 5.22. Similarly, instead of storing the result of that addition into memory and then moving it to the location assigned to variable w, we can simply store the contents of register 3 directly into @I5. By keeping track of the locations of operands within registers and storing and loading operands into registers only when necessary, a considerable savings in the

number of statements emitted is possible. In this case three statements
were saved by noting the locations of operands. In more complex assignment statements the savings may be even more substantial. The exercises
at the end of the chapter address the magnitude of the savings further.

We can also save instructions and space across statements, as well as
expressions. In Fig. 5-1:

$$b := w + -5 \bmod a; \hspace{3cm} (5.23)$$

follows statement 5.19. Applying our original code generation scheme,
this statement generates:

L	2,@I9	$-5 \bmod a$	(5.24)
SRDA	2,32		
D	2,@I2		
ST	2,@T0		
L	2,@I5	$w + @T0$	
A	2,@T0		
ST	2,@T0		
MVC	@I3(4),@T0	$b: = @T0$	

We can easily recode this as:

L	2,@I9	$-5 \bmod a$	(5.25)
SRDA	2,32		
D	2,@I2		
A	3,@I5	$@T0 + w$	
ST	3,@I3	$b: = @T0$	

reducing eight instructions to five. Note that at the conclusion of code
5.21, register 3 holds the value of w. If we do not overlay register 3 in
computing $-5 \bmod a$, then the faster register-register addition can be used
instead of the register-memory addition shown in 5.25:

L	4,@I9	$-5 \bmod a$	(5.26)
SRDA	4,32		
D	4,@I2		
AR	5,3	$@T0 + w$	
ST	5,@I3	$b: = @T0$	

In other situations a register load might be eliminated; for example, at the
conclusion of the code for:

$$z := b + -5 \bmod a; \hspace{3cm} (5.27)$$

Register 2 will hold the value of z; the next statement:

$$c := (b+z) * (a-b); \hspace{3cm} (5.28)$$

could directly reference that value in register 2 to perform the addition and avoid an unnecessary load! These facts motivate the allocation and assignment scheme described next.

5.6.4   Register Allocation and Assignment—Scheme Two

The second register allocation and assignment scheme:

1. uses general purpose registers 2 through 11, but allocates and frees them in even-odd pairs;
2. avoids needless stores into main memory;
3. avoids needless loads into registers.

By paying attention to these three points, the object code generated by CANTOR/1 will decrease significantly in size over that emitted by scheme one, a decrease which is significant enough to warrant the added complexity in the allocation and assignment scheme.

We shall say that a register pair is *allocated* when it contains the value of some quantity, either a compiler generated temporary or a program defined quantity such as a constant or literal. A register is said to be *assigned* to the name of the quantity it currently holds and conversely. Note that register pairs are allocated, but single registers are assigned. We allocate registers in pairs to simplify the bookkeeping and decision making in allocation policy, since some operations require single registers and others require double register pairs; however, a single register of the pair will, at the completion of the operation, hold the entire result. When the assignment of register to operand is broken, the register is *deassigned* from the operand and conversely; similarly, when a register pair is no longer allocated, it is *freed* or *deallocated*.

A single register will be assigned to at most one operand at a time. There are circumstances in which it is conceivable that more than one operand could be assigned to a single register at once; for example, if b is in register r, then the assignment statement:

$$c := b; \tag{5.29}$$

causes the current values of both c and b to be located in register r if the generated code is:

$$\text{ST} \quad r, @In \quad c := b$$

where @In is the internal name of c. However, our bookkeeping scheme will replace the assignment of r to b by an assignment of r to c. Identifier b will not be treated as if it were in a register after the execution of 5.29 until some later instruction forces b to be reloaded into a register (possibly not *r*). Although it would lead to more efficient object code, a scheme which permitted the assignment of sets of operands to single registers would be sufficiently more complex to obscure the presentation. This enhancement is left as an exercise for the reader.

Get_temp must be modified slightly for the new scheme. Each temporary in the first scheme names a main memory location. Accordingly, when a symbol table entry for a temp is created, the *alloc* field is always set to *yes*. Our new scheme will not allocate main memory for temporaries unless necessary, so that initially, the *alloc* field should be *no*. If necessary it will later be changed to *yes*. Other than that one change, the two *get_temps* are identical.

In section 5.6.3, we offered refinements of five operations using the simple allocation scheme presented in 5.6.2. We now offer five new refinements for these same operations under the new scheme presented as Figs. 5-18 through 5-22. The logic of the routines is complicated somewhat by considering whether the operands are originally in memory or registers. We are concerned about their location for two reasons:

```
procedure  emit_addition_code(operand1, operand2: string);
           {add operand2 to operand1.}
    var result_reg; 2 . . 11;
    begin
      if either operand is not an integer then
         process error—illegal type;
      if neither operand is in a register then
         allocate a register pair, assign one of the registers of that pair to operand1, and emit
            code to load operand1 into that register;
      if exactly one operand is in a register then begin
         call that register "result_reg";
         emit code to perform a register-memory addition; end;
      else {both operands are in registers so} begin
      if one register holds a temp and the other does not then
            {don't destroy non-temporary values unless necessary so}
         result_reg is the register holding the temp;
      else {both are temps or both are non-temps so}
        result_reg is either register;
      emit code to perform register-register addition with result_reg holding the result;
      end; deassign all temporaries involved and free these names for reuse;
        if result_reg had not held a temp then deassign it;
      assign result_reg the next available temporary name; and change the type of its
         symbol table entry to integer;
      push the name of the result onto operand_stk;
    end;
```

Fig. 5-18. *Emit_addition_code.*

```
procedure  emit_division_code(operand1, operand2: string);
        {divide operand2 by operand1.}
   var   result_reg: 2 .. 11;
   begin
      if  either operand is not an integer then
          process error—illegal type;
      if  operand2 is in an odd numbered register then
          expand its sign into the even half of its pair;
      else if  operand2 is in an even numbered register then begin
          shift it into the odd half of its pair;
          adjust books to show new location of operand2;   end;
      else  {operand2 is not in a register so}  begin
          allocate a register pair other than that occupied by operand1 (if it is assigned to one);
          assign operand2 to the odd register;
          emit instructions to load operand2 into the even register of that pair;
          shift operand2 into the odd half of its pair;   end;
          {operand 2 is now in the odd register of a pair. its sign has been propagated into the
            even register of that pair.}
      result_reg := register assigned to operand2;
      if  operand1 is in a register then
          emit code to perform a register-register division;
      else  emit code to perform a register-memory division;
      deassign all temporaries involved and free these names for reuse;
      if  operand2 is not a temporary then deassign it;
      result_reg := the next available temporary name and change the type of its symbol
          table entry to integer;
      push the name of the result onto operand_stk;
   end;
```

Fig. 5-19. *Emit division_code.*

1. If an operation requires that one operand be in a register, knowing it is already there can eliminate redundant loads.
2. If both operands are in registers, then faster (than register-memory) register-register operations may be applicable.

The first consideration is major, since, as we saw in the last section, the number of redundant loads and stores can be a large percentage of the code generated using the first simple scheme; the second consideration is more minor, depending on the exact timings of instructions. It is quite common for compilers to consider these two points in their allocation and assignment schemes.

We have taken advantage of the commutativity of addition and conjunction in Figs. 5-18 and 5-20, respectively. For both operations:

$$\text{operand2 op operand1} \qquad (5.30)$$

equals:

$$\text{operand1 op operand2} \qquad (5.31)$$

procedure   emit_and_code(operand1, operand2: **string**);
       {"and" *operand2* to *operand1*.}
  var   result_reg: 2 .. 11;
  begin
    if   *either operand is not boolean* **then**
      process error—illegal type;
    if   *neither operand is in a register* **then**
      allocate a register pair, assign operand2 to one of its registers, and emit code to load operand2 into that register;
    if   *exactly one operand is in a register* **then begin**
      call that register "result_reg";
      emit code to perform a register-memory "and";   **end;**
    else   {both operands are in registers so}   **begin**
      if   *one of the registers holds a temp and the other does not* **then**
         {don't destroy non-temporary values unless necessary so}
       result_reg is the register holding the temp;
      else
       result_reg is either register;
      emit code to perform register-register "and" with result_reg holding the result;   **end;**
    deassign all temporaries involved and free these names for reuse;
    if   *result_reg had not held a temp* **then** *deassign it;*
    assign result_reg the next available temporary name and change the type of its symbol table entry to boolean;
    push the name of the result onto operand_stk;
  end;

Fig. 5-20. *Emit_and_code.*

procedure   emit_equals_code(operand1, operand2: **string**);
       {test whether *operand1* equals *operand2*.}
  var   result_reg: 2 .. 11;
  begin
    if   *type of operands is not the same* **then**
      process error—incompatible types;
    allocate a register pair and call one of its registers "result_reg";   {we will put result here.}
    emit an instruction to load logical "false" into result_reg;
    emit an instruction to compare logically the two operands wherever they are located;
    emit an instruction to branch past the next assembler instruction if the condition code indicates operand1 ≠ operand2;
    emit an instruction to store logical "true" into result_reg; deassign all temporaries involved and free these names for reuse;
    assign result_reg the next available temporary name and change the type of its symbol table entry to boolean;
    push the name of the result onto operand_stk;
  end;

Fig. 5-21. *Emit_equals_code.*

procedure   emit_assign_code(operand1, operand2: **string**);
   {assign the value of *operand1* to *operand2*.}
 begin
  if *type of operands is not the same* **then**
   process error—*incompatible types;*
  if operand1 = operand2 **then return;**
  if *operand2 is in a register* **then** *deassign it;*
  if *operand1 is a register* **then begin**
   emit code to store the contents of that register into the memory location pointed to by
    operand2;
   deassign operand1;
   assign operand2 to that register; **end;**
  else {operand1 is in memory only so}
  emit code to perform a memory-memory movement of operand1 into operand2;
  if *operand1 is a temporary* **then** *free its name for reuse;*
 end;

In both cases we must also load one of the operands into a register before the operation can be executed. If *operand1* is already in a register and *operand2* is not, then instead of loading *operand2* into a register in order to perform 5.30, we just follow the simpler path by performing 5.31 instead. Note that for an operation such as division this is not possible since:

$$\text{operand2 } \textbf{div}\text{ operand1} <> \text{operand1 } \textbf{div}\text{ operand2}$$

WARNING.

One tricky situation occurs when both operands of a binary operation are the same. Consider the compilation of:

$$b * b$$

The first operand of a multiplication must reside in an odd numbered register. If *b* is assigned to an even register, it must be shifted into the odd register of the pair before the multiplication step can be executed. Normally this causes no problem, but because *b* is also the second operand, the correct positioning of the first operand has the subtle side-effect of altering the location of the second operand! The code for multiplication must allow for this fact. Addition and subtraction do not suffer from this side-effect, but **div** and **mod** do. We might be tempted to optimize '*b* **div** *b*' by performing the division during compilation to avoid the situation of concern. However, '*b* **div** *b*' only equals 1 if b ≠ 0. We are faced with the optimizer's eternal dilemma: Do we optimize on the premise the program is not erroneous, or do we exercise caution and perform the check for division by zero at execution-time? The code shown in Fig. 5-19 follows the latter course; hence, it must also carefully handle the situation where both operands are the same.

END OF WARNING.

Probably the two most confusing aspects of this new allocation and assignment scheme are the treatment of temporaries and the register allocation routine, *alloc_reg_pr*. The latter routine is defined in Fig. 5-23 and its further refinement, *forcibly_free_reg_pair*, is defined in Fig. 5-24. We shall explain them in turn.

Recall that all temporary quantities are useful or *"alive"* only from the time they are created until their first use as an operand in a call to *code*. Consequently, when each of the code emitting subroutines of *code* has finished its references to temporary quantities, it deassigns them so that:

1. The register (if any) occupied by that temporary is deassigned and hence the register pair to which that register belonged is deallocated.
2. The names given to these temporary quantities may be reused by new temporary quantities.

```
function   alloc_reg_pr(don't_free : reg_pr) : reg_pr;
            {returns a register pair as represented by the even numbered register of that pair
             between 2 and 10. Forcibly frees a register pair if none is available. Won't free
             dont_free.}
      var   i: reg_pr;
      begin
         {have all pairs been allocated?}
         i := 2;
         while   (i <= 10) do
            if   pair has been allocated then i := i + 2;
            else   {pair has not been allocated so}
               begin
                  set books to show pair has now been allocated;
                  alloc_reg_pr := i;
                  return;
               end;
         {no pair is free}
         forcibly free a register pair other than dont_free, assigning
         pair to alloc_reg_pr;
      end;
```

Fig. 5-23. *Alloc_reg_pr.*

function forcibly_free_reg_pair(dont_free : reg_pr) : reg_pr;
>{returns a register pair as represented by the even numbered register of that pair between 2 and 10. Forcibly removes an operand from an occupied register other than dont_free.}

begin
> **if** *any pair has a non-temporary assigned to one of its registers and pair not =
> dont_free* **then**
>>   **begin**
>>   *forcibly_free_reg_pair is any such pair;*
>>   *deassign the operand assigned to a register of forcibly_free_reg_pair;*
>>   **end;**
> **else**
>>   **begin**
>>>   **if** *any pair has a temp already allocated main memory
>>>   and is not = dont_free* **then**
>>>   *forcibly free_reg_pair is any such pair;*
>>>   **else**
>>>>   **begin**
>>>>   *forcibly_free_reg_pair is any pair not = dont_free;*
>>>>   *allocate main memory for the temp from the chosen pair;*
>>>>   **end;**
>>>   *emit code to store the temporary value into main memory;*
>>>   *deassign the temp from its register in forcibly_free_reg_pair;*
>>   **end;**
> **end;**

Fig. 5-24. *Forcibly_free_reg_pair.*

So, for example, in the latter part of *emit_addition_code,* there is an instruction which deassigns all temporary operands and their registers.

For certain operations, the result of the operation is placed in a register; so that whatever quantity, if any, formerly resided in this register (called *result_reg* here) no longer does. Hence, it is necessary to first deassign *result_reg* so that the old association is removed from the "books" and second to assign the name of the result to *result_reg.* Because *result_reg* will normally have a temporary name, it is important to first "release" the temporary names of the operands of the call to *code* prior to assigning *result_reg* a temporary name in order to minimize the number of temporaries actually needed. The third and fourth from the last lines of *emit_addition_code* modify the book entries for *result_reg* and its assigned operands as desired.

Alloc_reg_pr returns a register pair as represented by the even numbered register of that pair between 2 and 10; the pair it returns has no operands assigned to either of its registers. (Note that only one of the two registers of a pair can have an operand assigned to it at any one time.) It takes one argument which is a list of registers which should *not* be forcibly freed; we should, for example, never forcibly free a register holding one of the operands of the current operation.

Alloc_reg_pr first determines if any pair is not allocated. If there is such a pair, it simply marks the books to show that this pair has now become allocated and returns that pair. If there is more than one such pair, the choice of which to return is immaterial, but the code actually forces the return of the lowest numbered such pair. A problem arises if all of the pairs are allocated when *alloc_reg_pr* is called, in which case, a pair must be forcibly freed. Expression 5.18, as you will recall, illustrated a form of arithmetic expression which demanded an arbitrary number of temporaries. Under this new allocation and assignment scheme, the same unfortunate fact will still be true. If there were an arbitrary number of general purpose registers on the IBM 360/370 computer, then *alloc_reg_pr* would never have to forcibly remove an operand from a register, but with just five register pairs, expressions of only moderate complexity will fill all of the available pairs and request more. Furthermore, a sequence of assignment statements which has very little computation could also quickly fill all of the registers; for example, the sequence:

$$
\begin{aligned}
a &:= 1 + b; \\
c &:= 2 + b; \\
d &:= 3 + b; \\
e &:= 4 + b; \\
f &:= 5 + b;
\end{aligned}
\qquad (5.32)
$$

might leave variables a, c, d, e, and f in registers 3,5,7,9 and 11, respectively. One more statement following these:

$$
g := 6 + b; \qquad (5.33)
$$

and CANTOR/1 would have to clear a double register in order to perform the indicated addition. The routine *forcibly_free_reg_pair* is one strategy for deciding which of the five pairs to free. In Chapter 9 on *real* numbers, a similar problem and solution will be posed for the floating-point registers of the IBM 360/370 computer.

Forcibly_free_reg_pair always returns a register pair. It attempts to choose a pair which will be the least likely to increase the size of the object code generated by CANTOR. However, the routine operates under the major constraint that its choice cannot be based on statements in the source code not yet seen; a fact severely limiting the ability of *forcibly_free_reg_pair* to make "intelligent" choices.

Within an assignment statement, no program defined quantity can change value until, as a last step, the variable to the left of ':=' is assigned a value. Consequently, the value of a variable stored in memory is equal to the value stored in a register assigned to that variable (if any). Similarly, the value of a constant or literal stored in memory can never be different from its value in a register, so forcibly freeing a pair which holds a program defined variable, constant, or literal simply requires changing the compiler's books to deassign that quantity and the register which holds it. No assembly language code must be emitted to affect the deallocation of the pair. Consequently, the first choice of *forcibly_free_reg_pair* is to return a pair which had been holding a program defined quantity rather than a compiler generated temporary.

With this new scheme, no main memory allocation is made when a temporary quantity is named. The temporary normally "lives" in a register and is removed to main memory only when necessary. Hence, the more distinct temporaries which must be forcibly removed from registers, the more main memory storage space which is taken up by the object code. To minimize the storage space, we shall, as a second choice, forcibly free a pair which holds a temporary for which storage has already been emitted (an entry for it in the symbol table with *allocate* equal to *yes*). We shall also need to emit an assembly language instruction to store the contents of the register assigned to the operand into the main memory location created for it. Finally, as a last resort, we forcibly free a pair which holds a temporary for which no storage has already been emitted. We must set the *allocate field* of the symbol table entry for it to *yes* and emit an assembly language instruction as we did for our second choice. This last choice forces both data storage and assembly code to be emitted into the object text.

Figure 5-25 shows the code emitted by CANTOR/1 for the program in Fig. 5-1 resulting from the second allocation scheme. Including the standard prologue and epilogue, Fig. 5-17 has 75 lines of code, while Fig. 5-25 has 54 lines, a savings of 28%. Ignoring the standard prologue and epilogue which are constant for any program, Fig. 5-17 has 65 lines, while Fig. 5-25 has 44, a more significant savings of 32%!

Despite the savings in the number of loads and stores by intelligent bookkeeping, the second scheme described here is by no means optimal. Optimal allocation and assignment require a second pass over the program in which statements that follow the point where a register assignment is made may be taken into account. For example, if CANTOR is in a situation where it must forcibly free a register pair, it could, with the proper knowledge, choose to deassign an operand which it knows will not soon again be referenced. Instead, with our limited knowledge of the program (we can look backwards but not forwards) we could mistakenly deassign an operand and be forced to reference that operand immediately thereafter. In the worst case, the deassigned operand would have to be

```
HOHUM      CSECT
           STM      14,12,12(13)      save registers
           BALR     12,0              set up base register
           USING    *,12
           ST       13,@SAV+4         save loc old save area
           LA       13,@SAV           load addr new save area
           L        2,@I7             3 + 34
           A        2,@I8
           LR       3,2               five * @T0
           M        2,@I1
           ST       3,@I2             a := @T0
           AR       3,3               a + a
           ST       3,@I3             b := @T0
           L        4,@I9             −5 mod a
           SRDA     4,32
           D        4,@I2
           AR       5,3               @T0 + b
           ST       5,@I6             z := @T0
           AR       3,5               b + z
           L        6,@I2             a − b
           S        6,@I3
           MR       2,6               @T0 * @T1
           ST       3,@I4             c := @T0
           L        6,@I3             b div c
           SRDA     6,32
           DR       6,3
           A        7,@I2             @T0 + a
           ST       7,@I5             3 := @T0
           L        8,@I9             − 5 mod a
           SRDA     8,32
           D        8,@I2
           AR       9,7               @T0 + w
           ST       9,@I3             b := @T0
           SR       10,10             z > zero
           C        5,@I0
           BNH      *+10              branch if false
           BCTR     10,0              condition is true
           ST       10,@B0            d := @T0
@END       L        13,@SAV+4         restore loc old save area
           LM       14,12,12(13)      restore old registers
           BR       14                return
@SAV       DS       18F               @SAV
@I0        DC       1F'0'             zero
@I1        DC       1F'5'             five
@I2        DS       1F                a
@I3        DS       1F                b
@I4        DS       1F                c
@I5        DS       1F                w
@I6        DS       1F                z
@B0        DS       1F                d
@I7        DC       1F'3'             3
@I8        DC       1F'34'            34
@I9        DC       1F'−5'            −5
           END
```

Fig. 5-25. Object Code for Example Program in Fig. 5-1.

reloaded into a register. We might still be able to use it as the second operand of a register-memory instruction, but this is slower than the register-register instruction which might otherwise have been applicable. Section 5.7 examines some further possible optimizations.

5.7 Optimization

We have already incorporated a number of optimizing strategies into CANTOR. Our second register assignment and allocation scheme was designed specifically for efficient use of registers, temporaries being assigned main memory storage only when necessary. Data is physically located at the end of the object code to avoid branching around it. Other optimizations will be considered in this section, the first being *constant folding*.

If the values of all operands of an operation are known at compile-time and cannot change at execution-time, then the operation can be performed by the compiler and the result inserted in place of the code to perform the operation in the object code. Such operations are known as *compile-time arithmetic,* a very common optimization strategy. This particular strategy is called *constant folding*.

Evaluating operations at compile-time rather than at execution-time has two advantages:

1. The object code is reduced by the size of the code needed to perform the operation.
2. The operation is evaluated once at compile-time and not at all during execution, whereas, without this optimization, the operation would be performed every time this operation is referenced.

Hence, a significant savings in both the execution time of the compiled code and the space taken by the object code is possible. Of course, the size and speed of the compiler is adversely affected by this optimization, but on the premise that a program may be executed numerous times for many months or years after it is developed, during which time the program is not compiled at all, the increased compilation costs seem well worth the expense.

Compile-time arithmetic in RASCAL can be performed anytime all operands are either constants or literals. The result of such a computation is normally another literal which is inserted onto *operand_stk;* hence, the result of one compile-time computation can later be an operand of another compile-time computation. For example, the statement:

$$a := (3 \textbf{ div } 2) * (2 + 61)$$

can be compiled as if it were:

$$a := 63;$$

The reader may be wondering why any programmer would, in fact, write expressions which he himself could evaluate. The answer lies in two facts:

1. Programmers tend to be lazy.

and more importantly:

2. Certain relationships are more self-documenting if expressed un-evaluated.

The first fact needs no justification. To see the second is true, consider the simple computation:

$$\text{circumference} := 2 * \text{pi} * \text{radius} ;$$

Writing '$2 * pi$' (where pi is a constant) certainly reads more naturally than:

$$\text{circumference} := 6.28 * \text{radius} ;$$

When we incorporate arrays into RASCAL in Chapter 9, we shall see another very common example of compile-time arithmetic of a different sort—the compile-time computation of an array element's address when the subscript in the reference is a constant or compile-time computable value.

Modifying CANTOR to perform compile-time arithmetic is quite straightforward. Within the individual subroutines which emit code for the various operations, we can test whether the operands are either literals or symbolic constants; if they *all* are, then instead of emitting assembly code to perform the operation, CANTOR can perform it instead, name the result and push that name onto *operand_stk*.

Another optimization which is consistent with the one-pass organization of CANTOR is *constant propagation*. As an example of where this arises, consider the two statements:

$$a := \text{five} * (3+34); \qquad (5.34)$$
$$b := a + a; \qquad (5.35)$$

from Fig. 5-1. Since the addition in 5.35 involves two variables, the simple constant folding described earlier is not applicable, but the value of *a* in

5.35 can, in fact, be determined at compile-time. Constant folding in 5.34 leads us to assign 185 to a. Even though a is a variable, its value with respect to statement 5.35 is constant, *propagating* this constant value across statements allows b to be assigned the value 370 at compile-time.

Since RASCAL/1 has no input statements, constant propagation and folding can eliminate entirely the need for run-time arithmetic computation. CANTOR can execute (interpret) the entire program *hohum*. Once **read** and **readln** procedures are introduced in Chapter 7, however, this will no longer be true, although at certain points in a program's code, constant propagation may well be applicable.

A more sophisticated compiler might try to perform still further compile-time arithmetic by applying the mathematical axioms of the *integers* and *booleans*. For example, if b is a *boolean* variable then:

$$b \ \textbf{and} \ \textbf{true}$$

is just the value of b. Applying commutativity to:

$$6 * c * 4$$

it becomes:

$$24 * c$$

a reduction we would not detect with the compile-time arithmetic evaluation scheme described earlier. There is no limit to how "clever" a compiler writer can be in identifying ways to perform arithmetic or logical computation at compile-time. However, there is a point of diminishing returns, since, for even moderately sized expressions, the number of "reasonable" equivalent rearrangements is quite large.

Because CANTOR is a one-pass compiler, we have so far ignored the role which intermediate code normally plays in multipass compilers. At this point we digress briefly to consider how CANTOR might be reorganized into a two-pass compiler. The first pass generates intermediate level code; the second pass converts this into 360AL. This allows optimizations not possible in a one-pass compiler.

CANTOR's current structure offers an obvious format for intermediate code which is almost adequate for the job—the sequence of *calls* to *code* (as opposed to the *output* of those calls). Note that we do not mean the entire activity sequence, which includes calls to functions manipulating the symbol table, various stacks and possibly other supportive data structures; only the calls to *code* itself are considered. We do, of course, presume that the symbol table is available during the second pass to support code generation. Figure 5-26 shows the argument lists of the calls to *code* for the program emitted as Fig. 5-25. (We omit the word "code"

1.	(program, hohum)	12.	(*, @T1, @T0)
2.	(+, 34, 3)	13.	(:=, @T0, c)
3.	(*, @T0, five)	14.	(div, c,b)
4.	(:=, @T0, a)	15.	(+, @T0, a)
5.	(+, a, a)	16.	(:=, @T0, w)
6.	(:=, @T0, b)	17.	(mod, a, −5)
7.	(mod, a, −5)	18.	(+, @T0, w)
8.	(+, @T0, b)	19.	(:=, @T0, b)
9.	(:=, @T0, z)	20.	(>, zero, z)
10.	(+, z, b)	21.	(:=, @T0, d)
11.	(−, b, a)	22.	(end, .)

Fig. 5-26. Sequence of Calls to *Code*.

here to avoid clutter.) These 22 tuples express all of the operations which the object code must perform.

The only flaw in having Fig. 5-26 be the intermediate code is our inability, as it stands, to tell which computation any given temporary names. For example, which computation does @T0 in tuple 12 name? Although it might be difficult to match a temporary name to the tuple whose computation it names *after the intermediate code has been generated,* during the generation, the relationship is known explicitly by CANTOR. We, therefore, modify the tuples so that instead of including temporary names, they instead have *pointers* to other tuples. Figure 5-27 shows the revised code in which a pointer to tuple *n* is denoted '*#n*'.

The key optimization we shall discuss is *common subexpression elimination.* In Fig. 5-1 statements:

$$z : = b + −5 \bmod a ; \tag{5.36}$$

and

$$b : = w + −5 \bmod a ; \tag{5.37}$$

1.	(program, hohum)	12.	(*, #11, #10)
2.	(+, 34, 3)	13.	(:=, #12, c)
3.	(*, #2, five)	14.	(div, c,b)
4.	(:=, #3, a)	15.	(+, #14, a)
5.	(+, a,a)	16.	(:=, #15, w)
6.	(:=, #5, b)	17.	(mod, a, −5)
7.	(mod, a, −5)	18.	(+, #17, w)
8.	(+, #7, b)	19.	(:=, #18, b)
9.	(:=, #8, z)	20.	(>, zero, z)
10.	(+, z, b)	21.	(:=, #20, d)
11.	(−, b, a)	22.	(end, .)

Fig. 5-27. Revised Sequence of Calls.

both have the common subexpression:

$$-5 \ \mathbf{mod} \ a$$

The value of -5 is, of course, constant; furthermore, the value of a does not change between the execution of 5.36 and 5.37. Therefore, the value of '$-5 \ \mathbf{mod} \ a$' is the same in both statements. Instead of re-evaluating '$-5 \ \mathbf{mod} \ a$' again in executing 5.37, we could *save* the value computed for 5.36 and simply reference it when executing 5.37. Since the effort required to compute $-5 \ \mathbf{mod} \ a$ in 5.37 is ten bytes and three instructions, it seems worth the effort. In a more complex program, there might well be several occurrences of a common subexpression which have the same value. This would be especially likely in RASCAL/5 which has an array data-type. Subscripts are often repeated at several neighboring points such as in

$$b[i+1] := b[i+1] + 1 \ ;$$

In order to take advantage of a previously computed value, CANTOR must *know* that it needs to save it. This requires an examination of the entire program (block) for common subexpressions and a *flow analysis* to determine which of these subexpressions have the same value. In a language more complex than RASCAL/1, this analysis becomes somewhat involved. For the straight-line code of this chapter, it is simple enough to implement this optimization in two passes. We can construct a *dependency graph* during the first pass which shows the relationships between expressions and clearly marks which expressions are common.

The rules for constructing a dependency graph are:

1) Initially the graph is empty.

Suppose tuple $k = (\rho, b, c)$ is the next to be added to the graph:

2) If $\rho = ':='$ and c labels a *live* node, then *kill* that node and all nodes dependent on it.
3) If b (c) is not a tuple number and there is no *live* occurrence of b (c) in the graph, then create a *live* node labelled by c.
4) If there is no subgraph

already in the graph, where
   a) if b (d) is a tuple number, then b (d) is a tag of *live* node β (δ);
   b) if b (d) is not a tuple number, then b (d) is the label of *live* node β (δ);
   c) ρ labels α
then add subgraph

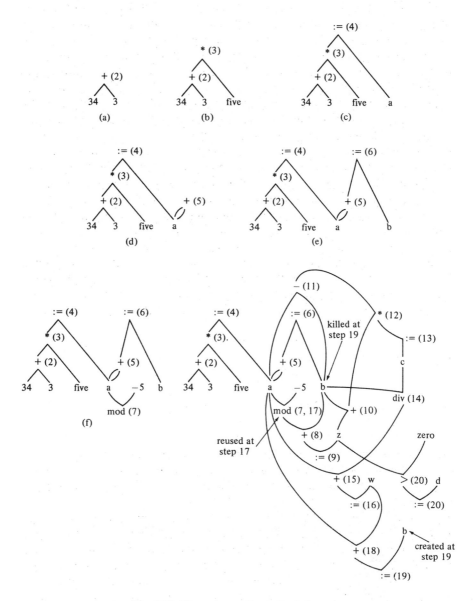

Fig. 5-28. Dependency Graph for *hohum*.

where

    a) if b (d) is a tuple number, then β (δ) is the *live* node whose tag is b (d);

    b) if b (d) is not a tuple number, then β (δ) is the *live* node whose label is b (d)

    c) ρ labels α and k tags α.

5) If there already is such a subgraph, the add tag k to α.

A node is *alive* just as long as its value is still valid for the current values of the variables. Once a variable changes value, all expressions which were computed using the old value are invalid; i.e., *killed*. Figure 5-28 shows several steps in the construction of the dependency graph for *hohum*. Because of the difficult topology of the graph, we have taken a few liberties with the angles at which subgraphs are drawn, but Fig. 5-28 contains all of the information required.

From this graph it is clear that tuple #17 is redundant and can be eliminated. The result of tuple #7 would be treated as if it were a permanent quantity until after tuple #18 were processed. This quantity would be stored in main memory before letting it be destroyed so that it could be referenced later in tuple #18. No code for tuple #17 would be emitted. After code for tuple #18 was emitted, the result of tuple #17 could be destroyed. Fig. 5-29 shows the resulting set of tuples. Note that the last-in first-out strategy employed for *get-temp* earlier in this chapter will no longer work because temporary quantities may now have to be saved for indefinite periods of time before release.

1.	(program, hohum)	12.	(−, b, a)
2.	(+, 34, 3)	13.	(*, #12, #11)
3.	(*, #2, five)	14.	(:=, #13, c)
4.	(:=, #5, a)	15.	(**div**, c, b)
5.	(+, a,a)	16.	(+, #15, a)
6.	(:=, #5, b)	17.	(:=, #16, w)
7.	(**mod**, a, −5)	18.	(+, _T0, w)
8.	(:=, #7, @T0)	19.	(:=, #18, b)
9.	(+, #7, b)	20.	(>, zero, z)
10.	(:=, #8, z)	21.	(:=, #20, d)
11.	(+, z, b)	22.	(end, .)

Fig. 5-29. Common Subexpression Elimination.

5.8   SUMMARY

RASCAL/1 adds the assignment statement to the features available to the programmer. This language, despite its seemingly simplicity, requires extensive effort to implement. The major additions to CANTOR/1, not found in CANTOR/0, are the operand and operator stacks, the extensive reliance on temporary variables to hold intermediate results, the variability in how registers are allocated and assigned to quantities and the optimizations possible by performing arithmetic and logical operations at compile-time rather than at execution-time. Because of the manner in which CANTOR/0 was designed, the implementation of CANTOR/1 required very little change in the shell which CANTOR/0 provided. For the most part, the changes were additions to existing code.

RASCAL/1

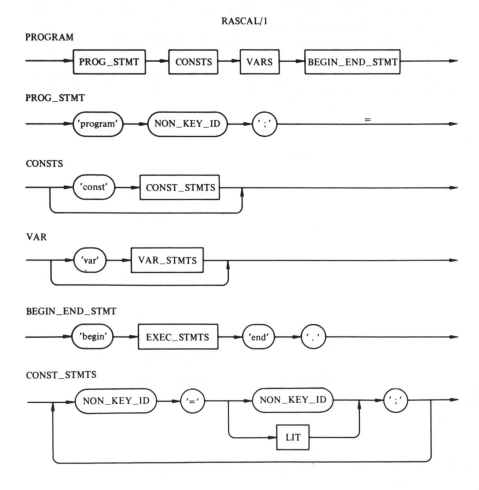

VAR_STMTS

IDS

TYPE

LIT

BOOLEAN

EXEC_STMTS

EXEC_STMT

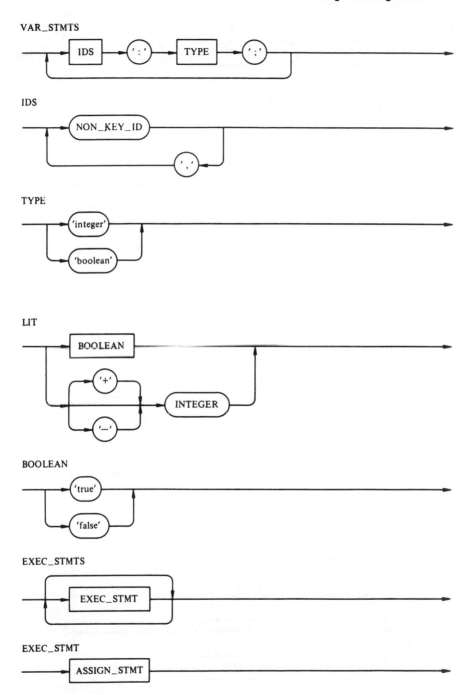

ASSIGN_STMT

EXPRESS

EXPRESSES

TERM

TERMS

FACTOR

FACTORS

PART

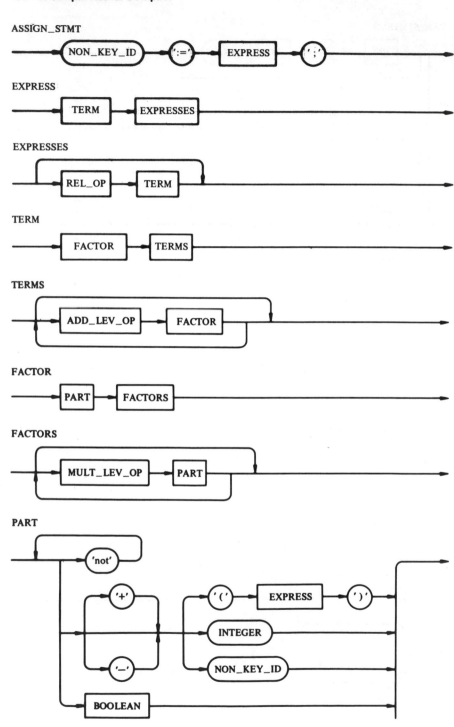

REL_OP

ADD_LEV_OP

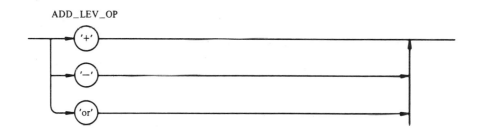

MULT_LEV_OP

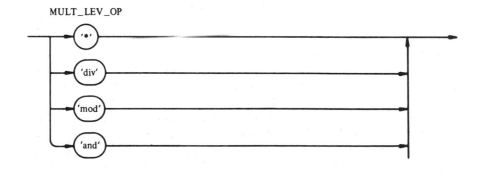

EXERCISES

5-1. Find out the precedence relations among the operators of:

FORTRAN,   ALGOL60,   PL/I

5-2. Find out if any implementations of languages available to you initialize variables implicitly at compile-time. Evaluate the wisdom of doing so in terms of programming ease and program reliability.

5-3. The **cand** operation is defined by:

b **cand** c = false if b is false
= c if b is true

This operation is similar to **and** but differs in the important case where the second operand is not defined if the first operand is false. Supposing **cand** is now available, construct an example expression in RASCAL/1. where **cand** is not equivalent to **and**. Is **cand** commutative or associative?

5-4. Modify the translation grammar of CANTOR/1 to implement **cand** in place of **and**. Presume **cand** has the same precedence as **and**. Define the necessary action routines to emit the proper 360AL code.

5-5. There is an operation, **cor**, which is to **or**, what **cand** is to **and**.

b **cor** c = true if b is true
= c if b is false

Construct an example which distinguishes **cor** from **or**. Is **cor** commutative? Associative?

5-6. Modify the translation grammar of CANTOR/1 to implement **cor** in place of **or**. Presume **cor** has the same precedence as **or**. Define the necessary action routines to emit the proper 360AL code.

5-7. Are the following expressions legal in RASCAL/1:

a. $--3$
b. $a+-3*-2$

If they are, then draw their parse trees. If they are not, indicate how you would modify the grammar for RASCAL/1 to allow them. Modify the translation grammar as well, changing action routines as needed.

5-8. Redefine RASCAL/1 so that the *boolean* operators **and, or** and **not** have a lower precedence than the relational operators and so that **not** is higher than **and** which is higher than **or**. Modify the LL(1) grammar and the translation grammar to accommodate these changes.

5-9. For our particular implementation of RASCAL/1, does it follow that if $b - c + d$ is defined, then $b + d - c$ is also defined? If so, why? If not, cite a specific case where the former is defined but not the latter.

5-10. Step through the changes to *operand_stk* and *operator_stk* for the following expressions:

a. $3 - b + c * 2$ {b,c are *integer*}
b. $(3 > y)$**and**$(t + 2 < 6)$ {y,t are *integer*}
c. z **or** b **and not** d   {z,b,d are *boolean*}

5-11. Is it possible for the following expresion to be legal RASCAL/1? If so, what data-types must *b, c,* and *d* have?

$$\textbf{not}(\ 3 > b \ \textbf{or} \ c \ \textbf{and} \ (4 <> b) \textbf{and} \ d)$$

5-12. Prove that there is no fixed number of temporaries which will suffice to compile all arithmetic expressions.

5-13. Modify the register allocation and assignment scheme so that single registers may be allocated for operations that do not require a double register, such as for addition operations. Describe all of the changes to the code generation routines. (Warning: efficient allocation can become quite involved. There are over half a dozen subcases for *integer* division depending on the location of the operands in registers and memory.)

5-14. On the premise that you were able to look ahead in the source code when allocating and assigning registers, devise a method which generates more optimal code than scheme two described in the chapter text; prove that your method generates more efficient code.

5-15. Determine what changes would have to be made to CANTOR/1 in order to take advantage of the commutative laws of addition and multiplication to perform more compile-time arithmetic than is described in the chapter text. So, for example, we would compile:

$$4 + x + 8$$

as if it were:

$$12 + x$$

5-16. Devise a strategy to perform compile-time simplification of *boolean* expressions, taking advantage of the fact that:

$$\textbf{true and} \ c = c$$
$$\textbf{false or} \ c = c$$
$$\textbf{false and} \ c = \textbf{false}$$
$$\textbf{true or} \ c = \textbf{true}$$

5-17. The **div** and **mod** operators are not completely defined in the chapter discussion. In particular, what is the value of m **div** n or m **mod** n, when m and n have different signs and the division is not exact? For example, does -3 **div** 2 equal -1 (with a remainder of $-.5$ which is lost) or does it equal -2 (with a remainder of $+.5$ which is lost)? In RASCAL, as in most languages, the answer is the former. Express more rigorously a formula which describes the desired functions, **div** and **mod,** using this example as the basis for your formulation.

5-18. *Integer* division in RASCAL is said to "truncate towards zero," because the truncated final result is always either equal to the original quotient or a value which is numerically closer to zero than the original. There is a commonly touted strategy to optimize some divisions which is incorrect if division truncates towards zero. The strategy is to equate a division by the n-th power of two to a shift right of the dividend by n bits. Show that for division which truncates towards zero, as is the case for ALGOL 60, FORTRAN IV, and RASCAL, such an optimization does not always work.

5-19. Revise the register bookkeeping system described in section 5.6.4 to permit sets of operands to be concurrently assigned to a single register.

5-20. Part of the responsibility of *push_operand* in CANTOR/1 is to enter a literal operand into the symbol table (unless an entry for that literal already exists). Centralizing the creation of symbol table entries for literals in this way simplifies the compiler design; however, it also has a detrimental effect on possible optimization of the object code. How? Support your explanation by an example. (Hint: think about compile-time arithmetic.)

5-21. State a necessary and sufficient condition for a series of assignment statements to fill all 5 register pairs as do statements 5.32. Generalize this condition to n pairs for arbitrary positive integer n.

TESTING HINTS

1. Test CANTOR/1 on all of your test programs for CANTOR/0 to ensure your expansion did not introduce a new bug or bring to the surface a latent one.

2. Test CANTOR/1 on one or more programs which:
   a. force the allocation of all register pairs;
   b. force main memory storage to be allocated for at least two temporaries;
   c. force repeated use of a temporary for which main memory has been allocated;
   d. have each binary operator in which both operands are the same;
   e. include compile-time arithmetic computation for each arithmetic operator;
   f. test all combinations of operand locations (memory and register) for each unary and binary operator;
   g. test the precedence of each operator.
   h. compute unary '+' and '−' of a variable, a parenthesized expression, and a constant;
   i. use parentheses to override all implicit precedences;
   j. have an arithmetic expression which references a literal, constant, and a variable;
   k. reference the same variable several times in a single expression;
   l. have an assignment statement in which the left-hand side is referenced on the right-hand side;

BIBLIOGRAPHY

Code generation for an optimizing compiler is discussed in [Waite 74] and in [Wulf, et al 75]. Special optimization strategies have been developed in [Floyd 61], [Sethi 75], and [Bruno and Lassagne 75], all dealing with register allocation, including analyses of their execution times in the latter two cases. The main bibliography in the back of this text cites a large number of studies of register assignment and allocation for varying machine models.

6

Stage 2: Control Structures

6.1 INTRODUCTION

Up to this point we have implemented a language which has no means to interrupt the normal sequential flow of control. All but the most trivial algorithms execute some of their steps conditionally, and nearly all such meaningful algorithms execute some of their instructions repeatedly. In stage 2, we offer three new control structures to allow conditional and repeated execution of RASCAL source code:

1. **if-then-else** statement
2. **while-do** statement
3. **repeat-until** statement

The first statement, which permits conditional execution of code, actually appears in two forms, with and without an **else** clause, while the second and third statements, employed for looping, have only one form. With their inclusion, RASCAL will almost become a viable language for simple but nontrivial programs. The only major component still missing will be input/output procedures which are presented in the next chapter.

Several new concepts will be introduced in this chapter. First, all of these new statements are *compound* statements. As such, we must be able to properly detect the end of each statement which may be arbitrarily far from its beginning. This problem is further compounded by the fact that these statements may be nested inside one another arbitrarily deep.

We shall presume in this chapter that register allocation and assignment scheme *two* was implemented by the reader in stage 1. As we shall soon see, additional complications arise in determining the correct location of operands in memory or registers in programs which exercise these new control structures. We call this the distinction between the *compile-time* and *run-time location* of operands.

6.2 RASCAL/2 LANGUAGE FEATURES

Seven new keywords are added to our language:

if,   then,   else,   repeat,   while,   do,   until

All of these keywords identify clauses of the three control structures augmenting RASCAL in this chapter, there being no new tokens added to RASCAL here. However, the token class of these seven keywords has been changed from NON_KEY_ID to KEYWORD.

We follow the pattern set in earlier chapters by presenting a context-free grammar for RASCAL/2 features along with the selection set of each alternative production. Again we shall not repeat a production unless it has somehow changed to accommodate the new language features. *In several cases, selection sets of productions not listed must be augmented.* We leave that task to the reader.

Revised Productions:

1. BEGIN_END_STMT→ 'begin'   EXEC_STMTS 'end'
                ('.' {'.'} ';' {';'})   {'begin'}

2. EXEC_STMT   → ASSIGN_STMT   {NON_KEY_ID}
                     → IF_STMT   {'if'}
                     → WHILE_STMT   {'while'}
                     → REPEAT_STMT   {'repeat'}
                     → NULL_STMT   {';'}
                     → BEGIN_END_STMT   {'begin'}

New Productions:

3. IF_STMT   → 'if'   EXPRESS 'then' EXEC_STMT
                     ELSE_PT   {'if'}

4. ELSE_PT   → 'else' EXEC_STMT   {'else'}
                     → λ   {'end', NON_KEY_ID, ';',
                            'until', 'begin', 'while', 'if', 'repeat'}

5. WHILE_STMT   → 'while' EXPRESS 'do' EXEC_STMT   {'while'}

6. REPEAT_STMT   → 'repeat' EXEC_STMTS 'until'
                     EXPRESS ';'   {'repeat'}

7. NULL_STMT   → ';'   {';'}

The additions of this chapter are not as numerous as those of Chapter 5, but their implementation is still a major task.

The only context-sensitive constraint on programs not expressed by the grammar is that the value of the expression in an **if, while,** or **repeat** statement must be of type *boolean*.

An example of a legal RASCAL/2 program is given in Fig. 6-1, while two examples of illegal RASCAL/2 programs are shown in Fig. 6-2. The comments within the latter two programs indicate why they are wrong.

The semantics of the **if** statement is shown in Fig. 6-3. We presume the reader is familiar with this nearly universal statement and do not belabor

```
program   gcd;
          {illustrate correct use of RASCAL/2 features.}
          {program computes the greatest common divisor of constants
             x and y.}
    const   x = 18;   y = 12;
    var   a,b : integer;
    begin
      if   (x > 0) and (y > 0) then        {x and y should be positive.}
        begin
          a := x; b := y;
          repeat
            while   a > b do a := a − b;
            while   b > a do b := b − a;
          until   a = b;
          {a = b = gcd(x,y).}
        end;
    end.
```

Fig. 6-1. Valid RASCAL/2 Program.

```
program   gobucks;
          {improper uses of RASCAL/2 features.}
    var   fortran,algol: integer;   why : boolean;
    begin
      if   fortran then algol := 0;        {predicate must be boolean valued.}
      else   snobol := −3; else            {extraneous 'else', 'snobol' not declared}
      while   why do begin;
        algol := fortran + 2;
        if   fortran = 3 then
        end;                               {improper nesting of if statement.}
      else   algol := fortran;
    end.
```

```
program   beatbo;
          {improper uses of RASCAL/2 features.}
    var   b,c,d: integer;
    begin
      b := 24;
      if   b > 0 then   else d := 4;    {then clause may not be empty.}
      else;                             {can use null statement, though.}
      begin;   if   b = d then; end;    {improper nesting.}
            else c := b;
    end.
```

Fig. 6-2. Two Illegal RASCAL/2 Programs.

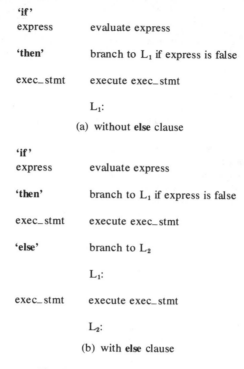

'if'

express   evaluate express

'then'   branch to L₁ if express is false

exec_stmt   execute exec_stmt

                 L₁:

(a) without **else** clause

'if'

express   evaluate express

'then'   branch to L₁ if express is false

exec_stmt   execute exec_stmt

'else'   branch to L₂

                 L₁:

exec_stmt   execute exec_stmt

                 L₂:

(b) with **else** clause

Fig. 6-3. Both Forms of **If** Statement.

its presentation, the RASCAL **if** statement being essentially the same as that found in PL/I or ALGOL 60. The object code emitted by CANTOR will perform the subtasks associated with the **if** statement pictured in Fig. 6-3. Code generation for this statement is given in section 6.4.

The **while** statement provides for conditional repetitive execution of a single (possibly compound) statement. When the expression following **'while'** is evaluated, if it is false, control resumes following the end of the **while** statement. If it is true, the statement following **'do'** is executed. When its execution is complete, control returns back to the point where the expression is again evaluated, and the entire process is repeated until the expression eventually turns false (or else the program is in an infinite loop). Figure 6-4 shows the **while** statement in operation.

The **repeat** statement is quite similar to the **while** statement in that both are used for looping, but with two major differences: The predicate is evaluated *after* the loop body has been executed, not *before,* as in a **while** statement. Consequently, the loop body (statements between **'repeat'** and **'until'**) is always executed at least once, even if the predicate is initially

'while'	L_1:
express	evaluate express
'do'	branch to L_2 if express is false
exec_stmt	execute exec_stmt
	branch to L_1
	L_2:

Fig. 6-4. The **While** Statement.

false. For a **while** statement, this is not true. If the predicate is initially false, the loop body (statement following '**do**') is skipped entirely. The second difference is that the **while** loop is executed repeatedly until the predicate is false, while the **repeat** statement is executed repeatedly until the predicate is true. The **repeat** statement is pictured in Fig. 6-5.

Unlike previous chapters, there are no special constraints imposed on RASCAL/2 by the implementation that have not already been mentioned for RASCAL/0 or RASCAL/1. However, the grammar just given for RASCAL/2 is special in a way not previously discussed. We digress here to examine this unusual situation. If the reader carefully examines the ELSE_PT production, he will note that part of one selection set is missing! The productions should actually be:

ELSE_PT → 'else' EXEC_STMT   {'else'}
         → λ   {'end', NON_KEY_ID, ';', 'until',
                                    'begin' 'while', 'if', 'repeat', 'else'}

Quite an omission! The 'else' has been omitted from the selection set of production 4.2. Note that with the full selection set listed, a key conflict results; hence, the grammar is not strictly LL(1), as we have promised. If the reader will forgive us, we shall explain why 'else' has been left out of

'repeat'	L_1:
exec_stmts	execute exec_stmts
'until'	
express	evaluate express
';'	branch to L_1 if express is false

Fig. 6-5. The **Repeat** Statement.

production 4.2's selection set. The **if** statement suffers from a classic ambiguity, called the "dangling **else**" problem, which manifests itself in the following code segment:

$$\text{if p } \textbf{then} \text{ if q } \textbf{then} \text{ r } \textbf{else} \text{ s} \qquad (6.1)$$

Both *p* and *q* are *boolean* predicates, while *r* and *s* are statements. Which **if** does the "dangling" **else** match? The question becomes clearer when we consider two alternative reformattings of 6.1:

$$\begin{array}{ll} \textbf{if} \text{ p } \textbf{then} & \qquad\qquad(6.2) \\ \quad \textbf{if} \text{ q } \textbf{then} \text{ r} & \\ \quad \textbf{else} \text{ s} & \end{array}$$

and

$$\begin{array}{ll} \textbf{if} \text{ p } \textbf{then} & \qquad\qquad(6.3) \\ \quad \textbf{if} \text{ q } \textbf{then} \text{ r} & \\ \textbf{else} \text{ s} & \end{array}$$

The first binds (in appearance) the **else** to the inner and closest **if,** while the second binds the **else** clause to the outer and farthest **if.** If we draw the parse trees for these two bindings, we have Figs. 6-6 and 6-7, corresponding to code segments 6.2 and 6.3, respectively. The grammar is ambiguous, with these two trees expressing the nature of the ambiguity.

We must resolve this ambiguity in the *language* first. This will dictate how to resolve the ambiguity in the grammar. RASCAL, like most languages, opts for the interpretation shown in Fig. 6-6 (we do not know of any language opting for Fig. 6-7). The grammar must allow *only* for this interpretation, but unfortunately, there is no unambiguous grammar for

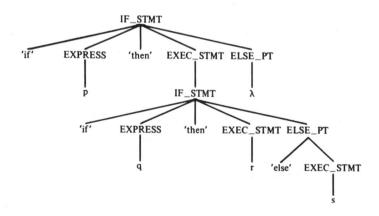

Fig. 6-6.

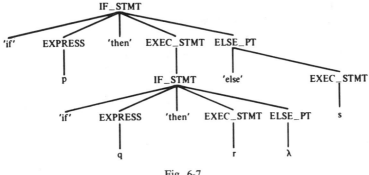

Fig. 6-7.

RASCAL which has this optional **else** clause. We rely upon an alternative which is occasionally taken by compiler writers—to force the choice of one production over another by deleting elements from selection sets, production 4.2 being an embodiment of this strategy. (An analogous strategy was developed for LR parsers in section 2.5, eliminating parsing action conflicts by "arbitrary" selection from among the choices.) By deleting 'else' from its selection set, the parse tree shown in Fig. 6-7 cannot be generated. A willingness to resolve selection set conflicts in this manner significantly increases the class of grammars to which the LL(1) parsing algorithm is applicable, even though these grammars are not strictly LL(1). The GDTGP requires the grammar writer to state the selection set of each production. He then has the freedom to resolve selection set conflicts by simply omitting an element of a set just as we have done in the translation grammar here.

6.3 CANTOR/2 TRANSLATION GRAMMAR

Revised Productions:

1. BEGIN_END_STMT→ 'begin'   EXEC_STMTS 'end'
   $('.'_x$ | $';'_x)$ $code$ ('end',x)

2. EXEC_STMT   → ASSIGN_STMT
                     → IF_STMT
                     → WHILE_STMT
                     → REPEAT_STMT
                     → NULL_STMT
                     → BEGIN_END_STMT

New Productions:

3. IF_STMT   → 'if'   EXPRESS   'then'
                     $code$('then', $pop\_operand$)
                     EXEC_STMT   ELSE_PT

4. ELSE_PT   → 'else' *code ('else', pop_operand)*
                        EXEC_STMT *code('post_if', pop_operand)*
                      → λ *pop_books code('post_if', pop_operand)*

5. WHILE_STMT   → 'while' *code('while')* EXPRESS 'do'
                        code('do', pop_operand) EXEC_STMT
                        code('post_while', pop_operand, pop_operand)

6. REPEAT_STMT   → 'repeat' *code('repeat')* EXEC_STMTS
                        'until' EXPRESS *code('until', pop_operand,*
                        pop_operand) ';'

7. NULL_STMT   → ';'

The only new action routine called directly from the translation grammar productions restores our register assignment books to an earlier status. It is detailed further in the next section. We have also added new calls to *code,* CANTOR's code generator. Since the pattern for modifying *code* was set in the last chapter, we shall not redefine it here. All that is needed is to add new alternatives to the **case** statement for the new arguments with which it can legitimately be called. In the next section we specify the code emitting routines called from *code* which generate object code for these new features.

6.4   CODE GENERATION

We begin with the revisions to *code* for the **end** statement since these are quite trivial. In revised production number one, if the punctuation following the keyword **'end'** is a period, then the entire program has terminated; otherwise, the punctuation is a semicolon, and a nested **begin-end** block has just been terminated, but the program should continue. Recall that all programs must end with a period and that the only legal way in which a statement may end with a period is if it is the final **'end'** of the program. No special action is required for a **begin-end** statement terminating with a semicolon. The more interesting refinements of the code emitters for the new control structures are given in Figs. 6-8 through 6-15.

In the past, *operand_stk* has held only operands of the various operators found in RASCAL source code such as ':=', '=', **'div'**, or **'and'**, among many others. We now extend the possible elements of *operand_stk* to include 360AL *labels* as well. Labels which CANTOR generates will have the form ''@L*n*'', where *n* is a non-negative integer. Initially, *n* is zero and is incremented by one with each call for a new label. The need for labels is illustrated back in Figs. 6-3 through 6-5, which show effectively how the 360AL implementations of these three statements appear. Branch instructions are issued either to skip over code which is to be conditionally executed or to return to the beginning of a loop from its end. In either case, the operand of the branch in 360AL is a

procedure   emit_then_code(operand: **string**);
   {emit code which follows '**then**' and statement predicate.}
 var   temp_label: **string;**
 begin
  push current status of "books" onto books_stk;
  assign next label to temp_label;
  emit an instruction to set the condition code depending on the value of operand;
  emit an instruction to branch to temp_label if the condition code indicates operand is
   zero {false};
  push temp_label onto operand_stk so that it can be referenced when emit_else_code or
   emit_post_if_code is called;
  if   *operand is a temp* **then begin**
   if *operand is in a register* then *deassign it;*
   free operand's name for reuse; **end;**
 end;

Fig. 6-8. *Emit_then_code.*

procedure   emit_else_code(operand: **string**);
   {emit code which follows **else** clause of **if** statement.}
 var   temp_label: **string;**
 begin
  assign next label to temp_label;
  emit instruction to branch unconditionally to temp_label;
  emit instruction to label this point of object code with the argument operand;
  push temp_label onto operand_stk;
  restore status of "books" saved in code('then', pop_operand) by popping books_stk;
 end;

Fig. 6-9. *Emit_else_code.*

procedure   emit_post_if_code(operand: **string**);
   {emit code which follows end of **if** statement.}
 begin
  emit instruction which labels this point of the object code with the argument operand;
  clear "books";
 end;

Fig. 6-10. *Emit_post_if_code.*

procedure   emit_while_code;
   {emit code following '**while**'.}
 var   temp_label: **string;**
 begin
  assign next label to temp_label;
  emit instruction labeling this point of object code as temp_label;
  push temp_label onto operand_stk;
  clear "books";
 end;

Fig. 6-11. *Emit_while_code.*

procedure   emit_do_code(operand: **string**);
          {emit code following '**do**'.}
   var   temp_label: **string**;
   begin
      assign next label to temp_label;
      emit instruction setting condition code depending on the value of operand;
      emit instruction to branch to temp_label if condition code shows operand is zero
         {predicate is false};
      push temp_label onto operand_stk;
      if   *operand is temp* **then begin**
         if   *operand is in a register*   **then** *deassign it;*
         free operand's name for reuse;   **end;**
   end;

Fig. 6-12. *Emit_do_code.*

procedure   emit_post_while_code(operand1,operand2: **string**);
          {emit code at end of **while** loop, *operand2* is the label of the beginning of the loop.
          operand1 is the label which should follow the end of the loop.}
   begin
      emit an instruction which branches unconditionally to the beginning of the loop, i.e., to
         the value of operand2;
      emit an instruction which labels this point of the object code with the argument
         operand1;
      clear "books";
   end;

Fig. 6-13. *Emit_post_while.*

procedure   emit_repeat_code;
          {emit code which follows '**repeat**'.}
   var   temp_label: **string**;
   begin
      assign the next label to temp_label;
      emit an instruction which labels this point in the object code with the value of
         temp_label;
      push temp_label onto operand_stk;
      clear "books";
   end;

Fig. 6-14. *Emit_repeat_code.*

procedure   emit_until_code(operand1,operand2: **string**);
　　　　　{emit code which follows '**until**' and the predicate of loop. *operand1* is the value
　　　　　of the predicate. *operand2* is the label which points to the beginning of the
　　　　　loop.}
begin
　emit an instruction which sets the condition code depending on the contents of the
　　register pointed to by operand1;
　emit an instruction which branches to the value of operand2 if the condition code shows
　　the predicate is false　　{i.e., branch to *operand2* if zero};
　if　*operand1 is a temp* **then begin**
　　if　*operand1 is in a register* **then** *deassign it;*
　　free operand1's name for reuse;　　**end;**
end;

Fig. 6-15. *Emit_until_code.*

label of some other 360AL statement which must be pushed onto
operand_stk. Aside from the need to create and process labels, the other
interesting feature of the implementation of these statements is the manner in which the bookkeeping system by which we keep track of the
location of operands in registers must be altered. This is discussed in
detail in the next section.

6.5   RUN-TIME VERSUS COMPILE-TIME LOCATION OF OPERANDS

In the last chapter, we developed an elaborate scheme for reducing the
number of loads and stores which must be included in the object code by
keeping track of which operands "lived" in registers and only performing
main memory references when needed operands could not be found in
registers. This scheme seemed to reduce the object code size
significantly—in our example program by about 28%. This scheme does
not extend without modification here, though, because of what we call the
"run-time versus the compile-time location" of operands, the topic of this
section. The modification is quite simple once we recognize where and
why we need it, the difficulty being in understanding the need for it at all.
We illustrate the problem with an example.

Figure 6-16 has two RASCAL/2 programs. Fig. 6-16a consists of a
sequence of five assignment statements which are executed sequentially.
Loopfree, as the program is called, fits the pattern of RASCAL/1 programs presented in the last chapter. Figure 6-16b is quite similar to *loopfree,* with one major difference: The fourth assignment statement is surrounded by a **while** loop; otherwise, the programs are identical. Consequently, one would expect the translation of these two programs to also
be identical, except for the explicit code necessary to implement the **while**

```
program  loopfree;
  var   x,y,z: integer;
  begin
    y := 3;
    x := y * y;
    y := y mod x;
    y := x + 1;
    z := y + 1;
  end;
```

(a)

```
program  looped;
  var   x,y,z: integer;
  begin
    y := 3;
    x := y * y;
    y := y mod x;
    while y < 10 do
      y := x + 1;
    z := y + 1;
  end.
```

(b)

Fig. 6-16. *Loopfree* and *Looped*.

loop structure. (Note: These programs have no useful function, so do not ponder what they compute.) Figure 6-17 shows the translation of *loopfree* using register allocation and assignment scheme *two* defined in Chapter 5. Fig. 6-18 gives the corresponding translation of *looped* using the same allocation and assignment scheme. The two translations are identical except for the lines in Fig. 6-18 marked with a dagger which explicitly concern the translation of the **while** statement. In addition, the internal name of the literal '1' has been changed from '@I4' to '@I5', reflecting the occurrence of '10' in the loop predicate which was assigned the internal name '@I4' by CANTOR. The comments to the right of the code indicate the purpose of each of the statements.

We claim that this translation is incorrect! That *looped* has been incorrectly translated becomes apparent when we trace its execution. The program terminates after executing the loop once with $x = 3, y = 10$, and $z = 11$. Figure 6-19 shows a history of the execution of the 360AL version of *looped*. The first time through the loop, the object code faithfully reflects the source code's behavior, but the second time that the loop predicate is evaluated in the 360AL version, it is still true! The reason is that the test whether y is less than 10 in Fig. 6-18 is made under the premise that the current value of y is in register 4, which is not true on the second iteration. The last statement of the loop body stores the contents of register 3 into y. Hence, register 3, not register 4, becomes the current value of y. The comparison code at the top of the loop erroneously makes no allowance for a change in the location of y during the execution of code in the rest of the loop. When we were executing sequential code, this problem could not arise. It is because statements are compiled sequentially (compile-time location of operands) but not necessarily executed sequentially (versus execution-time location of operands) that Fig. 6-18 is incorrect. Figure 6-20 shows the correction which we propose to this problem. At the beginning of the loop, we recognize that the location of various operands may change during loop execution so we "clear the books," by deassigning all operands from registers at the beginning of the loop. In this way, we are forced to reload operand y from memory in order to perform the comparison. No matter how the code in the loop body changes the location of y, we know that at the beginning of the loop, the current value of y must (by definition) be in main memory. Thus, the comparison instruction in Fig. 6-20 compares two memory locations, whereas in Fig. 6-18, a memory location was compared against a register which presuma-

```
LOOPFREE    CSECT
            . . .
            MVC     @I1(4),@I3      y := 3
            L       3,@I1           y * y
            MR      2,3
            ST      3,@I0           x := @T0
            L       4,@I1           y mod x
            SRDA    4,32
            DR      4,3
            ST      4,@I1           y := @T0
            A       3,@I4           x + 1
            ST      3,@I1           y := @T0
            A       3,@I4           y + 1
            ST      3,@I2           z := @T0
@END        L       13,@SAV+4       restore loc old sav area
            LM      14,12,12(13)    restore old registers
            BR      14              return
@SAV        DS      18F             @SAV
@I0         DS      1F              x
@I1         DS      1F              y
@I2         DS      1F              z
@I3         DC      1F'3'           3
@I4         DC      1F'1'           1
            END
```

Fig. 6-17. Translation of *Loopfree*.

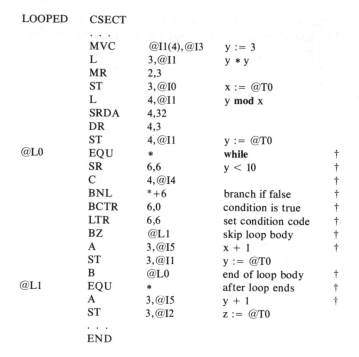

Fig. 6-18. Translation of *Looped*.

register 2 = undefined   register 3 = 9 = x   register 4 = 3 = y
register 5 = undefined   register 6 = undefined
x = 9   y = 3   z = undefined

(a) Status at Entry to Loop (@L0)

register 2 = undefined   register 3 = 10 = y   register 4 = undefined
register 5 = undefined   register 6 = true
x = 9   y = 10   z = undefined

(b) Status after Completion of First Loop Iteration

register 2 = undefined   register 3 = 10 = y   register 4 = undefined
register 5 = undefined   register 6 = true
x = 9   y = 11   z = undefined

(c) Status after Completion of Second Loop Iteration

---

loop execution should have terminated after first iteration, but register 4 still has a three left in it, even though it is unassigned, so loop execution continues indefinitely.

Fig. 6-19. Trace of *Looped*.

```
LOOPED      CSECT
            . . .
            MVC     @I1(4),@I3      y := 3
            L       3,@I1           y * y
            MR      2,3
            ST      3,@I0           x := @T0
            L       4,@I1           y mod x
            SRDA    4,32
            DR      4,3
            ST      4,@I1           y := @T0
@L0         EQU     *               while
            SR      2,2             y < 10
            L       4,@I1
            C       4,@I4
            BNL     *+6             branch if false
            BCTR    2,0             condition is true
            LTR     2,2             set condition code
            BZ      @L1             skip loop body
            L       5,@I0           x + 1
            A       5,@I5
            ST      5,@I1           y := @T0
            B       @L0             end of loop body
@L1         EQU     *               after loop ends come here
            A       5,@I5           y + 1
            ST      5,@I2           z := @T0
            . . .
            END
```

Fig. 6-20. First Revision of *Looped*.

bly held the value of y. Note also that the location of x in register 3 was also lost by deassigning all operands. Hence, in order to increment x by one, CANTOR first loads x into a register in Fig. 6-20, an instruction which is missing in Fig. 6-18.

Despite the changes made to the translation of *looped* in Fig. 6-20, the translation method given is still wrong (although the error will not be apparent from the behavior of *looped* itself). Suppose that instead of testing whether y were less than 10, *looped* tested whether y were less than 0; in that case, the loop predicate would initially be false, and so the entire loop body should be skipped. Our current implementation would do so correctly, but consider the code which follows the loop: It adds one to the current value of y and stores the sum in variable z. At the end of the *compilation* of the **while** loop, y was stored in register 5; hence, the code for the addition of one to y presumes that y is in register 5 already. If the body of the **while** loop is executed even once, this presumption is true, but if the loop body is skipped, then, since y was actually in register 4 at the beginning of the loop's execution, the code to increment y by one refers to the wrong register. Again the problem is simply that the code is compiled sequentially (compile-time location of operands) but not necessarily executed sequentially (versus execution-time location of operands). We can resolve this problem in the same way the entry to the loop was handled, by deassigning all operands on exit from the loop as well. With this second revision in assignment policy for **while** loops, we obtain the correct code shown in Fig. 6-21.

For each control structure a slightly different adjustment in register assignment is necessary. The pseudo-code refinements of the code emitters for these statements in Figs. 6-8 through 6-15 refer to these various adjustments. We have already seen the need to "clear the books" or deassign all operands in two places for **while** loops, at the beginning and at the end of the loop; for the **repeat** loop we need only clear the assignments at the beginning of the loop, since the loop body of a **repeat** statement must be executed at least once. The **if** statement is not a loop, and yet a similar problem arises because code can still be executed conditionally.

```
LOOPED      CSECT
            . . .
            MVC      @I1(4),@I3      y := 3
            L        3,@I1           y * y
            MR       2,3
            ST       3,@I0           x := @T0
            L        4,@I1           y mod x
            SRDA     4,32
            DR       4,3
            ST       4,@I1           y := @T0
@L0         EQU      *               while
            SR       2,2             y < 10
            L        4,@I1
            C        4,@I4
            BNL      *+6             branch if false
            BCTR     2,0             condition is true
            LTR      2,2             set condition code
            BZ       @L1             skip loop body
            L        5,@I0           x + 1
            A        5,@I5
            ST       5,@I1           y := @T0
            B        @L0             end of loop body
@L1         EQU      *               after loop ends come here
            L        2,@I1           y + 1
            A        2,@I5
            ST       2,@I2           z := @T0
            . . .
            END
```

Fig. 6-21. Second Revision of *Looped*.

Since either the **then** clause or the **else** clause of the **if** statement will be executed, but not both (for the more general **if** statement), the status of the "books" at the beginning of the execution of the **then** clause should be the same as the status at the beginning of the **else** clause. Hence, in *emit_then_code* there is a request to push the status of the register assignments onto a "books stack" and to pop it, thereby setting the assignment status to that found at the beginning of the **then** clause when *emit_else_code* is called. This stack is also popped if there is no **else** clause. When the end of the entire statement, with or without **else** clause, is reached, the simplest scheme is to simply clear the register assignments once more. The chapter exercises discuss more complex schemes for this and the other two statements, which do not erase all register assignments if some would be unaffected by the execution-time properties of the statements. Figure 6-22 shows the correct translation of the program in Fig. 6-1.

```
GCD         CSECT
            STM       14,12,12(13)      save registers
            BALR      12,0              set up base register
            USING     *,12
            ST        13,@SAV+4         save loc old save area
            LA        13,@SAV           load addr new save area
            SR        2,2               x > 0
            L         4,@I0
            C         4,@I4
            BNH       *+6               branch if false
            BCTR      2,0               condition is true
            SR        4,4               y > 0
            L         6,@I1
            C         6,@I4
            BNH       *+6               branch if false
            BCTR      4,0               condition is true
            NR        2,4               @T0 and @T1
            LTR       2,2               is @T0 true?
            BZ        @L1               skip then clause if false
            MVC       @I2(4),@I0        a := x
            MVC       @I3(4),@I1        b := y
@L2         EQU       *                 begin repeat loop
@L3         EQU       *                 begin while loop
            SR        2,2               a > b
            L         4,@I2
            C         4,@I3
            BNH       *+6               branch if false
            BCTR      2,0               condition is true
```

Fig. 6-22. Translation of Example Program in Fig. 6-1.

	LTR	2,2	is @T0 true?
	BZ	@L4	exit loop if false
	L	4,@I2	a − b
	S	4,@I3	
	ST	4,@I2	a := @T0
	B	@L3	cycle through **while** loop
@L4	EQU	*	exit point in **while** loop
@L5	EQU	*	begin **while** loop
	SR	2,2	b > a
	L	4,@I3	
	C	4,@I2	
	BNH	*+6	branch if false
	BCTR	2,0	condition is true
	LTR	2,2	is @T0 true?
	BZ	@L6	exit loop if false
	L	4,@I3	b − a
	S	4,@I2	
	ST	4,@I3	b := @T0
	B	@L5	cycle through **while** loop
@L6	EQU	*	exit point in **while** loop
	SR	2,2	a = b
	L	4,@I2	
	C	4,@I3	
	BNE	*+6	branch if false
	BCTR	2,0	condition is true
	LTR	2,2	is @T0 true?
	BZ	@L2	cycle through **repeat** loop
@L1	EQU	*	end of **if** statement
@END	L	13,@SAV+4	restore loc old save area
	LM	14,12,12(13)	restore old registers
	BR	14	return
@SAV	DS	18F	@SAV
@I0	DC	1F'18'	x
@I1	DC	1F'12'	y
@I2	DS	1F	a
@I3	DS	1F	b
@I4	DC	1F'0'	0
	END		

Fig. 6-22. Translation of Example Program in Fig. 6-1 (continued).

6.6   SUMMARY

With the addition of the **if, while** and **repeat** statements, RASCAL/2 has become a reasonably complex language. To implement these new statements, we extended the use of the operand stack to hold labels as well as the operands of operators, which have a direct analog in RASCAL source programs. The register assignment scheme presented in Chapter 5, while quite helpful in reducing the size of object code, also creates problems in correctly assigning registers to operands in the body of **if, while** and **repeat** statements. These problems were resolved by individually adjusting the register assignments as needed for each of the statement types.

RASCAL/2

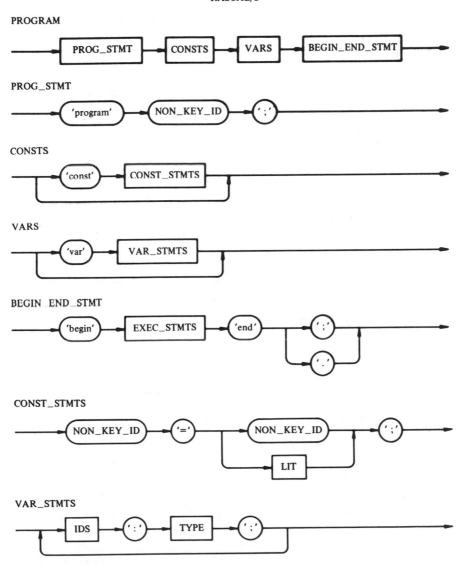

IDS

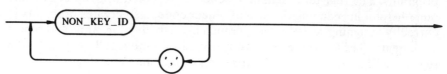

TYPE

LIT

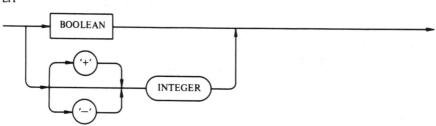

BOOLEAN

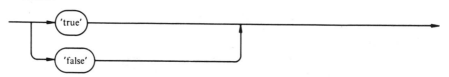

EXEC_STMTS

EXEC_STMT

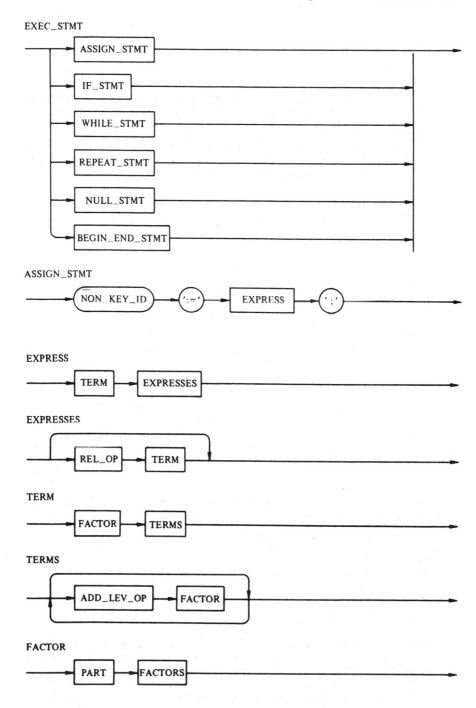

ASSIGN_STMT

EXPRESS

EXPRESSES

TERM

TERMS

FACTOR

FACTORS

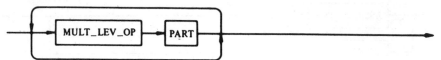

PART

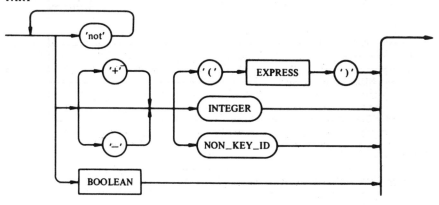

REL_OP

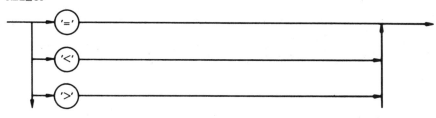

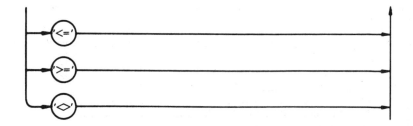

ADD_LEV_OP

MULT_LEV_OP

IF STMT

ELSE_PT

WHILE_STMT

REPEAT_STMT

NULL_STMT

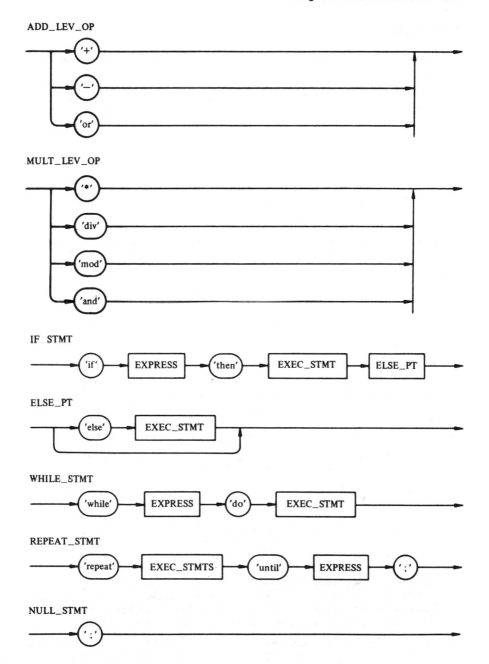

EXERCISES

6-1. The **case** statement with an **otherwise** clause was used extensively in defining CAN-TOR in your text. Describe how you would compile this statement if we added it to RASCAL. Recall that CANTOR is a 1-pass compiler, so your code must be generable in a single pass. Give a description of the compiler's action including how you would handle your register books. You may assume that a **case** statement has the form:

case	NON_KEY_ID **of**
label$_1$:	statement$_1$
label$_2$:	statement$_2$
. . .	
label$_n$:	statement$_n$
otherwise	statement$_{n+1}$

where each label i is an integer literal.

6-2. The **while** statement can be augmented to include a means to exit early from the loop's execution. The **exit** statement must be physically located inside the body of a **while** loop. For example,

```
while   p   do
      begin
            . . .
         exit;
            . . .
      end;
```

When **exit** is executed, control passes to the statement following the end of the loop body. If one **while** is nested inside another, the exit is from the innermost containing loop; for example,

```
while   p   do   begin
            . . .
   while   q   do   begin
                 . . .
            exit;
                 . . .
            end;
   {exit to here}
            . . .
      end;
```

In order to compile the original **while** statement of RASCAL/2, CANTOR/2 created labels and saved them for later reference on *operand_stk*. Show how you would compile the **exit** statement if we added it to RASCAL/2. In particular, give a pseudo-code description of the action routine executed when the **exit** is parsed.

6-3. The **exit** statement (see exercise 6-2) can also be extended to the **repeat-until** loop as well as the **while-do**. Modify RASCAL/2 to include this new form of **repeat-until**, making the necessary changes to the translation grammar and action routines.

6.4. Is the following RASCAL/2 program legal?

```
program isitlegal;
begin
  if true then;
        else;
end.
```

6-5. Is the following RASCAL/2 program legal?

```
program isitlegal;
begin
  repeat
  until true;
end.
```

6-6. Is the following RASCAL/2 program legal?

```
program isitlegal;
begin
  while true do;
end.
```

6-7. A *loop invariant computation* is one which is not affected by the number of iterations of the loop. For example, in the code segment:

```
while (x < 10) do
  begin
    y := 5 div z;
    x := x * y;
  end;
```

The value of z does not change during the iteration of the loop body, and the value of y changes only on the first iteration. Hence, the computation performed for the first assignment statement need not be inside the loop body where it will be executed with every loop iteration. An equivalent loop is:

```
if x < 10 then y := 5 div z;
while (x < 10) do x := x * y;
```

Moving code from inside a loop body to outside that loop is a form of *code migration*. Can this sort of optimization be performed in a one-pass compiler? If so then detail a plan to perform this type of optimization in CANTOR. If not, then pinpoint why it cannot.

6-8. The bookkeeping scheme for register contents detailed in the text "clears" the books upon entry to a **repeat** loop to avoid the problems associated with compile-time versus execution-time location of operands. This is somewhat of a brute force approach to solving this problem. A better solution would be to clear the books only for quantities which are referenced in the loop body. If, for example, the current value of d is in register r before:

```
repeat
  y := y * y;
until (y > 1000);
```

is executed, and register r is not needed for other purposes in the execution of this loop, then the current value of d could be available in register r after the loop has completed execution. Devise a method for incorporating this more sophisticated bookkeeping scheme into CANTOR/2, within the constraint that CANTOR/2 is a single-pass compiler.

6-9. Repeat the modification to the bookkeeping scheme developed in exercise 6-8 for the **while** loop.

6-10. A similar modification to the bookkeeping scheme developed in exercise 6-8 is applicable to the **if-then** and **if-then-else** statements. Determine what is possible, and incorporate it into CANTOR/2.

6-11. Add the **for** loop of PASCAL to RASCAL/2, modifying the translation grammar and action routines appropriately.

TESTING HINTS

1. Test CANTOR/2 on all of the programs used to test CANTOR/1 to ensure no new bugs have crept in or latent ones surfaced.

2. Test CANTOR/2 on one or more programs which:
   a. nest an **if-then-else** inside an **if-then** to ensure the **else** is associated with the correct **if** statement;
   b. nest control structures three deep, both homogeneous nesting and heterogeneous nesting;
   c. have both a simple statement and a **begin-end** statement as the object of a **while**-loop;
   d. have both a simple statement and a compound statement as the object of the **then** and **else** clauses of an **if-then-else** statement;
   e. have just the null statement for the **then** and **else** clauses of an **if-then-else** statement; for the loop body of a **while**-loop; for the **then** clause of an **if-then** statement.

BIBLIOGRAPHY

[Aho and Ullman 77] has an excellent elementary discussion of loop optimization. The strategies discussed there and elsewhere are primarily based on an analysis of the flow of control of the program. [Allen 69] treats the program as a set of strongly connected subgraphs, basing much of the work on the notion of a *dominator*. A node n of a flow graph dominates another node m, if every path from the initial node of the graph to m flows through n. [Lowry and Medlock 69] applied this notion to loop optimization. The "dangling else" problem arises from ALGOL 60, the first common language to offer both the **if-then** and the **if-then-else** constructs. This problem and its solution is treated in [Gries 71]. Many other control structures besides those offered here have been proposed, [Kosaraju 74] presenting a theoretical investigation of many of them. One of the most common control structures not offered here is the **case** statement, which is found in PASCAL ([Wirth 71]) and also in XPL ([McKeeman, et al 70]) among others.

7

Stage 3: Input/Output

7.1 INTRODUCTION

The last chapter of this part of the text deals with input and output procedures. RASCAL/3 has unformatted read and write procedures: **read
readln, write** and **writeln.** These four procedures are standard in PAS-
CAL. With these procedures *integer* and *boolean* values can be read from
the standard input data set, *SYSIN,* and printed to the standard output
data set, *SYSPRINT.* Although there is great utility in being able to print
literal *character* strings in the output, we opt for simplicity here and do
not include them.

The major problem in implementing input and output is *data conversion.* The format for storing data externally on an IBM 360/370 computer
is called *EBCDIC,* which stands for Extended Binary-Coded-Decimal In-
terchange Code. (Many other computers use *ASCII* instead.) Internally,
we have been storing *integers* as binary numbers and *booleans* as *integer*
0 and *integer* −1. Before a *boolean* value can be printed, it must first be
converted from its internal format into its EBCDIC equivalent. Similarly,
before a literal value read from a data set can be assigned to a variable, it
must first be converted from its external EBCDIC format into its binary
encoding. This is quite a tedious chore and, if done in a brute force
manner, is more an exercise in assembly language programming than in
compiling techniques; therefore, we shall take an alternative route to
perform the necessary conversions.

Calls to Input/Output procedures will not be compiled in the same
manner as other statements previously encountered. They will be translated into calls to separately written modules which must be available at
run-time. These *run-time support modules,* as they are called, need not be
written in assembly (machine) language! CANTOR/3 will originally be
written in a high-level language unless the reader is a masochist; it will
then be translated by a compiler for the language in which CANTOR/3 is
written. At that point, we will have a machine language version of
CANTOR/3 which can compile RASCAL programs. By the same token,
an I/0 support module can be written in a high-level language and compiled into machine language. The latter code can be linked to the object

program generated by CANTOR. This linked code forms a complete package which is the translation of the original RASCAL/3 code.

I/O is a very complex activity which is highly operating system dependent. Each operating system has its own interface for error recovery, conversion, and record-handling conventions and policies. Even within the IBM 360/370 environment, critical differences between DOS, OS, VS and various other operating systems make it virtually impossible to implement any compiler which does not show the marks of the operating system it will run under. Since I/O is complex, assembly code to perform it is quite long, compared to the code generation in this text so far. All of these factors support having a routine, not generated by CANTOR, perform the I/O. The routine is passed parameters which specify the particulars of the statements to be interpreted.

The price paid for calling I/O support routines is a degradation in the execution speed of the object program. The overhead of subroutine calls is not trivial in the IBM 360/370 architecture (this is less burdensome in some machines, such as the PDP-11). If the I/O module is originally written in a high-level language and then compiled, the resulting object code is probably not as efficient as a cleverly written hand-coded, assembly language routine would be. However, in this case the advantages of using support routines outweigh the disadvantages, and, of course, such a change in implementation strategies is informative in and of itself.

7.2 RASCAL/3 LANGUAGE FEATURES

Six new keywords have been added to our language:

read, write, readln, writeln, input, output

The first four begin the input and output procedures, respectively while the latter two are parameters of the **program** statement whose form is modified in this chapter. If a program performs any input, it must indicate so in the **program** statement by including a parameter (as defined in the grammar which follows) with the keyword 'input' included; if it performs any output, then the keyword 'output' must appear in the parameter list of the program statement.

Revised Productions:

1. PROG_STMT	→ 'program' NON_KEY_ID	
	(λ {';'} I '(' PROG_PARMS ')' {'('}) ';'	{'program'}
2. EXEC_STMT	→ ASSIGN_STMT	{NON_KEY_ID}
	→ IF_STMT	{'if'}
	→ WHILE_STMT	{'while'}
	→ REPEAT_STMT	{'repeat'}
	→ NULL_STMT	{';'}

→ READ_STMT	{'read', 'readln'}
→ WRITE_STMT	{'write', 'writeln'}
→ BEGIN_END_STMT	{'begin'}

New Productions:

3. PROG_PARMS	→ 'input' (λ {')'} ¦ ',output' {','})	{'input'}
	→ 'output' (λ {')'} ¦ ',input' {','})	{'output'}
4. READ_STMT	→ ('read' {'read'} ¦ 'readln' {'readln'}) READ_LIST ';'	
5. WRITE_STMT	→ ('write' {'write'} ¦ 'writeln' {'writeln'}) WRITE_LIST ';'	
6. READ_LIST	→ '(' IDS ')' {'('} ¦ λ {';'}	
7. WRITE_LIST	→ '(' EXPRESS EXPRESS_LIST ')' {'('} ¦ λ {';'}	
8. EXPRESS_LIST	→ ',' EXPRESS EXPRESS_LIST {','} ¦ λ {')'}	

There are several context-sensitive constraints on these new features not expressed within the grammar. Some concern the detailed execution-time behavior of the **readln** and **writeln** statements; these constraints will be explained shortly. The other three are:

1. All identifiers which appear in a I/O procedure argument list must be declared.
2. All variables which appear in a **write** or **writeln** argument list must have a value when the statement in which they appear is executed.
3. The **program** statement of a program which contains a **read** or **readln** statement must contain the parameter, **'input'**, and one with a **write** or **writeln** statement must contain the **'output'** parameter.

The first two constraints are the same restrictions observed elsewhere in RASCAL. The last restriction is peculiar to the I/O statements.

Both input and output are defined on sequential files only. An implicit file pointer (explicit in PASCAL) indicates the current position in the file being scanned. Suppose:

$$\textbf{readln}(a_1, \ldots, a_n);$$

were executed, where each a_i is a variable name. The program begins by scanning the sequential input file from the character following the last one it read in the previous input, skipping over blanks until it finds the next literal, which is assigned to a_1. The data-type of a_1 and the literal assigned to it must agree. *Integers* may be written either signed or unsigned, with or without leading zeroes. The *boolean* values **true** and **false** appear in the data set *without* quotation marks. No embedded blanks within values are allowed.

After the first variable has been assigned a value (presuming $n > 1$), the file is searched for a second value which is assigned to a_2. The same restrictions apply to the form of the literal and its type as applied to a_1. This cycle repeats until all n variables in the argument list have been assigned values. At this point, characters in the file up to the next *newline* are skipped, so that the file pointer points to the beginning of the next line. Then the execution of the **readln** statement ceases, and control resumes with the next statement in the flow of control. **Read** operates similarly except that the last step which skips to beginning of the next line is omitted.

Successive values in the data set must be separated by at least one blank. *A comma is not a valid separator.* If there are fewer than n values on the first line read, then the next line will be read when the first has been completely scanned for values. If the first two do not contain n values, then the third will be read, and so forth, until enough lines have been read from secondary memory to assign values to all n variables in the list. No value may cross a line boundary, since a *newline* is equivalent to a blank, the value separator. It is an error for the examined data set to contain fewer than n values. If the list is empty, then the file pointer is advanced to the beginning of the next line, but no values are assigned to variables.

The **write** and **writeln** statements output to a sequential file. Suppose

$$\text{writeln}(a_1, \ldots, a_n);$$

were executed, where each a_i is an expression. The value of each argument of the **writeln** statement is printed in a field m characters wide, where m is implementation dependent. *Integer* values are written right-justified in the field in decimal notation. *Boolean* values are also written right-justified in the field as either **'true'** or **'false'** but with no quotation marks. *Integers* are padded on the left with leading zeroes, *booleans* with blanks. All n arguments of the **writeln** statement are on a single line. After the values are printed a *newline* is written. If **write** is used instead, this latter step is omitted. Finally, the field width m must be large enough to hold the largest and smallest *integer* values and must be at least five since **'false'** has five characters.

Although the behavior of the assignment, **if, while,** and **repeat** statements in RASCAL are essentially identical to those found in numerous other languages, input/output details are peculiar to RASCAL. Each language typically has its own unique input/output facilities which differ in important details from those of other languages.

As in earlier chapters, we offer an example program in Fig. 7-1 which correctly illustrates the new input/output statements, which includes both the input data set on which it is executed and the output which it generates. This program computes the greatest common divisor of n pairs of *integers,* where n is a value which is read in from the data set. As such, it is an extension of the example program which illustrated RASCAL/2 features, Fig. 6-1. Figure 7-2 is a syntactically incorrect program, Fig. 7-3

```
program   gcd(input, output);
            {illustrate correct use of RASCAL/3 features.}
            {program computes the greatest common divisor of n pairs of integers, where n is
            read from the data file.}
   var   a,b,n: integer;
   begin
     readln  (n);  {how many pairs do we compute gcd for?}
     while   n > 0 do
       begin
         readln  (a,b);  writeln  (a,b);
         repeat
           while  a > b do  a := a − b;
           while  b > a do  b := b − a;
         until  a=b;
           {a = b = gcd of input pair}
         writeln  (a);
         n := n − 1;  {one less pair to process.}
       end;
   end.
input:   3
         4    2
         5    7
        12    8
output:  +0000000004   +0000000002
         +0000000002
         +0000000005   +0000000007
         +0000000001
         +0000000012   +0000000008
         +0000000004
```

Fig. 7-1. Valid RASCAL/3 Program with Input and Output.

```
program   syntacticallyincorrect;  {forgot 'input' and 'output'.}
            {illustrate incorrect syntactic usage of RASCAL/3 features.}
   const   y = 7;     var   x,w: integer;   z: boolean;
   begin
     readln, (x);       {no comma after 'readln'.}
     readln (y);        {argument must be variable.}
     readln (7);        {argument must be variable.}
     writeln  (x,wz);   {comma required between list elements.}
   end.
```

Fig. 7-2. Invalid RASCAL/3 Program.

```
program   runtimeincorrect(input,output);
          {illustrate run-time error in RASCAL/3 code.}
   var   p,q,r: boolean;
   begin
     readln  (p,q,r);
     if (p and q) or (not p and r) then writeln (true);
     else writeln  (false);
   end.
```

input set 1:   true   false ←————————(too few values)
input set 2:   true   3   false ←————(improper data type)

Fig. 7-3. Valid RASCAL/3 Program with Invalid Data.

is a legal RASCAL/3 program, but the two data sets shown for it violate the constraints of **readln** statements. In the first data set, there are only two values present where three are required; in the second data set, the second value which should be assigned to *boolean* variable *q* is an *integer*. Figure 7-4 gives the input/output behavior of *runtimeincorrect* on valid data sets.

7.3   CANTOR/3 IMPLEMENTATION FEATURES

The definition of RASCAL/3 left certain decisions on formatting up to the implementor. We make those decisions here; in particular, we:

1. set *m* to be 13   (print field width);
2. set the record size of SYSPRINT, the name of the standard output file, to be 133 characters long;
3. set the record size of SYSIN, the name of the standard input file, to be 80 characters long.

input set 1:	true	false	false	
output 1:	false			
input set 2:	false	false false	true	
output 2:	false			
input set 3:	false false	true	true	false
output 3:	true			
input set 4:	false			
	false			
	true			
output 4:	true			

Fig. 7-4. Input/Output Behavior of *runtimeincorrect*.

Obviously, these decisions are somewhat arbitrary but not totally so. The widest *integer* value occupies 11 characters; hence, *m* is 13, so that it will be relatively easy to distinguish visually between two adjacent *integers* printed on a page. The standard printer field on IBM 360/370 equipment is either 121 or 132 characters, but the student should adjust the field width to suit the equipment available to him. The standard input record size is 80 characters.

With these parameters, we can print at most ten values on a single printer line. The major deficiency in this input/output mechanism, besides the obvious lack of formatting, is the inability to print character string messages to improve the readability of the output. However, since we have not yet introduced the *character* data type into RASCAL (it first appears in Chapter 9), we shall forgo this input/output enhancement.

7.4 CANTOR/3 TRANSLATION GRAMMAR

Revised Productions:

1. PROG_STMT $\rightarrow$ 'program' NON_KEY_ID$_x$
                 $(\lambda_y \mid$ '(' PROG_PARMS$_y$ ')') ';'
                 code('*program*',*x*,*y*)

2. EXEC_STMT $\rightarrow$ ASSIGN_STMT
                 $\rightarrow$ IF_STMT
                 $\rightarrow$ WHILE_STMT
                 $\rightarrow$ REPEAT_STMT
                 $\rightarrow$ NULL_STMT
                 $\rightarrow$ READ_STMT
                 $\rightarrow$ WRITE_STMT
                 $\rightarrow$ BEGIN_END_STMT

New Productions:

3. PROG_PARMS $\rightarrow$ 'input' $(\lambda \mid$ ',output')
                  $\rightarrow$ 'output' $(\lambda \mid$ ',input')

4. READ_STMT $\rightarrow$ ('read'$_x$ $\mid$ 'readln'$_x$) READ_LIST$_y$ ';' *code*(*x*,*y*)

5. WRITE_STMT $\rightarrow$ ('write'$_x$ $\mid$ 'writeln'$_x$) WRITE_LIST$_y$ ';' *code*(*x*,*y*)

6. READ_LIST $\rightarrow$ '(' IDS ')' $\mid \lambda$

7. WRITE_LIST $\rightarrow$ '(' EXPRESS_LIST ')' $\mid \lambda$

8. EXPRESS_LIST $\rightarrow$ ',' EXPRESS EXPRESS_LIST $\mid \lambda$

```
procedure  emit_prologue(program_name, file_names: string);
        {emit the program prologue.}
    begin
      emit CSECT labeled by the first eight characters of program_name;
      emit(, 'STM', '14,12,12(13)', 'save registers');
      emit(, 'BALR', '12,0', 'set up base register');
      emit(,   'USING', '*+12');
      emit(, 'ST', '13,@SAV+4', 'save loc old save area');
      emit(, 'LA', '13,@SAV', 'load addr new save area');
      emit call to @IO telling it the file names;
    end;
```

Fig. 7-5. Emit_Prologue.

7.5   CODE GENERATION

There are five new calls to *code* in this revision of CANTOR:

$$code('program',x,y,)$$
$$code('readln',y)$$
$$code('writeln',y)$$
$$code('read',y)$$
$$code('write',y)$$

The first call is actually a modification of the earlier version:

$$code('program',x)$$

where the value of x is the name of the program. The new argument, y, is the parameter list which may either be **'input'**, **'output'**, or both. The refinement for this new version of *emit_prologue* is given in Fig. 7-5. It simply adds a call to @IO, the I/O module, which in this case transmits the name of each declared file.

Figures 7-6 and 7-7 show the specification of the routines which call @IO to perform reading and writing. @IO itself may easily be implemented in any high-level language. Note that if @IO is to perform error checks, it will need symbol table items about each argument of an I/O statement. This may be passed just for these items, or the entire table might be made available to @IO.

```
procedure emit_readln_code (arg_list : string);
    begin
      emit code which calls @IO passing
      it arg_list and a request
      to read;
    end;
```

Fig. 7-6. Emit_readln_code.

```
procedure  emit_writeln_code (arg_list : string);
  begin
    emit code to call @IO with arguments
    arg_list and a request to write to SYSPRINT;
  end;
```

Fig. 7-7. *Emit_writeln_code.*

7.6 SUMMARY

Input/output statements have been added to RASCAL. Their processing by CANTOR is largely an exercise in data conversion, operating system conventions, and assembly language programming rather than in new compiling techniques. Unfortunately, nearly all compilers suffer from this problem, since classical computers have very primitive input/output instructions and data conversion facilities.

PROGRAM

PROG_STMT

CONSTS

VARS

BEGIN_END_STMT

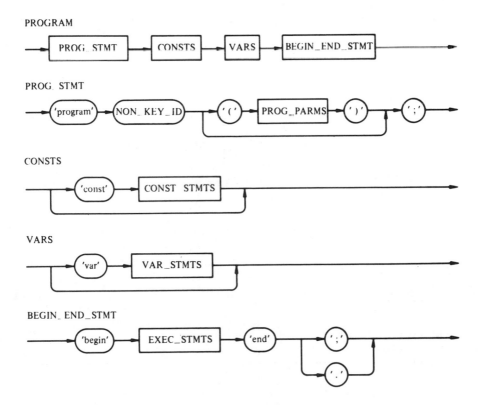

CONST_STMTS

VAR_STMTS

IDS

TYPE

LIT

BOOLEAN

EXEC_STMT

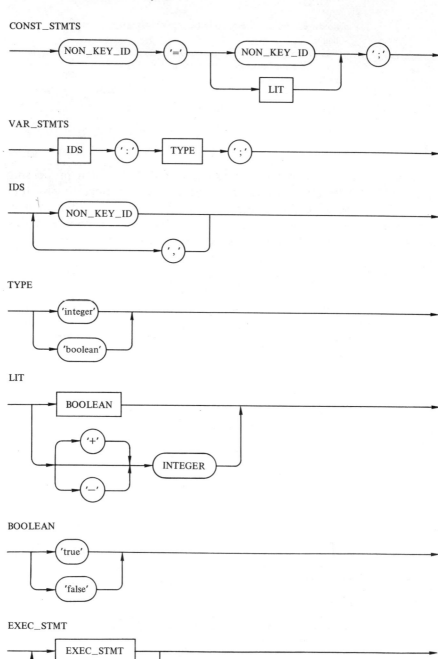

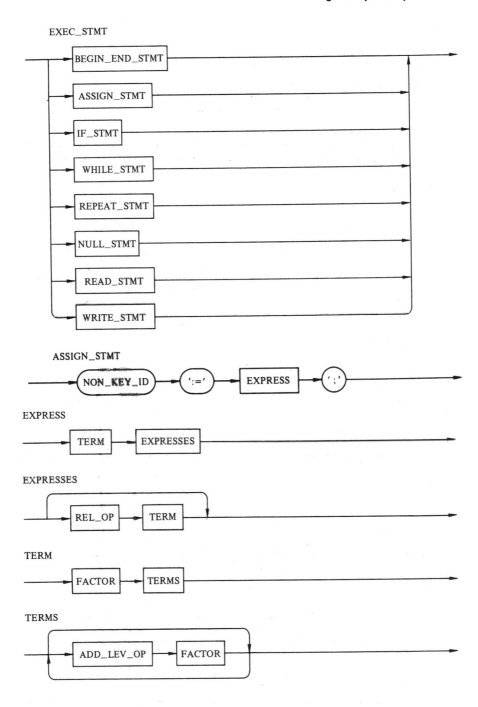

FACTOR

FACTORS

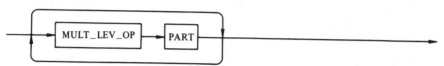

PART

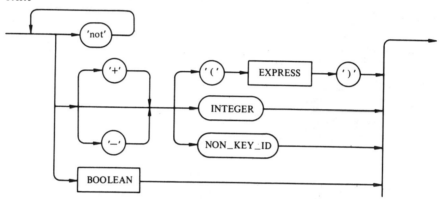

REL_OP

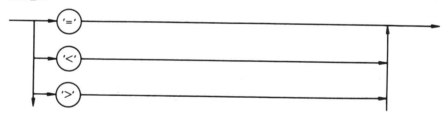

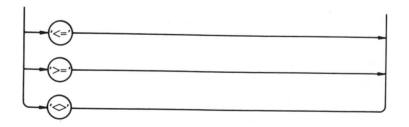

ADD_LEV_OP

MULT_LEV_OP

IF_STMT

ELSE_PT

WHILE_STMT

REPEAT_STMT

NULL_STMT

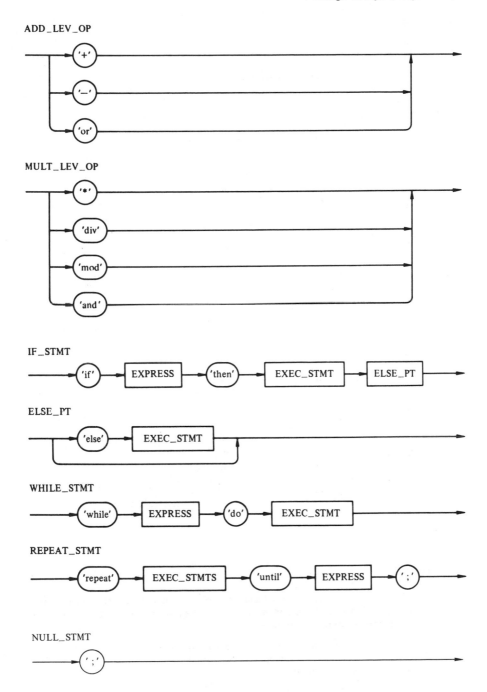

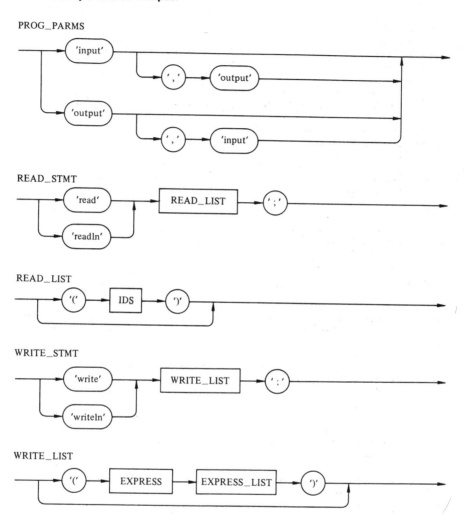

PROG_PARMS

READ_STMT

READ_LIST

WRITE_STMT

WRITE_LIST

EXERCISES

7-1. Add to RASCAL/3 the facility to read and write to non-standard files. The name of each file must be included in the argument list of the **program** statement. The **readln** and **writeln** statements are revised to be:

> **readln** (file-name,   argument-list);
> **writeln** (file-name,   argument-list);

and similarly for **read** and **write.**

Each non-standard file must be declared:

file-name: file **of char;**

We explicitly open a file for input by:

reset (file-name);

or for output by:

rewrite (file-name);

and close it by:

close (file-name);

7-2. Modify the **writeln** statement, so that if the length of the values being printed exceeds one record length, the output will be continued onto succeeding records as required.

7-3. Modify the **readln** statement so that a comma becomes a valid delimiter between input values along with the blank.

7-4. Suppose we wished to modify CANTOR so that it produced *machine* code directly rather than assembly code.

    a. What additional problems would arise? Be specific!
    b. How could we solve them?
    c. Do you believe it is really a good idea for a compiler to generate assembly code rather than machine code? Why?

7-5. Add a *boolean* function **eof** (file-name) which returns true if the last value has been read and false otherwise.

TESTING HINTS

1. Test CANTOR/3 on all of the programs you used to test CANTOR/2.

2. Test the **read** and **readln** statements on a data set which has:
    a. one completely blank line at the beginning of the file;
    b. one or more completely blank lines in the middle of the file;
    c. multiple values on a single line;
    d. single values on a single line;
    e. more values on a line than should be read in;
    f. a mix of both *boolean* and *integer* values on a single line;
    g. *integer* values with and without signs (both '+' and '−');
    h. a value beginning the first line of the file;
    i. a value ending the last line of the file;
    j. an empty file;
    k. a value ending the last character of a line;
    l. a value beginning the first character of a line;
    m. an *integer* with leading zeroes.

3. Test the **read** and **readln** statements with an argument list which:
    a. is empty;
    b. has fewer members than there are values on a single line;

c. has more members than there are values on a single line;
d. has only *boolean* arguments;
e. has only *integer* arguments;
f. has a mix of *boolean* and *integer* arguments.

4. Test the **write** and **writeln** statements with an argument list which:
   a. is empty;
   b. has fewer members than will occupy a complete line;
   c. has exactly enough members to occupy a complete line;
   d. has only *boolean* arguments;
   e. has only *integer* arguments;
   f. has a mix of *boolean* and *integer* arguments;
   g. has literals, constants, and variables of both data-types.

BIBLIOGRAPHY

Input/output is the black sheep of programming language definition. Because it seems so heavily dependent on the quirks of the implementation environment, it is often specified only vaguely in a language definition; the ALGOL 60 report ([Naur 63]) does not define the input/output features of that language at all! Their selection and implementation were left entirely in the hands of the compiler-writers. Even more recent efforts in language definition have not solved the input/output problem: PASCAL ([Wirth 71]) does not have an adequate set of input/output routines defined within it.

Part 3.
An Advanced
RASCAL Compiler

In Part 2, a compiler for a major subset of RASCAL was designed and developed. This subset was chosen to illustrate many features commonly found in programming languages and also to illustrate a number of considerations with which language implementors must concern themselves. In the third part, we build upon the foundation laid earlier by extending the features of RASCAL and CANTOR.

Chapter 8 introduces the topic of *error processing*. Throughout Part 2, we presumed that all RASCAL source programs submitted to CANTOR were completely correct with respect to the language specifications, an assumption which simplified the design and implementation of CANTOR considerably. However, all programmers make errors, and no implementation is complete without some ability to process those mistakes. Chapter 8 presents techniques for handling errors.

Chapter 9 augments RASCAL itself, not just its implementation. Here we shall add five new data-types to RASCAL: *real* numbers, *character* strings, *arrays, enumerated scalars* and *enumerated sets*. With the inclusion of these five data-types, RASCAL becomes almost as powerful a language as FORTRAN or PASCAL or other common languages. The one major feature which is missing is the ability to divide a program into simpler components. In RASCAL these take the form of *procedures* and *functions* which we introduce in Chapter 10. Two parameter passing techniques will be explored, *call by value* and *call by reference,* the two major methods implemented in most languages; in addition, we shall add the notion of *block structure* to RASCAL at this time.

The last chapter of the text addresses more diagnostic tools. Facilities to generate a *cross-reference map, dump variable values on request,* and *profile* the execution of a program's statements will be incorporated into CANTOR. In addition, we shall examine programmer-defined error conditions raised by embedding *assertions* into source code.

The chapters of Part 3 have been written independently; i.e., the student may study the material of Chapters 8 through 11 without regard to order, leaving both the student and the instructor with the greatest flexibility in organizing the presentation of this material. We strongly urge, however, that the student complete the study of all material in Parts 1 and 2 before reading further.

8
Stage 4: Error Processing

8.1 INTRODUCTION

In Part 2, we assumed that RASCAL source programs had no errors of any kind, a grossly unrealistic assumption with respect to the real world of programming. However, error processing is complex enough a topic that it was best to postpone its study until a basic compiler had been constructed. Now that this task has been completed, we turn to methods for handling the three stages of error processing:

1. detection
2. reporting
3. recovery

The first stage in error processing is the *detection* of an error. Errors can be detected either during compilation or during execution of the object code. The former are called *compile-time* errors, the latter *run-time* errors. Compile-time errors are, naturally enough, detected by the compiler during translation. In CANTOR, such errors may be detected by any major component including the scanner, parser, or action routines. Typical compile-time errors include mismatched parentheses and an illegal data-type for an operand. Run-time errors are detected either by the operating system in conjunction with the hardware (such as division by zero) or by code inserted into the target program by CANTOR specifically to test for certain error conditions (undefined variable value when referenced). Once an error is detected, it must be *reported* both to the user and to a routine which will process the error. The user must be informed of the nature of the error and its probable location, as well as the action which was taken in response to its detection, which is normally done by printing a diagnostic message on the program listing.

In addition to reporting the error, some action must be taken to *recover* from it, since normal processing is, by definition, impossible. This action can be as abrupt as the termination of program processing (compiler or object code), or it can be as sophisticated as an intelligent "guess" as to the probable intent of the programmer and suitable modifications to the program to effect that guess. Typically, the response to errors will vary between these extremes, depending on the nature and severity of the detected error and the sophistication of the implementation.

8.2   DETECTION

The first stage of error processing is *detection,* where the error is uncovered, and is broken into two major categories: those suited for compile-time and those suited for execution-time.

8.2.1   Detecting Compile-Time Errors

Each major compiler component can detect a different class of errors. The first of these is the scanner, which can detect *lexical* errors.

8.2.1.1   *Detecting Lexical Errors*

Within the scanner, which is called *next_token* in CANTOR, there are several places where it tests whether the tokens encountered are legal in any possible context. The scanner does not attempt to determine whether a token it encounters is legal in the context in which it appears, a task reserved for other compiler components.

An example of an error detected by the scanner is an unterminated comment. The scanner must remove all comments from the source code. It is erroneous, of course, to begin a comment but never terminate it, an act which would be detected by encountering the end of the source file before encountering the end of the comment denoted by '}'. Similarly, there is a well-defined set of characters which may belong to any token. The scanner detects the presence of an unexpected character by the **otherwise** clause of the **case** statement around which the entire scanner is organized.

8.2.1.2   *Detecting Syntactic Errors*

In each chapter of Part 2, we presented an LL(1) context-free grammar which defined the syntactic aspects of that chapter's changes to RASCAL. In Figs. 4-10 through 4-17, we explicitly defined a parser in pseudo-code constructed from the grammar given in that chapter. In all cases the parser expects certain tokens or token classes to appear at certain points in the source code. In each case, the parser explicitly tests whether its expectations are satisfied. If so, then it continues with its normal processing; otherwise, the normal routine of the parser is interrupted, and an error processing routine is called. If tests such as those just described are made at each point where a token is expected, the parser will be able to detect all syntactic errors in this manner. Hopefully, the reader, in his extensions to the parser given in Chapter 4, made the same tests for errors.

A GDTGP will detect all errors except syntactic ones in the same manner as a recursive descent processor. Syntactic errors are always detected at the earliest possible moment with no special effort on the part of the grammar writer. When comparing a source terminal in the current sentential form against the next token, a failure to match is detected immediately, as will be an attempt to expand a nonterminal in the current sentential form against the next token, if that token in not the selection set of an alternative production for that nonterminal.

8.2.1.3 Detecting Semantic Errors

Semantic errors are detected by the action routines called within the parser; for example, *insert* tests whether a name which is to be inserted into the symbol table already has an entry there. A violation of the semantic constraint within RASCAL that a name may be declared just once would be detected by this check within *insert*.

The adequate detection of semantic errors is a place where most commercial compilers fail. For example, in FORTRAN it is illegal for a statement to branch from outside the scope of a DO-loop into the interior of the scope of that loop. This constraint cannot be expressed by any context-free grammar of FORTRAN and, as such, is by definition a semantic constraint. Neither the IBM FORTRAN G nor the FORTRAN H compilers detect violations of this constraint; on the other hand, the WATFIV implementation of FORTRAN does.

Because the context-sensitive constraints of RASCAL as defined in Part 2 can all be easily checked—usually by a reference to the symbol table, it is quite easy to include this error detection capability in CANTOR. The pseudo-code definitions of the relevant action routines already contain some of these checks. The reader should identify where checks for errors are missing and isolate the appropriate routines and code needed to perform these tests.

RASCAL has been designed in part to facilitate easy detection of semantic errors, but in some languages there are features which require more effort on the compiler's part to detect errors; the branch into the scope of a DO-loop cited earlier is one such feature. In order to detect this error, the compiler must analyze the structure of the program in order to determine from what points in the code references to labels are legal. While the amount of work required for this task is not inordinate, it is nontrivial. FORTRAN has numerous other semantic constraints, each of which requires special handling in order to detect violations—and FORTRAN is a rather simple language. This is the primary reason why most implementations ignore at least some semantic constraints of the source language being compiled.

8.2.1.4   Detecting Compiler Errors

The last category of compile-time errors deals with malfunctions within the compiler itself rather than in RASCAL source programs. A correct program could be incorrectly compiled because of a bug in CANTOR, in which case, the user has little choice but to report the error to the system staff and to "massage" his program in such a way as to eliminate the error, a course of action possible only if the user is aware there is a bug in the compiler! Unless the compiler is instrumented with code to check itself periodically for errors, it may not detect malfunctions. Without detection and subsequent reporting of such errors, the user might not even become aware of a problem, or he might waste time trying to debug *his* program, mistakenly believing it is an error on his part.

Although we have not made extensive efforts to instrument CANTOR with self-checking code, at a few key places, self-checking code has been inserted. For example, the push and pop routines for *operand_stk* and *operator_stk* check for overflow and underflow, respectively. An overflow error may not be too serious in that all that may be necessary is an increase in the stack size. An underflow error indicates a compiler malfunction, since there should be one push executed for each pop. Of course, the compiler executes under the guiding hand of the operating system to which it, for example, calls for I/O. A nasty compiler problem is a failure which is detected by the operating system, such as an intermediate file overflowing or perhaps a division by zero attempted during botched compile-time arithmetic. This problem pervades compiler writing in all environments and machines.

8.2.2   Detecting Run-Time Errors

Run-time errors can be detected either by i) the *execution environment* (hardware + operating system); or by ii) code inserted into the object program by the compiler specifically to perform certain checks.

8.2.2.1   Errors Detected by the Execution Environment

The object program executes within an *environment* which we shall define as the hardware plus the operating system. The environment interfaces with the user program and has certain expectations about its behavior. When these expectations are not met, the environment may treat that as an error. For example, on the IBM 360/370 family and on nearly all computers, it is illegal to attempt an *integer* division by zero. In general, it is not possible to determine at compile-time whether such an error will ever arise. The hardware itself, in the case of the IBM machines, will detect any attempt to perform an *integer* division by zero.

The other half of the environment is the operating system, whose complexity can vary from literally nothing on some microcomputers to an immense system such as OS/360. We presume in this chapter that CANTOR emits programs which will be run under OS. One of the important functions of OS/360 is to assist the user program in its input/output operations. If the user program attempts to read past the end of a data file, the operating system will treat this attempt as an error.

8.2.2.2   Errors Detected by Compiler-Embedded Code

The final class of errors which we shall consider are detected by 360AL code inserted into the object program by the compiler specifically for the purpose of error detection. The need for such code arises when the object code version of a source program is expected to obey certain constraints which are part of the source language or implementation definition but are not constraints imposed by the execution environment itself. For example, each program variable of a RASCAL program is represented in the object version as a location in memory. Logically, a program variable has no defined value until it is given one during execution, either as the result of an input or an assignment statement. Physically, however, the location which represents that variable has some binary value stored in it at all times, including when the object program is loaded into main memory. Thus, an illegal reference to an undefined variable (with respect to RASCAL) is translated into a perfectly legal reference to a memory location (with respect to 360AL). This deficiency in the output of CANTOR/3 could cause erratic program behavior, since each time the program is loaded into memory, a different value may be stored in the location reserved for the undefined program variable. To overcome this particular problem, CANTOR can insert code into the object program which tests whether a variable has been assigned a value when it is referenced. This code may be emitted at the beginning of the relevant code emitting procedures called within *code*. Figure 8-1 shows a revised version of *emit_addition_code*, which does precisely this through a call to *is_defined*, a routine which emits the necessary test code:

$$\begin{array}{lll} \text{CLI} \quad @T\text{nDF, X'00'} & \text{if variable is defined,} & (8.1) \\ \text{BNE} \quad *+k & \text{branch around error code} \\ \textit{code, k-4 bytes long,} \\ \textit{which reports and} \\ \textit{recovers from error} \end{array}$$

where T is 'I' if the variable is **integer** and 'B' if it is **boolean.** The code which reports and recovers from the error will be discussed in the sections of this chapter dealing with those topics.

The detection code just given references a flag, $@T\text{nDF}$. For each variable which is declared in the program, such a flag must be created. This can be accomplished by modifying the translation grammar production for variable declarations to be:

$$\text{VAR\_STMTS} \rightarrow \text{IDS}_x \quad \text{':'} \quad \text{TYPE}_y \quad \text{';'}$$
$$\textit{insert(x,y,mutable,,yes,1)}$$
$$\textit{create\_flag(x)} \text{ (VAR\_STMTS} \mid \lambda \text{)}$$

where *create_flag* is an action routine which inserts an entry into the symbol table for each variable in x. For variable 'z' in x, the fields of this entry have the values:

mode=mutable, data_type=byte, alloc=yes,
units=1, internal_name='$@T\text{nDF}$', value=X'00'

where $@T\text{n}$ is the internal name of 'z'. Note that the flag defined for each variable is initialized to X'00' indicating that the variable is undefined. When a value is assigned to the variable, either through an assignment or an input statement, code should be emitted which changes the flag's value to X'FF' or any other non-zero value. Such code is easily inserted into the

```
procedure   emit_addition_code(operand1,operand2: string);
            {add operand2 to operand1, checking whether both operands have values.}
    var    result_reg: 2 . . 11;
    begin
       emit code which tests whether operand1 is defined;
       emit code which tests whether operand2 is defined;
       if   either operand is not an integer then
           . . .    {same code as in Fig. 5-18}
    end;
```

Fig. 8-1. *Emit_addition_code.*

code emitters for the assignment and input statements:

MVI   @TnDF,X'FF'   show variable is defined

This is just one example of where an error can be detected at run-time by compiler generated object code. The chapter exercises address others, but in the main chapter body, we shall consider only this one run-time error in depth.

It should be obvious to the reader that it is much easier for the compiler to detect errors rather than the object program. The compiler is (presumably) written in a high-level language with tools to assist the compiler writer in expressing the concepts with which he is modeling his solutions to compiling problems. Typically, assembly languages hinder such abstraction, and, in this respect, 360AL is no exception. From the viewpoint of how easy a task the implementor faces, it is better for him to be able to detect errors during compilation when the tools he has available for that detection are more sophisticated. Aside from simply easing the implementor's burden, there is another reason for wishing to detect errors during compilation rather than during execution. Efficiency of the object code is adversely affected by the insertion of instructions which test for errors, both with respect to program size and execution speed. Once a program has been debugged, it normally is compiled one last time and its object code version is saved. This object program may be executed dozens, perhaps hundreds or even thousands of times without ever needing recompilation. Error checking during the execution of this code is very expensive because it must be repeated during every run of the program (perhaps many times per run). The compiler, on the other hand, performs a test just once on a program, a cost that is borne only during program development, not after installation.

For the sake of both object code efficiency and implementation ease, it is usually best to perform as many error checks as possible during compilation. In the case of RASCAL, the language has been designed to facilitate compile-time error checking. For example, in RASCAL the data-type of a variable is declared at the beginning of a program and once declared may not change during the course of program execution. Furthermore, the language does not provide for automatic conversions between data-types when a value other than of an expected type is encountered (with an exception noted in Chapter 9 on *real* numbers). By examining the program text alone, it is possible to tell whether the result of an expression will have type *boolean* or type *integer* in RASCAL/3. Hence, in an **if, while,** or **repeat** statement, where a *boolean* valued expresion is expected, the compiler can determine whether the source code meets those expectations. In a language not oriented to compile-time error checking, one could imagine a different situation: The *integer* one could be converted to *true* and the *integer* zero to *false,* in accordance with rather standard conventions. In that case a statement such as:

if x **then** . . .   {x is an *integer.*}

could be syntactically and semantically correct at compile-time but erroneous at execution-time, if *x* ever takes on a value other than *integer* zero or one when this statement is executed.

The implementation of a language which permits more automatic conversions between data-types than RASCAL must insert more run-time checks into the object code. RASCAL trades a certain degree of flexibility in program design for an added measure of simplicity in the behavior of RASCAL programs and the effort it takes to implement RASCAL compilers. We have just stressed the fact that it is more efficient to check for errors at compile-time rather than at run-time. With this fact in mind, we shall briefly re-examine the scheme just presented for detecting when a variable has been declared, but not defined, prior to referencing its value. The scheme inserts additional 360AL statements into the object code which performs this check. This code is inserted just prior to the occurrence of *each* variable reference in the program. While this is certainly a valid approach to determining whether a variable is defined, it is not as efficient as it might be. Upon reflection, we shall see that much of this code is redundant, in that at some points in a program, it is impossible for a variable to be undefined. By detecting those points at compile-time, we can avoid emitting the run-time detection code, thereby reducing the size of the object code and increasing its execution speed with no loss of error-detection capabilities.

Our strategy for reducing the amount of run-time checking rests on the notion of a *flow path.* At each *decision point* of a program (the predicate of an **if, while,** or **repeat** statement which determines the flow of control to the next statement), we choose between two paths to follow; for example, at the beginning of a **while** loop, we choose either to execute the loop body or to skip past that body entirely. Until the next decision point is reached, the flow of control is entirely determined by the physical ordering of the program statements. By making a series of decisions at successive decision points, the flow control through a program is determined. A *flow path* is simply the sequence of statements executed in a program by one particular series of decisions at the decision points encountered during program execution. A program which has no decision points, as is true for all programs written in RASCAL/1, has only one flow path. A program with a single **if** statement has two paths. A program with either a **while** or a **repeat** statement has an infinite number of paths, each one corresponding to a different number of iterations of the loop. Figure 8-2 shows some of the flow paths for the GCD program of Fig. 7-1.

On any given flow path, if variable x is defined when statement i is executed, then for all statements executed later, variable x is still defined. This may seem absurdly obvious, but it is not true in all languages. For example, in FORTRAN, after a DO-loop has terminated normally, the loop index variable becomes undefined! RASCAL has no such feature, nor any other feature which could cause a defined variable to become undefined. Since no variable can become undefined on a single flow path, if variable x is undefined at reference i, then it was undefined at all earlier references (1 . . (i-1)) along that path as well. In order to determine whether a variable is undefined, we need only guarantee that the first reference to that variable along each path is tested. The particular strategy for doing this depends upon the language features. In our case, we shall presume only the features of RASCAL/3.

The algorithm which determines whether or not testing code should be emitted at any given point requires a stack which represents the various paths through the program. Each stack element will be a list of variable names. As decision points are reached, new elements will be pushed onto the stack, and at the end of those control statements, elements will be popped off. We shall find it convenient in this case to have a separate stack just for this purpose, rather than to overcrowd the already heavily worked *operand_stk* or *operator_stk*. We call our new stack *test_stk* to indicate its purpose in error-testing.

When the first **begin** statement of the program is encountered, all variable names are pushed onto the stack as a single element. These are the

flow path 1:
  readln (n);   **readln** (a,b);   **writeln** (a,b);   a := a − b;
  writeln (a);   n := n − 1;

flow path 2:
  readln (n);

flow path 3:
  readln (n);   **readln** (a,b);   **writeln** (a,b);   b := b − a;
  b := b − a;   a := a − b;   **writeln** (a);   n := n − 1;
  readln (a,b);   **writeln** (a,b);   a := a − b;   b := b − a;
  b := b − a;   b := b − a;   a := a − b;   **writeln** (a);
  n := n − 1;

flow path 4: . . .   (there is an infinite number of paths)

Fig. 8-2. Flow Paths for the Program in Fig. 7-1.

names of all variables which must be undefined at this point in the program (initially all variables are undefined, since there is no compile-time initialization in RASCAL/3). As each variable name is encountered in a statement, we take one of three actions, depending on whether that encounter references the current value of the variable or assigns it a value:

> **if** *variable x is being referenced* **and** *x is*
> *in the top of test_stk* **then begin**
>   *emit test code;*
>   *remove x from top of test_stk;* **end;**
> **else if** *variable x is being defined* **and** *x*
>   *is in the top of test_stk* **then**
>   *remove x from top of test_stk;*
> **else** {x has already been defined or tested
>   on this path so do nothing}
>   ;

If a variable has already been assigned a value or been tested along this flow path, we do not bother to emit test code because the program could never fail the test.

It is obvious that this scheme works properly for code in which there are no decision points; i.e., no **if, while,** or **repeat** statements. It can be inserted at the beginning of each code generator routine which references one or more operands, rather than emitting the unconditional emission code shown in Fig. 8-1; however, this scheme will not work without modification when control statements are present. The only changes necessary are the pushing and popping of stack elements when these control statements are encountered. The actions to be taken when variable names are encountered do not change.

The simplest control statement to analyze is the **repeat.** It turns out that we must do nothing special when encountering this statement because the code in the loop body must be executed at least once; hence, for purposes of testing, we compile the **repeat** loop as if it were sequential code. The **while** statement differs from the **repeat** in that the loop body may be skipped. After the loop predicate is compiled, we create a copy of the current top of *test_stk* and push it onto *test_stk.* At this point the top two stack entries are identical. We are *saving* the current testing environment which we shall restore after compiling the loop body. Inside the loop body, we reference the new top of *test_stk.* Variables which either become defined or are tested have their names removed from the top of *test_stk.* When the end of the loop body is encountered, *test_stk* is popped, restoring the old testing environment which existed prior to encountering the **while** statement. We created a local testing environment for the **while** statement which is lost after the end of the loop is encountered, because the loop is conditionally executed. If it is skipped, then the tests and assignments made in the loop body will not be applicable to the code which is subsequently executed. The only variables which we can presume have either been defined or tested are those which were defined or tested prior to entering the **while** loop.

The **if** statement is similar to the **while** in that code is conditionally executed. After the statement predicate has been compiled, we create a copy of the current top of *test_stk* and push it onto the top of *test_stk*. Again, at this point the top two stack entries are identical. Inside the **then** clause we reference the new top of *test_stk*. Variables which either become defined or tested inside this clause have their names removed from the top of *test_stk*. When the end of the **then** clause is encountered, we take one of two actions depending on whether an **else** clause is present. If no **else** clause is indicated, we simply pop *test_stk* to restore the environment to its status prior to entering the **then** clause. We must do so because the **then** clause, like the **while** loop body, is conditionally executed. If an **else** clause is present, then we not only pop *test_stk*, we also push a fresh copy of the new top of *test-stk* (environment prior to encountering the **then** clause) back onto *test_stk*. The same logic which applied to the **then** clause applies to the **else** clause. When the entire **if** statement has been compiled, we again pop *test_stk*, restoring the environment we had prior to encountering the **then** clause. More succinctly:

encounter	*action*
repeat	nothing special;
while	after compiling predicate, push a copy of current top of *test_stk* onto *test_stk*;
end of **while**	pop *test_stk*;
if	after predicate, push a copy of current top of *test_stk* onto *test_stk*;
end of **then** clause — no **else**	pop *test_stk*;
end of **then** clause — with **else**	pop *test_stk*; push a copy of current top of *test_stk* onto *test_stk*;
end of **else** clause	pop *test_stk*;

```
program   runtimetest(input, output);
          {show places where code is inserted to test
            whether a variable is defined when referenced.}
   const   size = 10;
   var   b,c,d: integer;
   begin
     readln (b);
        {from this point on no tests for b.}
     if b > 0   then begin
       readln (c);
          {from this point on in the then clause, no tests for c;}
       while (c > size) do begin  {don't check on constants.}
         if c < b   then readln (d);
         if c < d   then   {test for d here.}
           writeln (d); {don't test for d here.}   end;
       end;
     if c < 7 then writeln (d);   {must test for d and c here.}
     else   writeln (b);   {don't test for b here.}
   end;
```

Fig. 8-3. Sample RASCAL/3 Program Showing Points Where Run-Time Checking Code Must Be Inserted.

Figure 8-3 shows a RASCAL/3 program indicating the points where testing code would be inserted.

This strategy for inserting testing code is nearly optimal for RASCAL/3. One improvement centers around the **if** statement. The strategy described for **if** statements will not eliminate all redundant tests. We leave it as an exercise for the reader to identify under what circumstances improvement is possible, and to make the necessary modifications.

8.3   REPORTING

Once an error is detected, it must be reported both to the user and to whatever agent will handle that error. Typically, the user receives one or more messages on his program listing informing him of the detection of that error. In this section we shall concentrate on the form of these messages and how they are generated.

8.3.1   Compile-Time Reporting

An error detected by the compiler should be reported by the compiler as well. The style and content of the message presented to the user can have a considerable impact on his ability to correct the cause of that error. Several characteristics of proper messages are:

1. The messages should be specific, pinpointing the place in the program where the error was detected as closely as possible; furthermore, this reference should be with respect to the user's source program, not the object code generated by the compiler (or perhaps both as an option). For normal debugging of a high-level language program, a user should never have to refer to the object code.

2. The messages should be written in clear, unambiguous English phrases and complete sentences, never in cryptic terms significant only to language experts or persons familiar with the implementation details (with the possible exception of compiler errors, to assist the people who must debug the compiler). Never list just a message code number such as "error number 34," forcing the user to refer to a manual he may not have handy or even available at all at the time he is debugging the program.

3. The messages should not be redundant. Certain compilers (PL/I F is notorious for this) tend to repeat the same message over and over for what is essentially the same single error; for example, if a variable is not declared, it is only necessary to print that fact once, not every time it is referenced.

4. The messages should indicate to the extent possible, the nature of the error discovered; for example, if a colon were expected but not found, then the message should say just that and not "syntax error" or "missing symbol."

5. The messages should indicate the exact action taken by the compiler in response to an error; for example, a compiler might choose to ignore an erroneous statement, attempt to "patch" the error with a guess as to the programmer's intentions or even terminate compilation altogether if the error is severe enough, such as a compiler error.

There are two common formats for presenting error messages, some implementations offering a mixture of the two styles. In the first format, messages are interspersed with the program source statement listing; in the second, the messages are clustered at the end of the listing. The advantage of the first method is that the message appears at the same point where the error is detected so that the programmer can see both the message and the cause of that message without having to flip through sheets of paper on his listing. The advantage of the second method is that by clustering all messages at one place, it is unlikely that a programmer would overlook a message in the listing. There is a danger that in a long program, he could overlook an interspersed message, especially if the format of that message did not make a strong visual distinction between it and normal source code.

CANTOR prints messages interspersed in the program listing as they are discovered. Errors which cannot be detected until the entire program has been scanned will be reported at the end of the program listing. Since the input routine will print the source line image as it is read in from the source file, an error message will be printed immediately below the line of the program in which that error was detected. To assist the programmer in distinguishing an error message from other listed information, the message itself will be preceded and followed by asterisks. Figure 8-4 shows a revision of Fig. 7-1 in which several errors have been inserted along with the corresponding messages which CANTOR will print. The program is shown in the output format of CANTOR.

For semantic errors, we shall also have no problem pinpointing precisely where the difficulty is encountered; for example, if a variable is not declared, we shall be able to recognize that by referencing the symbol table and discovering that it has no entry. The data-type of an expression can be determined when that expression is compiled (in fact, it must be determined in order to compile it properly). Here again, any discrepancy between expected and encountered data-type will be reported immediately below the offending code.

The second, fourth, and fifth points of the list of qualities of a good error message can best be addressed by presenting the list of messages generated by CANTOR/0E (with error processing), shown in Fig. 8-5. Most messages must be 'customized' to include information peculiar to the particular erring statement. For example, error message number 9 should be printed when the final statement of a program is not the **end** required by the grammar rules. The blank is filled with the token actually encountered so that the message pinpoints precisely where the error was detected and its nature. The former helps support point one of proper error message writing, the latter supports point four.

Each message is divided into two sentences, the first sentence pinpointing the location and nature of an error, the second indicating the recovery action taken by CANTOR/0E. Message number one indicates that CANTOR/0E merely continues processing a program after discovering that the **program** statement is missing; message number 6 tells us that the remainder of an erroneous statement is skipped. Scanning resumes with the next statement. Techniques for recovering from errors must wait until the next section, however, so we shall not dwell on the various recovery actions given in Fig. 8-3.

LL(1) parsing guarantees that at each step of the parse CANTOR/0E knows which are legitimate next tokens in the source program. The error messages indicate the set of alternatives being sought when the error is encountered, if the error is syntactic in nature. For example, after the

CANTOR COMPILER: STAGE 4   JAN 11, 1978   21:37

LINE NO.   SOURCE STATEMENT

```
 1 |     program       gcd(input,output);                                      |
 2 |                   {illustrate error detecting capabilities of CANTOR/4.}  |
 3 |                   var  a,b,n: intger;                                     |
   ***   ERROR 15.     Data-type of variable must be 'integer' or 'boolean',  ***
   ***                 but 'intger' encountered.  Skipping to beginning of    ***
   ***                 next statement.                                        ***
 4 |                   begin                                                   |
 5 |                     readln, n;  {how many pairs do we compute gcd for?}   |
   ***   ERROR 30.     (expected after 'readln', but ',' encountered.         ***
   ***                 skipping to next statement.                            ***
 6 |                     while n > 0                                          |
 7                        begin                                               
   ***   ERROR 28.     'do' expected after predicate of 'while', but 'begin'  ***
   ***                 encountered.  'do' inserted into text.                 ***
 8 |                       readln  (a,b)     writeln  (a,b);                   |
   ***   ERROR 34.     ';' expected after readln argument list, but 'writeln' ***
   ***                 encountered. Skipping to beginning of next statement.  ***
 9 |                         repeat                                           |
10 |                           while  a > b  do  a := a − b;                   |
11 |                           while  b > a  do  b := b − ;                    |
   ***   ERROR 31.     Operand expected after '−' in expression, but ';'      ***
   ***                 encountered. Skipping to beginning of next statement.  ***
12 |                         until  a=b;                                      |
13 |                           {a = b = gcd of input pair}                    |
14 |                         writeln  (a);                                    |
15 |                         n := n − 1;  {one less pair to process.}         |
16 |                       end.                                               |
   ***   ERROR 33.     Unterminated 'begin' statement. End statement is in-   ***
   ***                 serted.                                                ***
```

COMPILATION TERMINATED   6 ERRORS ENCOUNTERED.
                                1 ERROR REPAIRS MADE.
                                5 FATAL ERRORS.
EXECUTION ABORTED BECAUSE OF FATAL ERRORS.

Fig. 8-4. Invalid Variant of Fig. 7-1.

1. First statement should be a program statement. Compilation continues.

2. 'const', 'var' or 'begin' expected, but _____ encountered. 'begin' inserted into text.

3. No text may follow 'end.'. This text is ignored.

4. Program name should follow 'program', but _____ encountered. Skipping to beginning of next statement.

5. Semicolon expected after program name, but _____ encountered. Semicolon added to text.

6. Non-keyword identifier must follow 'const', but _____ encountered. Skipping to beginning of next statement.

7. Non-keyword identifier must follow 'var', but _____ encountered. Skipping to beginning of next statement.

8. Period should follow 'end', but _____ encountered. _____ ignored and period inserted.

9. Last statement of program should be 'end'. End statement inserted into text.

10. An *integer* must follow '+' or '−' in the value assigned to a literal. Skipping to beginning of next statement.

11. Semicolon expected after value assigned to constant, but _____ encountered. Semicolon inserted into text.

12. Value assigned to constant must be either a literal or a previously defined constant, but _____ encountered. Skipping to beginning of next statement.

13. '=' should follow name of constant, but _____ encountered. Skipping to beginning of next statement.

14. Semicolon expected after data-type of variable list, but _____ encountered. Semicolon inserted into text.

15. Data-type of variable must be 'integer' or 'boolean', but _____ encountered. Skipping to beginning of next statement.

16. ':' must follow variable name list, but _____ encountered. Skipping to beginning of next statement.

17. The name _____ has previously been declared. Second declaration is ignored.

18. Keyword _____ may not be used as the program name or declared as a variable or symbolic constant. Use here is ignored.

19. Compiler error. Code generator has been called with illegal arguments _____. Compilation aborted.

20. Compiler error. Symbol table has illegal value _____ stored under name _____. Compilation aborted.

21. End of file unexpectedly encountered while processing an unterminated comment. '}' inserted into text.

22. It is illegal to begin a token with '}'. Symbol ignored.

23. Illegal symbol _____ encountered. Symbol skipped.

Fig. 8-5. Error Messages.

24. Compiler error. Parser routine called with next token not in selection set. Compilation aborted.

25. Token following a constant declaration must be 'begin', 'var', or a non-keyword identifier beginning another constant declaration, but _____ encountered. Skipping to beginning of next statement.

26. Token following a variable declaration must be 'begin' or a non-keyword identifier beginning another variable declaration, but _____ encountered. Skipping to beginning of next statement.

27. Token following a comma in a list of identifiers must be another non-keyword identifier, but _____ encountered. Skipping to beginning of next statement.

Fig. 8-5. Error Messages (cont.)

program statement, the next statement must begin with one of 'var', 'const', or 'begin' as stated in message number two. This information should help the programmer to correct the problem by not only telling him where he committed the error, but also what would have been acceptable in that context. Most compilers, unfortunately, do not offer this information to the user.

Each error message is numbered, so that at each point in CANTOR where there is a pseudo-code statement:

process error - . . .

a procedure call can be issued to a routine which processes the error; i.e., causes the appropriate message to be printed and recovers from the error. This routine, *process_error*, has one argument, the error code number. It is given in Fig. 8-6. *Process_error* references an array of error messages, obtains the desired message, inserts any necessary information into blank spaces in the message and emits it to the listing file. If main memeory storage were limited, these messages could be stored on secondary memory and read into main memory as needed. For a larger language with many more features, a good diagnostic compiler would have literally hundreds of messages; one version of WATFIV having 305 different messages

```
procedure   process_error(error_code: integer);
            {report and recover from error indicated by error_code.}
   const   message = array of messages given in Fig. 8-3 indexed by error codes;
   begin
      print message[error_code]   formatted with preceding and trailing asterisks on listing
         file, so that current token appears in the proper place;
      recover [error_code];
   end;
```

Fig. 8-6. *Process_error*.

which are normally stored on an error message file and brought into main memory as needed.

We have given just the messages for CANTOR/0E because it is only for CANTOR/0 that we have explicitly presented the parser, the particulars of which motivated many of the messages. The reader must provide his own messages for the many additions to RASCAL/0 given in RASCAL/1 through RASCAL/3. We have also not explicitly identified which message is associated with a particular error, leaving this as an exercise for the reader as well.

As an example of how difficult it is to write clear messages, we draw on a compiler which is justifiably noted for its superior diagnostic capabilities—WATFIV. The following two WATFIV statements declare variable PI to have a REAL type and initialize its value at compile-time to 3.1415927:

$$\text{REAL \quad PI}$$
$$\text{DATA \quad PI/3.1415927/}$$

It is, in fact, erroneous for a very subtle reason; however, the message, emitted at the bottom of the program which caused the error:

TYPE OF VARIABLE AND CONSTANT DO NOT AGREE

is nonsense to those not familiar with the quirks of WATFIV. (Can the reader spot the error?) The error occurs because WATFIV distinguishes between two types of REAL numbers, those requiring four storage bytes and those requiring eight. PI has been declared to hold numbers requiring four bytes, while the initial value specified is too precise to fit into four bytes; eight significant digits require the longer form. In this case WAT-FIV does not store a less precise answer; rather, it treats the initialization as erroneous. The quite similar initialization :

$$\text{DATA \quad PI/3.141593/}$$

compiles properly. This example is not intended as a criticism of WATFIV (it is far and away the best implementation available for teaching FOR-TRAN) but simply to indicate how difficult it is to write messages. The message is very clear in a situation such as:

$$\text{REAL \quad PI}$$
$$\text{DATA \quad PI/ .TRUE. /}$$

where we try to store the *boolean* value *true* into a REAL variable; it is only the subtle distinction between long and short REAL numbers which leads to confusion.

8.3.2   Run-Time Reporting

Reporting an error at run-time is somewhat more troublesome, because the error must be reported by executing 360AL code from within the object program rather than from a high-level language module within the compiler. Because more effort is required for reporting run-time errors, some commercial compilers do a poor job. However, the five criteria stated in section 8.3.1 on what constitutes a good error message apply to run-time messages as well. It is not uncommon to have a dump of main memory along with register contents and some other bookkeeping information as the format for reporting an error detected at run-time. With today's understanding of how to write a compiler, such a strategy is an abomination. The run-time error message should be in English, should identify the source program statement which caused the error and should identify, as clearly as possible, the nature of the error. For certain errors this is not possible, but, to the extent that it is possible, it should be done.

In section 8.2.2.1, we briefly discussed errors detected by the environment. Depending on the severity of the error and the flexibility the environment offers in returning control to the user's program after detecting such an error, the user may be able to report from within the object program itself; for example, an attempted *integer* division by zero is trapped by the IBM 360/370 hardware. Control is wrenched from the user's program and given to the operating system, which, in this case, prints an error message and terminates the execution of the user's program. To a certain extent this is profitable. The environment detects, reports and recovers from the error without any effort on the part of the user's program. If we accept both the report format and content and the recovery policy, then the compiler writer can safely ignore this error entirely. If we object to this error processing, our only recourse is to regain control from the environment after the error is detected, which for this particular error, and in fact for most environment-detected errors, is possible. Execution within the user's program can resume at a special entry point designated for that error. Special error reporting and recovery code inserted by the compiler within the object program can then be executed, but we shall not detail here how this transpires. Depending on the quirks of the environment in which a program is run, the number of detected errors for which the user's program can regain control will vary.

Another source of run-time problems is a *compiler* error which causes a legal but unfaithful translation to be emitted. Strange assembly code (or machine code in other compilers) could lead to totally unexpected run-time behavior. This error type is particularly nasty because the programmer who writes the RASCAL source will probably blame *his* code for the error, wasting long hours vainly trying to spot the error. Even if he dumps the assembly version of the code, the error may be so subtle that discovery would be painful.

Section 8.2.2.2 dealt with run-time errors detected by compiler-generated code; for such cases, the user's program never loses control to the operating system. The insertion of such reporting and recovery code into the object program is more straightforward than for environmentally-detected errors. Recall that we showed how an undefined variable reference could be detected quite easily. When this error is detected, we would like to print:

VARIABLE _____ IS UNDEFINED IN LINE NUMBER _____.

where the first blank is filled in with the *external name* of the undefined variable and the second blank is the *source program* line number where the error is detected. In order to accomplish this, both values must be known at object code execution-time. In the code emitted by CANTOR/3 this will not be the case, so we must alter the code emission routine appropriately.

In order to make the external name available within the object code, we create a *character* constant at the time the variable name is declared, @*nEN*, where @*n* is the internal name of the variable:

$$@n\text{EN} \quad \text{DC} \quad \text{C'} \quad external\ name\ here\ \text{'}$$

This constant can be created by modifying *create_flag* to emit @*nEN*, as well as @*nDF*. The pseudo-360AL code given in segment 8.1 can now be refined further into:

$$\begin{aligned} &\text{MVC} \quad @\text{RUNERR}+10(20),@n\text{EN} &&(8.2)\\ &\text{MVC} \quad @\text{RUNERR}+60(3),=\text{CL3'}\ line\ number\ \text{'}\\ &CALL \quad @IO\ to\ print\ @RUNERR\ ; \end{aligned}$$

where @*RUNERR*+*10* is the blank spot for the external name in the constant which defines the error message, and @*RUNERR*+*60* is the other blank spot in @*RUNERR* reserved for the line number. Note that the line number is known at compile-time, when code segment 8.2 would be generated, so that the second MVC instruction can be generated.

Alternatives to these strategies exist which can significantly improve the storage requirements for this check. Looking ahead to the recovery strategy we shall take for this error—stop program execution—we know that at most one reference to a variable name will ever be made. Because no such reference will ever take place if this error never occurs, it seems extravagant to store long character names in main memory, perhaps tying up thousands of bytes of storage. These names could be written to a file on secondary memory by the compiler which is treated as an integral part of the object code module. When the program is executed, this file would be available for reference if needed but not kept in main memory. We can also eliminate many of the moves of line numbers to @RUNERR+60. If we assume for the sake of simplification that a RASCAL program has no more than 255 lines, then at the beginning of the object code emitted for each executable statement, we insert:

$$\text{MVI} \quad \text{@LNNUM, X}\text{'}h\text{'}$$

where h is the hex coding of the line number and @LNNUM is referenced at @PRTERR described next. With these simplifications, the reporting code becomes:

$$\text{MVI} \quad \text{@HLDINDX, X}\text{'}i\text{'} \qquad (8.3)$$
$$\text{B} \qquad \text{@PRTERR}$$

where i is the hex encoding of the index into the external name file. @PRTERR labels the one place in the object code where the blanks in the error message are filled and @IO, the basic I/O routine, is called. Via @PRTERR the value of @HLDINDX is converted into EBCDIC character format for printing.

8.4 RECOVERY

The final stage of error processing concerns the actions taken after an error has been reported. By the very nature of "error" processing, normal execution may not simply continue; some exceptional action is required.

8.4.1 Compile-Time Recovery

There are four strategies for recovering from compile-time errors exercised by CANTOR. These four are fairly typical of the range of techniques commonly employed in commercial compilers. The particular strategy selected depends upon the nature and severity of the error:

1. *Abort* compilation entirely.
2. *Ignore* the remainder of a statement in which an error is detected, and make no attempt to execute the resulting object code generated.
3. Attempt to *continue* processing the statement in which the error occurred, and make no attempt to execute the resulting object code generated.

4. Attempt to *repair* the statement in which the error occurred by modifying the incorrect code; execution of the resulting object code is attempted.

The first strategy is extremely severe and should be exercised only for the most *catastrophic* errors. CANTOR terminates compilation abruptly only when an error within the compiler itself is detected, such as an overflow in *operand_stk* or a call to *code* with illegal arguments. The second and third strategies are quite popular among compiler writers. In both cases, compilation continues after error processing is completed. Strategy two, also referred to as *panic mode recovery* in the literature, presumes that when an error in a statement is encountered, it is pointless to continue processing the remainder of the statement. In a statement in which there are a number of ways in which the error could have occurred, such as having an extra comma or omitting a period, it may be difficult to determine how to continue the analysis of the statement at the point past the error. For those errors, it is probably best to simply skip past the remainder of the statement and resume the scanning after the end of statement marker which in this case is a semicolon.

The third strategy does attempt to continue the analysis of a statement past the point where an error is detected. The value of this policy is the possible uncovering of errors later in the statement which would go undetected if the simpler panic mode were used instead. The danger in continuing the analysis of an erroneous statement is that by misjudging how to analyze the remainder of the statement, the compiler could issue a rash of misleading error messages. An example of a fairly "safe" place to continue the parsing is in a variable declaration in which an illegally formatted identifier has been found. By reporting the error and skipping to the ',' or ':', the parser can *synchronize* with the productions of the grammar which define the correct form of variable declarations.

The fourth strategy goes one step further than the third in attempting to more elegantly recover from errors. In the fourth method, we actually *attempt to correct* the encountered error by changing the illegal program into one which is legal; of course, such an attempt is only an "intelligent guess" on the part of the compiler writer as to the most likely intended code at the point at which the error was located. For example, if '=' is found in a variable declaration rather than ':', the compiler could make a "reasonable" assumption that the programmer meant to write ':', but committed a small, mental error and wrote '=' instead. Rather than merely flagging this statement as erroneous and continuing the analysis with the next token or next statement, the compiler could actually substitute the ':' for a '=' and continue the processing as if the ':' had been there originally. An error message would still be issued, informing the programmer of the detected error and the action taken by the compiler, but compilation of that statement would proceed normally, and, presuming no *fatal* errors existed elsewhere in the source code, the object program would be considered executable after compilation had terminated.

There is disagreement among compiler writers as to the wisdom of attempting to correct erroneous programs, a tactic also called *program repair* (with no guarantees of a correct repair). The advantage of this strategy is that trivial errors do not waste a programmer's time. Nearly correct programs are executed, providing feedback to the user about the run-time behavior of his program, rather than simply indicating compile-time problems. On the other hand, this strategy suffers from several major handicaps: An incorrectly repaired error might not be recognized as such by the programmer. He could mistakenly believe the compiler had *corrected* the error, not merely *repaired* it, when the repair may not, in fact, reflect the intentions of the programmer. Compilation time may be bloated significantly if the repairs are numerous or sophisticated (PL/C is an excellent example of this, with compilation time often doubling when a slightly "buggy" program is compiled). Catastrophe could strike if a repair is made at run-time; data sets could be destroyed if the repair is erroneous. Repair is mostly suited for the running of small student programs in a batch-oriented environment. Run-time repair is too dangerous in a commercial environment, and, in a snappy interactive system, turnaround time is not a significant factor.

Repair of syntactic errors where the meaning is clear is not nearly as difficult as those errors which have semantic impact; for example, if a variable declaration were mistakenly written as:

$$\textbf{var} \quad y : \quad integr ;$$

then what is the best way to repair this error? The data-type of y clearly will impact all references to y later in the code. Using information theoretic measures of "distance", it is possible to determine that the "closest" valid type name is "integer." Similarly, if a variable name is misspelled, we can measure the "distance" between it and all declared variables and treat the misspelled variable as if it were actually the declared variable closest to it; clearly, such strategies will err a significant percentage of the time. Compile-time errors which are practically impossible to correctly repair include a missing operator or operand (which one do we insert?) or improper nesting (how do we restructure the source code?). Repairs in these cases have such little likelihood of succeeding that attempting repair at all is a dubious strategy. Practically no run-time errors can be reasonably repaired. If a variable's value is undefined, it is just nonsense to choose a value (such as 0.0) and arbitrarily assign it to that variable. If the end of a data file is encountered, what value can be assigned to the input variable? Again, automatic run-time repair is probably not worth the effort and, as stated earlier, is actually dangerous in a commercial environment. CANTOR repairs some simple compile-time errors such as a missing **end** statement to terminate the program. The reader should select a small set of errors for RASCAL/3 programs, decide on a reasonable repair for each such error and implement this strategy.

Figure 8-7 shows the structure of the recovery procedure and the details of the recovery strategy for the first six errors. In the first and fourth errors, both related to the **program** statement, we create a compiler-defined name for the program since the program source code fails to do so. The second error requires that a new token be "squeezed" in front of the remaining source text, in this case **'begin'**. To recover from encountering extraneous text after the logical end of the program, we simply skip past all tokens until the end of the source file is reached. The fifth error arises when the closing semicolon is left off of a **program** statement. We simply insert it into the text, repairing the code, and continue on. The last

```
procedure   recover(error_code: integer);
   begin
      case   error_code   of
         1:   begin
                 code('program','@SPECNAM');
                 insert('@SPECNAM', prog_name, immutable, '@SPECNAM', no,);
                 if token in ['const'] then consts(token);
                 if token in ['var'] then vars(token);
                 if token not in ['begin'] then process_error(2);
                 begin_end_stmt (token);
                 if token not in [end-of-file] then process_error(3);
              end;
         2:   insert 'begin' into text, resetting token to be 'begin';
         3:   while token <> end-of-file do next_token(token);
         4:   begin
                 code('program', '@SPECNAM');
                 insert('@SPECNAM', prog_name, immutable, '@SPECNAM', no,);
                 advance token pointer past next semicolon or to end-of-file;
              end;
         5:   insert ';' into text, resetting token to be ';';
         6:   begin
                 advance token pointer past next semicolon or to end-of-file;
                 if end-of-file then terminate parsing;
              end;
         . . .
```

Fig. 8-7. *Recover.*

```
procedure  parser;
   var   token: string;
            {token is the next token.}
   begin
            {a call to next_token has two effects: (1) the variable, token, is assigned the value of
            the next token; (2) the next token is read from the source file in order to make the
            assignment. The value returned by next_token is also the next token.}
      if  next_token(token) not in ['program'] then begin
         process_error(1);   return;   end;
      if next_token(token) in [end-of-file] then return;
      prog(token);
   end;
```

Fig. 8-8. *Parser* with Error Processing.

recovery detailed in Fig. 8-7 is a panic recovery. We skip past code until we either come to the beginning of the next statement (token following a semicolon) or reach the end of the source file. If we reach the end of the file, then we simply terminate the parsing action; otherwise, we shall return to the calling point in procedure *consts*. Note that *consts* has a **goto** statement in it, as do several other procedures which have been modified in Figs. 8-8 through 8-15 to reflect the error processing. Although we, in general, discourage the use of **goto** statements, this is an exception, motivated by the fact that we are recovering from an abnormal situation. In this case, after skipping past what was an erroneous constant declaration, we should expect to encounter either the beginning of another constant declaration, the beginning of the variable declarations, or a **begin** statement. We determine if this is in fact the case; if not, then we print another

```
procedure   prog(var   token: string);
               {process production 1}
               {token should be 'program'}
   begin
      if token not in ['program'] then
         process_error(24);
      prog_stmt(token);
      if token in ['const'] then consts(token);
      if token in ['var'] then vars(token);
      if token not in ['begin'] then
         process_error(2);
      begin_end_stmt(token);
      if token not in [end-of-file] then
         process_error(3);
   end;
```

Fig. 8-9. *Prog.*

error message for this next statement and repeat the cycle. Eventually, we should either encounter **'var', 'begin',** a non-keyword identifier, or the end of the source file.

Note how the changes to the parser procedures (originally Figs. 4-10 through 4-17) shown in Figs. 8-8 to 8-15 are limited to the places in the code which we designated for processing errors. There are only two exceptions: The first is the possible labeling of a statement so that it can be the target of a **goto** statement; the second variation appears in *var_stmts* and *ids*. *Var_stmts* calls *ids* to obtain the list of identifiers in the current variable declaration. If *ids* fails to find a proper id list, it processes the error in the standard way by calling *process_error* with the appropriate argument. For other than a compiler error, *ids* recovers by skipping to the beginning of the next statement (errors 16 and 27). It cannot simply **return** to *var_stmts* at this point, however, because *var_stmts* would have no way of knowing that an error occurred in *ids*. Without this knowledge it would continue normal execution and not branch to statement 10 as it should. The problem lies in the fact that *var_stmts* performs statement-level analysis, *ids* performs expression-level analysis, and yet the error

```
procedure   const_stmts(var   token: string);
            {process production 6}
            {token should be NON_KEY_ID}
  var x,y: string;
  begin
    if token not in [NON_KEY_ID] then
      process_error(24);
    x := token;
    if next_token(token) not in ['='] then begin
      process_error(12);   goto 10;   end;
    y := next_token(token);
    if y not in ['+', '-', NON_KEY_ID, 'true', 'false', INTEGER] then
      begin process_error(12);   goto 10;   end;
    if y in ['+', '-'] then begin
      if next_token(token) not in [INTEGER] then begin
        process_error(10);   goto  10;   end;
      y := y ∥ token;   end;
    if next_token(token) not in [';'] then
      process_error(11);
    insert(x, which_type(y), immutable, which_value(y), yes, 1);
 10:  if next_token(token) not in ['begin', 'var', NON_KEY_ID] then begin
        process_error(25);   goto 10;   end;
      if token in [NON_KEY_ID] then   const_stmts(token);
  end;
```

Fig. 8-10. *Const_stmts.*

```
procedure   consts(var   token: string);
            {process production 3}
            {token should be 'const'}
    begin
        if token not in ['const'] then   process_error(24);
        if next_token(token) not in [NON_KEY_ID] then begin
          process_error(6);
     10:   if token not in ['var', 'begin', NON_KEY_ID] then begin
              process_error(25);   goto  10;  end;
          if token not in [NON_KEY_ID] then return; end;
        const_stmts(token);
    end;

procedure   vars(var   token:   string);
            {process production 4}
            {token should be 'var'}
    begin
        if token not in ['var'] then   process_error(24);
        if next_token(token) not in [NON_KEY_ID] then begin
          process_error(7);
     10:   if token not in ['begin', NON_KEY_ID] then begin
              process_error(26);   goto  10;  end;
          if token not in [NON_KEY_ID] then return; end;
        var_stmts(token);
    end;
```

Fig. 8-11. *Consts* and *Vars*.

```
procedure   begin_end_stmt(var   token: string);
            {process production 5}
            {token should be 'begin'}
    begin
        if token not in ['begin'] then
          process_error(24);
        if next_token(token) not in ['end'] then
          process_error(9);
        if next_token(token) not in ['.'] then
          process_error(8);
        next_token(token);
        code('end', '.');
    end;
```

Fig. 8-12. *Begin_end_stmt*.

```
        procedure  prog_stmt(var  token: string);
                {process production 2}
                {token should be 'program'}
     var  x: string;
     begin
       if token not in ['program'] then
          process_error(24);
       x := next_token(token);
       if token not in [NON_KEY_ID] then  begin
          process_error(4);  return; end;
       if next_token(token) not in [';'] then
          process_error(5);
       next_token(token);
       code('program', x);
       insert(x, prog_name, immutable, x, no, );
     end;
```

Fig. 8-13. *Prog_stmt.*

```
procedure  var_stmts(var  token: string);
        {process production 7}
        {token should be NON_KEY_ID}
  var  x,y; string;
  begin
    if token not in [NON_KEY_ID] then
       process_error(24);
    x := ids(token);
    if  x = error-16 then begin process_error(16);
           goto 10 ; end ;
    if  x = error-27 then begin process_error(27);
           goto 10 ; end ;
    if token not in [':'] then begin
       process_error(16);   goto 10; end;
    if next_token(token) not in ['integer', 'boolean'] then  begin
       process_error(15);   goto 10; end ;
    y := token ;
    if next_token(token) not in [';'] then
       process_error(14);
    next_token(token);
    insert(x, y, mutable, , yes, 1);
10:  if next_token(token) not in ['begin', NON_KEY_ID] then
           process_error(26); goto 10; end;
       if token in [NON_KEY_ID] then var_stmts (token);
  end;
```

Fig. 8-14. *Var_stmts.*

```
function  ids(var   token: string): string ;
              {process production 8}
              {token should be NON_KEY_ID}
      var   temp: string;
      begin
          if token not in [NON_KEY_ID] then
             process_error(24);
          ids := token;
          temp := token;
          if next_token(token) not in [',', ':'] then begin
             ids := error-16{establish error return}; return; end;
          if token in [','] then begin
             if next_token(token) not in [NON_KEY_ID] then   begin
                ids := error-27; return;   end;
             ids := temp ∥ ',' ∥ ids(token);   end;
      end;
```

Fig. 8-15. *Ids.*

recovery policy in this case has statement-level impact. If *ids* were to repair the error, then the impact of error recovery would not propagate to the statement-level, and *var_stmts* need not become aware of an error which occurred at a deeper level; however, we want to skip past the rest of the erroneous statement. Organizationally, it seems wrong for an *expression-level* routine to advance the token pointer past the rest of a *statement;* also the statement-level routine will have to be notified of the error. Furthermore, *ids* might be called from several different, higher level parser routines (in later compiler versions), each of which demands a *different* recovery action for the same error. For all of these reasons, we detect the error in *ids* but report it back to *var_stmts,* which initiates recovery action. To report the error, we assign x the special value *error-16* or *error-27,* depending on which error was encountered.

This last example reveals a general strategy for error processing in more complex situations. Each parser routine is responsible for some form(s) of expression, statement, block, subprogram, or other program segment(s). The calling structure is nested so that routines responsible for larger segments invoke those which handle smaller segments. To maintain the integrity of this structure and to ensure maximum flexibility in recovery strategies, no routine should ever initiate a recovery which extends beyond its intended scope; rather, a routine should report such an error to a "higher authority," which will either handle the recovery itself or, in turn, report it to a still higher authority.

Unfortunately, there is one important aspect of error recovery which cannot be adequately explained by relying upon the features of

RASCAL/0, for example. When an error is encountered in the middle of certain statements, the partial processing of those statements up to the point where the error is detected will have modified the two primary stacks of the compiler, *operand_stk* and *operator_stk*. For other compilers, the details may vary, but the principle remains the same so that data structures will have been modified by the partial processing of certain statements, such as an assignment statement. In order to complete panic mode recovery, we must not only skip past further tokens within the erroneous statement, we must also adjust the stacks so that they resume the status they had before compilation of the erroneous statement began.

The easiest way in which to restore *operand_stk* and *operator_stk* is to have a *synchronization element* already on the stacks when the error is encountered. This element is inserted into each stack when the compilation of a new statement begins and is removed when its compilation is completed. In this way, to remove all stack elements inserted because of the partial compilation of an erroneous statement only requires emptying the stacks down to the first synchronization element encountered.

Error recovery in the grammar driven translation grammar processor (GDTGP) described in Chapter 3 is quite primitive—abort on the first detected error. We must extend this error capability so that the user can have much greater control over what recovery policy is taken by his compiler. To do so we must extend the grammar syntax to include *patch* code in which error recovery information will be placed. The following is a translation grammar for RASCAL/0 complete with error recovery code using the syntax explained in Chapter 3:

```
%a AX
%n PROG PROG_STMT CONSTS VARS BEGIN_END_STMT
%n CONST_STMTS VAR_STMTS
%n IDS TYPE LIT BOOLEAN
%n NEW1 NEW2 NEW3
%l program
%l const var
%l begin end
%l =
%l :
%l ,
%l integer boolean
%l + −
%l true false
%g NON_KEY_ID INTEGER SEMICOLON
%%
```

PROG   = {synch: program => 2, const => 3, var => 5, begin => 7}
   PROG_STMT
   {synch: const => 4, var => 5, begin => 7} CONSTS
   {synch: var => 6, begin => 7} VARS
   {synch: begin => 8, . => *} BEGIN_END_STMT [any]

PROG_STMT   = program NON_KEY_ID SEMICOLON {!squeeze(';');}
   {code ('program', $2); insert($2,prog_name,immutable,$1,
   no);}[program]

CONSTS   = const CONST_STMTS [const]
   = [var begin]

VARS   = var VAR_STMTS [var]
   = [begin]

BEGIN_END_STMT   = begin end {!squeeze('end');} . {!replace('.');}
   {code('end', '.');} [begin]

CONST_STMTS   = {synch: SEMICOLON NON_KEY_ID => 6, var => *, begin
   => *}
   NON_KEY_ID = NEW1 {insert($2,which_type($4),immutable,,
   which_values($4),yes,1);} SEMICOLON {!squeeze(';');}
   CONST_STMTS [NON_KEY_ID]

NEW1   = NON_KEY_ID [NON_KEY_ID]
   = LIT [true false INTEGER + −]

VAR_STMTS   = {synch: SEMICOLON NON_KEY_ID => 6, begin =>*} IDS :
   TYPE {insert($2,$4,mutable,yes,, 1);} SEMICOLON
   {!squeeze(';');} NEW2 [NON_KEY_ID]

NEW2   = VAR_STMTS [NON_KEY_ID]
   = [begin]

IDS   = NON_KEY_ID NEW3 [NON_KEY_ID]

NEW3   = , IDS [,]
   = [:]

TYPE   = integer [integer]
   = boolean [boolean]

LIT   = INTEGER [INTEGER]
   = BOOLEAN [BOOLEAN]
   = + INTEGER [+]
   = − INTEGER [−]

BOOLEAN   = true [true]
   = false [false]

%%

There are a number of special constructions in this new grammar which
define the error recovery policy. First we will explain only those features
relevant to the repair, deletion, or insertion of a token in the candi-

date string, after which, we will address panic and continue recoveries.

The selection set element *any* is a special symbol used in error processing that matches any token. It is found in the first production of the sample grammar. Its use will become clear when panic and continuation recoveries are discussed.

A new type of action routine is specially created to handle errors—*patch*—which may appear after any literal or group. Superficially, a patch looks like any other action code—a sequence of PASCAL statements surrounded by curly brackets—except that the patch routine begins with '{!'. The translation grammar analyzer (TGA) processes a patch routine exactly as it does an ordinary action routine, except that it marks the style of the patch as "patch", not "action".

The complete compiler (CC) will not execute patch code during normal parsing. When it is a patch routine's "turn" to be executed, CC skips past it. However, if a syntactic error is detected while trying to match a terminal, CC looks ahead in the sentential form to see if a patch immediately follows the errant symbol in the sentential form. If not, the default action is to abort compilation, but if a patch is found, its code is executed instead. The patch should contain a call to one of the built-in error processing procedures:

1) replace(newvalue: string)
2) squeeze(newvalue: string)
3) remove

Replace will replace the current token with the string specified as its argument. *Squeeze* will push the string specified in its argument list just in front of the current token, while *remove* will pull the current token from the candidate. After executing any of these procedures, CC will resume parsing in the state it was just prior to detecting the error. The patch code can also contain calls to any other routines as necessary to manipulate the data structures of the compiler, and in fact, if the compiler writer wishes, he does not have to call these built-in routines. They are provided for his convenience only, and an arbitrary recovery action can be initiated. However, the current system is not designed to facilitate this, so the writer must be familiar with the details of CC's parsing structures and processing algorithms if he is to write his own recovery strategy.

For even greater flexibility, the user can also specify a panic or continue policy by inserting special action code, which is not valid PASCAL code, but which will be translated by the TGA into executable PASCAL for inclusion in CC. The format of this special code is:

'{' 'synch' ':' RECOVERY ';' PASCAL code '}'

where RECOVERY specifies both how far in the candidate string to advance the token pointer, and how far in the sentential form to jump ahead ("synch" stands for "synchronize"). RECOVERY is a list of synchronization specifications, separated by commas, each having the form:

TOKENS '=>' INTEGER

The tokens in TOKENS are separated by one or more blanks or *newlines*. The semicolon and PASCAL code at the end of the synch routine is optional. Any production can have an arbitrary number of synch action routines, but only the latest one executed, called the active synch, will be in effect at any given time. The active synch dictates future error recovery policy for all vocabulary symbols in the production in which it occurs. That policy remains in effect either until another synch in that production becomes active or the processing of that production is completed. For example, the first right-hand side element in production 1 is a synch. If an error occurs in processing PROG_STMT, this synch will dictate recovery for this error. However, if PROG_STMT is successfully processed, a second synch is executed which establishes a new recovery policy. If that second synch were not present, then an error in CONSTS would recover using the synchronization policy established by the first action routine.

The three recovery strategies specified earlier are all local in effect; i.e., only the area around the current token can be affected, and the parsing always continues where it left off just prior to detecting the error. For continuation this is not true. The token pointer may be advanced arbitrarily far into the candidate string, and the sentform pointer, sentptr, may be advanced to any symbol in the production in which the active synch appears.

When synch is executed, it merely establishes how to respond to an error if one occurs. Provided there is no error, the synchronization information will be ignored, and processing will continue normally. Suppose, however, that in processing a vocabulary symbol, a syntactic error is detected. At that point, the action taken will depend on several factors. If there is an active synch in the production in which the errant symbol occurs, and there is no patch immediately following the errant symbol, then tokens in the candidate will be skipped until the current token becomes one of those to the left of a '=>' in that synch. For example, production 6 for CONST_STMTS includes a synch as the first right-hand side element. This synch is active when CC tries to match '=' in the sentential form to a token in the candidate. If '=' does not follow the NON_KEY_ID, CC will detect the error and initiate the active synch recovery. Tokens will be skipped until either a semicolon immediately followed by a NON_KEY_ID is found, or 'var' is found, or 'begin' is found. If the end of the candidate is reached before one of these three token strings is found, CC prints an appropriate message and aborts compilation. If a semicolon followed by a NON_KEY_ID is found first, the parser resumes by looking for the fifth element on the right-hand side of the production, in this case a semicolon. This synchronizes the parser with the beginning of what we expect to be the next constant declaration. The constant declaration being processed when the error was detected is ignored.

If 'var' is discovered first, the parser presumes the entire production has been processed as indicated by the '*' to the right of '=>'. Similarly so if 'begin' is found first. Since 'var' and 'begin' are reserved words, the only way in which they could legitimately appear is as the beginning of the variable declaration section or the beginning of the executable code, respectively. If either is seen before another SEMICOLON NON_KEY_ID, then the constant declaration section is presumed ended.

If the semicolon is missing from a constant declaration, CC will follow a different path. After SEMICOLON in the production there is a patch which corrects the problem. The presence of this patch overrides synch recovery so that CC squeezes a semicolon into the candidate and continues processing where it left off. If that patch had been left off, synch recovery would have been activated instead.

A more interesting case arises when a production does not itself have an active synch, but an ancestral nonterminal which led to that production appearing in the sentential form does have one. Production 2 for PROG_STMT is such a case. It is easiest to see how synch works in this situation by referring to the derivation tree which is, in effect, derived by CC in parsing the candidate string.

Suppose a program omits the name from the program statement. CC detects this error when trying to match NON_KEY_ID against the current token. There is no active synch in production 2, but there is one in production 1 from which production 2 was generated. PROG_STMT in production 1 is the parent node of the right-hand side of production 2 in which the error was detected. This right-hand side inherits the synch policy of its parent. Since it does not override that policy by executing a synch of its own, when the error in production 2 is detected, the recovery is dictated by actions taken in processing production 1. In particular, tokens in the candidate are skipped until either 'program', 'const', 'var', or 'begin' is found. CC will then in effect erase all of the derivation tree which hangs below PROG_STMT and resume parsing at the point dictated by the synch in production 1. For example, if 'var' is encountered first among the alternatives, then parsing will resume with element 5 of the right-hand side of production 1, where a new synchronization policy which is appropriate for variable declarations will be established. All symbols up to that synchronization point in the right-hand side are treated by CC as if they had been successfully matched.

The special token *any* is defined to allow the user to force CC to accept the first production independent of the candidate string in order to establish the synchronization policy in case there is an error in the first token of the program. If 'program' were not the first token, and we used only the normal selection set of PROG; i.e., ['program'], then the compilation of the entire program would be aborted.

The only feature of the error processing facilities not yet explained is the PASCAL code which can follow the RECOVERY specification in a synch. When a synchronization takes place, not only must the sentform be adjusted, but so must any user-defined data structures which would otherwise be left in an inconsistent state. For example, operand_stk or optor_stk might have to be cleared of certain elements if we were specifying the error recovery for CANTOR/1. Any PASCAL code following RECOVERY will be executed just after the synchronization activities, and before parsing resumes.

To better illustrate the recovery policy, we will follow the actions of CC on program *badegg* in Fig. 4-2. The derivation begins with:

PROG ===> {synch: . . .} PROG_STMT {synch: . . .} CONSTS {synch: . . .} VARS
{synch: . . .} BEGIN_END_STMT

The **program** statement is successfully compiled, as is the empty constant declaration section. When the processing of VARS begins, the third synch in the production is active. We then have:

PROG =$\overset{*}{=}$=> . . . {synch: . . .} var VAR_STMTS . . .

===> . . . {synch: . . .} var {synch: . . .} IDS : TYPE
{insert. . .} SEMICOLON {!squeeze. . .} NEW2 . . .

At this point the synch just prior to IDS becomes active. Continuing with the derivation:

PROG =$\overset{*}{=}$=> . . . {synch: . . .} x : integer {insert. . .}

SEMICOLON {!squeeze. . .} NEW2 . . .

Expanding NEW2, still another synch becomes active and we finally detect an error in IDS:

PROG =$\overset{*}{=}$=> . . . VAR_STMTS . . .
=$\overset{*}{=}$=> . . . {synch: . . .} IDS : TYPE {insert. . .}
SEMICOLON {!squeeze. . .} NEW2 . . .
===> . . . {synch: . . .} y, z NEW3 : TYPE {insert. . .}
SEMICOLON {!squeeze. . .} NEW2 . . .

At this point the current token is '+', and the nonterminal to be expanded is NEW3. Neither alternative production for NEW3 has '+' in its selection set, so CC detects the error. Since no patch follows NEW3, synchronization recovery is initiated. The active synch is part of the production for VAR_STMTS. Tokens are skipped up to the next SEMICOLON followed by a NON_KEY_ID (since that occurs before 'begin') which is ';' 'asis', the beginning of the next variable declaration. The parser resumes with the semicolon as the current token, and SEMICOLON as the current sentential form in the production for VAR_STMTS. We leave the rest of the program's compilation to the reader as an exercise.

8.4.2   Run-Time Recovery

For CANTOR, as for most implementations, there is just one recovery strategy exercised when encountering a run-time error—terminate program execution. For the case of undefined program variables which we have been studying, this is easily effected by:

$$B \quad @END \qquad (8.4)$$

Instead of terminating the program's execution, we might offer the programmer the option of specifying a point in his program to which control should be transferred when an error occurs. This option is not found in RASCAL but is available in PL/I, which offers the *ON ERROR* statement:

$$ON\ ERROR \quad statement \qquad (8.5)$$

Whenever a run-time error occurs which is not so severe that the environment wrenches control from the user's program and will not return it, the statement following 'ON ERROR' is executed. This gives the programmer the flexibility to respond to run-time errors in his own fashion, allowing him to print diagnostic information which may be helpful in correcting the error or even permit him to "patch" the error on the "fly" and resume normal processing elsewhere within his program.

To implement an *ON ERROR* feature added to RASCAL would be relatively straightforward. Instead of branching to *@END* when recovering from a run-time error, the 360AL code could simply branch to the address where the translated version of the *ON ERROR* code is located. We leave the details of both the RASCAL extension and its implementation in CANTOR to the interested reader as an exercise.

8.5 SUMMARY

Error processing capabilities have been added to CANTOR, which enable it to *detect, report* and *recover* from errors both at compile-time and at run-time. Detecting syntactic compile-time errors in a properly structured compiler is relatively straightforward. Semantic errors, such as branching into the scope of a control structure is considerably more difficult. Detecting run-time errors is even harder because the detection must be performed either by the program *environment* or by code explicitly inserted into the object program for error checking.

Error messages should be written in clear, unambiguous English prose, never in cryptic or abbreviated format. They should pinpoint the location and nature of the error and, wherever possible, also indicate how that error might be repaired by the programmer (i.e., what was expected at the point the error was found). The message should also indicate the recovery action taken.

There are several recovery strategies ranging from attempting to *repair* an erroneous program to *aborting* execution of the compiler or object code. CANTOR/4 (also called CANTOR 0/E) uses both of these extremes along with more moderate policies. The "best" recovery strategy varies with the nature and severity of the error and partly with the judgement of the compiler writer as well.

EXERCISES

8-1. Analyze the error-detection abilities of a compiler available at your installation. Obtain the language definition, and determine how many violations the compiler detects, especially run-time errors.

8-2. What advantage is there in terms of error-detection capability in not allowing a conversion between *integer* and *boolean* objects, such as is defined in some languages?

8-3. Devise a scheme to keep CANTOR from issuing an error message below each reference to an undeclared identifier. CANTOR should emit a message only for the first such reference.

8-4. Modify RASCAL/4 so that the 'on eof(input)' statement of PL/I is available, making all necessary changes to the translation grammar and the action routines.

8-5. Modify CANTOR/4 so that it checks whether the input data is valid for the arguments of the **read** and **readln** statement. Note that this must be a run-time check.

8-6. The Stonybrook PASCAL compiler initializes all *integer* variables to zero at compile-time. Hence, no *integer* variable is ever undefined.
   a. Evaluate the wisdom of such a policy in terms of programming ease and program reliability.
   b. Modify CANTOR/4 to have this policy and to initialize *boolean* variables to **true** as well.

8-7. Modify CANTOR to emit all error messages at the end of the program listing. This will probably require writing the messages out to a temporary disk file until the entire program has been processed.

8-8. Analyze the quality of the error messages of a compiler available from your installation in terms of the 5 criteria stated in the chapter. How often, for example, does a message seem to mislead you as to the actual cause of the error?

8-9. Write a list of six errors for which you feel the best recovery strategy is a repair, indicate what that repair is, and how you would implement it in CANTOR/4.

8-10. Write a list of six errors for which you feel that a repair is probably unwise, because it is unlikely to reflect the programmer's actual desires, and indicate why you believe this to be so.

8-11. The strategy specified in section 8.2.2.2 which eliminates many redundant tests for an undefined variable does not remove *all* redundant tests. Modify the strategy for **if** statements so that further tests are eliminated at run-time.

8-12. Prove that the strategy for eliminating redundant tests is correct; i.e., that it is never possible to reference the value of an undefined variable.

8-13. The strategy for removing redundant tests for undefined variables relies upon the fact that the only control structures are the **if, while,** and **repeat.** Extend this strategy to the **case** and **for** statements of PASCAL.

8-14. If a **goto** statement is added to RASCAL, the strategy for removing redundant tests is severely restricted; explain why this is so. Can this restriction be corrected in a multi-pass compiler? How?

8-15. When a compile-time error in a statement is detected, two reasonable recovery strategies are: 1) skip the rest of the statement ("panic" mode); and 2) attempt to repair the error and continue normal processing. The parsing method employed affects the compiler's ability to perform strategy 2) over 1). Explain the characteristics of LL(1) parsing which enable it to repair more easily than "panic" when a compile-time error is encountered.

8-16. In Chapter 7, we introduced the notion of a run-time support package to aid in I/O; explain how this concept could be helpful in error processing as well. Cite specific errors in RASCAL/3 and other languages where such a package would help.

8-17. Finish the compilation of *badegg* begun in section 8.4.

8-18. Show how CC would handle the errors in *evenworse* in Fig. 4.2.

8-19. Compare the error recovery policy of CC and the recursive descent compiler described in the chapter for RASCAL/0. Find all differences and determine how to change each to match the other.

TESTING HINTS

1. Test CANTOR/4 on all of the programs used to test CANTOR/3.

2. Test CANTOR/4 on one or more programs which violate each and every error which the compiler is capable of detecting. Introduce errors into the compiler (on the premise, of course, that you have no bugs already) which cause compiler errors to be detected by the self-diagnostic code.

BIBLIOGRAPHY

Error processing has received much attention in the literature. [Irons 63] description of a syntax-directed compiler mentioned the added error detection capabilities it offered over ad hoc compiling methods. [Bauer and Eickel 74] have a lengthy discussion of the proper form and style of error messages. [Graham and Rhodes 75], [Barnard 76], [James 72], [LaFrance 70], [Leinius 70], [Levy 71], and [Fischer, Milton, and Quiring 77] all address error recovery techniques.

The PL/C compiler is a striking example of error repair carried to an extreme ([Conway and Wilcox 73], [Cornell 74]). In nearly every case, some repair is attempted, so that processing may continue.

[Elson 73] and [Pratt 75] both discuss in some length methodologies for error processing at an abstract level.

The WATFIV implementation of FORTRAN, while not attempting to repair errors to the degree which the PL/C compiler does, is an excellent example of a good diagnostic compiler [Cress, et al 70]. The messages are clear, complete and the compiler detects many run-time and semantic compile-time errors missed by many implementations. [Pyster and Dutta 78] analyzes the effectiveness of four FORTRAN implementations at detecting both semantic and run-time errors.

9
Stage 5: Data-Types

9.1 INTRODUCTION

Integers and *booleans* represent only a fraction of the data-types commonly available in current programming languages. In this chapter, we augment RASCAL to allow the manipulation of several new data-types:

1. *real* numbers
2. *character* strings
3. *arrays*
4. *enumerated* scalars
5. *enumerated* sets

Several new problems arise in the implementation of these new features: first, we must perform conversions between objects of different types, most notably, *integer* and *real* values; second, we must manipulate objects which do not fit into a single register and which, in fact, can have an arbitrary length. Finally, we must consider objects which are compound in that they may be composed of other objects. For each data-type, we shall discuss general implementation problems and alternative solutions but at a more abstract level than in Chapters 4 through 7 where detailed code segments were presented.

9.2 RASCAL/5 LANGUAGE FEATURES

9.2.1 *Real* Numbers

A *real* number is a limited, precision, rational number. The range of permissible values along with the numerical precision are implementation dependent. *Real* literals have the form:

$$\text{REAL} \rightarrow (\text{SIGN} \mid \lambda) (\text{INTEGER '.' INTEGER})$$
$$(\text{'e' SIGN INTEGER} \mid \lambda)$$

If an 'e' is present, then the value to its left is multiplied by ten raised to the signed *integer* to its right.

    Real symbolic constants are declared in the same manner as *integer* constants, except that the token to the right of '=' is either a *real* literal or a previously declared *real* constant. *Real* variables are declared exactly as are *integer* or *boolean* variables, except that the data-type to the right of ':' is **'real'**.

All arithmetic and relational operators are extended from *integer* to *real* objects in the natural way, except for **'div'** and **'mod'**, which are not defined on *real* operands. One of the most common errors made in arithmetic computation is the unexpected truncation of a fraction by performing *integer* division. To alleviate this problem, RASCAL/5 (as does PASCAL) has a separate operator for division of *real* quantities, '/'. There is no corresponding **'mod'** operator for *reals*. The operands and result of '/' are all *real;* the quotient is not truncated.

Real values are read and written by the natural extensions of **read, readln, write** and **writeln** statements to *real* literals, constants, and variables. The form of I/O statements does not change at all. With the addition of such complex data values to the language, the virtues of a support package for I/O should be even clearer now.

9.2.2 Character Strings

A *character* (or just *char*) is any element of the available alphabet. It might, for example, be all of the characters in the ASCII or EBCDIC character sets. The character of length zero is λ.

A *char* literal is written as:

$$CHAR \rightarrow \text{''' } any\ character \text{ '''}$$

Since the character set includes ', we need a special way to unambiguously write a quote as a character literal. Letting two adjacent quotes stand for a lone quote, we get:

$$''\quad \text{- empty string}$$
$$''''\quad \text{- a quote}$$
$$'\ '\quad \text{- a blank}$$

This is an unfortunate "kluge". The C programming language offers another solution—the *escape* character. A '\' indicates that the next character is to be taken literally, not as part of the metalanguage; thus, in C a quote would be:

$$'\backslash'$$

The escape character finds extensive use in the UNIX text editor, where characters such as '.' and '$' have a special meaning.

Char constants are declared in the usual manner, with the token to the right of '=' being a *char* literal or previously defined *char* constant. Similarly for variables, with the type of a *character* variable being denoted by 'char'.

In addition to a *char* datatype, RASCAL also supports a *string* datatype as well. A *string* is a sequence of zero or more chars up to a maximum of 255. A string literal is just:

$$\text{STRING} \rightarrow \text{'' } any \ sequence \ of \ chars \ \text{''}$$

Strings of length one are also *chars*. *String* constants and variables are also defined in the obvious way, except that *string* variables are declared by:

$$\text{IDS ':' 'string' ('[' LENGTH ']' } |\lambda) \text{ ';'}$$

The length field is an unsigned *integer* literal or a symbolic constant whose value is a positive *integer*. The length field's value, which must be less than 256, indicates the maximum length *string* which may be assigned to that variable. The default is 255 if the length field is missing.

There are no built-in operators especially for *strings*. Procedures to concatenate or analyze *strings* can be readily constructed in RASCAL once subprograms are introduced in Chapter 10.

Relational operators are extended in the natural way to *strings* and *chars*. The collating sequence which determines < and > is implementation dependent, and a major source of headaches when transporting code across machines; for example, 'b' < 'A' in EBCDIC, but 'A' < 'b' in ASCII. Two *strings* must have the same length in order to be compared. Assignment is also extended to *strings* and *chars* in the obvious way, with the restriction that it is illegal to assign to a *string* variable a *string* value longer than the length specified in that variable's declaration. *Strings* of length zero or one can be assigned to *char* variables and conversely.

Input and output of *chars* and *strings* is also simple. Executing **read**(c), where c is a *char* variable, will advance the input file pointer by one character and assign it to c. If **readln**(c) is used instead, then after reading in a value for c, the file pointer will be advanced to the beginning of the next line. For string valued expression e, **write**(e) and **writeln**(e) are handled analogously. Input and output of *strings* is more difficult because they have variable length. We will let **read**(s) and **readln**(s) both assign the sequence of *chars* up to the next *newline* to string variable s. **Write**(e) will output the current value of string expression e, while **writeln**(e) will output a *newline* after the value as well.

9.2.3 *Arrays*

An *array* is an ordered set of objects of the same type, indexed by an n-tuple of *integer* values. In RASCAL/5 we restrict *arrays* so that each object in an *array* is either a *real, boolean, integer, char* or *string*. These five types are called *scalar* data-types to denote the fact that they are not composed of other objects. An *array,* on the other hand, is a *compound* data-type because it is structured from other objects. While there is no reason why the elementary objects of an *array* cannot themselves be compound, we do not allow this for the sake of simplicity here. In RASCAL/5 we do not have any means to write a literal *array* value. This constraint is common to many languages including PL/I, ALGOL60, SNOBOL4, FORTRAN, BASIC, and COBOL. In fact, among the "common" languages, only APL permits the programmer to write an *array* literal; i.e., a self-defining term which represents the value of an entire *array*. Since we cannot write an *array* literal, neither can we declare an *array* symbolic constant. The only means for referencing an *array* is through an *array* variable. An *array* variable is declared by:

IDS ':' 'array' '[' SIZE ']' 'of' SCALAR _TYPE ';'

where *SIZE* is an n-tuple of positive *integer* literals or symbolic constants whose values are positive *integers* or some combination of them. The components of the tuple are separated by commas. SCALAR_TYPE may be any of **'real'**, **'integer'**, **'boolean'**, **'char'** or **'string'**. In the latter case, **'string'** may be qualified by the length of the *strings*.

In RASCAL/5 there are no operators which act on *arrays* as a whole other than assignment, which is defined only between variables with identical SIZE and SCALAR_TYPE. All other operations are defined on the individual elements of the *array* in a manner similar to that of FORTRAN or ALGOL 60. To reference an individual element we write:

NON_KEY_ID '[' TUPLE_EXPRESS ']'

where the non-key identifier is the name of the *array,* and TUPLE_EX-PRESS is a tuple of *integer* valued expressions which agree in number with the declaration of the *array*. In addition, the value of the tuple must be within the range specified in the declaration. An *array* element may appear anywhere that a simple variable of the same type as that element may appear in a program and has the same effect as if a simple variable of that type were to appear there instead.

9.2.4   Enumerated Scalars and Sets

An *enumerated set* in RASCAL/5 is an ordered enumeration of scalar literals. Each literal is an identifier which is not otherwise used as a variable or symbolic constant. A scalar literal may occur in a new class of declaration—the *type* declaration. *Type* declarations have the form:

TYPES   → 'type' TYPE_DCLS

TYPE_DCLS → TYPE_DCL TYPE_DCLS ⎮ TYPE_DCL

TYPE_DCL   → NON_KEY_ID '=' ENUM_SET ';'

ENUM_SET → '(' IDS ')'

This section must follow all constant declarations. A single identifier can appear in just one *type* declaration. The elements of the enumeration are ordered in increasing order from left to right and are incomparable to all other objects. PASCAL has a slightly more general *type* definition facility which we do not include here for the sake of simplicity.

Three sample *type* declarations are:

> **type** day = (mon,tues,wed,thurs,fri,sat,sun);
> city = (santabarbara,chicago,columbus);
> sport = (basketball,football,baseball);

Having created a new data-type, a programmer can now reference either members or subsets of the defining enumeration through literals or variables. A literal has one of two forms depending on whether it is a scalar or a set. The scalar is simply a non-keyword identifier which is a member of some enumeration, its type being that of the enumeration from which it is drawn. A set literal has the definition:

SET_LITERAL → '[' ELEMENTS ']' ⎮ '[' ']'
ELEMENTS   → ELEMENT ',' ELEMENTS ⎮ ELEMENT
ELEMENT   → NON_KEY_ID ' .. ' NON_KEY_ID ⎮ NON_KEY_ID

Each non-keyword identifier is an element of an enumeration of some type. All members of the same literal must belong to a single enumeration; i.e., must have the same type. The elipsis notation is taken directly from PASCAL. It denotes all of the elements of the enumeration between and including the boundary identifiers. If the first identifier is greater than the second, then that sequence is empty. The null set is denoted by '[ ]'.

Variables can also be declared to have the new data-types:

> **var**   weekday: day;
> homes: city;
> major,minor,college: sport;

In addition to enumerated scalar variables, we also have enumerated set variables, as well. The value of a set variable is any subset of a programmer-defined type; for example, we can declare:

days: **set of** day;
cities: **set of** city;
sports: **set of** sport;

The value of each of these variables is a set whose elements are chosen from the enumeration of *day, city,* or *sport.* We shall often use the term *enum* to describe objects and the names of objects whose type is programmer-defined, as opposed to one of the built-in types. Thus, *weekday,* in addition to being of type *day,* is also an *enum scalar* variable, just as *cities,* besides being a variable of type *set of city,* is also an *enum set* variable. Enumerated *sets* give us the ability to model concepts within our programs in their abstract form rather than through some encoding. For example, instead of having the type *day* in a FORTRAN program, we would probably have *integers* 1 through 7 represent the seven days of the week. *Weekday* would be an integer variable which could be assigned one of these seven *integer* values. We would be forced in FORTRAN to model days of the week as if they were *integers,* a process which detracts from the aesthetics of the program, as well as its reliability. A *set* variable would probably be modeled as an *array* of logical elements, where a logical *true* indicates a member is present in the set; a logical *false* indicates its absence. This again detracts from the beauty of the program by forcing the programmer to bend his view of the problem to the constructs of the language, instead of extending the language constructs to meet the programmer's needs. RASCAL/5, makes some attempt to extend the base language as required by the problem being solved.

An ordering is defined on the elements of a *set* enumeration, as dictated by their order of appearance in the enumeration from left to right. To make this ordering truly useful, we need two functions, *pred* and *succ,* which return the element, if any, which precedes or follows their argument in the enumeration. **Pred** is undefined on the first element of the enumeration, just as **succ** is undefined on the last.

Since we have enumerated *sets,* it is natural to define operators on both individual *set* elements and on the *sets* themselves. For *sets* we define union, intersection, difference, and membership test, using the tokens:

$$\text{`+', `*', `-', `in'}$$

to denote these infix operators. Note that '−' is now used for five different operations: *integer* subtraction, *real* subtraction, *integer* negation, *real* negation, and *set* difference. For scalar objects the relational operations are determined by the ordering of the *set* enumerations. It is illegal to compare two objects which are not from the same enumeration. Of course, in addition to the operations mentioned above, we can also *assign* one scalar or *set* object to a scalar or *set* variable of the same type. Deviating from the simple view taken by PASCAL, we shall also permit output of any object which is either a member of an enumerated set or a set of such members, and input of *enum* scalars. Scalar literals will appear as character *strings* in both the input and the output data streams. An enumerated *set* will appear *without elipsis* as a *set* literal in the output. The elements of the *set* will be separated by an implementation dependent number of blanks on output. '[' will appear before the first element and ']' after the last element.

Adding the ability to read and write abstract data-types, is a major improvement over PASCAL. We have extended the abstract view of the problem directly to the data preparation and output analysis. The person preparing the input can think in terms of *days, cities,* and *sports* and not have to translate those thoughts into some encoding; similarly, the people analyzing the program output need not handle some encoding of the abstract concepts.

9.2.5 Conversions

We permit just a handful of type conversions in RASCAL/5 programs. Automatic conversions are defined between *integer* and *real* quantities, and conversions are also defined between *strings* of length one or zero and *chars*.

Wherever a *real* value is expected, but an *integer* is found, that *integer* is converted into its *real* equivalent. There is no implicit conversion from *real* to *integer,* even for the assignment statement. One of the most common arithmetic errors is the unexpected truncation of a fraction when converting a *real* value into an *integer.* PASCAL safeguards against this error by prohibiting implicit *real* to *integer* conversion. In PASCAL, the programmer must explicitly order the conversion via the **trunc** or **round** functions, which have a *real* argument, returning an *integer* result. Actually, the policy of requiring explicit syntactic markers to show conversion is a throwback to FORTRAN II, where mixed type arithmetic expressions were not allowed. However, RASCAL/5 is not as restrictive as was FORTRAN II, in that implicit *integer* to *real* conversions (which are not nearly as often a source of error) are permitted.

Figure 9-1 shows a valid RASCAL/5 program, while Fig. 9-2 presents an erroneous one.

```
program   payroll(input, output)
        {illustrate correct usage of new types.}
   const  rate = 6.50;  {hourly average}
          size = 7;     {# of employees}
   type   days = (mon, tue, wed, thu, fri, sat, sun);
   var    i, j: integer;
          dayworked: days;
          m, hours: real;
          k: string[25];
          salary: array[size] of real;
          name: array[size] of string[25];
          bonus: set of days; {days receiving bonus pay}
   begin
        {compute salaries}
     readln (bonus);   {which days earn bonus pay?}
     i := 1;
     while (i <= size) do   begin
       readln (name[i]);
       readln (hours);
       readln (dayworked);
       if (dayworked in [sat, sun] or (dayworked in bonus) then
          salary[i] := 2 * rate * hours;  {double pay}
     else   salary[i] := rate * hours;
     i := i + 1; {process next employee}  end;
       {sort salaries}
   i := 1;
   while (i <- size) do begin
     j := i + 1;
     while (j <= size) do begin
       if name[i] > name[j] then begin
          {exchange}
          k := name[i];  m := salary[i];
          name[i] := name[j];  salary[i] := salary[j];
          name[j] := k;  salary[j] := m;  end;
       j := j + 1;  end;
     i := i + 1;  end;
       {print salaries}
   i := 1;
   while (i <= size) do begin
     writeln (name[i], salary[i]);
     i := i + 1;  end;
```

Fig. 9-1. A Valid RASCAL/5 Program.

```
program  hardlyanyeffort(input,output);
         {illustrate incorrect usage of RASCAL/5 features.}
  type  hobbits = (bilbo, samwise, frodo);
        magicians = (merlin,gandalf, saruman);
        rabbits = (marli,bilbo,bigwig,hazel);  {bilbo appears twice.}
        numbers = (3,4,1.5);  {only identifiers in enumeration.}
  var  travelers: hobbits;
       magicians: integer;  {magicians already a type name.}
       wild:  set of rabbits;
       i: integer;  r: real;
       greatest: set of habits;
  begin
    readln  (greatest);
    if greatest = bilbo then;                  {cannot compare a set to a scalar.}
    readln  (wild, travelers, i, r);
    if i in wild then i := i + 1;            {integer cannot be in a set of rabbits.}
    else  wild := wild + marli;                   {cannot "union" a set to a scalar.}
     i := r;                           {cannot assign a real to an integer variable.}
  end.
```

Fig. 9-2. An Invalid RASCAL/5 Program.

9.3 CANTOR/5 IMPLEMENTATION FEATURES

In Chapter 4 we set restrictions on the range of legal *integer* values in CANTOR/0; we must repeat this process for *real* values here. On the IBM 360/370, *real* numbers (also called *floating-point* numbers) are represented internally in fraction times exponent format. Figure 9-3 shows the breakdown of the full-word representation of a *real* number into its component fields: sign, fraction, and exponent. The machine architecture also supports a larger 64-bit floating point number which offers greater precision,

0	1000000	10000000 00000000 00000000
sign	characteristic	fraction

value is computed by formula:

sign = 0 => positive
     = 1 => negative

exponent = characteristic − 64
fraction = unsigned binary number with leading binary point
value = sign   fraction × 16^{exponent}

so for this example,

value = $+\ 0.5 \times 16^0 = +0.5$

Fig. 9-3. Internal Representation of *Real* Numbers.

but we shall not consider such *double precision floating-point* numbers here. Since the IBM 360/370 hardware is organized to support operations on *real* numbers stored in the format shown in Fig. 9-3, this is the format which we shall follow here.

The IBM 360/370 architecture supports the convenient relocation of up to 256 contiguous bytes in memory with a single instruction. (The IBM 370 supports much larger relocation, but we wish to remain compatible with the IBM 360.) Consequently, we shall restrict the length of *strings* to be less than or equal to 255. This is not as arbitrary as it might seem, since a very popular implementation of PL/I, namely, PL/C, has this same restriction.

We restrict the size of *arrays* to $2^{31} - 1$, since that is the largest *integer* which can be held in a full-word. However, another constraint on the compiler actually restricts the size of *arrays* to a small fraction of this value. The entire object program must be addressable by a single base register; i.e., no more than 4096 bytes. However, since the exact size of the largest *array* will vary with the other code in the RASCAL/5 source program, we do not set an explicit upper bound here other than that the *array* size must fit into a full-word.

Some of the readers may be bothered (appalled ?) by the fact that the amount of data, and even the size of an array which we can have, is a function of how much executable 360AL object a program is compiled into. This compiler quirk arises because we have chosen to address both the code and the data via one base register, and the data physically follows the code in memory. Many computers maintain physically separate areas for code and data. They are addressed by two distinct base registers (or something equivalent); in this way, the size of the "easily addressable" code and data are independently determined. We could have chosen to maintain separate base registers for code and data but opted for simplicity in compiler design. We have also ignored how programs which require more than 4096 bytes are, in fact, compiled. Clearly, one simple option is to allocate more base registers as needed. This, of course, has a strong impact on the size of the code generated, because such a strategy decreases the number of general purpose registers free for arithmetic and other such operations. Furthermore, this policy cannot be extended indefinitely, since there are only sixteen such registers available; every commercial compiler writer faces this problem, which is really one of architecture. If the IBM 360 designers had been willing to extend each instruction (perhaps optionally) which references memory by another byte, the maximum displacement would be increased from 4096 to 1,048,576 bytes, a figure more than adequate for nearly every program running today. It has been said that there is no greater architectural flaw than not allowing enough addressing bits. This is evidenced quite clearly in the instruction set of the IBM 360.

To sidestep the addressing limitations we sketch one general solution which requires a two pass compiler and one permanent base register. Two passes are needed in order to resolve forward references properly. Up to two *temporary* base registers are needed to handle SS instructions such as:

$$\text{MVC DATA1, DATA2}$$

where DATA1 and DATA2 require different base registers. One of the functions of the first pass is to break the program up into segments, each of which (except possibly the last) is 4096 bytes long. Numbering each segment from 1, suppose we have a program with 4 segments. Within each segment we shall insert a data area which contains the address of the beginning of each segment which is referenced from that segment except itself; in the case of our example, segment 1 would contain:

```
SA100002 DC  A(SEG00002)
SA100004 DC  A(SEG00004)
```

if it had references to segments 2 and 4.

Each segment establishes addressability in the normal manner, labeling each segment:

```
            BALR     12.0
            USING    *,12
   SEGn     EQU      *
```

where the n is the segment number. Note that each segment uses the same base register. Suppose segment 1 contains a reference to a location in segment 2:

$$\text{L r,DATAIN2}$$

As it stands, DATAIN2 is not addressable; to establish addressability, we instead issue:

```
   L         q,SA10002
   USING     SEG00002,q
   L         r,DATAIN2
```

where q is a register which is allocated just for this one code segment. After this segment is emitted, register q can be freed for other purposes. To assure addressability, a statement such as:

$$\text{MVC   DATAIN2,DATAIN4}$$

becomes:

```
L        q,SA10002
USING    SEG0002,q
L        s,SA10004
USING    SEG0004,s
MVC      DATAIN2,DATAIN4
```

Again, after this segment is emitted, registers q and s can both be freed.

The only other constraint which must be set here is the size of the print fields for *real* and *boolean* values. We shall keep the same value as that used for printing in Chapter 7; i.e., 13.

In this chapter, we do not present an LL(1) grammar which formally defines the extensions to RASCAL/3 presented here. We instead offer new features in a much more informal manner. We shall, however, indicate the nature of the routines which must be defined to process these new features and how they are embedded into CANTOR/5. We begin with the processing of declarations.

9.4   Processing Declarations

The first class of declarations encountered in a RASCAL/5 program will be **const** declarations. Symbolic constants are easily handled as shown in Fig. 9-4. Because **type** declarations follow the **const** declaration section, constants can be of type **integer, boolean, real, char,** and **string** only.

The second class of declarations establish programmer-defined types. We shall need to reference the individual elements of an enumeration later in the compilation; hence, each element must be saved. Furthermore, we shall map the elements of the enumeration into an internal representation more convenient for manipulation in the object code, just as we mapped logical **true** and **false** to integer -1 and 0, respectively. The simplest encoding is to map a set of n enumerated elements into the first n non-negative *integers*. Figure 9-5 shows the mapping for the **type** declaration of *days* in Fig. 9-1. Although the programmer manipulates abstract ob-

```
insert('rate',real,immutable,6.50,yes,1)
insert('size', integer, immutable, 7, yes, 1)

@R0  DC  E'6.50'    rate
@I0  DC  F'7'       size
```

Fig. 9-4. Calls to *Insert* for The Declaration of Symbolic Constants in Fig. 9-1 Along with The Storage Generated.

day = (mon, tues, wed, thurs, fri, sat, sun)
  1 2 3 4 5 6 7

Fig. 9-5. Mapping Type Declarations to Their Integer Representation.

jects, such as days of the week or various cities and sports, the implementation will convert all references to these abstract objects into references to "concrete" *integer values,* with the additional property that the ordering of abstract objects is preserved in the representation.

Two types of entries are made in the symbol table for each *type* declaration: First, we create an entry for the name of the *type* itself, and second, for each element of the enumeration. The *value* field gives the *integer* representation of that element; the *type* field shows the name of the new data-type. Figure 9-6 shows the calls to *insert* for the *type* declaration of Fig. 9-1. They create entries in the symbol table as described. We shall also emit a storage structure which will enable us to map the abstract names to their representation at object code execution time, which is necessary for the input and output of abstract objects. A simple structure shown in Fig. 9-7 has two components. The first is a list of *n* addresses, where *n* is the cardinality of the enumeration. Each address points to a second component, which is a *string*—the abstract name. The *i*-th address points to the *i*-th name of an element in the enumeration. With such a structure available in the object code, it is easy to imagine routines which

from *day* type declaration:

 insert('days',prog.defined,immutable,'mon,tue,wed,thu,
  fri,sat,sun',no,)
 insert('mon','day',immutable,1,no,)
 insert('tue','day',immutable,2,no,)
   . . .
 insert('sun','day',immutable,7,no,)

for input/output:

@A0	DC	A(@T2)	address of mon
	DC	A(@T3)	address of tue
		. . .	
	DC	A(@T8)	address of sun
@T2	DC	C'MON'	from type day
@T3	DC	C'TUE'	from type day
		. . .	
@T8	DC	C'SUN'	from type day

Fig. 9-6. Calls to *Insert* for The *Type* Declaration of Fig. 9-1 Along with Storage Emitted.

insert('i,j', integer, mutable,, yes, 1)
insert('dayworked', days, mutable,, yes, 1)
insert('m,hours', real, mutable,, yes, 1)
insert('k', varying, mutable,, yes, 25)

@I1	DS	F	i
@ 2	DS	F	j
@I4	DS	F	dayworked
@ 1	DS	E	m
@ 2	DS	E	hours
@ V0	DS	CL25	k
@LNV0	DS	F	length of @V0

Fig. 9-7. Calls to *Insert* for The Declaration of Scalar Variables, along with Emitted Storage.

map between internal *integer* and external *string* formats for abstract objects.

Finally, variable declarations are reached. **Real** and **char** variables are handled using standard assembly language conventions. *String* variables, on the other hand, are somewhat different, because the length of the value assigned to the variable may change at execution-time. We must allocate *two* storage components in 360AL to correspond to the declaration of a single **string** variable: one for the value; the other for the length of the current value. We shall allocate enough storage to hold the longest *string* which can be assigned to the variable, based on the length specified in the declaration. At times, the *string* value will occupy less than the full amount of storage allocated to it. The length field will indicate exactly how many characters are in the current value.

The other scalar variable *dayworked* has type *days*. Because *days* is implemented as an integer value, its storage is a full-word.

Figure 9-7 shows the calls to *insert* for the scalar variable declarations, along with the storage eventually emitted by *emit storage* for these entries. The correspondence between the names of the length and value fields of a *string* variable will simplify coordinating their use in code generation.

Figure 9-1 also includes a set variable. We can represent a *set* of enumerated literals as a *linked list,* where the value field of each node is a representation of a *set* element. However, given the simple nature of the *set* member representation, namely, as a positive *integer,* encoding a *set* in this manner would waste time and space. We instead represent the current value of a *set* variable by a bit vector: one bit per potential member. The vector is n bits long, where n is the number of elements in the enumerated *set* in the declaration of this variable. A zero value for the i-th bit of the vector indicates that the i-th element of the enumerated *set* is not in the variable's current value; a one indicates it is. Since we cannot allocate single bits in the IBM 360/370 family, we shall allocate $(n+7)$ **div** 8 bytes of contiguous storage to hold the value of a variable whose value can have cardinality at most n.

In order to process the declaration of an *array* variable, we must store the dimensions of the *array* into the symbol table entry for the *array* name. This is necessary for three reasons, two related to error processing. The storage for the *array* will be one contiguous block large enough to hold the value of every element of the *array*. An element of the *array* is mapped to a set of contiguous locations within that block. In order to compute the offset from the beginning of the block associated with any given *array* element, we shall need to know the values of the *array* dimensions. A second reason is to ensure that each reference has the number of values in the subscript required by the declaration. Finally, a third is to guarantee that the subscript is within the bounds of the *array* as specified in the declaration.

Figure 9-8 shows the way in which storage will be allocated and elements referenced. The formula shown works for *arrays* of arbitrary dimension, provided that only the lower bound for each dimension is one, a slight generalization of this formula working for arbitrary lower bounds, as well. Generating this more general form is left to the reader as an exercise.

Every time an *array* element is referenced in the program, a fairly long computation must be carried out to find the address of that element within the *array* block. By a bit of simple algebraic manipulation, this computation can be reduced. Figure 9-9 shows both the revised form of the formula and a comparison of the amount of computation required for the two schemes. The key difference between the two rests on the compile-time computation of a value, which is *constant* at execution-time. By factoring

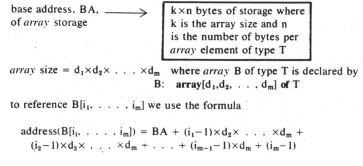

base address, BA, $\longrightarrow$ of *array* storage

$k \times n$ bytes of storage where k is the array size and n is the number of bytes per *array* element of type T

array size = $d_1 \times d_2 \times \ldots \times d_m$ where *array* B of type T is declared by
B: **array**$[d_1, d_2, \ldots, d_m]$ **of** T

to reference B$[i_1, \ldots, i_m]$ we use the formula

$$\text{address}(B[i_1, \ldots, i_m]) = BA + (i_1-1) \times d_2 \times \ldots \times d_m + (i_2-1) \times d_3 \times \ldots \times d_m + \ldots + (i_{m-1}-1) \times d_m + (i_m-1)$$

Fig. 9-8. Referencing Elements of An *Array*.

This can be broken into two parts: cpart + vpart where

$$\text{cpart} = BA - d_2 \times' . \ . \ . \times d_m - d_3 \times \ . \ . \ . \times d_m - . \ . \ . - d_m - 1$$

$$\text{vpart} = i_1 \times d_2 \times \ . \ . \ . \times d_m + i_2 \times d_3 \times \ . \ . \ . \times d_m + . \ . \ . + i_{m-1} d_m + i_m$$

Vpart can be conveniently computed by factoring

$$d_m(i_{m-1} + d_{m-1}(i_{m-2} + d_{m-2}(i_{m-3} + . \ . \ . + d_2 i_1) . \ . \ .))) + i_m$$

Cpart can be computed once during compilation. Vpart must be computed at execution time for each *array* reference.

Original formula has   m subtractions, $(m-2)(m-1)/2$ multiplications, and m+1 additions.

Revised formula has   0 subtractions, $m-1$ multiplications, and m additions at execution-time presuming cpart is computed once at compile-time.

Fig. 9-9. Optimized Referencing Elements of An *Array*.

this constant out and performing the computation just once at compile-time, repeated computation at execution-time is avoided. In addition to storing the *array* dimensions in the symbol table, we should also compute and save *cpart*, as we call the constant part of the address computation. We organize all of the new information which must be stored in the symbol table under a single new field—*dope vector*, the term commonly given to describe such a collection of information. Figure 9-10 shows the calls to *insert* for the *array* and set variables declared in the program of Fig. 9-1, along with the storage generated for those entries. Note that the last field of each call to *insert* is itself a *record* which contains the number of dimensions, each dimension value and *cpart*. Note also that the *type* field of the entry for an *array* is a *record* as well, having two fields, one indicating that the variable is indeed an *array,* the second indicating the data type of each *array* element.

insert('salary', (array, real), mutable,, yes, (1,7,−1))
insert('name', (array, varying), mutable,, yes, 25, (1,7,−1))
insert('bonus', (set, days), mutable,, yes, 1)

@R3	DS	7E	salary
@ V1	DS	175C	name
@LNV1	DS	25F	length of name ←
@S1	DS	1X	bonus

Note that this is an *array*, too.

Fig. 9-10. Calls to *Insert* for The Declaration of *Array* Variables in Fig. 9-1 Along with Storage Generated.

9.5　PROCESSING REFERENCES

The last section established the storage structures we shall use to hold the representation of objects of our new data-types. Now we must determine how to handle references to these new objects within the main body of the RASCAL/5 source code. The discussion centers around the various operators for which these new objects are operands.

All operands, independent of their data-type, are pushed onto a single operand stack by the parsing action routines, the stack created for CANTOR/1. These stack elements become arguments in the calls to the various subroutines nested inside *code,* the code generator of CANTOR. Each subroutine which receives such arguments must now check their data-type so that:

1. 360AL code which converts an operand's value into another type can be emitted if necessary (note that the conversion is performed in the object code);
2. if the data-types of the arguments are illegal for this particular operation, that can be detected by CANTOR (see Chapter 8 for more details);
3. if a single operator token, such as '+', actually stands for more than one operation at the object code level, such as *integer* or *real* addition, the code generating routine can determine which operation is applicable in this case.

If a literal or symbolic constant must be converted into a different data-type, that conversion can be done at *compile-time,* rather than at *execution-time,* since the value of the operand will not change during program execution. This is just another example of a simple but quite useful optimization which can be performed with little effort. The expression:

$$3 + bc \quad \text{\{where bc is a \textit{real} variable\}}$$

can be compiled as if it were:

$$3.0 + bc$$

saving the execution of the conversion routine in the object code. For *real* operands, we can perform compile-time arithmetic wherever possible without much additional effort; thus, we can compile:

$$3.0 + 7 * 23.1$$

as if it were 164.7 instead.

Operations on *real* operands are normally handled through a set of four floating-point registers and a related set of operations which manipulate values in those registers. These registers and instructions are part of the architecture of the IBM 360/370 family. We must establish a bookkeeping system for these registers in exactly the same way we did for the fixed-point registers earlier. This new bookkeeping system should operate in a manner consistent with the philosophy that the fewer perturbations of operands in registers and memory when allocating a register, the better. We do not elaborate further on this bookkeeping scheme.

Because the compilation of references to *chars* is somewhat easier than that to *character strings,* we consider *chars* first. A "CLC" 360AL instruction can compare two *chars* directly; for example, to compare *chars* x and y for equality, we could use the following 360AL code:

$$\text{CLC} \quad @Cn(1), @Cp$$

where @C*m* is the internal name of x and @C*p* the internal name of y. Assignment is handled in just as easy a manner with an "MVC" instruction.

Comparing two *strings* is more complex because *string* lengths vary at execution time. RASCAL requires the two *strings* to have the same length, so that we can perform the comparison without having to pad or truncate either operand. The code to perform the comparison between *strings* x and y is:

$$\text{EX} \quad r, @\text{COMPARE}$$

where @COMPARE labels

$$\text{CLC } x(0), y$$

and register r holds the length of x. An EXECUTE instruction is needed to accommodate the variable length. If *strings* could be longer than 255 characters, this scheme would not work. Assignment 'x := y;' also requires an EXECUTE instruction:

$$\text{EX} \quad r, @\text{ASSIGN}$$

where @ASSIGN labels

$$\text{MVC } x(0), y$$

where r holds the length of x.

An enumerated scalar is represented internally as an *integer*. Hence, references to *enum* scalar variables are essentially handled as if they were references to *integer* variables. Similarly, references to enumerated scalar literals are handled as if they were *integer* literals. Thus, the implementation of comparison and assignment operations is quite straightforward. They are compiled essentially as if they were *integer* operations. Of course, the date-type of an *enum* scalar is *not integer,* so the compiler must disallow any such illegal references (presuming error detection capability as described in Chapter 8). The type field of the symbol table entries for the elements of an enumerated type permits us to determine whether two enumerated scalar operands have the same type. For input and output of enumerated scalars, references to the table of storage shown in Fig. 9-5 must be made. The external identifier name of an abstract quantity must be available at execution-time in order for input/output of abstract quantities to be possible.

An enumerated *set,* you will recall, is represented by a bit vector, one bit per possible element of the *set.* With this representation, the basic *set* operations become trivial to implement. Union is simply the "oring" of bit vectors; intersection is their "anding;" and 'A-B' is simply the bitwise computation of 'A **and not** B'. Membership is decided by checking whether the i-th bit of the vector is one or zero, where i is the representation of the element being tested. Assignment is accomplished by replacing one bit vector with another. There are no relational operations defined on *sets,* except for '=' and '<>', which are easily implemented by a "CLC" operation on the two operands, which have the same length, because both operands must have the same type. Output is also accomplished through references to the table which maps internal representation to abstract names for *set* elements.

9.6   SUMMARY

Six new classes of data-types have been added to RASCAL: *reals, char, strings, arrays,* enumerated scalars and enumerated *sets*. The compilation of these new types offers a number of problems not faced in earlier versions of RASCAL. In particular, we are forced to use the floating-point hardware and instruction set of the IBM 360/370 family for the first time. This involves establishing a register allocation and assignment scheme for floating-point registers on a par to the one created in Chapter 5 for the fixed point registers of the machine. We must also handle operands which cannot be placed into a single register because their length can be arbitrarily long. Furthermore, the length of string variables can change during program execution, a possibility not previously encountered, forcing us to postpone certain computations until execution-time which otherwise would be made during compilation. *Arrays* offer new challenges in that they are *compound* objects; i.e., an object composed of other objects. We must devise a mechanism for referencing single elements of the *array* in a reasonably efficient manner. Finally, we extend RASCAL to permit programmer-defined data-types and allow both *scalar* and *set* variables to be defined over these new types. Because of our relatively efficient representation of an enumerated type as a sequence of positive *integers,* the compilation of references to objects with these new types is relatively simple.

EXERCISES

9-1. If we did not allow input/output of programmer-defined objects, what reductions in storage would be possible in the object code of CANTOR/5?

9-2. PASCAL permits *array* indices to have arbitrary lower bounds. Extend RASCAL/5 and CANTOR/5 to incorporate this new feature. Motivate its inclusion by several examples where an arbitrary lower bound for an *array* dimension improves the aesthetics of the programs.

9-3. PASCAL permits *array* indices to be any scalar type except *real,* including enumerated scalars. Extend RASCAL/5 and CANTOR/5 to incorporate such a feature. Motivate its inclusion by several examples where arbitrary scalar indices improve the aesthetics of the programs. Why do you think *reals* were excluded, even though they are ordered?

9-4. Suppose an implicit conversion were defined between *integers* and *strings* so that an *integer* was always converted into a *string* when a *string* was expected, and a *string* was converted into an *integer* if the conversion made sense, when an *integer* was expected. So, for example,

$$'3' + 5$$

would be well-defined and equal *integer* 8, while:

$$concat('ho', 5, result);$$

would also be well-defined, assigning 'ho 5' to *result.* What changes to our ability to detect errors at compile-time would result from such an extension in conversion policy?

9-5. Add the *record* data-type of PASCAL to RASCAL/5 and CANTOR/5.

9-6. How would you implement a FORTRAN-like EQUIVALENCE statement in RASCAL/5?

9-7. Extend the operations on sets to include subset '<=', proper subset '<', superset, '>=', and proper superset '>'.

9-8. Extend RASCAL/5 to allow array literals so that, for example,

$$array[1, 3, 7]$$

is an array of three integers. Allow such literals in expressions.

TESTING HINTS

1. Test CANTOR/5 on all programs used to test CANTOR/3 (or CANTOR/4 if you have also built error processing capabilities into your compiler).

2. Test CANTOR/5 on one or more programs which:
   a. Have an enumerated type which has just one element; one which has eight elements; and one which has nine elements. The programs should include literals, and variables, both scalar and *set,* of each type.
   b. Include all operations on *sets.* The bit vectors should be both one and two bytes long.
   c. Have *real* literals, constants, and variables. The literals should use both the 'e' format and the simpler form without 'e' and should include both signed and unsigned *real* literals. Test to ensure that zero is properly represented.
   d. Fill all floating-point registers to test your register allocation and assignment code. You should force the creation of temporaries in main memory as you did in testing the scheme devised for *integers* in Chapter 5.
   e. Have *char* literals, constants, and variables. Include the literal empty string and a literal which has an embedded quotation mark.
   f. Have *string* variables. At run-time assign these variables *strings* of length zero up to their maximum length. Print each value as it is assigned to ensure the correct value is being stored.
   g. Have *arrays* of each permissible type of one, two, and three dimensions. Step through each element of each *array* to ensure that the proper values are referenced.
   h. Read and write all new types in all various forms.

BIBLIOGRAPHY

[Knuth 68] is an excellent source for general information on data structures. More recent texts include [Horowitz and Sahni 76] and [Tremblay and Sorenson 76]. [Pratt 75] offers an excellent study of the structures required to implement many programming language data-types, such as strings, records and so forth.

A more efficient implementation of *strings* requires dynamic storage management, a topic not broached in this text except for subprogram calls. [Gries 71] has a short discussion of this topic. [Griswold 71] is a lucid, detailed look at a SNOBOL interpreter and covers this topic more fully.

10
Stage 6: Subprograms and Block Structure

10.1 INTRODUCTION

The need to divide large programs into smaller modules was recognized from the earliest days of programming. Such a division:

1. improves readability;
2. improves testability;
3. enhances organization;
4. makes recursion possible.

RASCAL supports two forms of subprogram: the *procedure* and the *function*. These two forms differ chiefly in that the function returns a value to the calling expression, while a procedure does not. Hence, a procedure is a restricted form of function. A program must contain one *main* module but can have any number of subprograms. Within executable code, we can insert calls to activate any or all subprograms, any number of times. The calling discipline, called *block-structure,* is explained in detail in this chapter.

The implementation of subprograms is the most complex problem we tackle in this text; consequently, we introduce it piecemeal. The first part deals with parameter passing and subprogram communication in a non-block-structured language (such as FORTRAN). We continue with the implementation of a non-recursive block structured RASCAL. Finally, we offer the full power and generality of recursion and block structure in RASCAL. Block structure and recursion are especially difficult to implement, because of the change in storage policy they necessitate. In earlier chapters, we could allocate all of the storage required by a program at compile-time. In a block structured language this simple allocation policy is not adequate. Memory must be *dynamically* allocated at run-time in a stack discipline. As each new subprogram is called, storage for quantities local to it must be allocated. When that routine returns to its caller, the allocated storage must be released. In a recursive program, where a single routine may be activated many times simultaneously, an indefinite number of copies of that routine's data area may exist concurrently.

10.2 SUBPROGRAMS IN A NON-BLOCK STRUCTURED ENVIRONMENT

10.2.1 Physical Organization

In this section subprograms are physically separate entities. As such, they will be compiled separately as well; i.e., no information used in the compilation of one module will affect the compilation of another module. Figure 10-1 shows the physical organization of such a program, including the form of subprogram definition and call. The main module is followed by any number of subprograms, either functions or procedures, in any order. Any subprogram may be called by another module. The only restriction is

```
program   m(input,output);
               {illustrate non-block structured RASCAL with subprograms.}
   const   age = 21;
   var   x,y: integer;   z: boolean;
         f: function(boolean): integer; forward;
         s: procedure(integer,integer); forward;
   begin
     readln   (x,z);
     y := f(z);
     writeln (y);
     s(age,x);
     writeln (x,y);
   end.

procedure   s(howold: integer; var status: integer);
   var   x: boolean;   {new variable with same name as in m.}
   begin
     readln (x);
     if x then status:=howold;
     else   status := 0;
   end.

function   f(q: boolean): integer;
   var   age: integer;
   begin
     if q then readln (age);
     else   age := 0;
     f := age + 21;
   end.
```

Fig. 10-1. Physical Organization of Subprograms in Non-Block Structured RASCAL/6.

that no subprogram may directly or indirectly call itself; i.e., *recursion* is not allowed. Figure 10-2 shows two forbidden calling structures. Procedure *c* has a call to *c* inside it. Since *c* calls itself, it is *directly recursive;* furthermore, *c* also calls *d,* which then calls *c* again. Routine *c* is also said to be *indirectly recursive.* A routine which is either directly or indirectly recursive is said to be *recursive.* Recursive routines cannot be implemented without dynamic storage allocation, since a data area must be created for each activation of the routine. We therefore postpone consideration of recursive routines until section 10.4.

A subprogram communicates with its caller through a *parameter* or *argument* list, as shown in Fig. 10-1. The subprogram header statement, which begins the definition of the subprogram, includes a list of variable names called *formal parameters* or *formal arguments.* Each call to a subprogram must include a list of arguments equal in number to those of the subprogram header. The arguments in the call, the *actual arguments* or *actual parameters,* may be any arithmetic, relational or logical expressions. A correspondence is defined between the *i*-th formal and *i*-th actual argument at the time the call is made. This correspondence lasts only for the duration of the call, being broken once the call is completed. The transfer of information to and from the calling and called routines is termed *parameter passing* and centers around the correspondence between formal and actual arguments.

```
procedure   c(x: integer);
                {illustrate recursion, which is illegal in this version of RASCAL.}
        var   d: function(integer): boolean;
        . . .

        begin
        . . .
        c(y);
        z := d(arg);
        . . .
        end.

function   d(n: boolean): integer;
                {d will call c, so that c indirectly calls itself.}
        var   c: procedure(integer,integer);
        . . .
        begin
        . . .
        c(arg);
        . . .
        end.
```

Fig. 10-2. A Recursive Subprogram.

There are at least seven commonly discussed methods for passing arguments between a subprogram and its caller:

1. value
2. reference or address
3. result
4. value-result
5. name
6. text or string
7. dummy argument

The differences in passing techniques affect program behavior, often in subtle ways. RASCAL and its parent language PASCAL support only the first two methods. As such, these are the only two which we shall examine here. For further information on the other five methods, the reader is urged to see [Elson 73], [Pratt 76] or one of the other general language references cited in the bibliography.

All names of a module, except a subprogram name, are *local* to the containing module. We say that the *scope* of names defined within a module is just that module. In later sections describing block-structure, this scoping policy will change, but here a simple scoping policy is adopted. Hence, in Fig. 10-1, we have both subprogram s and main program m declaring variable x. This is perfectly valid. Note that even the data-types of the two variables are different! The two names have no relationship to one another whatsoever. The reference to x from within s addresses the variable declared in s. Similarly, the reference to x from m addresses a distinct x. The only name associated with a module which is not local to it is the module name itself. Module s is *global* in that it is known to all other routines so that they may call it.

The value of restricting the scope of identifier names is that subprograms can be developed independently without having to coordinate the selection of identifier names to avoid overlap. However, if two routines need to share a large amount of storage, this can lead to very long parameter lists. This is bad on two counts: First, the programmer can get writer's cramp having to mark down all those parameters; secondly, long lists are error-prone. It is easy to forget a parameter or to permute the order of two arguments. Block structure and FORTRAN COMMON blocks are methods designed to reduce the need to explicitly pass information between routines via parameter lists. Block structure will be studied in section 10.3.

10.2.2   Call By Reference

The first parameter passing technique we shall discuss is call by *reference*. In this method, the address of the actual argument is passed to the sub-program. There is no physical storage allocated for the formal argument; instead, it is bound to the address of the actual argument which is passed to the subprogram. The formal and actual arguments become *aliases* or synonyms for the same memory location for the duration of subprogram execution. Upon return of control to the calling routine, the bond between formal and actual argument is broken. As a consequence of this correspondence, any change to the value of the formal argument has the effect of simultaneously changing the value of the actual argument. Figure 10-3 shows the effects of call by reference. Procedure *p* is called from main program *m* with actual argument *x*. The formal argument of *p* is *u*. Because the value of *x* is 12 at the time of the call, when subprogram *p* begins execution, the value of *y* is also 12. The first assignment statement of *p* changes the value of *y* to 1. The value of *x* is simultaneously changed to 1 as well since *x* and *y* refer to the same location in memory. When *p* returns control to *m*, the value of *x* remains modified as 1, and the value of formal argument *y* becomes undefined.

With call by reference, the calling program has no direct way to protect an actual argument from being accidentally and improperly changed by a subprogram. For example, suppose the programmer of *m* did not wish variable *x* changed by *p*, although *p* would be free to reference the current value of *x* as needed for its computation. The calling routine cannot guarantee that the actual argument will not be modified. One way to ensure that the value of *x* is not modified is to assign it to a temporary variable, *t* and use *t* as the actual argument instead of *x*. Any changes to

```
program   m(output);
          {illustrate call by reference.}
    var   x: integer;
          p: procedure(integer);
    begin
      x := 12;     {set value of x to 12.}
      p(x);        {change value of x.}
      writeln (x); {the value printed is 1.}
    end.

procedure   p(var   y: integer);
    begin
      y := 1; {change formal argument, simultaneously changing actual argument.}
    end.
```

Fig. 10-3. Call by Reference.

the value of *t* do not matter. Another more satisfying solution is to specify in the subprogram that the value of the formal argument is to be initialized to that of the actual argument when the subprogram is called but that changes to the formal argument are not to be reflected as changes to the value of the actual argument. This solution is our second parameter passing technique, call by *value*.

10.2.3   Call By Value

When an argument is passed by *value,* the address of the actual argument is passed into the subprogram just as for call by reference. In the call by reference, the formal parameter is bound to that address for the duration of the call, but in a call by value the formal argument is allocated storage in the subprogram. The value of the actual argument, through its address, is copied by the subprogram into the storage reserved locally for the formal argument. The formal argument can then be manipulated independent of the actual argument. When the subprogram ceases execution, the value of the actual argument is unchanged, and the value of the formal argument becomes undefined. In this way, the value of the actual argument is protected from change. Figure 10-4 demonstrates the difference between call by value and reference. Subprogram *q* has both a value and a reference argument which are distinguished by the appearance of 'var' in the specification of the reference arguments and the absence of 'var' in the value arguments. Within *q,* the change to the value of reference argument

```
program   m(output);
          {illustrate difference between call by value and call by reference.}
   var   b,c: integer;
          q: procedure(integer, integer);
   begin
          {set values of actual parameters prior to call.}
      b := 12;
      c := 3;
      q(b,c);
         {value of b printed is 0; value of c printed is still 3.}
      writeln (b,c);
   end.

procedure   q(var w: integer; v: integer);
   begin
      w := 0;   {change actual parameter too.}
      v := 0;   {change only formal parameter.}
   end.
```

Fig. 10-4. Difference Between Call by Value and Call by Reference.

w causes a simultaneous modification to actual argument *b,* while the change to value argument *v* has no effect on actual argument *c.* As far as the *calling* routine is concerned, there is no difference between call by value and result. In both cases the address of the actual argument is passed to the subprogram. It is the subprogram's handling of that address which differs in the two methods. (PASCAL constrains call by reference so that the actual argument of a reference parameter must be a variable, not an arbitrary expression. We have extended PASCAL here for the sake of generality, since this restriction is quite arbitrary and not found in most programming languages which offer call by reference parameter passing. The actual argument may be any arbitrary expression.)

10.2.4   Processing a Subprogram Definition

Except for the code to link them to their callers, subprograms are compiled in exactly the same manner as the main program. The only physical difference between them is in the program header. The main program begins with a **program** statement, which names the program and identifies the input/output files. A subprogram begins with either a **function** or a **procedure** statement which identifies the name of the routine and its formal arguments, along with their data-types and whether they are reference or value arguments. In addition, if the subprogram is a function, the header indicates the type of the returned value. All of this information is mandatory in RASCAL.

When the subprogram header is encountered, three tasks must be performed. First, the information in that statement must be stored in the symbol table; in particular, the subprogram name, its arguments and their attributes, and the type of the returned value must be entered into the table for later reference. Second, the addressability of the routine must be established, just as we did for the main program. Third, if an argument is passed by value, local storage for that value must be allocated, and the value of the actual argument copied into it. We shall address these tasks in turn, except for the first, which is so simple that we shall not explain it any further.

The revisions to the symbol table are relatively straightforward. The most important factor is that the subprograms will be compiled independently; i.e., all counters, stacks, tables, and other data values maintained by CANTOR will be re-initialized for each new subprogram encountered, including the symbol table. Consequently, only one occurrence of an identifier name will ever occur in the table at any time, even if several modules have many of the same local names. Whenever a module references a subprogram, the header information about that subprogram, including the expected data-types of its arguments and the type of the returned value, if any, will not be available. For each subprogram referenced in any module, there must be a declaration of the subprogram header inside that module following the variable declaration section:

'procedure' NON_KEY_ID '(' SUB_PARMS ')' ';'

or

'function' NON_KEY_ID '(' SUB_PARMS ')' ':' RETURN_TYPE ';'

where NON_KEY_ID is the subprogram name, SUB_PARMS is the list of *types* of the formal parameters, and RETURN_TYPE is the type of the result returned by the function. The parenthesized list of types is omitted if the subprogram has no parameters.

Note that only the number and type of the formal arguments is important in the *calling* routine, not the formal argument names, so the names are excluded here. By having the type of each argument, the compiler can perform additional error checking to ensure that the actual arguments match the expected types and the number of actual arguments equals the number of formal arguments. (See Chapter 8 for details on error processing.) Since there are no default data-types in RASCAL, the specification of the type to be returned by a function is mandatory.

The type field of each entry must be changed so that it is a *record* with two fields: *store_class* and *store_type*. For purposes of this chapter, the permissible values of *store_type* are all of the types defined for CANTOR/3 except for *prog_name*. *Store_class* indicates whether the name is locally declared, a formal parameter or a module name:

local, var_parm, main, funct, proc

indicating that the name is that of local storage, a variable parameter, the main program name, a function name or a procedure name, respectively. Because a value parameter is initialized to the current value of the actual argument and then treated as if it were a local variable, there is no special entry under *storage_class* for value parameters.

Figure 10-5 is a sample program whose compilation we shall examine closely in the rest of this section. It has a main routine, one procedure, and one function. Both of the function arguments are called by value. One of the two procedure arguments is passed by value, the other by reference. The main routine calls procedure *p* which calls function *f*. Figure 10-6 shows the symbol table entries made when the procedure statement is encountered. Figure 10-7 shows this same table as it would appear after the declaration specifying that the function header has been processed. Note the additional entries for the constant and previously declared variables. The symbol table appearance after encountering the beginning of the definition of *f* is in Fig. 10-8. There are no routines called from *f*, so there are no subprogram headers declared inside it.

When the keyword **'procedure'** or **'function'** is encountered, and the name of the routine is seen by the parser, it can then emit 360AL code to establish addressability. This code is identical to that emitted for the main program earlier:

```
name     CSECT
         STM       14,12,12(13)
         BALR      12,0
         USING     *,12
         ST        13,@SAV+4
         LA        13,@SAV
```

```
program  m;
             {a program illustrating all basic features of non-block-
              structured RASCAL/6.}
    var   p: procedure(integer,boolean);
          x: integer;
          y: boolean;
    begin
      x := 3;
      y := true;
      p(x+2,y);
    end.

procedure   p(m:integer; var n: boolean);
    const   two = 2;
    var   z: integer;
          f: function(integer, integer): integer;
    begin
      z := two;
      if   n then
        begin
          z := f(m,z+3);
          n := not n;
        end;
    end.

function   f(n,x: integer): integer;
    const   ten = 10;
    begin
      f := n + x + ten;
    end.
```

Fig. 10-5. A Sample RASCAL/6 Program without Block-Structure.

internal name	type	mode	value	alloc	units	args
@P0	proc_name	immutable	—	no	—	(integer,integer)
@SAV	integer	mutable	—	yes	18	—
@I0	[integer, value, parm]	mutable	—	yes	1	—
@B0	[boolean, ref, parm]	mutable	—	no	—	—

'p'
'@SAV'
'm'

'n'

Fig. 10-6. Symbol Table after Processing Procedure Definition in Fig. 10-5.

internal name	type	mode	value	alloc	units	args
@P0	proc name	immutable	—	no	—	(integer,integer)
@SAV	integer	mutable	—	yes	18	—
@I0	[integer, value, parm]	mutable	—	yes	1	—
@B0	[boolean, ref, parm]	mutable	—	no	—	—
@I1	integer	immutable	'2'	yes	1	—
@I2	integer	mutable	—	yes	1	—
@F0	func. name	immutable	—	no	—	(integer,integer):integer

'p'
'@SAV'
'm'

'n'

'two'
'z'
'f'

Fig. 10-7. Symbol Table after Processing Function Header in Procedure p of Fig. 10-5.

internal name	type	mode	value	alloc	units	args
'f' @F0	func_name	immutable	—	no	—	(integer,integer):integer
'@SAV' @SAV	integer	mutable	—	yes	18	
'n' @I0	[integer, value, parm]	mutable	—	yes	1	
'x' @I1	[integer, value, parm]	mutable	—	yes	1	

Fig. 10-8. Symbol Table after Processing Function Statement in Program of Fig. 10-5.

Parameters are passed into a subroutine indirectly. The calling routine assembles a contiguous list of their addresses and passes the address of that list to the subprogram. The advantage of this scheme is that all parameters can, in essence, be passed via one register and the length of the argument does not affect the length of the list being passed, since all addresses are four bytes long. (For this chapter we are interested only in *integer* and *boolean* arguments, but this scheme is easily extended to *strings, records, sets, arrays,* and so forth, where the lengths of the various arguments will differ.) The convention on IBM 360/370 computers is to pass the address of this list in register 1 as shown in Fig. 10-9. If the parser encounters a value parameter in its scan of the header statement, it creates local storage for it and copies the value of the actual parameter into that reserved storage:

$$
\begin{array}{ll}
\text{L} & r,k(1) \\
\text{MVC} & @Tn(4),0(r)
\end{array}
$$

where r is a register into which the address of the value parameter is loaded, $@Tn$ is the compiler-generated name of the local storage reserved for the formal parameter, and k is the offset in bytes from the beginning of the parameter list, where the address of the value parameter is located.

```
* CALLING ROUTINE
      . . .
* SET UP PARAMETER LIST: (A1,A2, . . . , An)
            LA      1,PARMLIST     ready register one
            LA      r,A1           store address of A1
            ST      r,0(1)         in first slot
            LA      r,A2           store address of A2
            ST      r,4(1)         in second slot
            . . .
            LA      r,An           store address of An
            ST      r,k(1)         in n-th slot where k=(n-1)*4
            L       15,=V(SUB)     load address of subprogram
            BALR    14,15          branch to routine
            . . .
PARMLIST    DS      nA             storage for parameter list
```

```
* CALLED ROUTINE — SUB
      . . .
* LOAD A1 INTO REGISTER s
            L       s,0(1)         address of A1 into s
            L       s,0(s)         value of A1 into s
```

Fig. 10-9. Parameter Passing in 360AL.

After the header has been processed, references to value parameters are through temporaries such as $@Tn$, while reference parameters are addressed through register 1.

If the subprogram is a function, we must establish a means of returning a value to the calling routine. This is done by simply increasing the length of the parameter list by one. The final member of the list will hold the address of the computed result. This address is stored in that list by the caller. The function will treat this location as if it were an ordinary reference parameter. Figure 10-10 shows the difference between a parameter list for a procedure and for a function.

In this chapter, we are considering only *boolean* and *integer* data-types, but the parameter passing scheme described here works equally well on other types. If the beginning address of an array, string, sets or any other data-type is passed to a subprogram in a parameter list, it can be accessed in the subprogram just as easily as *integer* or *boolean* objects.

A reference parameter may be addressed in several different ways: First, the value of that parameter may be in a register; second, the address of that parameter may be in a register; third, the address of the address of that parameter is accessible through register 1. The first situation corresponds to that encountered in the main program; the last two situations

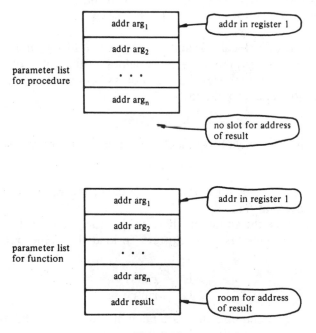

Fig. 10-10.

are new. We must augment the register bookkeeping system to account for these new situations. When requesting the status of a quantity, the bookkeeping system now responds with a *record,* rather than simply a register number or lambda. The first field, *addr_nature,* describes the register quantity; the second field, *number,* pinpoints which register is assigned. The options for *addr_nature* are: *value, address, parm_address.* The second field, *number*, may vary from 1 to 11. Register 1 has been added to the list of assignable registers since the address of the parameter list is passed to the subprogram in this register. This is the reason we did not allow register 1 to be used for other purposes earlier. Register 1 cannot be freed to hold other operands.

If the value of a local variable is in a register, it is handled as in the main program. The same holds true for references to the existing value of a reference parameter which resides in a register. Because a change to the value of a reference parameter must be immediately reflected by a modification to the actual argument as well, the compiler must also emit code which stores the new value in the actual parameter:

$$L \qquad r,k(1)$$
$$ST \qquad s,0(r)$$

where k is the offset in the parameter list to the address of the relevant actual argument, and register s holds the new value of the formal argument.

If the value of a local variable is not in a register, it is referenced through its internal symbolic name as before. If the value of a reference parameter is not in a register, but its address is in register s, then to load that value into register r requires:

$$L \qquad r,0(s)$$

while updating that value to reflect the contents of r requires:

$$ST \qquad r,0(s)$$

When the value is loaded into r for reference, the books should be adjusted to show that fact.

Finally, we face the situation where neither the value nor the address of a reference parameter is in a register. To load the value into register r emit:

$$L \qquad r,k(1)$$
$$L \qquad r,0(r)$$

where k is the offset into the parameter list where the address of the indicated argument is found. Alternatively, we could emit:

$$L\ r,\ k(1)$$
$$L\ s,\ 0(r)$$

to save address of *r* in a register for possible later use.

When the end of the subprogram is reached, the compiler emits the same epilogue that it did for the main program:

```
@END    L     13,@SAV+4
        LM    14,12,12(13)
        BR    14
```

This is, of course, followed by the local storage for that routine.

10.2.5 Calling a Subprogram

When a subprogram call is encountered, several things must happen: First, the current value of register 1 must be saved; second, the argument list must be constructed; third, the address of that list must be loaded into register 1; fourth, the address of the subprogram must be loaded into register 15; fifth, the subroutine must be invoked; sixth, the value of register 1 must be restored. After a function returns control to the caller, the caller will have the returned value in its local storage (the location pointed to by the last address in the parameter list generated to call the function). The only possible complication is if one of the actual arguments in the call itself calls a function. This merely implies that the compiler code to handle subprogram calls is potentially recursive. The scheme for calling just described will work properly no matter how deeply nested subprogram calls are written.

This completes our examination of subprogram definition and calling in a FORTRAN-like, non-block structured language. Figure 10-11 shows the translation of the entire program of Fig. 10-5, excluding input/output related code, which is omitted to avoid clutter.

10.3 SUBPROGRAMS IN A BLOCK STRUCTURED NON-RECURSIVE ENVIRONMENT

10.3.1 Physical Organization

The only means for subprograms to communicate in the last section was through an explicit list of arguments and a lone returned value from a function call. Even at the time FORTRAN was designed, people recog-

```
M              CSECT
               STM      14,12,12(13)        save registers
               BALR     12,0                establish addressability
               USING    *,12
               ST       13,@SAV+4
               LA       13,@SAV
               MVC      @I0(4),@I1          x := 3
               MVC      @B0(4),@B1          y := true
               LA       1,@PARM0            create parm list
               L        2,@I0               x+2
               A        2,@I2
               ST       2,@T0               store @T0
               LA       4,@T0               put addr x into parm list
               ST       4,0(1)
               LA       4,@B0               put addr y into parm list
               ST       4,4(1)
               L        15,=V(P)            call subprogram p
               BALR     14,15
@END           L        13,@SAV+4           restore registers
               LM       14,12,12(13)
               BR       14                  return
@SAV           DS       18F                 @SAV
@I0            DS       1F                  x
@B0            DS       1F                  y
@I1            DC       1F'3'               3
@B1            DC       1F'0'               true
@PARM0         DS       2A                  @PARM0
@I2            DC       1F'2'               2
@T0            DS       1F                  @T0
               END


P              CSECT
               STM      14,12,12(13)        save registers
               BALR     12,0                establish addressability
               USING    *,12
               ST       13,@SAV+4
               LA       13,@SAV
               L        2,0(1)              copy value of m
               MVC      @I0(4),0(2)
               MVC      @I2(4),@I1          z := two
               L        2,4(1)              addr of n into reg 2
               CLC      0(4,2),=F'-1'       is predicate true?
               BNE      @L0                 skip then clause if false
               ST       1,@T0               store addr of parm list
               LA       1,@PARM0            create parm list
               LA       4,@I0               put addr m into parm list
               ST       4,0(1)
               LA       4,@I2               put addr z into parm list
```

Fig. 10-11. Translation of Program in Fig. 10-5.

	ST	4,4(1)	
	LA	4,@T1	put addr return
	ST	4,8(1)	value into parm list
	L	15,=V(F)	call subprogram f
	BALR	14,15	
	L	1,@T0	restore addr of parm list
	MVC	@I2(4),@T1	z := @T1
	L	4,0(2)	not n
	X	4,=F'−1'	
	ST	4,0(2)	n := @T0
@L0	EQU	*	end **then** clause
@END	L	13,@SAV+4	restore registers
	LM	14,12,12(13)	and
	BR	14	return
@SAV	DS	18F	@SAV
@I0	DS	1F	m
@I1	DC	1F'2'	two
@I2	DS	1F	z
@PARMNO	DS	3A	@PARMNO
@T0	DS	1F	@T0
@T1	DS	1F	@T1
	END		
F	CSECT		
	STM	14,12,12(13)	save registers
	BALR	12,0	establish addressability
	USING	*,12	
	ST	13,@SAV+4	
	LA	13,@SAV	
	L	2,0(1)	copy value of n
	MVC	@I0(4),0(2)	
	L	2,4(1)	copy value of x
	MVC	@I1(4),0(2)	
	L	2,@I0	n + x
	A	2,@I1	
	A	2,@I2	@T0 + ten
	L	4,8(1)	f := @T0
	ST	2,0(4)	
@END	L	13,@SAV+4	restore registers
	LM	14,12,12(13)	and
	BR	14	return
@SAV	DS	18F	@SAV
@I0	DS	1F	n
@I1	DS	1F	x
@I2	DC	1F'10'	ten
	END		

Fig. 10-11. Translation of Program in Fig. 10-5 (continued).

nized that if two routines shared a large amount of data, the parameter lists could grow quite long. This is bad on two counts: first, no one wants to type lists with 15 or 20 members; second, a long list is error prone in that a programmer could easily permute the order of arguments or leave one out. To solve this problem, FORTRAN permits a programmer to define one or more COMMON blocks of storage which is global to all routines. Any module may access any or all values in a COMMON block, simply by including a statement telling which values are to be accessible. This scheme permits easy sharing of large blocks of data between routines, without having to explicitly write long parameter lists. The great weakness of this approach to sharing is that *any* module can have access to the COMMON storage without the knowledge of any other module. One module cannot prohibit access nor even become aware of potential access by other routines, which often causes confusing module interfaces, damages program reliability and increases debugging time.

RASCAL offers a more structured way for modules to share data. This approach, called *block structure,* uses the physical organization of the program as nested modules to dictate which modules share data. Each module is called a *block*. The block currently being executed is called the *active* block. Within any block can be defined any number of other blocks, either procedures or functions, all subprograms being physically nested inside the main program. An identifier is *local* to the block which contains its declaration. A subprogram name is defined in the block which contains its definition. The rule on resolving an identifier reference to a declaration is that the name is bound to the declaration for that identifier occurring within that block, if such a declaration exists; otherwise, the name is bound as if it occurred in the containing block. A name which is not bound to any declaration by this rule is undeclared, and its occurrence is erroneous. Figure 10-12 shows a sample RASCAL program with block structure. Note that the form of a subprogram is the same as in the last section, except now the subprograms are nested one inside another, and only the main program ends with a period. Figure 10-12 has a main program and three subprograms: f, p, and q; f is a function; the other two are procedures; p is nested inside f; q is contained directly in main program m. Identifiers x, y, and z are declared locally in m; f redeclares x; p redeclares y; and q redeclares both x and z. The reference to x inside m refers to the x declared in m. The reference to x in f is to the variable declared in f, but the reference to y inside f is to the variable declared in m, since m surrounds f, and y is not declared in f. Similarly, the reference to x inside p is to the variable declared in f, while y refers to the variable declared in m. When p calls q, control is transferred to q; upon completion, q returns control back to p. While q is executing, a reference to x and z is resolved locally within *q*. A reference to variable *y*, however, is resolved to the declaration in *m* (not *p!*). Even though *p* called *q*, references to non-local names are resolved through the *physical* nesting of the program blocks, not their *logical* relationships. (Other languages, such as APL do resolve references through the calling structure.) As a consequence of this resolution policy, *at compile-time*, we can decide to which declaration a name is bound.

The advantage of this data sharing method over COMMON is that by nesting blocks, a programmer can isolate routines which he does not want others to see and share storage in any manner he wishes with those isolated modules. For example, block *p* cannot be accessed from outside *f* (why?). Consequently, all implicit storage shared between *p* and *f* (in this case just *x*) cannot be accessed by other modules. Normally, block-structured languages are implemented using dynamic storage allocation. One copy of the module code is always available; however, storage for the

```
program   m;      {block # 1}
          {illustrate RASCAL/6 with block-structure but without recursion.}
      var   x,y,z: integer;
        procedure q (var s: integer); forward;   [block # 2]
        function f(t: integer): boolean;      {block # 3}
          var   x: integer;
            procedure p(r: integer);      {block # 4}
              var   y: boolean;
              begin
                y := true;   x := 3;
                q(r);
              end;
          begin
            x := 2;   z := 0;
            y := −2
            p(t);
            f := y;
          end;
        procedure   q;
          var   x,z: integer;
          begin
            x := 0;   y := −1;   z := 4;
            s := 5;
          end;
      begin
        x := −3;
        y := −2;
        z := f(x);
      end.
```

Fig. 10-12. A Sample RASCAL/6 Program Illustrating Block-Structure.

data items of a module is allocated only when that block is activated and is released when that block is deactivated. This can bring about a major savings in storage space, since the data area for a module exists only when that module is active and also permits us to incorporate recursion into a language. In this section, we discuss how this allocation is managed and the effects it has on our ability to address names.

Despite the fact that most block structured languages are implemented by dynamic storage allocation, it need not be so. From a linguistic viewpoint, block structure is an intermodule communication strategy. Recognizing that this scoping policy could also be implemented to save storage, compiler writers have traditionally used dynamic rather than static storage allocation when implementing block structure, but unless the language allows recursive subprogram calls or has other features which require dynamic allocation (such as list processing), a compiler could simply allocate enough storage for all subprograms at compile-time and enforce the accessing discipline of block structure.

10.3.2   Block Structured Symbol Tables

Before we delve into storage management, we consider how to determine which block a non-local reference should be resolved to. The memory management policy will let us reference the correct object once we have decided which one we want. To reference non-local names requires a reorganization of the symbol table into a *block-structured* symbol table. Referring back to Fig. 10-12, we have numbered each block according to the order of appearance of its block header statement in the program. Figure 10-13 shows the format of the symbol table used to store informa-

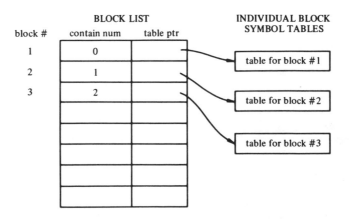

Fig. 10-13.

tion about the program names. It actually has two components: The first is an index into the second; the second is a symbol table as we have defined it in the last part of the text. There is one entry for each block of the program. Binding a name to a declaration is accomplished by searching through the tables in a manner which corresponds to the binding rule for a block-structured language. The *block list,* which is the index into the symbol table of any given block, is a table of k rows, where k is the maximum number of blocks in a single program which the implementation permits. Each row of the table has two entries:

$$contain\_num, \qquad table\_ptr$$

Contain_num indicates the block number of the containing block. *Table_ptr* points to the symbol table of that block, whose structure is identical to that studied in the last section.

When a block header is encountered, it is assigned a number, and an entry for it is created in the block list. The name of that block is inserted into the symbol table of the containing block, and then the processing of the containing block is suspended until the new block has been completely processed. All entries are made in the symbol table of the new block until another block is entered or the new block's definition is terminated. If the former happens, the process repeats itself, with the creation of another entry in the block list. In the latter case, the processing of the new block is complete, and the processing of the containing block is resumed. Figure 10-14 shows a series of snapshots of the block-structured symbol table as it is filled in during the processing of part of Fig. 10-12, excluding compiler-generating quantities.

In the last section the symbol table was cleared between the compilation of each subprogram so we had to insert into the code of each module the header information about each routine it called. With the block-structured environment, however, this is no longer true. The only subprogram headers which must be declared in a routine are for subprograms which have not been defined prior to the call. For the others, the necessary information will already be in the symbol table.

Routines which have not been defined before they are referenced are said to be *forward* referenced. *q* is such a procedure in Fig. 10-12. It is referenced in line 10, but its definition doesn't appear until line 18. We add a **forward** declaration of the procedure heading to *m* in line 3 so that when the call is encountered, the compiler can check whether the number and type of the arguments are correct. Following PASCAL, the **forward** declaration is the normal **procedure** statement followed by '**forward;**'. The beginning of the procedure definition just has the keyword **procedure** and the procedure name.

Once a block has been compiled, we shall never reference its symbol

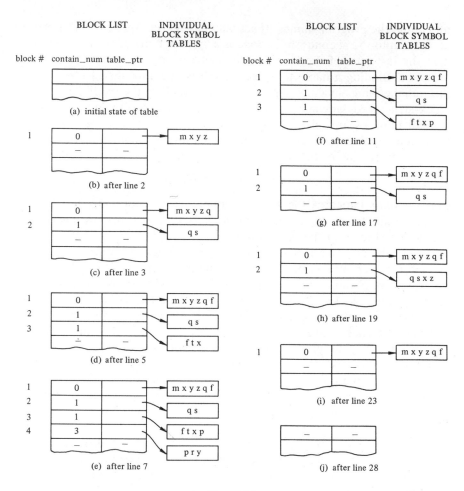

Fig. 10-14.

table again (why?). It is, therefore, only sensible to erase that block's symbol table after block exit, so it can be reallocated for other purposes. Fig. 10-14 reflects this strategy. Note that if a cross-reference map of a block is to be printed, it must be done before that block's table is erased.

10.3.3   Storage Management

We turn next to the storage management required for a block structured language. When a block is activated, it will be allocated a fixed amount of storage atop a *data stack*. The potential size of the stack is, of course, implementation dependent. The amount of storage allocated will depend on the declarations in the block, but the total needed will be computed at compile-time. This storage remains assigned to that block as long as it is activated. When the block is exited, that storage will be freed for reuse as the storage area for other blocks. In this way, the total amount of storage allocated for data is limited by the number of blocks currently activated, independent of how many blocks there are in total in the program. As a consequence of this scheme, the particular section of the stack in which the data area of a block may reside will vary during program execution in a manner which cannot be predicted at compile-time. Each activation of the same block could be in an entirely different section of the stack.

The storage area will hold the values of variables, compiler-generated temporaries and several compiler-generated pointers. The values of all but the symbolic constants and literals are determined at run-time. The value of a symbolic constant is fixed at compile-time and cannot change for successive activations of a block. Instead of storing constants in the stack, we could just leave them as part of the block code; however, this would mean two addressing schemes, one for constants, and one for everything else. Such a distinction does not seem worth the additional complexity it would entail here, although, for an optimizing compiler, this might not be true. However, we do wish to avoid the inefficiencies which result from reinitializing constants and literals with every block entry. A convenient way to maintain the stack discipline is to create an imaginary block external to the main program. The storage for *all* literals and constants through the *entire program* will be allocated as if they were declared in this outmost block; this storage is allocated and inititalized once by the *compiler*. It can never be deallocated since the block is never left during the lifetime of the program's execution. It is important to note that the scope of a symbolic constant is not changed by this optimization. Its storage is simply moved to a more convenient section of the stack.

The physical location in memory reserved for an identifier will change during program execution, but the relative offset from the beginning of the area reserved for the block in which it is declared will be fixed. If the location of the beginning of the block's data area is known, the location of the identifier's storage can then be computed at run-time. Figure 10-15 shows the organization of the data area for the main program of Fig. 10-12. The storage for variable x is offset k bytes from the beginning of the data area. Variable y begins four bytes later and z four bytes after that. There are several compiler-generated temporaries in the area, as well, along with several pointers necessary for the stack manipulation. If the address of the beginning of the data area were in register r, then in order to load variable x into register s, we need only emit:

L   s,k(r)

| storage for result of call to f |
| parmlist for call to f |
| z |
| y |
| x |
| register save area |
| compiler-generated quantities for storage management |

Fig. 10-15. Organization of Data Area for Main Program of Fig. 10-12.

If we knew the beginning address of each data area currently activated, then any variable in any block could be located by this relative addressing scheme. A collection of such addresses is called a *display*. A separate display is created every time a new block is activated holding the address of each data area which can be referenced from the new active block. When only the imaginary and main program is activated, the display has two entries. When m calls f, storage for f is allocated and a display for the new activation is created. The new display is simply the old display with an entry added to the top, holding the address of f's data area. When f calls p, still one more entry is placed on the top of a new display. Finally, when p calls q, a display having only the address of the data area for m and q is established. Since storage within f and p is not addressable from q, the address of their data areas is omitted from the display. A natural question to ask is where do we put the displays? They could be placed in a separate area specifically for them, but a cleaner solution is to store the display as an entry in that block's data area. Figure 10-16 shows the stack when f calls p.

The size of the display for any block is known at compile-time, even if the particular addresses to be placed into the display are not. Hence, a fixed amount of storage can be reserved for the display in any data area; for p, this is 10 bytes, holding four addresses. At block activation time, when the data area is allocated, those addresses will be known and can be stored into the display. When f calls p, f's display contains all of the addresses needed for p's display, except for the address of p's own data area. The rule for creating the new display from the old is quite simple. First, we define the *nesting level* of a block to be one plus the nesting level of its surrounding block, except for the imaginary block, whose nesting level is always one. If the nesting level of the old data area minus the level of the new data area is k, then the new display is simply the $k+1$ bottom-most entries of the old display, with the address of the new data area placed on top. Because of the scoping rules, k can never be less than -1. The copying is executed as part of the prologue during block entry.

With the display included as part of the data area, it is quite straightforward to reference any addressable quantity. Register 13, which held the address of the register save area in earlier versions of the compiler, now holds the address of the active data area. The register save area is now part of that data area, so its address need not be saved. Suppose p is the active block. Local quantity y is referenced by its offset from the address

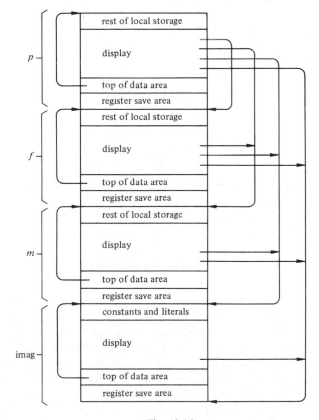

Fig. 10-16.

in register 13. Variable x, whose declaration is in f, is loaded into register r indirectly by:

$$L \qquad r,4(13)$$
$$L \qquad r,d(r)$$

where d is the offset from the beginning of f's data area where x is located. Similarly, to load z into register r:

$$L \qquad r,8(13)$$
$$L \qquad r,n(r)$$

where n is the proper offset into m's data area. With this scheme, no matter how many levels removed a non-local identifier is declared, there is only one level of indirection to load its value into a register.

Five activities are necessary upon block entry: First, the value of the old block's registers must be saved; this is accomplished exactly as before, since the register save area is the beginning of the data area. Note that the old value of register 13 is the address of the data area we wish to make active when the current block is exited. Second, the code's addressability must be established as always. Third, the data area for the currently active block must be allocated and register 13 set. The amount of storage which must be allocated was computed at compile-time. The address of the first available location in the stack beyond the current data area must be stored so that when the next block is entered, that block's entry routine will know where to begin its data area. Fourth, the display must be initialized. Fifth, value parameters must be copied into local storage.

The only aspect of this scheme which must still be specified is how a block exit is handled. As part of the block entry prologue, the address of the previous active data area is stored in the current active area. (It is the old value of register 13.) When the active block is exited, the value in register 13 is simply updated to point to this last data area, as part of the standard policy of restoring registers to their old values upon subprogram exit. Figure 10-17 shows the entire translation of the program of Fig. 10-12; Fig. 10-18 shows its data areas; again, input/output code has been left out to avoid clutter. We presume that the compiled version of each subprogram is a physically separate 360AL CSECT, despite the fact that the RASCAL/6 code has the subprograms nested. We do this for two reasons: First, separation increases greatly the total permissible size of the program, since the restriction to addressability by a single base register then means only that each subprogram individually must be addressable by a single base register. With a nested organization, the code in the main program which follows the subprogram definitions could easily be more than 4096 bytes from the base register contents, which would make it inaccessible on the IBM 360/370 family. Second, by having separate CSECTs for the subprograms, the compiler-generated names can be re-used freely across subprograms. Because nested subprogram declarations occur before any executable code of the block which contains the declaration, emitting separate CSECTs is no problem. It can be achieved by postponing the emission of any code for either the main program or a subprogram until the first **begin** of that routine is encountered. For languages such as PL/I which allow declarations in blocks positioned anywhere in the executable code, this scheme will not work.

10.4 BLOCK-STRUCTURE PLUS RECURSION

If a subprogram either directly or indirectly calls itself, it is said to be *recursive*. RASCAL/6 supports recursion. When a subprogram calls itself, a new copy of the data area for that program is created. If a subprogram is nested n levels deep in recursion, then there are n copies of its data area on the data stack. The scheme we have constructed for implementing subprograms calls in the last section works with only a single modification when the subprograms are recursive. We merely have to distinguish occurrences of the function name on the left-hand side of an assignment statement from all others. Such an appearance assigns a value to the function result for when it returns to its caller, while all other occurrences are recursive calls. This is easily effected in the parser. Since the code itself does not change from call to call, merely the data values, it is enough to have one copy of the code and multiple copies of the data area.

10.5 SUMMARY

Subprograms add a new dimension to RASCAL. Arbitrarily large and complex programs can be subdivided into small manageable modules, independent of the overall size of the program. *Block structure* allows implicit information sharing without long lists of parameters. Normally this is implemented by dynamic storage allocation: As each block is entered, a data area for it must be allocated in a pushdown stack; this area is released upon block exit. By use of *displays,* the effort required to reference non-local identifiers is independent of how many levels removed from the reference that identifier is defined. *Recursion,* where a subprogram calls itself, is supported in RASCAL/6. The implementation method chosen for non-recursive RASCAL/6 extends with trivial change to recursive programs, since the code is *reentrant;* i.e., does not change during execution.

```
@IMAG       CSECT
            STM     14,12,12(13)            save registers
            BALR    12,0                    establish addressability
            USING   *,12
            ST      13,4(13)
            LA      13,@STK
            LR      2,13                    set top of stk pointer
            A       2,@STKTOP
            ST      2,72(13)
            ST      13,76(13)               create display
            MVC     80(4,13),=F'-1'         set constants
            MVC     84(4,13),=F'3'
            MVC     88(4,13),=F'2'
            MVC     92(4,13),=F'0'
            MVC     96(4,13),=F'4'
            MVC     100(4,13),=F'5'
            MVC     104(4,13),=F'-3'
            MVC     108(4,13),=F'-2'
            L       15,=V(M)                call M
            BALR    14,15
@END        L       13,4(13)                restore register
            LM      14,12,12(13)            and
            BR      14                      return
@STKOP      DC      F'112'                  top of area
@STK        DS      1000F                   stack
            END

M           CSECT   -
            STM     14,12,12(13)            save registers
            BALR    12,0                    establish addressability
            USING   *,12
            ST      13,4(13)
            LA      13,72(13)
            LR      2,13                    set top of stk pointer
            A       2,@STKTOP
            ST      2,72(13)
            L       2,4(13)                 create display
            MVC     76(4,13),76(2)          copy level 1
            ST      13,80(13)               store level 2
            MVC     80(4,13),104(2)         x := -3
            MVC     84(4,13),108(2)         y := -2
            LA      1,92(13)                create parm list
            LA      4,80(13)                store addr of x
            ST      4,92(13)                into parm list
            LA      4,100(13)               store addr of result
            ST      4,96(13)                into parm list
            L       15,=V(F)                call f
            BALR    14,15
```

Fig. 10-17. Translation of Program in Fig. 1-12.

	MVC	84(4,2),108(4)	y = −2
@END	L	13,4(13)	restore registers
	LM	14,12,12(13)	and
	BR	14	return
@STKTOP	DC	F'104'	top of area
	END		

F	CSECT		
	STM	14,12,12(13)	save registers
	BALR	12,0	establish addressability
	USING	*,12	
	ST	13,4(13)	
	LA	13,72(13)	
	LR	2,13	set top of stk pointer
	A	2,@STKTOP	
	ST	2,72(13)	
	L	2,4(13)	create display
	MVC	76(8,13),76(2)	copy levels 1 − 2
	ST	13,84(13)	store level 3
	L	4,0(1)	copy t
	ST	84(4,13),0(4)	
	L	4,76(13)	x := 2
	MVC	88(4,13),88(4)	
	MVC	88(4,2),92(4)	z :− 0
	MVC	84(4,2),108(4)	y := −2
	ST	1,92(13)	save register 1
	LA	1,96(13)	create parm list
	LA	6,84(13)	store addr of t
	ST	6,96(13)	
	L	15,=V(P)	call P
	BALR	14,15	
	L	1,92(13)	restore register 1
	L	8,4(1)	f := y
	MVC	0(4,8),84(2)	
@END	L	13,4(13)	restore registers
	LM	14,12,12(13)	and
	BR	14	return
@STKTOP	DC	F'100'	top of area
	END		

P	CSECT		
	STM	14,12,12(13)	save registers
	BALR	12,0	establish addressability
	USING	*,12	
	ST	13,4(13)	
	LA	13,72(13)	
	LR	2,13	set top of stk pointer
	A	2,@STKTOP	

Fig. 10-17. Translation of Program in Fig. 1-12 (continued).

```
            ST        2,72(13)
            L         2,4(13)              create display
            MVC       76(12,13),76(2)      copy levels 1 – 3
            ST        13,88(13)            store level 4
            L         4,0(1)               copy r
            MVC       88(4,13),0(4)
            L         4,76(13)             y := true
            MVC       92(4,13),80(4)
            MVC       88(4,2),84(4)        x := 3
            ST        1,96(13)             save register 1
            LA        1,100(13)            create parm list
            LA        6,88(13)             store addr of r
            ST        6,100(13)
            L         15,=V(Q)             call Q
            BALR      14,15
            L         1,96(13)             restore register 1
@ ND        L         13,4(13)             restore registers
            LM        14,12,12(13)         and
            BR        14                   return
@STKTOP     DC        F'104'               top of area
            END


Q           CSECT
            STM       14,12,12(13)         save registers
            BALR      12,0                 establish addressability
            USING     *,12
            ST        13,4(13)
            LA        13,72(13)
            LR        2,13                 set top of stk pointer
            A         2,@STKTOP
            ST        2,72(13)
            L         2,4(13)              create display
            MVC       76(8,13),76(2)       copy levels 1 – 2
            ST        13,84(13)            store level 3
            L         4,76(13)             x := 0
            MVC       84(4,13),92(4)
            MVC       84(4,2),80(4)        y := −1
            MVC       88(4,13),96(4)       z := 4
            L         6,0(1)               s := 5
            MVC       0(4,6),100(4)
@END        L         13,4(13)             restore registers
            LM        14,12,12(13)         and
            BR        14                   return
@STKTOP     DC        F'92'                top of area
            END
```

Figure 10-17. Translation of Program in Fig. 1-12 (continued).

100–103	temp for storing f			
92–99	parm list	96–99	parm list
88–91	z	92–95	temp for storing reg 1
84–87	y	88–91	x
80–83	x	84–87	t
76–79	display	76–83	display
72–75	top of stack	72–75	top of stack
0–71	register save area	0–71	register save area

(a) data area of m (b) data area of f

100–103	parm list			
96–99	temp for storing reg 1			
92–95	y	88–91	z
88–91	r	84–87	x
76–87	display	76–83	display
72–75	top of stack	72–75	top of stack
0–71	register save area	0–71	register save area

(c) data area of p (d) data area of q

Fig. 10-18. Data Areas for Blocks of Programs in Fig. 10-12.

EXERCISES

10-1. Build the data area and step through the execution of the following program:

```
program driver;
    var n: integer; z: integer;
        function fact(n: integer): integer;
            begin
                if n = 1 then fact := 1;
                else fact := n * fact(n − 1);
            end;
    begin
        n := 3;
        z := fact(n);
    end.
```

10-2. Build the data area and step through the execution of the following program:

```
program m;
    var x,s: integer; u: boolean;
        procedure t(x: integer; var y: integer);
            var z: integer;
            begin z := x + y; y := 3 * z; end;
        function g(d: integer) :boolean;
            begin
                if d = 0 then g := u;
                else g := false;
            end;
```

```
begin
    u := true; x := 4; s:= x +6;
    t(s,x+6);
    u := g(x + s);
end.
```

10-3. Step through the construction of the symbol table for each of the programs in 10-1 and 10-2.

10-4. Explain why the storage for an individual symbol table can be released as soon as that block is closed.

10-5. Devise a scheme for implementing a variant of RASCAL in which blocks are not physically nested, but the calling sequence determines a logical nesting dynamically; i.e., block B is considered to be nested in block C whenever C calls B. The nesting lasts only until B returns control back to C (this is how APL behaves).

10-6. Why must register 1 be saved and restored for a subprogram call in section 10.2?

10-7. In Fig. 10-17 the quantity @STKTOP is added to the contents of register 13 in the beginning of each routine. Even though @STKTOP is constant for each routine, we cannot simply replace:

$$A \quad 2,@STKTOP$$

by:

$$A \quad 2,=F'n'$$

where n is the value of @STKTOP. Why not?

10-8. How would you add a FORTRAN-like COMMON statement to RASCAL for a non-block structured programming environment?

TESTING HINTS

1. Test CANTOR/6 on all of the programs used to test CANTOR/3.
2. Test CANTOR/6 on a program which:
   a. is recursive;
   b. is non-recursive;
   c. redeclares every variable (i.e., no non-local storage);
   d. redeclares no variables;
   e. has function calls within the actual argument list;
   f. has boolean and integer formal arguments in a procedure and in a function;
   g. has a boolean value returned by a function;
   h. has an integer value returned by a function;
   i. has a subprogram reference a subprogram not yet defined;
   j. has literals, constants and variables as actual arguments;
   k. has both call by reference and call by value arguments;
   l. has one routine call another routine whose nesting level is one greater;
   m. has one routine call another routine whose nesting level is equal;
   n. has one routine call another routine whose nesting level is less;
   o. has a subprogram reference a previously defined subprogram.

BIBLIOGRAPHY

Virtually all high-level languages support some form of subprogram. Many languages support block structure, including: ALGOL 60, PASCAL, PL/I, SNOBOL, and LISP (see [Naur 63], [Jensen and Wirth 75], [ANSI 76], [Griswold, et al 71], and [McCarthy, et al 65], respectively). The concept of block structure first appeared in ALGOL 60; [Evans 64] describes an ALGOL 60 compiler; [Grau, A.A., et al 67] is an entire book devoted to the description of one such compiler. Section 9 of the bibliography contains references to many example compilers of languages which support block structure and recursion.

11
Stage 7: Diagnostic Tools

11.1 INTRODUCTION

We once heard it said that "with enough incompetence in the right places, who needs saboteurs?" Barring even such a cynical view of the world, programming efforts, even trivial ones, inevitably lead to errors. It is best to anticipate mistakes and create a set of tools to facilitate detecting and correcting them. *Diagnostic tools,* as they are called, are those components of a computer system which aid the programmer in error detection and correction. Chapter 8 examined the most common form of diagnostic tool; namely, compile-time and run-time error processors. The errors discussed in that chapter were violations of i) language rules; ii) implementation restrictions on the language; or iii) environmental constraints outside the language processor. In this chapter, we turn instead to tools which provide information independent of any errors defined in Chapter 8. We examine four classes of diagnostic tools which are available in varying degrees in many implementations of common programming languages:

1. cross-reference map
2. dump of program variables
3. execution profile
4. assertions

These tools assist the programmer by providing information other than that which he would receive from the normal error processing facilities of the compiler. The last category of tools, *assertions,* stands out from the others in that they are *programmer-defined* error detectors. A programmer has certain expectations about the behavior of his program at various times in its execution. Embedded assertions are an expression of those expectations in a form which permits the implementation to determine whether they are being met. When they are violated, this is detected and reported. Depending on the nature of the tool, the recovery process will vary. The other tools simply offer additional information to the user but are not explicitly tied to error conditions. Often they are included in a program at the discretion of the programmer by means of *switches* or other explicit controls.

11.2 CROSS-REFERENCE MAP

A *cross-reference map* is a table which has an entry for each non-keyword identifier in the program (with some variation). The information which is commonly included in each entry is the data-type of the identifier and a list of the location of each reference to this identifier. This location is normally either a source code line number or the number of the statement in which the reference occurs. In CANTOR, we uniformly reference line numbers rather than statement numbers, a better indicator since a single statement may spread over many lines. Figure 11-1 is the output of CANTOR/7 on the indicated program. Using the cross-reference map, a programmer can easily isolate any and all references to identifiers of interest.

Implementing the cross-reference map feature is quite simple, given the structure of CANTOR in the seventh chapter. The symbol table contains all of the necessary information, except for the line numbers of the identifier references. We can simply create a new field for each entry of the table which holds the list of line numbers where references are found. Furthermore, if we always add the latest reference to the end of the list, then that list is always in increasing order by line number reading from front to back. By printing the list in the map from front to back, we shall write the line numbers in increasing order, without any need to sort them. The routine should be called from the main procedure following the call to *create_listing_trailer*.

A cross-reference map could contain information other than that shown here, including for example, the number of bytes of memory allocated to each identifier. It might also give the address where the first byte of the identifier's storage is located. If the compiler produces relocatable code, as does CANTOR, the address is relative. If not, that address could be an absolute machine location. For languages which do not require the declaration of all variables and constants, the cross-reference map could indicate whether an identifier were declared. One simple scheme would be to put an asterisk in front of a row of the map if that identifier had not been declared. This would alert the programmer to the fact that the attributes were assigned by default and might be other than what were expected. That entry would, of course, show the attributes actually assigned to that identifier. Since RASCAL requires the declaration of all variables and constants, this feature is not needed in the cross-reference map of CANTOR.

CANTOR COMPILER: STAGE 7   FEB 13, 1978   23:26

```
1 |        program   gcd(input,output)                                    |
2 |                  {illustrate diagnostic tools.}                        |
3 |                  {program computes the greatest common divisor of n pairs of   |
4 |                     integers, where n is read from the input data file.}       |
5 |        var   a,b,n: integer;                                           |
6 |        begin                                                           |
7 |           readln (n);   {how many pairs do we compute gcd for?}        |
8 |           while   n > 0 do                                             |
9 |              begin                                                     |
10 |                readln  (a,b);   writeln  (a,b);                        |
11 |                repeat                                                  |
12 |                   while   a > b   do   a := a − b;                     |
13 |                   while   b > a   do   b := b − a;                     |
14 |                until a=b;                                              |
15 |                   {a = b = gcd of input pair.}                         |
16 |                writeln   (a);                                          |
17 |                n := n − 1;   {one less pair to process.}               |
18 |              end;                                                      |
19 |        end.                                                           |
```

COMPILATION TERMINATED   0 ERRORS ENCOUNTERED

CROSS-REFERENCE MAP

NAME	TYPE	REFERENCED IN LINE NUMBER
gcd	program name	1
a	integer	5,10,10,12,12,12,13,13,14,16
b	integer	5,10,10,12,12,13,13,13,14
n	integer	5,7,8,17,17

note multiple occurrences of a name on a single line
result in multiple entries in the cross-reference map

Fig. 11-1. A Sample RASCAL/7 Program with Cross-Reference Map.

It is important to recognize that the format of the cross-reference map, what information it provides, or even whether there is such a map at all, is normally a decision left entirely to the implementor. Language definitions normally do not mandate any diagnostic tools which must accompany an implementation. The selection of tools and their nature and quality is an implementor's prerogative, but nearly all commercial implementations offer a cross-reference map in some form.

11.3 DUMPING PROGRAM VARIABLES

A cross-reference map presents a static view of a source program. Although helpful in locating references to identifiers, it offers no real help in understanding the dynamic behavior of the source code, which is where most errors occur. One of the simplest and most helpful aids in understanding a program's run-time behavior is a facility which dumps the values of program variables on demand. This facility can either provide for selective dumping of specific variable values or simply dump the value of every variable in the program. The former is certainly preferred with an option for an easy expression of the latter. CANTOR/7 has the **dump** statement which has the form:

'**dump**' '(' list of variables ')' ';'

or

'**dump**' '**all**' ';'

Dump statements of the first form cause the current value of each variable in the list to be printed when the **dump** statement is executed. If the second format is used, the current value of every variable is printed. The values are printed one per line in the form:

name '=' *value*

where *name* is the external name of a program-defined variable. Internal compiler-defined variables are not printed. If the value is not defined, a string of question marks, '??????', are printed instead. By labeling each value with its name, the programmer's task of interpreting the information presented is eased considerably. This format corresponds to the "PUT DATA" statement of PL/I, but we offer it just as part of the package of diagnostic tools, not as part of the host language.

The utility of "**dump all**" may be obvious. It saves the programmer from having to write the name of each variable explicitly in a list in order to have its value printed. The advantage of the selective dump over a simple **writeln** statement may be less apparent. There are three chief advantages to having a separate **dump** statement for debugging purposes:

1. The keyword '**dump**' identifies the purpose of the statement to the programmer, not confusing him as a **writeln** statement might. He knows this statement is for debugging only.
2. The name of the value is printed along with the value without any special effort on the programmer's part.
3. We shall provide a *switch* in CANTOR which the programmer can use to turn off the printing of values from **dump** statements. Debugging data is only printed during a *test* run of the program, not during *production* use.

The latter point is especially important. If a programmer instruments a program himself with standard language constructs, such as **writeln** statements as a debugging aid, there is no easy way to "turn off" the effects of these statements after the debugging phase is completed. CANTOR includes a control mechanism which at one place in the program can turn off the printing caused by subsequently occurring **dump** statements. It must physically precede any occurrence of a **dump** in order to affect it, and has the simple form:

$$\{\$\textbf{dump } -\}$$

This *pseudo-comment* has the lexical form of a comment, yet is specially interpreted by CANTOR. Pseudo-comments have the advantage of being transparent to other implementations which may not support **dump.** If the programmer wishes, he may also explicitly indicate that he wishes to execute subsequent **dump** instructions by

$$\{\$\textbf{dump } + \}$$

He can selectively execute **dump** instructions in various program parts by placing {**$dump** +} before the segment of code where the printing is needed, and following that code with {**$dump** −}. The default value if no pseudo-comment is specified, is {**$dump** −}.

The **dump** instruction is easily implemented using the same basic methods presented for printing data in Chapter 7. The external name of every variable is available in the symbol table, so the implementation of a **"dump all"** instruction presents no more difficulty than that for selective dumping. That all variables are declared in RASCAL is critical to the implementation of **"dump all".** Since CANTOR is a one-pass compiler, if a **"dump all"** instruction were encountered prior to the first reference to a variable (physically), the compiler could not easily generate code to print the current value of that variable. Since that variable must be declared at the beginning of the program, before a **"dump all"** instruction could be encountered, the symbol table entry for that variable will be available when needed.

Note that there is one further advantage to the **dump** instruction over the **writeln** statement not yet discussed. If a programmer attempts to print the value of an undefined variable via a **writeln** statement, that is an error which, using the guidelines established in Chapter 8, will cause program execution to terminate. We explicitly do not wish this to happen when debugging a program. We might *expect* that a variable's value is undefined at a particular moment and merely wish to check our expectations. There is no convenient way to accomplish this in RASCAL. The **dump** instruction makes a check for undefined variables quite simple and straightforward. Note that **dump** requires that a scheme such as that described in Chapter 8 for dynamically checking whether a variable is defined must be

```
$dump- on ;
program  gcd(input,output);
              {illustrate dumping of variable values.}
              {program computes the greatest common divisor of n pairs
               of integers, where n is read from the input data file.}
      var  a,b,n: integer;
      begin
        readln (n);  {how many pairs do we compute gcd for?}
        dump(n);
        while  n > 0 do
          begin
            readln  (a,b);  writeln  (a,b);
                {note that with writeln statement, dumping of
                 a and b would be superfluous.}
            repeat
              while  a > b  do  a := a - b;
              while  b > a  do  b := b - a;
              dump(a,b);
            until  a=b;
              {a=b=gcd of input pair.}
            writeln  (a);
            n := n - 1;  {one less pair to process.}
            dump(n);
          end,
      end.
```

Fig. 11-2. A Sample RASCAL/7 Program with Variable Dumps.

implemented. Figure 11-2 is a modified version of the program in Fig. 11-1, which has been instrumented with **dump** instructions. Its output on the data set given in Fig. 11-3 is shown in Fig. 11-4.

11.4 EXECUTION PROFILE

Judiciously instrumenting a program with **dump** statements can give the programmer excellent feedback on the detailed behavior of the program with respect to variable values. However, the dumping facility will not present a global perspective of the program flow of control. This data could be valuable in detecting code which is executed too frequently or too little, indicating a possible logical error. For example, a **while** loop which the programmer expected would iterate just twice, may in fact iterate three times instead. Ready access to this fact would help the pro-

3   8   6   13   5   26   13

Fig. 11-3. Data Set for Program of Fig. 11-2.

```
n = + 0000000003
+ 0000000008   + 0000000006
a = + 0000000002   b = + 0000000002
+ 0000000002
n = + 0000000002
+ 0000000013   + 0000000005
a = + 0000000003   b = + 0000000002
a = + 0000000001   b = + 0000000001
+ 0000000001
n = + 0000000001
+ 0000000026   + 0000000013
a = + 0000000013   b = + 0000000013
+ 0000000013
```

Fig. 11-4. Output of Sample RASCAL/7 Program on Input Data Set of Fig. 11-3.

grammer identify this loop as a possible problem point. The *profile* option causes a modified second copy of the program listing to be printed after program execution has terminated, showing the number of times each executable statement or sub-statement was, in fact, executed for that particular run. Figure 11-5 shows the profile listing of the program given in Fig. 11-1 run on the data set shown in Fig. 11-2. It is important to recognize that the compiler *cannot* create the profile, since the necessary information can only be known *after* the generated object code has completed its execution on a particular data set.

PROFILE OF PROGRAM EXECUTION

```
program   gcd(input,output);
    var   a,b,n: integer;
  1—begin
    1—readln  (n);
    4—while  n > 0 do
      3—begin
        3—readln  (a,b);
        3—writeln  (a,b);
        4—repeat
          9—while  a > b  do
            5—a := a − b;
          8—while  b > a  do
            4—b := b − a;
        4—until a=b;
        3—writeln  (a);
        3—n := n − 1;
      3—end;
  1—end.
```

note that comments have been removed and statements reformatted so that the execution of a sub-statement of a compound statement may be separately indicated.

Fig. 11-5. Profile of Sample Program of Fig. 11-1 on Data Set of Fig. 11-2.

The profile module is obviously a non-trivial string processing program. It must format a listing of the program and insert an integer in front of each line of the program, ignore comments, blanks lines and so forth. This task is not easily accomplished in assembly language, with its primitive data-types, instruction set, and control structures. There is another language, however, which is almost ideally suited to the task. It has reasonable string processing facilities, data-types, a powerful set of operations, and a structured set of control statements—RASCAL/5! Actually, RASCAL/5 is not quite up to the task, since it lacks the ability to read and write non-standard files. If we extend RASCAL/5 so that non-standard files can be input and output, then we can write the profile module in extended RASCAL/5, call it RASCAL/5+, compile it on CANTOR/5+, and incorporate this object code into the total object program generated by CANTOR/7 for a program exercising the profile option. Figure 11-6 shows the creation of the profile module in 360AL from RASCAL/5+ and how it is incorporated into the code emitted by CANTOR/7.

The profile module needs two sets of data. First, it needs access to the source code of the program it must profile. This should be available from a non-standard input data set, the file which the compiler itself referenced earlier. The second data set holds the number of times each line in the source program was executed on this particular run. This data set is generated in core by the main program of the object code and is stored in k cor ious full-words, where k is the number of lines in the source program. This block is then written onto a second, non-standard file just prior to the call to the profile module. The profile module reads this file when it

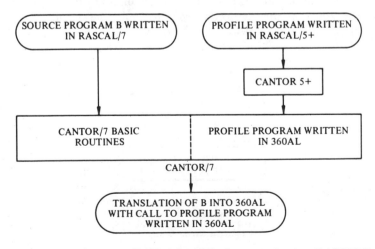

Fig. 11-6. Creation of Profile Module and Its Incorporation into RASCAL/7.

is called, processing it in conjunction with the RASCAL source program file to print the profile of that program.

We can easily give the programmer greater flexibility by allowing him to turn off the profile option. The format is similar to the switch given earlier for the dump statement:

$$\{\$profile\ +\}$$

or

$$\{\$profile\ -\}$$

The default for the profile option is **off.**

The reader should recognize that the process for generating the 360AL version of the profile module is quite different from anything suggested here earlier. We are creating a new version of a compiler from an older version! This particular process is called *bootstrapping,* in reference to the old adage about "pulling oneself up by the bootstraps." Bootstrapping is a general method for creating successively larger, more complex systems from smaller, simpler ones. Figure 11-7 shows the general bootstrapping process. Language version i already exists and has a working implementation, compiler i. We would like to create a new version of language i, call it language $i+1$, but would like to avoid having to begin from scratch with the implementation. If we can express implementation $i+1$ in terms of features in language i, then the implementation of language $i+1$ can be written as a language i program and compiled on implementation i, yielding an object code version of implementation $i+1$. RASCAL/5 fell a little short of our needs in order to build the profile module for CANTOR/7, but it was close enough to illustrate the utility of such a scheme.

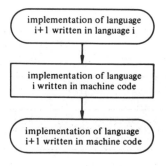

Fig. 11-7.

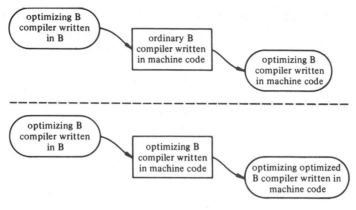

Fig. 11-8.

An interesting variation of the bootstrapping idea concerns different implementations for the *same* language. Suppose our eventual goal is to write a compiler for language B which produces extremely efficient object code with respect to time and space. We may already have a compiler for language B which works correctly but does not generate optimal code. If we write an optimizing compiler for B in language B itself, it can be compiled on the unoptimizing compiler, yielding an optimizing compiler which is itself not optimized but which is in object code form. The source code of the optimizing compiler is written in B. Hence, the source code of the optimizing compiler can be compiled directly by the object code, unoptimized version of the optimizing compiler! The result is an optimized, optimizing compiler for language B! This last step would be impossible if the optimizing compiler were not written in the language it compiles. Figure 11-8 shows the generation of the optimizing optimized compiler from the original compiler.

11.5 ASSERTIONS

A programmer has certain expectations about the behavior of that program at various points in its execution. For example, at a specific line of code, he may expect that variable x is greater than 7, or that z equals y. Normally, these expectations are in the programmer's subconscious when he writes the code, not explicitly within the code itself. He might even write some of these expectations as comments, but (alas) probably not too often.

Suppose a programmer could assert his expectations within the program in a format which an implementation could both recognize and process. Then the implementation could insert machine instructions into the object code it generates which test whether the assertions are in fact satisfied during the run of that program. Depending on the outcome of those tests, the implementation could create diagnostic messages, take corrective action or perhaps simply terminate the execution of the object program. Such a facility could make it possible for the programmer to easily identify logical error conditions within his program beyond those predefined within the language, implementation or environment. These programmer-defined error conditions could cause the implementation to report as errors situations which would otherwise cause no exception in program behavior. Figure 11-9 shows the program of Fig. 11-1 with assertions about its behavior embedded into it. The program has been modified slightly so that the data required for the assertions is available. These assertions have the form of relational and *boolean* predicates with op-

```
$assert = on;
program   gcd(input,output);
              {illustrate embedding of assertions into code.}
              {program computes the greatest common divisor of n pairs
               of integers, where n is read from the input data file.}
    var   a,b,x,y,n: integer ;
    begin
      readln (n);   {how many pairs do we compute gcd for?}
      while  n > 0 do
        begin
          readln  (a,b);   writeln  (a,b);
          assert   (a > 0) and (b > 0);
          x - a; y - b;
          repeat
            while   a > b do begin
              a - a - b;
              assert  x mod b = a mod b;
              end;
            while   b > a do begin
              b - b - a;
              assert  y mod a = b mod a ;
              end;
          until   a = b;
          {a = b = gcd of input pair}
          writeln  (a);
          n := n - 1;
          end;
    end;
```

Fig. 11-9. A Sample RASCAL/7 Program with Assertions.

tional quantification. For quantifiers we allow any of:

1. **'for all'**
2. **'there is'**
3. **'not for all'**
4. **'there is no'**

not shown in Fig. 11-9. The predicates are compiled in exactly the same manner as we would for other language constructs, such as the predicate of an **if** or **while** statement. An assertion of the form:

assert B ;

where B is a predicate with optional quantification is, in effect, compiled as if it were:

if not B **then** *process_error;*

For this implementation, the action taken when an assertion is violated is to simply print an informative message indicating which assertion was violated and to terminate program execution. If the implementation includes a **dumping** option, then the current value of all variables at the time that the assertion was violated might also be printed to provide greater help to the programmer in debugging. The quantifiers are easily converted into loops; e.g., the assertion:

assert for all $1 <= i <= 10$, b[i] < 0;

is translated as if it were:

```
i := 1;
while i <= 10 do begin
  if not(b[i] < 0) then process_error;
  i := i + 1;
  end;
```

The strategies which the implementor needs in order to include an **assert** statement have clearly been discussed under other topics; i.e., the chapters on control structures, predicates, and error processing, so we shall not repeat those methods here.

The assertions are included as an aid in testing a program under development. Once development has been completed, the programmer may choose to turn off or disable their effects omitting the **$assert** switch:

{**$assert** +}

The default for the switch is off. The programmer may, for the purposes of clarity and documentation, explicitly indicate that the switch is off by including the control card:

$$\{\$\textbf{assert} \ -\}$$

at the beginning of his program. If the switch is **off,** then the compiler may simply ignore the program assertions, not generating any code which will perform run-time checks, reducing the size of the object code over that generated when the assertions are checked.

We have only sketched the motivation for program assertions. Their value and proper usage really require an extended examination, which is not appropriate for this text. We urge the interested reader to consult one of the several references in the bibliography for more details on assertions.

11.6 SUMMARY

An implementation of a language which does not offer debugging aids is inexcusable. The most obvious *diagnostic tool* is a means for handling normal errors, at both compile and run-time, a topic discussed in detail in Chapter 8. Other tools are of interest, and as a package presented to the compiler user, can make a tremendous difference in the time it takes to develop a program. Among the many common tools are the:

1. cross-reference map
2. variable dump
3. execution profile
4. run-time assertions

These four are hardly a complete list of the diagnostic tools offered in the literally thousands of implementations currently available but do indicate their essential character.

The cross-reference map is really just an index into the program to help a programmer conveniently locate any or all references to one or more program identifiers. Perhaps because it is so simple to implement, it is almost universally available. The other three tools assist the programmer to understand the dynamic behavior of his program. By *dumping* the value of variables at specific points in the program execution, the programmer can observe the detailed execution of his program at key places. By *profiling* the execution of the program, he can see the overall flow of control for a particular run. Finally, by *asserting* that certain conditions hold within the program text, he can embed programmer-defined error conditions into the code which are checked dynamically via code generated by the implementation. This package of tools gives the programmer considerable flexibility in the style of debugging he chooses with little or no cost once development is complete.

EXERCISES

11-1. Modify the general predicates of RASCAL to include quantifiers as described for assertions, changing CANTOR as needed to accommodate the extended feature.

11-2. Survey the diagnostic tools available from three compilers or interpreters available at your installation. Evaluate them for quality with respect to the nature and form of information they provide. If two or more implementations have the same feature, then contrast the particulars of each version.

11-3. Go back to each valid RASCAL program given in the text as an example since Chapter 4 and embed assertions in places where you feel it will improve debugging capabilities, then run these programs through CANTOR/7.

11-4. How would you implement the cross-reference map for a block-structured language? Explain why it differs from that of a non-block-structured language.

TESTING HINTS

1. Test CANTOR/7 on all programs used to test CANTOR/3. If in addition, you have a compiler which has extensions, as specified in other chapters of this part of the text, then test CANTOR/7 on those programs as well.

2. Test your cross-reference map feature when the source program has no constants or variables.

3. Test your cross-reference map feature when the symbol table is full.

4. Test your variable dumping feature when values are undefined and defined. Test both formats of the dump statement. Test the same program with the $dump switch off and on.

5. Test the profile feature when some code is not executed at all. Test it with code which exercises *all* features of RASCAL/7 to ensure the format is correct, and with the $profile switch off and then on.

6. Test the assertion feature with simple and with complex predicates, just as you did when testing predicates in Chapter 5. Test the same program first with *$assert* off and then on. Test it with a program which has no violated assertions and then with one which has an assertion violated. Make sure that you test the quantifiers, since these are not part of the original predicate format described in Chapter 5.

BIBLIOGRAPHY

Studies of diagnostic tools are scarce indeed, with the exception of the assertion which has generated tremendous enthusiasm in the past few years. [Bauer and Eickel 74] has a cursory treatment of the subject. None of the other major compiler texts discuss diagnostic tools to any extent ([Lee 74], [Lewis, et al 76], [Aho and Ullman 77], and [Gries 71]).

The notion of an assertion is often attributed to Floyd in a classic paper on language semantics ([Floyd 67]). This notion was applied in [King 71] to proving programs to be correct with respect to a specified set of input/output assertions. A number of researchers have examined the utility of embedding assertions into code both for improved testing capabilities and the possibility of a proof of correctness ([Dijkstra 76], [Gries 76], [Manna 76,77], [Wegbreit 77]). These efforts have been only partially successful, leaving this area as one of tremendous vitality and importance in the future.

Appendix A
Compiler User's Manual

A product without adequate documentation is a lemon, because no one but its authors will know how to properly use it without a great deal of pain and patience. Certain implementors are absolutely notorious for the poor quality of their software documentation. Generating software documentation is one of the most important tasks in the total software development process and unfortunately also one of the least glamorous aspects as well.

The product of interest here is CANTOR. The documentation is a user's manual for the compiler. Although there is no one right way to write a manual, there are important guidelines. First and foremost, the documentation should be *user-oriented;* i.e., written with the potential reader audience in mind. In our case, we shall presume that the user community consists of college students and researchers, familiar with general programming and with PASCAL in particular. This document will be presented to them as the primary source for information on RASCAL, the variant of PASCAL implemented, and the various features such as a cross-reference map, which the compiler itself offers. It should be written to explain the compiler as a "black box." The user has no need to understand the internal organization or structure of CANTOR. A separate document, a *compiler logic manual,* should be written to explain the internal workings of CANTOR for system programmers who may have to repair bugs or modify its behavior. We do not present a table of contents for a logic manual, but the student may wish to write one as well, using several of the logic manuals available from his computer center for various implementations as models.

Perhaps the most critical information in the user's manual in this case is a definition of RASCAL, since it differs from PASCAL in many important details. This definition should take two forms. First a context-free grammar of the language should be included, perhaps as an appendix. This grammar need not be the same grammar which drives CANTOR, since the latter grammar was chosen for its efficient parsing properties, not its expository power. The second form should be an English narrative explaining features with examples of their proper usage, just as given in this book. It is just as important to indicate what is *not* legal, as to pinpoint what is valid RASCAL in this exposition; e.g., a statement which illustrates that keywords are reserved is critical. After the language definition has been presented, the features of the compiler itself should be listed. Depending on how many components of CANTOR were actually implemented this could include a discussion of the cross-reference map, profile option, and so forth, complete with an example of each listed feature.

Following this discussion should be the job control language statements which must be included with the source RASCAL program in order to compile it. Since

CANTOR outputs 360AL code, the job control language might also include information on how to assemble the resultant object code and execute the output of the assembler. Again, an example is extremely helpful here, especially since job control language is for many students (the user community) a difficult and confusing subject.

The entire list of error messages, by number, should be included in a section of the manual. Accompanying the complete text of the message should be any additional information which the manual writer may know about possible causes or corrections for the error. This may include references to other points in the manual where a feature is discussed in more detail, such as the section of the manual dealing with the correct form of assignment statements for an error raised within an assignment statement.

Finally, the manual must have an index. It is terribly frustrating to leaf through a manual looking for the single critical sentence simply because the authors generated a poor (or perhaps no) index. Selecting indexing terms is quite tedious but important to the overall quality of the manual. Of course, if the manual is quite small, then an index may be unnecessary, but for a project of the magnitude of CANTOR, it is quite appropriate since the user's manual would have to be relatively long in order to be complete. As a general guideline, any document over fifteen pages should probably have an index.

TABLE OF CONTENTS

1. Purpose of Manual
2. Overview of Manual Contents
3. RASCAL Language Definition with Examples
4. Compiler Features
5. Running CANTOR and The Object Code It Generates
6. Error Messages
7. References to Other Pertinent Documents
8. Index

Appendix B
The Structure of the IBM
360/370 Computer Family

The IBM 360/370 computer is actually a family of over twenty different computer systems whose processing speeds vary by over two orders of magnitude. The dozen different 360 CPUs have the same instruction set, differing primarily in processor speed and the main memory which size they can support. The 370 family, released throughout the seventies, executes all of the instructions of the earlier 360 models and, in addition, offers new instructions to facilitate operations found awkward on the 360. The 370 family was designed to support a virtual memory operating system (although a conventional system is supported by IBM), whereas only the 360/67 processor includes the necessary hardware to efficiently support virtual memeory. Since the operating system is peripheral to our interests in this text, we shall not dwell on the important flexibility that a virtual memeory operating system allows, concentrating instead on the instruction set.

By offering a large family of upward compatible computers, IBM has enabled the user to upgrade an installation without the costly software conversion problems which ordinarily result from changing processors. Software can be moved from one family member to another essentially without change. (There are exceptions which we shall not consider here; see [Case and Padegs 78] for details.) The wide variation in system power and cost with minimal conversion difficulties has made the IBM 360/370 computer immensely successful, as demonstrated by its overwhelming dominance of the large computer market.

Figure B-1 shows the functional architecture of the IBM 360 machine. The main storage is organized into *bytes,* each of which is 8 bits long. Each byte is addressable, with a maximum of 2^{24} different bytes addressable on any machine, although on most models the actual maximum is much smaller. For a variety of operations, bytes are grouped into half-words (2 bytes), full-words (4 bytes), and double-words (8 bytes). On most of the 360 models, half-words must begin on even numbered addresses, full-words on an address divisible by four and double-words on an address divisible by eight. This constraint, imposed to simplify the hardware design, was removed for all 370 models (but with a time penalty).

Together with main memory, there are 16 general purpose registers numbered 0 to 15, all addressed independently from memory. Most arithmetic, logical and relational operations reference one or two such registers, which are 32 bits long (one full-word). In addition, four floating-point registers, each 64 bits long (one double-word) allow direct floating-point computation.

The five basic instruction formats of the 360 are shown in Fig. B-2. Instruction length varies from two to six bytes, depending on the number of main memory

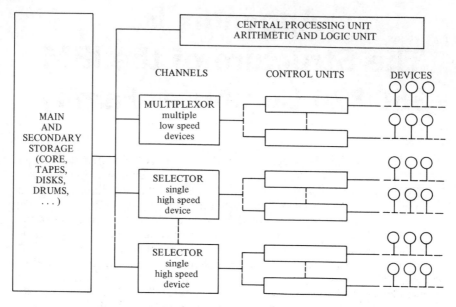

Fig. B-1. Functional Schematic of IBM 360 Computer.

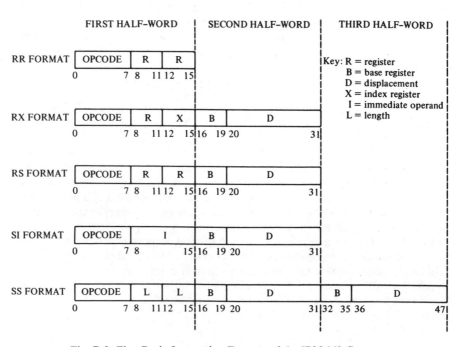

Fig. B-2. Five Basic Instruction Formats of the IBM 360 Computer.

references, and whether there is an immediate operand in the instruction. The longest instruction is the Storage-Storage format which references two main memory locations; the shortest is the Register-Register format which makes no main memory references at all.

Main memory can be referenced via general purpose registers configured by the programmer as base and index registers offset by a fixed, non-negative displacement. The base and index registers are chosen by the programmer from among general purpose registers 1 to 15; register 0 cannot be used for this purpose. The displacement can vary from 0 to 4095. There is no indirect addressing, except through the base and index registers.

Certain operations involve *immediate* operands, which are fixed operands included in the actual instruction. The immediate operand is one byte. For example, the "Move Immediate" instruction moves one byte of information specified in the instruction to a memory location also given as part of the operand.

Numbers are stored in three different formats: binary, decimal, and floating-point. Each binary number is either a half-word or full-word long, represented in two's complement format.

Each decimal digit can be represented in four bits in BCD, so that two digits are packed into a single byte. Decimal operations reference operands directly in memory, rather than through the general purpose registers. Operand lengths vary from 1 to 16 bytes on the 360, including one half-byte for the sign, numbers being represented in sign-magnitude format.

Floating-point numbers are stored either in full or double-word lengths, representing approximations to real numbers. Each number has three components: sign, fraction and exponent. The fraction, always less than one, can be either 24 or 56 bits, depending on the overall length of the number. The exponent is a power of sixteen, whose effective range is 16^{-64} to 16^{63}. The ALU executes instructions which manipulate all three numeric formats, in addition to other instructions which reference storage as literal character or binary data, including shifts, logical comparisons, and memory to memory moves.

Input/output is performed through the operating system, never directly by the user. For programmer convenience, a series of system macros have been defined by IBM to facilitate input/output operations.

IBM has established a set of conventions for subroutine calls to which we adhere in this text. The 360 and 370 computers have a fairly conventional Von Neumann architecture, rather than the stack architecture typical of even today's microcomputers. Consequently, the programmer is responsible for saving the register values of the calling routine when entering a subroutine and restoring those values upon subroutine exit and return to the calling module. This is normally accomplished by having each routine establish a "save area," where register contents are stored. The called routine, as its first activity, stores the values of the caller's registers into the *caller's* save area. Of course, if this subroutine itself calls still another routine, the other routine must repeat these same steps. Just prior to returning to the calling routine, the subroutine restores the register contents of the caller to what they were prior to the subroutine's activation. In this way, all changes made to the registers by the subroutine are transparent to the calling routine. Normally, routines pass information between themselves via parameter lists. The IBM 360/370 standard is to pass the address of a contiguous list of addresses between routines; each address in the list points to a parameter. Figure B-3 shows the code which might appear in a program having a subroutine.

```
* CALL SUBROUTINE "SUB" WHICH HAS TWO ARGUMENTS: ARG1 & ARG2
            LA        1,PARMAREA      prepare parameter list
            LA        2,ARG1          put addr ARG1 into list
            ST        2,0(1)
            LA        2,ARG2          put addr ARG2 into list
            ST        2,4(1)
            L         15,=V(SUB)      branch to subprogram
            BALR      14,15
* SUBROUTINES RETURNS HERE
            . . .
CALLSAVE    DS        18F             save area where subroutine
*                                     stores registers of caller
PARMAREA    DS        2A              addresses of parms go here
            . . .


* SUBROUTINE "SUB" WHICH EXPECTS TWO ARGUMENTS: ARG1 & ARG2
SUB         CSECT
            STM       14,12,12(13)    store registers of caller
*                                     in save area established
*                                     by caller
            BALR      12,0            establish addressability
            USING     *,12            using register 12 as base
            ST        13,SUBSAV+4     store location of caller's
*                                     save area in subroutine's
*                                     save area
            LA        13,SUBSAV       load location of subroutine's
*                                     save area
            . . .
            [subroutine's code goes here]
            . . .
* PREPARE TO RETURN TO CALLING ROUTINE
            L         13,SUBSAV+4     load location of caller's
*                                     save area
            LM        14,12,12(13)    restore caller's registers
            BR        14              return
            . . .
SUBSAV      DS        18F             subroutine's save area
            . . .
```

Fig. B-3. Subroutine Linkage Conventions.

Appendix C
LL(1) Parsing

The first algorithm presented computes the selection set. Originally presented in [Lewis, et al, 76], it has thirteen steps:

1. Find the set of "alive" nonterminals.
2. Find the nullable nonterminals and productions.
3. Construct the BEGINS-DIRECTLY-WITH relation.
4. Compute the BEGINS-WITH relation.
5. Compute the FIRST set of each symbol.
6. Compute the FIRST set of each production.
7. Compute the IS-FOLLOWED-DIRECTLY-BY relation.
8. Compute the IS-DIRECT-END-OF relation.
9. Compute the IS-END-OF relation.
10. Compute the IS-FOLLOWED-BY relation.
11. Extend IS-FOLLOWED-BY to include endmarker '¢'.
12. Compute the FOLLOW set of each nullable nonterminal.
13. Compute the selection set of each production.

We shall explain each step in turn:

Step 1. Alive Nonterminals. A nonterminal is *alive* if it can derive one or more terminal strings; otherwise, it is *dead*. To determine which nonterminals of a grammar are alive:

a. List all nonterminals which appear on the left-hand side of at least one production which has no nonterminals on the right-hand side.
b. Add to the list any nonterminal which appears on the left-hand side of at least one production for which all nonterminals on the right-hand side already belong to the list. Repeat this step until it can no longer be applied

The members of the final list produced are all of the alive nonterminals, while all nonterminals not on that list are dead.

Step 2. Nullable Nonterminals and Productions. A nonterminal is *nullable* if it derives lambda; a production is *nullable* if it derives lambda. To determine which nonterminals and productions are nullable, simply:

Delete all productions whose right-hand side includes a terminal symbol. (Recall that lambda is not a terminal symbol.)

The nullable nonterminals are those alive in the resulting grammar, while the nullable productions are those from the resulting grammar, all of whose right-hand side nonterminals are nullable.

Step 3. BEGINS-DIRECTLY-WITH. Nonterminal B BEGINS-DIRECTLY-WITH vocabulary symbol C, if and only if there is a production:

$$B \to \alpha\, C\, \beta$$

where α is nullable, and β is an arbitrary string. We shall summarize the relation in a n×n matrix, where n is the cardinality of the vocabulary and the i,j-th entry is one, if the i-th vocabulary symbol BEGINS-DIRECTLY-WITH the j-th vocabulary symbol and zero, otherwise.

Step 4. BEGINS-WITH. Nonterminal B BEGINS-WITH vocabulary symbol C, if and only if there is a string beginning with C which can be derived from B. This relation, also represented by a matrix, is the reflexive, transitive closure of the BEGINS-DIRECTLY-WITH matrix.

Step 5. FIRST of each symbol. Terminal C is in the FIRST of nonterminal B, if and only if B BEGINS-WITH C. Terminal C is the FIRST of C.

Step 6. FIRST of each production. The FIRST of production $B \to \nu_1 \ldots \nu_m$, where each ν_i is a vocabulary symbol, is

$$\text{FIRST}(\nu_1) \cup \text{FIRST}(\nu_2) \cup \ldots \cup \text{FIRST}(\nu_n)$$

Either each of $\nu_1, \ldots, \nu_{n-1}$ is nullable and ν_n is not, or n = m and $\nu_1, \ldots, \nu_m$ are all nullable. FIRST $(B \to \lambda) = \Phi$.

Step 7. IS-FOLLOWED-DIRECTLY-BY. B IS-FOLLOWED-DIRECTLY-BY C, if and only if there is a production:

$$D \to \alpha\, B\, \beta\, C\, \gamma$$

where B and C are vocabulary symbols, α and γ are arbitrary strings and β is a nullable string. This is easily computed from the productions and the list of nullable nonterminals computed in Step 2.

Step 8. IS-DIRECT-END-OF. B IS-DIRECT-END-OF C, if and only if there is a production of the form:

$$C \to \alpha\, B\, \beta$$

where β is a nullable string and α is an arbitrary string.

Step 9. IS-END-OF. B IS-END-OF C, if and only if the entry corresponding to B,C in the reflexive transitive closure of IS-DIRECT-END-OF is one.

Step 10. IS-FOLLOWED-BY. IS-FOLLOWED-BY is:

$$\text{IS-END-OF} \times \text{IS-FOLLOWED-DIRECTLY-BY} \times \text{BEGINS-WITH}$$

B IS-FOLLOWED-BY C, if and only if there is a string derived from the axiom in which BC is a substring.

Step 11. Extend IS-FOLLOWED-BY. We extend the matrix representation of IS-FOLLOWED-BY to include a column labelled by the endmarker '$\not{c}$'. B IS-FOLLOWED-BY '$\not{c}$', if and only if B IS-END-OF S, where S is the grammar axiom. The latter relation was computed in Step 9.

Step 12. FOLLOW set of each nullable nonterminal. Terminal B is in the FOLLOW set of nullable nonterminal C, if and only if the C,B entry of IS-FOLLOWED-BY is one. The list of nullable nonterminals was computed in Step 2.

Step 13. SELECTION set of each production. For production B → β, SELECT (B → β) = FIRST (B → β), if β is not nullable, and is FIRST (B → β) ∪ FOLLOW (B), if it is.

This completes the algorithm which computes selection sets. It is tedious to perform by hand but quite amenable to computer implementation, since it is essentially no more than simple matrix manipulation.

When a grammar is not LL(1) because the selection sets of alternative productions are not disjoint, the compiler writer must either modify the grammar, remove a conflicting selection set element or change parsing methods. Sometimes it is necessary to try an alternative method, because the language is not LL(1). However, this is not often the case in practice, the grammar being modifiable into an LL form. Alternatively, the writer might alter the language being parsed to become a superset of the original. New sentences not in the original language can be excluded by the semantic processor, rather than the syntactic component. If the resulting language does have an LL grammar which the writer can discover, then this new grammar can be employed to drive the parser.

Here we examine two methods for eliminating conflicts in alternative productions. A third method, eliminating left recursion, was discussed in Chapter 2. The first method explored is called *left factoring*. Suppose a grammar contains two productions:

$$B \rightarrow \alpha \beta$$
$$B \rightarrow \alpha \gamma$$

where α is a string which derives at least one terminal string (not lambda) and $\beta \neq \gamma$. Then their selection sets cannot be disjoint, since they will both contain FIRST(x) where x is the terminal string derived from α. If FIRST(β) (FIRST(β) ∪ FOLLOW(B), if β is nullable) is disjoint with FIRST(γ) (FIRST(γ) ∪ FOLLOW(B), if γ is nullable), then we can rewrite these two productions as:

$$B \rightarrow \alpha C$$
$$C \rightarrow \beta$$
$$C \rightarrow \gamma$$

where C is a new nonterminal. The selection sets of the two productions whose left-hand side is C will be disjoint so there is no selection set conflict.

Another modification frequently made to grammars is called *corner substitu-*

tion, or more specifically, *left corner substitution.* The leftmost symbol on the right-hand side of a production is its *left corner.* A lambda production has no left corner. Given a production:

$$B \rightarrow C \, \alpha$$

and n productions:

$$C \rightarrow \beta_1$$
$$\cdots$$
$$C \rightarrow \beta_n$$

whose left-hand side is C (and no others), then we can replace $B \rightarrow C \, \alpha$ by

$$B \rightarrow \beta_1 \, \alpha$$
$$\cdots$$
$$B \rightarrow \beta_n \, \alpha$$

Note that we cannot remove the n productions whose left-hand side is C, unless there is now no sentential form containing a C.

Left corner substitution is helpful when combined with left factoring. Consider grammar G with productions:

1. S → 'x' C
2. S → 'B' y
3. C → 'a' S
4. C → 'x' 'a'
5. B → 'x'

It is not LL(1) because the selection sets of productions 1 and 2 both contain 'x'. By first performing left corner substitution, we obtain:

1. S → 'x' C
2'. S → 'x' 'y'
3. C → 'a' S
4. C → 'x' 'a'
5. B → 'x'

Since B is no longer on the right-hand side of any production, production 5 can now be eliminated, although this is not necessary in order to obtain an LL(1) grammar. Note that this revised grammar is still not LL(1) because the first two productions both have right-hand sides which begin with 'x'. By left factoring we obtain:

1'. S → 'x' D
3. C → 'a' S
4. C → 'x' 'a'
6. D → C
7. D → 'y'

which is LL(1).

Bibliography

1. OPTIMIZATION AND REGISTER ALLOCATION

Abel, N. E., and Bell, J. R. 1972. "Global optimization in compilers." *Proc. First USA-Japan Computer Conf.* AFIPS Press, Montvale, N.J.

Aho, A. V., and Johnson, S. C. 1976. "Optimal code generation for expression trees." *J. ACM* **23**:3, 488–501.

Aho, A. V.; Johnson, S. C.; and Ullman, J. D. 1977. "Code generation for expressions with common subexpressions." *J. ACM* **24**:1, 146–160.

Aho, A. V., and Ullman, J. D. 1972. "Optimization of straight line code." *SIAM J. Computing* **1**:1, 1-19.

Aho, A. V., and Ullman, J. D. 1972. "Optimization of LR(k) parsers." *J. Computer and Systems Sciences* **6**:6, 573–602.

Aho, A. V., and Ullman, J. D. 1973. "A technique for speeding up LR(k) parsers." *SIAM J. Computing* **2**:2, 106–127.

Aho, A. V., and Ullman, J. D. 1976. "Node listings for reducible graphs." *J. Computer and Systems Sciences* **13**:3, 286–299.

Allen, F. E. 1969. "Program optimization." *Annual Review of Automatic Programming* **5**, 239–307.

Allen, F. E. 1975. "Bibliography on program optimization." *RC-5767,* IBM T. J. Watson Research Center, Yorktown Heights, N.Y.

Allen, F. E., and Cocke, J. 1972. "A catalogue of optimizing transformations." In Rustin 1972, pp. 1–30.

Allen, F. E.; Cocke, J.; and Kennedy, K. 1974. "Reduction of operator strength." *TR 476-093-6,* Dept. of Mathematical Sciences, Rice Univ., Houston.

Bagwell, J. T. 1970. "Local optimizations." *SIGPLAN Notices* **5**:7, 52–66.

Beatty, J. C. 1972. "An axiomatic approach to code optimization for expressions." *J. ACM* **19**:4, 613–640. *Errata,* **20**:1 (Jan. 1973) 180 and **20**:3 (July 1973) 538.

Beatty, J. C. 1974. "Register assignment algorithm for generation of highly optimized object code." *IBM J. Research and Development* **5**:2, 20–39.

Branquart, P.; Cardinael, J. P.; Lewi, J.; Delescaille, J. P.; and Vanbegin, M. 1976. *An Optimized Translation Process and Its Application to ALGOL 68. Lecture Notes in Computer Science,* **38**, Springer-Verlag, New York.

Breuer, M. A. 1969. "Generation of optimal code for expressions via factorization." *Comm. ACM* **12**:6, 333–340.

Bruno, J. L., and Lasagne, T. 1975. "The generation of optimal code for stack machines." *J. ACM* **22**:3, 382–397.

Busam, V. A., and Englund, D. E. 1969. "Optimization of expressions in FORTRAN." *Comm. ACM* **12**:2, 666–674.

Cocke, J. 1970. "Global common subexpression elimination." *SIGPLAN* Notices **5**:7, 20–24.

Cocke, J., and Miller, R. E. 1969. "Some analysis techniques for optimizing computer programmers." *Proc. 2nd Hawaii Intl. Conf. on Systems Sciences,* pp. 143—146.

Earnest, C. 1974. "Some topics in code optimization." *J. ACM* **21**:1, 76–102.

Floyd, R. W. 1961. "An algorithm for coding efficient arithmetic expressions." *Comm. ACM* **4:**1, 42–51.

Fong, A. C. 1977. "Elimination of common subexpressions in very high-level languages." *Proc. 4th ACM Symposium on Principles of Programming Languages,* pp. 48–57.

Frailey, D. J. 1970. "Expression optimization using unary complement operators." *SIGPLAN Notices* **5:**7, 67–85.

Freiburghouse, R. A. 1974. "Register allocation via usage counts." *Comm. ACM* **17:**11, 638–642.

Gear, C. W. 1965. "High speed compilation of efficient object code." *Comm. ACM* **8:**8, 483–488.

Geschke, C. M. 1972. "Global Program Optimization." Ph.D. dissertation, Dept. of Computer Science, Carnegie-Mellon Univ., Pittsburgh.

Harrison, W. 1975. "A class of register allocation algorithms." *RC-5342,* IBM T. J. Watson Research Center, Yorktown Heights, NY.

Harrison W. 1977. "A new strategy for code generation—the general purpose optimizing compiler." *Proc. 4th ACM Symposium on Principles of Programming Languages,* pp. 29–37.

Horowitz, L. P.; Miller, R. M.; and Winograd, S. 1966. "Index register allocation." *J. ACM* **13:**1, 43–61.

Huxtable, D. H. R. 1964. "On writing an optimizing translator for ALGOL 60." In *Introduction to System Programming,* Academic Press, New York.

IBM 1968. *FORTRAN (h) Compiler Programming Logic Manual.* Form Y28-6642, IBM, New York.

Johnsson, R. K. 1975. "An Approach to Global Register Allocation." Ph.D. dissertation, Carnegie-Mellon Univ., Pittsburgh.

Kennedy, K. 1972. "Index register allocation in straight line code and simple loops." In Rustin 1972, pp. 51–64.

Kildall, G. A. 1973. "A unified approach to global program optimization." *Proc. ACM Symp. on Principles of Programming Languages.* pp. 194–206.

Kim, J., and Tan, C. J. 1976. "Register assignment algorithm—II." *RC-6262,* IBM T. J. Watson Research Center, Yorktown Heights, NY.

Loveman, D. B. 1976. "Program improvement by source to source transformation." *Proc. 3rd ACM Symposium on Principles of Programming Languages,* pp. 140–152.

Lowry, E., and Medlock, C. W. 1969. "Object code optimization." *Comm. ACM* **12:**1, 13–22.

Luccio, F. 1969. "A comment on index register allocation." *Comm. ACM* **10:**9, 372–374.

McKeeman, W. M. 1965. "Peephole optimization." *Comm. ACM* **8:**7, 443–444.

Mendicino, S., and Zwackenberg, R. 1965. "A FORTRAN code optimizer for the CDC 6600." *UCRL-14162,* Lawrence Radiation Lab.

Neel, D., and Amirchahy, M. 1975. "Removal of invariant statements from nested loops in a single effective compiler pass." *SIGPLAN Notices* **10:**3, 87–96.

Newcomer, J. M. 1975. "Machine-Independent Generation of Optimal Local Code." Ph.D. dissertation, Computer Science Dept., Carnegie-Mellon U., Pittsburgh.

Nievergelt, J. 1965. "On the automatic simplification of computer code." *Comm. ACM* **8:**6, 366–370.

Paige, R., and Schwartz, J. T. 1977. "Reduction in strength of high level operations." *Proc. 4th ACM Symposium on Principles of Programming Languages,* pp. 58–71.

Palm, R. C., Jr. 1975. "A portable optimizer for the language C." M.Sc. Thesis, Massachusetts Institute of Technology, Cambridge, MA.

Pyster, A. 1977. "Using assertions to improve language translators." *National Computer Conference,* June 1977, Dallas, pp. 665–668.

Rustin, R. 1972. *Design and Optimization of Compilers*. Prentice-Hall, Englewood Cliffs, NJ.

Schaefer, M. 1973. *A Mathematical Theory of Global Program Optimization*. Prentice-Hall, Englewood Cliffs, NJ.

Schneck, P. B., and Angel, E. 1973. "A FORTRAN to FORTRAN optimizing compiler." *Computer J.* **16**:4, 322–330.

Schneider, V. B. 1971. "On the number of registers needed to evaluate arithmetic expressions." *BIT* **11**:1, 84–93.

Schwartz, J. T. 1975. "Optimization of very high level languages." *J. Computer Languages*, Part I: "Value transmission and its corollaries," **1**:2, 161–194; Part II: "Deducing relationships of inclusion and membership." **1**:3, 197–218.

Sethi, R. 1975. "Complete register allocation problems." *SIAM J. Computing* **4**:3, 226–248.

Sethi, R., and Ullman, J. D. 1970. "The generation of optimal code for arithmetic expressions." *J. ACM* **17**:4, 715–728.

Stockhausen, P. F. 1973. "Adapting optimal code generation for arithmetic expressions to the instruction sets of present day computers." *Comm. ACM* **16**:6, 353–354. *Errata,* **17**:10 (Oct. 74) 591.

Waite, W. M. 1974. "Optimization." In Bauer and Eickel 1974, pp. 549–602.

Wasiew, S. G. 1971. "A Compiler Writing System with Optimization Capabilities for Complex Order Structures." Ph.D. dissertation, Northwestern University, Evanston, IL.

Wulf, W.; Jonsson, R. K.; Weinstock, C. B.; Hobbs, S. O.; and Geschke, C. M. 1975. *The Design of An Optimizing Compiler*. American Elsevier, New York.

Yhap, E. F. 1974. "Global register assignment using interval partition and piecewise processing." *RC-5015*, IBM T. J. Watson Research Center, Yorktown Heights, NY.

Yhap, E. F. 1975. "General register assignment in presence of data flow." *RC-5645*, IBM T. J. Watson Research Center, Yorktown Heights, NY.

Zelkowitz, M. V., and Bail, W. G. 1974. "Optimization of structured programs." *Software—Practice and Experience* **4**:1, 51–57.

2. TEXTS ON GENERAL COMPILING METHODS

Aho, A. V., and Ullman, J. D. 1972. *The Theory of Parsing, Translation and Compiling*. Vol. 1, *Parsing*, Prentice-Hall, Englewood Cliffs, NJ.

Aho, A. V., and Ullman, J. D. 1973. *The Theory of Parsing, Translation and Compiling*. Vol. II, *Compiling*, Prentice-Hall, Englewood Cliffs, NJ.

Aho, A. V., and Ullman, J. D. 1977. *Principles of Compiler Design*. Addison-Wesley, Reading, MA.

Bauer, F. L., and Eickel, J. 1974. *Compiler Construction: An Advanced Course*. Springer-Verlag, New York.

Cheatham, T. E., Jr. 1967. *The Theory and Construction of Compilers*. Computer Associates, Wakefield, MA.

Cocke, J., and Schwartz, J. T. 1970. *Programming Languages and Their Compilers, Preliminary Notes*. 2nd. rev. ed. Courant Institute of Mathematical Sciences, New York.

Gries, D. 1971. *Compiler Construction for Digital Computers*. Wiley & Sons, New York.

Hopgood, F. R. A. 1969. *Compiling Techniques*. American Elsevier, New York.

Lee, J. A. N. 1974. *Anatomy of A Compiler*. Van Nostrand, New York.

Lewis, P.; Rosenkrantz, D.; and Stearns, R. 1976. *Compiler Design Theory*. Addison-Wesley, Reading, MA.

Pollack, B. W., ed. 1972. *Compiler Techniques*. Auerbach, Philadelphia.

3. PROGRAMMING LANGUAGES: PRINCIPLES, HISTORY, AND SURVEY

Elson, M. 1973. *Concepts of Programming Languages.* Science Research Associates, Palo Alto, CA.

Galler, B. A., and Perlis, A. J. 1970. *A View of Programming Languages.* Addison-Wesley, Reading, MA.

Genuys, F. 1968. *Programming Languages.* Academic Press, New York.

Higman, B. 1967. *A Comparative Study of Programming Languages.* MacDonald Elsevier, New York.

Nicholls, J. E. 1975. *The Structure and Design of Programming Languages.* Addison-Wesley, Reading, MA.

Pratt, T. 1975. *Programming Languages: Design and Implementation.* Prentice Hall, Englewood Cliffs, NJ.

Rosen, S., ed. 1967. *Programming Systems and Languages.* McGraw-Hill, New York.

Sammet, J. E. 1969. *Programming Languages: History and Fundamentals.* Prentice-Hall, Englewood Cliffs, NJ.

Sammet, J. E. 1972. "Programming languages: history and future." *Comm. ACM* **15**:7, 601–610.

4. DEFINITIONS OF PROGRAMMING LANGUAGES

ANSI. 1966. "American national standard FORTRAN." (ANS X3.9-1966), American National Standards Institute, New York.

ANSI. 1968. "American national standard COBOL." Form X3.23-1968, New York.

ANSI. 1976. "American national standard programming language PL/I." (ANS X3.53-1976), American National Standards Institute, New York.

ANSI. 1976. "Draft proposal ANS FORTRAN." (ANS X3J3-1976), *SIGPLAN Notices* **11**:3.

Backus, J. W. 1959. "The syntax and semantics of the proposed international algebraic language of the Zurich ACM-GAMM Conference." *Proc. Intl. Conf. on Information Processing,* UNESCO, pp. 125–132.

Conway, R. W.; Gries, D.; and Zimmerman, E. C. 1976. *A Primer on PASCAL.* Winthrop, Cambridge, MA.

Conway, R. W., and Maxwell, W. L. 1963. "CORC—the Cornell computing language." *Comm. ACM* **6**: 317–321.

Conway, R. W., et al. 1970. "PL/C. A high performance subset of PL/I." *TR 70-55,* Computer Science Dept., Cornell Univ., Ithaca, NY.

Griswold, R. E., and Griswold, M. 1973. *A SNOBOL4 Primer.* Prentice-Hall, Englewood Cliffs, NJ.

Griswold, R. E.; Poage, J.; and Polonsky, I. 1971. *The SNOBOL4 Programming Language.* Prentice-Hall, Englewood Cliffs, NJ.

Hoare, C. A. R., and Wirth, N. 1973. "An axiomatic definition of the programming language PASCAL." *Acta Informatica* **2**:4, 335–356.

IBM, 1969. *PL/I Language Specifications.* Form GY33-6003, Hursley Park, England.

Iverson, K. 1962. *A Programming Language.* John Wiley & Sons, New York.

Jensen, K., and Wirth, N. 1975. *PASCAL User Manual and Report.* Springer-Verlag, New York.

Kernighan, B. W. 1975. "RATFOR—a preprocessor for a rational FORTRAN." *Software—Practice and Experience* **5**:4, 395–406.

Kieburtz, R. B., and Barabash, W. 1976. *Stonybrook PASCAL/360 User's Guide, Release 1 Edition*. State University of New York at Stonybrook.

Lauer, P. E. 1968. "Formal definition of ALGOL 60." *TR 25.088*, IBM Laboratory, Vienna.

McCarthy, J., et al. 1965. *LISP 1.5 Programmer's Manual*. MIT Press, Cambridge, MA.

Naur, P. 1963. "Revised report on the algorithmic language ALGOL 60." *Comm. ACM* **6**:1, 1–17.

Pagan, F. G. 1976. *A Practical Guide to ALGOL 68*. John Wiley & Sons, New York.

Pakin, S. 1972. *APL/360 Reference Manual*. 2nd ed. Science Research Associates, Chicago.

Ritchie, D. M., Kernighan, B. W.; and Lesk, M. E. 1975. "The C Programming Language." *CSTR 31*, Bell Laboratories, Murray Hill, NJ.

Schwartz, J. T. 1973. *On Programming: An Interim Report on The SETL Project*. Courant Institute, New York.

Shaw, C. J. 1963. "A specification of Jovial." *Comm. ACM* **6**:12, 721–735.

Van Wijngaarden, A., et al. 1969. "Report on the algorithmic language, ALGOL 68." *TR MR 101*, Mathematisch Centrum, Amsterdam.

Van Wijngaarden, A., et al. 1974. "Revised report on the algorithmic language, ALGOL 68." *Acta Informatica*, **5**:1, 1–236.

Weissman, C. 1967. *LISP 1.5 Primer*. Dickenson, Encino, CA.

Wirth, N. 1968. "PL360, a programming language for the 360 computers." *J. ACM* **15**:1, 37–74.

Wirth, N. 1971. "The programming language PASCAL." *Acta Informatica* **1**:1, 35–63.

Wirth, N., and Weber, H. 1966. "EULER: a generalization of ALGOL and its formal definition: Part I." *Comm. ACM* **9**:1, 13–23.

Wirth, N., and Weber, H. 1966. "EULER: a generalization of ALGOL and its formal definition: Part II." *Comm. ACM* **9**:2, 89–99.

5. LANGUAGE DEFINITION TOOLS

Bar Hillel, Y.; Perles, M.; and Shamir, E. 1961. "On certain formal properties of simple phrase structure grammars." *Z. Phonetik, Sprachwissenschaft und Kommunikationsforschung* **14**: 143–172.

Chomsky, N. 1956. "Three models for the description of language." *IRE Trans. on Information Theory* **2**:3, 113–124.

Chomsky, N. 1959. "On certain formal properties of grammars." *Information and Control* **2**:2, 137–167.

Cleaveland, J. C., and Uzgalis, R. C. 1977. *Grammars for Programming Languages*. American Elsevier, New York.

DeChastellier, G., and Colmerauer, A. 1969. "W-grammar." *Proceedings of the ACM National Conference*. New York, pp. 511–518.

Galler, B. A., and Perlis, A. J. 1970. *A View of Programming Languages*. Addison-Wesley, Reading, MA.

Gill, A. 1962. *Introduction to the Theory of Finite-State Machines*. McGraw-Hill, New York.

Ginsburg, S. 1962. *An Introduction to Mathematical Machine Theory*. Addison-Wesley, Reading, MA.

Ginsburg, S. 1966. *The Mathematical Theory of Context-free Languages*. McGraw-Hill, New York.

Gross, M., and Lentin, A. 1970. *Introduction to Formal Grammars*. Springer-Verlag, Berlin.

Hopcroft, J. E., and Ullman, J. D. 1969. *Formal Languages and Their Relation to Automata*. Addison-Wesley, Reading, MA.

Jazayeri, M.; Ogden, W. F.; and Rounds, W. C. 1975. "The intrinsically exponential complexity of the circularity problem for attribute grammars." *Comm. ACM* **18**:12, 697–706.

Johnston, J. 1971. "The Contour Model of Block Structured Processes." *SIGPLAN Notices* **6**:2, 55–82.

Knuth, D. E. 1968. "Semantics of context-free languages." *Math Systems Theory* **2**:2, 127–145.

Knuth, D. E. 1971. "Examples of formal semantics." *Lecture Notes in Mathematics.* Engler (ed.), No. 188, Springer-Verlag, Berlin.

Lucas, P., et al. 1968. "Method and notation for the formal definition of programming languages." *TR 25.087,* IBM Laboratory, Vienna.

Kosaraju, S. R. 1974. "Analysis of structured programs." *J. Computer and Systems Sciences* **9**:3, 232–255.

Rustin, R., ed. 1972. *Formal Semantics of Programming Languages.* Prentice-Hall, Englewood Cliffs, NJ.

Salomaa, A. 1973. *Formal Languages.* Academic Press, New York.

Van Wijngaarden, A. 1965. "Orthogonal design and description of a formal language." *TR MR 76,* Mathematisch Centrum, Amsterdam.

6. PARSING

Aho, A. V., and Johnson, S. C. 1974. "LR Parsing." *Computing Surveys* **6**:2, 99–124.

Aho, A. V.; Johnson, S. C.; and Ullman, J. D. 1975. "Deterministic parsing of ambiguous grammars." *Comm. ACM* **18**:8, 441–452.

Aho, A. V., and Ullman, J. D. 1972. *The Theory of Parsing, Translation and Compiling, Vol. I: Parsing.* Prentice-Hall, Englewood Cliffs, NJ.

Aho, A. V., and Ullman, J. D. 1972. "Optimization of LR(k) parsers." *J. Computer and Systems Sciences* **6**:6, 573–602.

Aho, A. V., and Ullman, J. D. 1973. "A technique for speeding up LR(k) parsers." *SIAM J. Computing* **2**:2, 106–127.

Anderson, T.; Eve, J.; and Horning, J. J. 1973. "Efficient LR(1) parsers." *Acta Informatica* **2**:1, 12–39.

Backhouse, R. C. 1976. "An alternative approach to the improvement of LR parsers." *Acta Informatica* **6**:3, 277–296.

Birman, A., and Ullman, J. D. 1973. "Parsing algorithms with backtrack." *Information and Control* **23**:1, 1–34.

Colmerauer, A. 1970. "Total precedence relations." *J. ACM* **17**: 14–30.

Culik, K., II. 1968. "Contribution to deterministic topdown analysis of context-free languages." *Kubernetika* **5**:4, 422–431.

DeRemer, F. L. 1969. "Practical Translators for LR(k) Languages." Ph.D. dissertation, M. I. T., Cambridge, MA.

DeRemer, F. L. 1971. "Simple LR(k) parsing." *Comm. ACM* **14**:7, 453–460.

Demers, A. J. 1974. "Skeletal LR Parsing." *IEEE Conf. Record of the 15th Annual Symp. on Switching and Automata Theory,* pp. 185–198.

Demers, A. J. 1975. "Elimination of single productions and merging of nonterminal symbols in LR(1) grammars." *J. Computer Languages* **1**:2, 105–119.

Earley, J. 1970. "An efficient context-free parsing algorithm." *Comm. ACM* **13**:2, 94–102.

El Dijabri, N. 1973. "Reducing the size of LL(1) parsing tables." *TR-119,* Dept. of EECS, Princeton Univ., Princeton, NJ.

El Djabri, N. 1973. "Extending the LR parsing technique to some non-LR grammars." *TR-121,* Dept. of EECS, Princeton Univ., Princeton, N.J.

Fischer, M. J. 1969. "Some properties of precedence languages." *Proc. ACM Symposium on Theory of Computing,* pp. 181–188.

Fischer, C. N.; Milton, D. R.; and Quiring, S. B. 1977. "An efficient insertion-only error-corrector for LL(k) parsers." *Proc. 4th ACM Symposium on Principles of Programming Languages,* pp. 97–103.

Floyd, R. W. 1963. "Syntactic analysis and operator precedence." *J. ACM* **10**:3, 316–333.

Floyd, R. W. 1974. "Bounded context syntactic analysis." *Comm. ACM* **7**:2, 62–67.

Geller, M. M., and Harrison, M. A. 1973. "Characterizations of LR(0) languages." *IEEE Conf. Record of 14th Annual Symposium on Switching and Automata Theory,* pp. 103–108.

Graham, S. L., and Rhodes, S. P. 1975. "Practical syntactic error recovery in compilers." *Comm. ACM* **18**:11, 639–650.

Hammer, M. H. 1974. "A new grammatical transformation in LL(k) form." *Proc. Sixth Annual ACM Symp. on Theory of Computing,* pp. 266–275.

Ichbiah, J. D., and Morse, S. P. 1976. "A technique for generating almost optimal Floyd-Evans productions for precedence grammars." *Comm. ACM* **13**:8, 501–508.

Irons, E. T. 1963. "An error correcting parse algorithm." *Comm. ACM* **6**:11, 669–673.

Johnson, W. L.; Porter, J. H. ; Ackley, S. I.; and Ross, D. T. 1968. "Automatic generation of efficient lexical analyzers using finite state techniques." *Comm. ACM* **11**:12, 805–813.

Joliat, M. J. 1974. "Practical minimization of LR(k) parser tables." *Proc. IFIP Congress 74,* North Holland, Amsterdam, pp. 376–380.

Joliat, M. L. 1976. "A simple technique for partial elimination of unit productions from LR(k) parsers." *IEEE Trans. on Computers,* C-**25**:7, 763–764.

Knuth, D. E. 1965. "On the translation of languages from left to right." *Information and Control* **8**:6, 607–639.

Knuth, D. E. 1971. "Top down syntax analysis." *Acta Informatica* **1**:2, 79–110.

Korenjak, A. J. 1969. "A practical method for constructing LR(k) processors." *Comm. ACM* **12**:11, 613–623.

Kurki-Suonio, R. 1966. "On top-to-bottom recognition and left recursion." *Comm. ACM* **9**:7, 527–529.

Kurki-Suonio, R. 1969. "Notes on top down languages." *BIT* **9**:3, 225–238.

LaLonde, W. R. 1976. "On directly constructing LR(k) parsers without chain reductions." *Proc. 3rd ACM Symposium on Principles of Programming Languages,* pp. 127–133.

LaLonde, W. R.; Lee, E. S.; and Horning, J. J. 1971. "An LALR(k) parser generator." *Proc. IFIP Congress 71,* North Holland, Amsterdam, pp. 153–157.

Lesk, M. E. 1975. "LEX—a lexical analyzer generator." *CSTR 39,* Bell Laboratories, Murray Hill, NJ.

Loeckx, J. 1969. "An algorithm for the construction of bounded-context parsers." *Report R99,* Manufacture Belge de Lampes et de Materiel Electronique.

Madsen, O. L., and Kristensen, B. B. 1976. "LR parsing of extended context-free grammars." *Acta Informatica* **7**:1, 61–74.

Martin, D. 1968. "Boolean matrix method for the detection of simple precedence matrices." *Comm. ACM* **11**:10, 685–687.

Martin, D. 1972. "A Boolean matrix method for the computation of linear precedence functions." *Comm. ACM* **15**:1, 35–38.

Pager, D. 1974. "On eliminating unit productions from LR(k) parsers." *Automata, Languages and Programming.* J. Loeckx, ed., Springer-Verlag, New York.

Pager, D. 1977. "A practical general method for constructing LR(k) parsers." *Acta Informatica* **7**:3, 249–268.

Rosenkrantz, D. J., and Stearns, R. E. 1970. "Properties of deterministic top-down grammars." *Information and Control* **17**:3, 226–256.

Stearns, R. E. 1971. "Deterministic top-down parsing." *Proc. 5th Annual Princeton Conf. on Information Sciences and Systems,* pp. 182–188.
Valiant, L. 1975. "General context-free recognition in less than cubic time." *J. Computer and Systems Sciences* **10:**2, 308–315.
Weingarten, F. W. 1973. *Translation of Computer Languages.* Holden-Day, San Francisco.
Wharton, R. M. 1976. "Resolution of ambiguity in parsing." *Acta Informatica* **6:**4, 387–396.
Younger, D. H. 1967. "Recognition and parsing of context-free languages in time n-cubed." *Information and Control* **10:**2, 189–208.

7. FLOW ANALYSIS

Allen, F. E. 1970. "Control flow analysis." *SIGPLAN Notices* **5:**7, 1–19.
Allen, F. E. 1974. "Interprocedural data flow analysis." *Proc. IFIP Congress 74,* North Holland, Amsterdam, pp. 398–402.
Allen, F. E., and Cocke, J. 1972. "Graph theoretic constructs for program control flow analysis." *RC-3932, IBM T. J. Watson Research Center, Yorktown Heights, NY.*
Allen, F. E., and Cocke, J. 1976. "A program data flow analysis procedure." Comm. ACM **19:**3, 137–147.
Barth, J. M. 1977. "An interprocedural data flow analysis algorithm." *Proc. 4th ACM Symposium on Principles of Programming Languages,* pp. 119–131.
Fosdick, L. D., and Osterweil, L. J. 1976. "Data flow analysis in software reliability." *Computing Surveys* **8:**3, 305–330.
Hecht, M. S., and Ullman, J. D. 1975. "A simple algorithm for global data flow analysis programs." *SIAM J. Computing* **4:**4, 519–532.
Kam, J. B., and Ullman, J. D. 1976. "Global data flow analysis and iterative algorithms." *J. ACM* **23:**1, 158–171.
Kam, J. B., and Ullman, J. D. 1977. "Monotone data flow analysis frameworks." *Acta Informatica* **7:**3, 305–318.
Kennedy, K. 1971. "A global flow analysis algorithm." *Intl. J. Computer Math.* **3,** 5–15.
Kennedy, K. 1975. "Node listings applied to data flow analysis." *Proc. 2nd ACM Symposium on Principles of Programming Languages,* pp. 10–21.
Lomet, D. B. 1975. "Data flow analysis in the presence of procedure calls." *RC-5728,* IBM T. J. Watson Research Center, Yorktown Heights, NY.
Rosen, B. K. 1975. "Data flow analysis for procedural languages." *RC-5211,* IBM T. J. Watson Research Center, Yorktown Heights, NY.
Ullman, J. D. 1975. "Data flow analysis." *Proc. 2nd USA-Japan Computer Conference,* pp. 335–342, AFIPS Press, Montvale, NJ.

8. SYNTAX-DIRECTED TRANSLATORS

Aho, A. V., and Ullman, J. D. 1969. "Syntax-directed translations and the pushdown assembler." *J. Computer and System Sciences* **3:**1, 37–56.
Aho, A. V., and Ullman, J. D. 1969. "Properties of syntax directed translations." *J. Computer and System Sciences* **3:**3, 319–334.
Aho, A. V., and Ullman, J. D. 1971. "Translations on a context-free grammar." *Information and Control* **19:**5, 439–475.
Aho, A. V., and Ullman, J. D. 1972. *The Theory of Parsing, Translation and Compiling, Vol. I: Parsing.* Prentice-Hall, Englewood Cliffs, NJ.
Aho, A. V., and Ullman, J. D. 1973. *The Theory of Parsing, Translation and Compiling, Vol. II: Compiling.* Prentice-Hall, Englewood Cliffs, NJ.

Brooker, R. A., MacCallum, I. R., Morris, D.; and Rohl, J. S. 1963. "The compiler-compiler." *Annual Review of Automatic Programming* **3**: 229–275.

Brooker, R. A., and Morris, D. 1962. "A general translation program for phrase structure languages." *J. ACM* **9**:1, 1–10.

Brooker, R. A.; Morris, D.; and Rohl, J. S. 1967. "Experience with the compiler compiler." *Computer J.*, **9**: 345–349.

Buttelmann, H. W. 1974. "Semantic-directed translation." *Amer. J. of Computational Linguistics* **2**: Microfiche 7.

Cheatham, T. E., Jr. 1965. "The TGS-II translator generator system." *Proc. IFIP Congress 65*, North Holland, Amsterdam, pp. 592–593.

Cheatham, T. E., Jr., and Sattley, K. 1964. "Syntax directed compiling." *Proc. AFIPS 1964 Spring Joint Computer Conf.*, Spartan Books, Baltimore, pp. 31–57.

Feldman, J. A. 1966. "A formal semantics for computer languages and its application in a compiler-compiler." *Comm. ACM* **9**:3–9.

Feldman, J. A., and Gries, D. 1968. "Translator writing systems." *Comm. ACM* **11**:2, 77–113.

Irons, E. T. 1961. "A syntax directed compiler for ALGOL 60." *Comm. ACM* **4**:1, 51–55.

Irons, E. T. 1963. "The structure and use of the syntax-directed compiler." in *Annual Review in Automatic Programming, 3*:207–227.

Johnson, S. C. 1974. "YACC—yet another compiler compiler." *CSTR 32*, Bell Laboratories, Murray Hill, NJ.

Krishnaswamy, R., and Pyster, A. 1977. "On the correctness of semantic-syntax-directed translations." *TR77-5*, Dept. of Computer Science, Iowa State University, Ames.

Lewis, P. M., II; Rosenkrantz, D. J.; and Stearns, R. E. 1974. "Attributed translations." *J. Computer and Systems Sciences* **9**:3, 279–307.

Lewis, P. M., II, and Stearns, R. E. 1968. "Syntax-directed transduction." *J. ACM* **15**:3, 465–488.

McClure, R. M. 1965. "TMG—a syntax directed compiler." *Proc. 20th ACM National Conf.*, pp. 262—274.

McKeeman, W. M.; Horning, J. J.; and Wortman, D. B. 1970. *A Compiler Generator.* Prentice-Hall, Englewood Cliffs, NJ.

Pyster, A., and Buttelmann, H. W. 1978. "Semantic-syntax-directed translation." *Information and Control, 36*:3.

Rosen, S. 1964. "A compiler building system developed by Brooker and Morris." *Comm. ACM* **7**:7, 403–414.

Schorre, D. V. 1964. "META-II: a sumtax-oriented compiler writing language." *Proc. 19th ACM National Conf.*, D1. 3-1–D1.3-11.

Wasilew, S. G. 1971. "A Compiler Writing System with Optimization Capabilites for Complex Order Structures." Ph.D. dissertation, Northwestern Univ., Evanston, IL.

9. EXAMPLE COMPILERS

Bauer, H.; Becker, S.; and Graham, S. 1968. "ALGOL W implementation." *CS 98*, Computer Science Dept., Stanford Univ. Stanford, CA.

Bron, C., and de Vries, W. 1976. "A PASCAL compiler for PDP11 mini-computers." *Software—Practice and Experience* **6**:1, 109–116.

Conway, R. W., and Wilcox, T. R. 1973. "Design and implementation of a diagnostic compiler for PL/I." *Comm. ACM* **16**:3, 169–179.

Cress, P.; Dirkson, P.; and Graham, J. W. 1970. *FORTRAN IV with WATFOR and WATFIV.* Prentice-Hall, Englewood Cliffs, NJ.

Dijkstra, E. W. 1960. "ALGOL 60 translation." *Supplement ALGOL Bulletin 10.* Also see "Recursive programming." *Numerische Math.* **2:** 312–318 (1960), reprinted in Rosen 1967.

Evans, A. 1964. "An ALGOL 60 compiler." In *Annual Review in Automatic Programming,* Pergamon Press.

Freeman, D. N. 1964. "Error correction in CORC—the Cornell computing language." *Proc. AFIPS 1964 Fall Joint Computer Conf.,* Spartan Books, Baltimore, pp. 15–34.

Freiburghouse, R. A. 1969. "The Multics PL/I compiler." *AFIPS Conf. Proc. Fall Joint Computer Conference* **35:** 187–208.

Grau, A. A.; Hill, U.; and Langmaack, H. 1967. *Translation of ALGOL 60.* Springer-Verlag, New York.

Gries, D.; Paul, M.; and Wiehle, H. R. 1965. "Some techniques used in the ALCOR ILLINOIS 7090." *Comm. ACM* **8:**8, 496–500.

Griswold, R. E. 1972. *The Macro Implementation of SNOBOL4.* W. H. Freeman, San Francisco.

IBM 68. "FORTRAN IV (H) compiler program logic manual." Form Y28-6642-3, IBM, New York.

Irons, E. T. 1961. "A syntax directed compiler for ALGOL 60." *Comm. ACM* **4:**1, 51–55.

Randell, B., and Russell, L. J. 1964. *ALGOL 60 Implementation.* Academic Press, New York.

Rosen, S.; Spurgeon, R. A.; and Donnelly, J. K. 1965. "PUFFT—the Purdue University fast FORTRAN translator." *Comm. ACM* **8:**11, 661–666.

Russel, D. L., and Sue, J. Y. 1976. "Implementation of a PASCAL compiler for the IBM 360." *Software—Practice and Experience* **6:**3, 371–376.

Schneck, P. B., and Angel, E. 1973. "A FORTRAN to FORTRAN optimizing compiler." *Computer J.* **14:**4, 322–330.

Sheridan, P. B. 1959. "The FORTRAN arithmetic-compiler of the IBM FORTRAN automatic coding system." *Comm. ACM* **2:**2, 9.

Spillan, T. C. 1971. "Exposing side effects in a PL/I optimizing compiler." *Proc. IFIP Congress 71,* North Holland, Amsterdam, pp. 376–381.

Welsh, J., and Quinn, C. 1972. "A PASCAL compiler for the ICL 1900 series computers." *Software—Practice and Experience* **2:**1, 73–76.

Wirth, N. 1971. "The design of a PASCAL compiler." *Software—Practice and Experience* **1:**4, 309–333.

Wortman, D. B.; Khaiat, P. J.; and Laskar, D. M. 1976. "Six PL/I compilers." *Software—Practice and Experience* **6:**3, 411–422.

10. DATA STRUCTURES AND REPRESENTATIONS

Berztiss, A. 1971. *Data Structures: Theory and Practice.* Academic Press, New York.

Flores, I. 1969. *Computer Sorting.* Prentice-Hall, Englewood Cliffs, NJ.

Harrison, M. 1973. *Data Structures and Programming.* Scott, Foresman, Glenview, IL.

Hoare, C. A. R. 1968. "Record handling." in *Programming Languages,* Academic Press, pp. 291–347.

Horowitz, E., and Sahni, S. 1976. *Fundamentals of Data Structures.* Computer Science Press, Woodland Hills, Ca.

Ingerman, P. Z. 1961. "Thunks." *Comm. ACM* **4:** 55–58.

Knuth, D. E. 1968. *The Art of Computer Programming, Vol. 1: Fundamental Algorithms.* Addison-Wesley, Reading, MA.

Knuth, D. E. 1973. *The Art of Computer Programming, Vol. III: Sorting and Searching.* Addison-Wesley, Reading, MA.
Morris, R. 1968. "Scatter storage techniques." *Comm. ACM* **11**:1, 38–44.
Sattley, K. 1961. "Allocation of storage for arrays in ALGOL 60." *Comm. ACM* **4**:1, 60–65.
Stone, H. 1972. *An Introduction to Computer Organization and Data Structures.* McGraw-Hill, New York.
Tremblay, J. P., and Sorenson, P. G. 1976. *An Introduction to Data Structures with Applications.* McGraw-Hill, New York.
Wagner, P. 1968. *Programming Languages, Information Structures and Machine Organization.* McGraw-Hill, New York.

11. DIAGNOSTIC TOOLS

Aho, A. V., and Peterson, T. G. 1972. "A minimum distance error-correcting parser for context-free languages." *SIAM J. of Computing* **1**:4, 305–312.
Barnard, D. T. 1975. "A survey of syntax error handling techniques." *Computer Science Research Group,* Univ. of Toronto.
Dijkstra, E. W. 1976. *A Discipline of Programming.* Prentice-Hall, Englewood Cliffs, NJ.
Fischer, C. N.; Milton, D. R.; and Quiring, S. B. 1977. "An efficient insertion-only error-corrector for LL(k) parsers." *Proc. 4th ACM Symposium on Principles of Programming Languages,* pp. 97–103.
Freeman, D. N. 1964. "Error correction in CORC—the Cornell computing language." *Proc. AFIPS 1964 Fall Joint Computer Conf.,* Spartan Books, Baltimore, pp. 15–34.
Gerhart, S. L. 1975. "Knowledge about programs: a model and case study." *Proc. Intl. Conf. on Reliable Software,* pp. 88–95.
Gerhart, S. L. 1975. "Correctness-preserving program transformations." *Proc. 2nd Symp. on Principles of Programming Languages,* Palo Alto, CA.
Gerhart, S. L. 1976. "Theory of partial correctness verification systems." *Siam J. of Computing* **5**:3, 355–377.
Graham, S. L., and Rhodes, S. P. 1975. "Practical syntactic error recovery in compilers." *Conf. Record ACM Symposium on Principles of Programming Languages,* Boston, pp. 52–58.
Gries, D. 1976. "An illustration of current ideas on the derivation of correctness proofs and correct programs." *I.E.E.E. Trans. on Software Engineering* SE-2:4, 238–243.
King, J. 1969. "A program verifier." Ph.D. Dissertation, Carnegie-Mellon University, Pittsburgh.
Manna, Z. 1969. "The correctness of programs." *J. Computer and System Sciences* **3**:, 119–127.
Morgan, H. L. 1970. "Spelling correction in system programs." *Comm. ACM* **13**:2, 90–94.
Moulton, P. G., and Muller, M. E. 1967. "DITRAN—a compiler emphasizing diagnostics." *Comm. ACM* **10**:1, 45–52.
Pyster, A., and Dutta, A. 1978. "Error checking compilers and portability." *Software—Practice and Experience,* 8:1 Jan–Feb 1978; see also *TRCS77-1,* Dept. of Elec. Engr. and Comp. Sci., Univ. of California, Santa Barbara.
Stucki, L. G. 1977. "New directions in automated tools for improving software quality." Computer Science Dept., McDonnel Douglas Corp.
Stucki, L. G. 1972. "A prototype automatic program testing tool." *AFIPS Conference Proc,* Part 2, **41**: 829–836.

12 IBM 360/370 ARCHITECTURE AND MACHINE LANGUAGE

Amdahl, G. M.; Blaauw, G. A.; and Brooks, F. P. 1964. "Architecture of the IBM System/360." *IBM J. of Research and Development* **8**:2, 87–101.

Amdahl, G. M. 1964. "The structure of System/360, Part III: processing unit design considerations." *IBM System J.* **3**:2, 144–164.

Bell, C. G., and Newell, A. 1971. *Computer Structures: Readings and Examples.* McGraw-Hill, New York.

Blaauw, G. A., and Brooks, F. P. 1964. "The structure of System/360, Part I: outline of the logical structure." *IBM System J.* **3**:2, 119–135.

Case, R. P., and Padegs, A. 1978. "Architecture of the IBM System/370." *Comm. ACM* **21**:1, 73–96.

Struble, G. 1969. *Assembler Language Programming: The IBM System/360.* Addison-Wesley, Reading, MA.

Index